MW00750116

Combining Minds

HOW TO THINK ABOUT COMPOSITE SUBJECTIVITY

Luke Roelofs

OXFORD
UNIVERSITY PRESS

Oxford University Press is a department of the University of Oxford. It furthers
the University's objective of excellence in research, scholarship, and education
by publishing worldwide. Oxford is a registered trade mark of Oxford University
Press in the UK and certain other countries.

Published in the United States of America by Oxford University Press
198 Madison Avenue, New York, NY 10016, United States of America.

© Oxford University Press 2019

CIP data is on file at the Library of Congress
ISBN 978-0-19-085905-3

9 8 7 6 5 4 3 2 1

Printed by Sheridan Books, Inc., United States of America

COMBINING MINDS

PHILOSOPHY OF MIND

SERIES EDITOR: David J. Chalmers, *Australian National University*

The Conscious Brain
Jesse Prinz

Simulating Minds
The Philosophy, Psychology, and
Neuroscience of Mindreading
Alvin I. Goldman

Supersizing The Mind
Embodiment, Action, and Cognitive
Extension
Andy Clark

Perception, Hallucination, and Illusion
William Fish

*Phenomenal Concepts and Phenomenal
Knowledge*
New Essays on Consciousness and
Physicalism
Torin Alter and Sven Walter

Phenomenal Intentionality
George Graham, John Tienson, and
Terry Horgan

The Character of Consciousness
David J. Chalmers

The Senses
Classic and Contemporary Philosophical
Perspectives
Fiona Macpherson

Attention Is Cognitive Unison
An Essay in Philosophical Psychology
Christopher Mole

The Contents of Visual Experience
Susanna Siegel

Consciousness and The Prospects of Physicalism
Derk Pereboom

Consciousness and Fundamental Reality
Philip Goff

The Phenomenal Basis of Intentionality
Angela Mendelovici

Seeing and Saying
The Language of Perception and the
Representational View of Experience
Berit Brogaard

Perceptual Learning
The Flexibility of the Senses
Kevin Connolly

This book is dedicated to all the particles that composed my brain while I was writing it. Ultimately, they did all the work.

Contents

Preface

DIFFERENT READERS MAY want to take different routes through the chapters of this book. The first chapter poses a philosophical question, "Can minds combine?," whose importance I think has been underestimated. Many philosophers have explicitly said no, and many more have implicitly assumed the answer is no without quite recognizing the question. I think the answer is yes, and over the course of the book I argue for that. Chapter 2 considers the most general reasons that can be given for saying no, but there is a limit to how far the question can be addressed in a wholly general way, without asking "What sort of minds?" or even "What are minds?" For people attracted to different answers to those questions, I've broken the rest of the book into three divisions, sketching three different theories of mental combination. If you're interested in recognizably human minds, and their struggles over self-knowledge, agency, and inner conflict, you should jump from chapters 1 and 2 straight to chapters 7 and 8, where I outline "psychological combinationism." If you're interested in a more cognitive-science perspective, focused on minds as information-processing machines, you should go from chapters 1 and 2 to chapters 5 and 6, where I outline "functionalist combinationism." If you're interested in panpsychism, then chapters 3 and 4 are for you. The three theories aren't entirely separate from each other, since some topics that are relevant to all three are addressed in the particular division that they're *most* relevant to, but they're equally good starting points.

Acknowledgments

THIS BOOK COULD not have been written without the support and input of a huge number of people over the past seven years, to whom I am endlessly grateful.

I am especially grateful to Jessica Wilson, Bill Seager, Diana Raffman, Benj Hellie, David Chalmers, Daniel Stoljar, and Philip Goff: they have simultaneously enriched its contents intellectually while also helping to shepherd it and me through the long journey from conception to publication.

The book began life as my doctoral thesis at the University of Toronto, where it was supervised by Jessica, Bill, Diana, and Benj. It was then rewritten as a book during a two-year appointment at the Australian National University, under Daniel's supervision. David and Philip reviewed versions of the manuscript, as well as providing essential theoretical input and inspiration.

Among corporate persons, I owe a special debt to the philosophy departments of the University of Toronto, where the book was born; the Australian National University, where it matured; and the Ruhr-University Bochum, where the finishing touches were made.

Along the way many friends, colleagues, and fellow travelers have given their time and mental energy, in writing or in conversation, to improve the various parts which compose the book and the multifarious papers and conference presentations they spawned or absorbed. Among them are Miri Albahari, Dominic Alford-Duguid, Timothy Bayne, Bianca Bosman, Joshua Brandt, Jed Buchanan, Monima Chadha, Sam Coleman, Elena Rabinoff Derksen, Mark Fortney, Greg

Glatz, Reier Helle, Aaron Henry, Jeff Hilderly, Greg Horne, Matthew Ivanowich, Ole Koksvik, Uriah Kriegel, Takashi Kurihara, Pat Lewtas, Erick Llamas, Tom McClelland, Victoria McGeer, Angela Mendelovici, Greg Miller, Garrett Mindt, Hedda Hassel Mørch, Mark Moyer, Bhaskarjit Neog, Don Nordblom, Adam Pautz, Steve Pearce, Philip Pettit, Daniel Derksen Rabinoff, Carol Rovane, Alex Sandgren, Elizabeth Schechter, Eli Shupe, Holger Thiel, and Benjamin Wald.

Persons whom I must thank by description rather than acquaintance include anonymous referees for *Thought: A Journal of Philosophy*, the *Journal of Consciousness Studies*, *Philosophical Studies*, *Dialectica*, *Erkenntnis*, Routledge, and Oxford University Press.

Finally, I want to thank my family: my sisters, Aurora and Portia; my brother, Jacob; and my parents, Ann and Andrew. Their love and support has been inestimably valuable. And I must above all thank Katlyn Beattie, my partner, companion, and best friend, and the book's cover artist.

COMBINING MINDS

1 Introducing Combinationism

1 A Universe of Composite Subjectivity

NOTHING IN NATURE is an absolute unit. Human bodies, and everything around them, are built up out of smaller things, themselves built up out of smaller things, and they are parts of larger wholes, which are themselves parts of larger wholes. Moreover, they overlap with other things marked out by other ways of drawing boundaries: the world can be carved up in many different ways, but it is the same world however we carve it. This compositional structure is central to our ability to make sense of the physical world: both scientifically and in everyday life, we understand things by breaking them down into simpler components and putting them together into new and more complex wholes.

Are our minds likewise wholes made of mental parts, themselves made of smaller and smaller minds, which can be divided in many alternative ways or recombined into more complex mental wholes? If they are, that would be a deep and interesting continuity between mind and matter; if they are not, that would be a deep and interesting discontinuity. But there is something puzzling about the thought of minds composed of, contained in, and overlapping with other minds: How should I relate to these other minds that I contain, or are contained within, or overlap with? Are they "self" or "other"? Do they know that I exist? Does it really make sense for my point of view to be nothing over and above theirs? In this book I defend and explain this idea: that each of us has a composite subjectivity, formed of many individually conscious parts.

To bring out what is at issue, consider an everyday physical object, like a rock. Theories in physics never mention rocks, but this is no shortcoming: rocks fit neatly into the world described by physics because they are made up of parts (electrons, quarks, etc.) that physics does mention, and these parts combine with each other in intelligible ways to yield a rock. In particular, note three things. First, many key properties of the rock are "division-invariant" (a "division" is simply a certain way of organizing things into larger or smaller units): its mass or volume, however, remains constant whether you treat it as one thing, or as two halves, or as trillions of atoms. Carve it up however you like, when you add up the features of the parts, you will get the same result.[1] Of course, many of the rock's other properties are not like that: the rock's texture or solidity or symmetry is not automatically shared by its halves, let alone its component atoms. But—and this is the second key point—these properties are typically "intelligibly division-relative": when we analyze them we can see that their nature explains why the same set of division-invariant properties would support them on one way of carving but not another. Suppose the rock is striped when considered as a whole rock, but not when considered as a set of atoms (atoms are not striped, after all). But it is not as though stripedness mysteriously pops into existence at the rock-scale: analyzing what "being striped" means reveals that having thin adjacent regions of different colors is all it takes to be striped, and it is obvious why the whole can satisfy that description even though slices of it do not. Third, the relations that hold within the rock (its structure of "internal relations") can equally well be viewed as external relations between distinct objects, namely its parts. If its different-colored slices are chemically bonded together, we can equally well describe this as several objects, each of which is bonded to another, external object, or as a single object, which is internally tightly bound.

The idea of combining minds is challenging because these three things seem to be absent when we start to think about the mental world, and in particular about consciousness, about what it feels like to be me at a given moment. I may be a part of a club, or be made of many neurons, but consciousness seems, at first glance, to be present only at the human-being level, not at the level of the club (even though it has conscious parts) or the level of the neurons (even though they form

---

[1] Of course, we need to make sure to consider the parts *in their specific relations* to each other: a rock may take up more space than all of its component atoms would, if they were arranged differently. But that is simply to say that the rock takes up more space as it actually is than it would if it were restructured somehow.

a conscious whole).[2] So consciousness does not seem to be division-invariant, like mass, but it is also far from clear whether consciousness is intelligibly division-relative, like being striped. When I consider a club which has conscious people as parts, I do not know how to redescribe the consciousness of those people as a property of the club, the way I can redescribe the rock's parts being differently colored as the rock being striped. Likewise it is hard to see how my consciousness could be redescribed as some fact about my many neurons. And, most strikingly, the relations that hold within my mind seem very different from those that hold between my mind and the minds of others. My desires can motivate my decisions, my perceptions can inform my beliefs, my thoughts can conjure up imaginings, all apparently *directly*. By contrast, any interaction between me and other people is strikingly *indirect*: my desires and perceptions and thoughts seem radically cut off from theirs and can affect them only by first producing some outward movement of my body that they can perceive. In these ways the conscious mind seems like an anomaly, an absolute unit in a world of endless division and composition.

It is because composite subjectivity seems so challenging that I want to defend it. Historically, many philosophers have gone the opposite way and deemed it impossible. In fact, this supposed impossibility has sometimes been used to argue that consciousness requires an indivisible, immaterial soul, separated from the material world and from all other souls by unambiguous boundaries. At other times the challenge of composite subjectivity influences philosophical debates more subtly, by obscuring possibilities which would rely on it. But I think that denying composite subjectivity is a mistake, an illusion of indivisibility that misattributes the imperfect unity that our brains manage to achieve to a fundamental inner unity at the heart of the mind. It is also human-centric: we are too used to thinking about the minds of things with centralized brains, highly integrated internally and separated from all other brains by thick layers of bone. But there are creatures on earth whose nervous systems are not packaged into such neat units, and for all we know even more such creatures elsewhere. Developing brain technologies offer the prospect that we might be able to forge connections between human brains just as strong as the connections within a human brain, or establish divisions within a human brain just as sharp as those between different brains. If we want

---

[2] The metaphor of "levels" in nature, which I use here and throughout the book, can be defined in a variety of ways (see, e.g., Wimsatt 1976; Marr 1982; Bechtel 1994; Rosenberg 1994; Craver 2015). I use it to mean a set of entities of similar sizes, interacting in distinctive ways that might be studied by a specific science (as sociology studies group-level goings-on, psychology studies human-being-level goings-on, and neurobiology studies neuron-level goings-on) and typically but not always composed of "lower level" entities and composing "higher level entities."

to understand all of these possibilities, and free our imaginations from the narrow bounds of present-day-human-like minds, we need to think about composite subjectivity.

I analyze the idea that compositive subjectivity is impossible in terms of a principle I call "anti-combination," which in turn employs the notion of a "mere combination" and is opposed to a doctrine I will call "combinationism," defined thus:

Anti-combination: The experiential properties of a conscious subject cannot be mere combinations of the experiential properties of other subjects which compose it.

Combination$_{df}$: One property-token P is a "combination" of other property-tokens $p_1, p_2, p_3, \ldots$, if and only if (i) P is fully grounded in the ps, and the real relations[3] obtaining among them, and (ii) P is fully explained by the ps, and the real relations obtaining among them.[4]

Combinationism: The experiential properties of a conscious subject are sometimes mere combinations of the experiential properties of other subjects which compose it.

A more intuitive way to put the definition of "combination" is to say that a feature of me is a combination of features of my parts if those other features, and the way they are connected, both suffice to ground my having the feature in question and could be appealed to in an explanation of why I have it. Obviously we still need to unpack terms like "grounded," "explanation," "parts," and "experiential properties"; in section 1.3 I do so, but for now I will leave the idea rough. Anti-combination claims that when something is conscious in a certain way, this is always a further fact "over and above" the fact that its parts are conscious in certain ways and related in certain ways: combinationism denies this. Combinationism allows for composite subjectivity: experiential properties of x that are mere combinations of the experiential properties of the parts of x. Combinationism also implies the possibility of partial overlap of consciousness: three subjects such that

---

[3] Here and below I use the phrase "real relation" just to exclude a certain sort of trivialization-by-creative-definition. For instance, consider the relation "composing-a-composite-subject-together-with." From the fact that two minds stand in this relation to one another, it follows *a priori* that there is a composite subject they compose. Yet clearly this has not really achieved anything. A "real relation" is one that, unlike "composing-a-composite-subject-together-with," actually pertains to the relata themselves, so that our understanding of it is not parasitic upon our understanding of what it is meant to explain.

[4] What if P is entirely grounded in, and explained by, just *one* of the ps? This arguably satisfies the definition of combination given, but there is clearly a sense in which no actual "combining" is going on. I will call a case like this "trivial combination": combination that is not trivial is "substantive." For brevity, all references to "combination" should be read as meaning "substantive combination" unless otherwise specified.

A is a part of both B and C, and its experiential properties contribute to grounding and explaining both of theirs. The opposite of a mere combination (a property of a whole which is neither grounded in nor explained by any properties of its parts or their interrelations), I will call an "emergent" property.[5] It is often thought that there are no genuinely emergent properties in nature, and there seem to be none in the physical realm.

I think anti-combination is deeply intuitive to many people and has a powerful grip on our thinking about consciousness. I also think it is false; each of us in fact has a composite subjectivity, built up out of the consciousness of the parts of our brains. But it is hard to make sense of combinationism, of the idea that "what it is like to be me [is just] what it is like to be each of those [parts] (somehow experienced all at the same time)" (Goff 2006, 59). How can my perspective be nothing over and above what it is like for many other beings to stand in some relation? What does it mean to talk about "what it is like to be all of them" and to identify that with the apparently unitary consciousness I enjoy?

My aim in this book is to make it plausible that anti-combination is false; equivalently, it is to defend combinationism and the possibility of composite subjectivity. This will require theorizing mental combination so that it shares the three features, mentioned above, that make physical combination so satisfying: mental properties should be either division-invariant or intelligibly division-relative, and mental relations should be simultaneously within-subject and between-subjects. We should be able to see how, for each component subject in a composite subject, the other parts are external things and its relations to them are relations of self to other, even though for the whole, none of the parts is external, and their relations are just the internal structure of its own mind.

This chapter sets the stage by defining and contextualizing this project: Why does composite subjectivity matter? Who has endorsed anti-combination? And what do these various terms ("part," "consciousness," etc.) mean, exactly?

1.1. The Anti-Combination Intuition

The reason for this book's existence is the breadth and strength of the anti-combination intuition. The idea that consciousness, or mental properties more generally, cannot combine is often asserted as obvious, as a premise that can be assumed without argument (e.g., Van Inwagen 1990, 118; Lowe 1996, 39; Merricks

---

[5] This kind of emergence is sometimes called "strong emergence," to distinguish it from "weak emergence," where the whole's property is, in principle, explained by and grounded in some properties of its parts, but cannot easily, or in practice, be deduced from them (see Bedau 1997; Chalmers 2006b; Wilson 2010; Seager 2017). I am unsure what to call properties that are grounded but not explained, or vice versa.

2001, 111; cf. Bechtel 1994, 16). Other writers assume it implicitly in the way they frame or defend their views. And there is certainly something compelling in the idea that a conscious point of view has a special, indivisible wholeness. This widespread and powerful conviction makes composite subjectivity seem impossible.

In this section I review some of the ways that I believe the anti-combination intuition has influenced philosophical thought on a range of topics; in the next section I examine in more detail a topic which has recently occasioned especially focused attention to questions of mental combination, namely panpsychism and the "combination problem" thought to face it.

1.1.1. THE "ACHILLES" ARGUMENT AND ANTI-NESTING PRINCIPLES

First, anti-combination has a long and prominent history in the form of what is sometimes called the "Achilles" argument, so christened by Kant (1997, A351) for being the strongest argument of its kind. The argument maintains that because "representations that are divided among different beings . . . never constitute a whole thought" (A353), conscious minds must be simple and without parts, and therefore cannot be material. Versions of this Achilles argument appear in authors stretching from Plotinus (1956, 255–258, 342–356) to Brentano (1987, 290–301).[6] And for these authors, since physical things are always divisible, the indivisibility of conscious minds proves that they lie outside the physical world.

In recent philosophy of mind, most explicit discussion of anti-combination has dealt with the combination problem for panpsychism (treated in section 1.2), but that does not mean that other theories of mind are not influenced by it. For one thing, advocates of both machine-state functionalism (Putnam 2003, 215–216) and integrated information theory (Tononi 2012, 59, 67–68) have stipulated "anti-nesting" principles, by which no system can qualify as conscious if it is contained within, or contains as parts, other conscious systems: consciousness can be in the part or in the whole but not both. (This claim is of course not equivalent to the claim that conscious minds must be simple, i.e., without any parts at all, but both show the same sense of a special difficulty in mental combination.)

1.1.2. CONSCIOUSNESS IN SOCIAL GROUPS

The anti-combination intuition exerts a strong but sometimes unrecognized influence when philosophers consider the status of large groups like nations or crowds. Although many philosophers vigorously debate the possibility and nature of

---

[6] Other users of this style of argument include Proclus (1963, 163), Avicenna (1952, 47ff.), Descartes (1985, 2:59), Butler (1860), Mendelssohn (2002), Clarke (1978, 3:759), Bayle (1991, 128–134), and Lotze (1894, 158). See also Mijuskovic (1984) and Lennon and Stainton (2008).

collective *intentionality*—collective beliefs, collective goals, collective intentional actions, etc. (e.g., Velleman 1997; Gilbert 2000; Bratman 1997; List and Pettit 2011; Tollefsen 2014)—the proponents of this kind of collective mentality will generally resist the idea of collective *consciousness*. While a group might plan, or investigate, or deploy strategies to achieve goals, it is assumed that there could not be something it is like to *be* a group: whatever we may do together, surely there is nothing it is like to be us. Even those who go furthest in defending genuinely collective mental states stop short of collective consciousness: Gilbert (2002) and Huebner (2011) both argue in support of collective emotions, but do so by trying to break the link between emotion and consciousness, arguing that genuine emotions may be devoid of phenomenology. Thus they seek to prevent "the implausibility of collective consciousness . . . impugn[ing] the possibility of collective emotions" (Huebner 2011, 102).

The intuition that groups are not conscious is so strong, in fact, that it has been used to argue against particular theories on behalf of others. For instance, Block (1992) offers thought experiments in which we are supposed to find consciousness in certain beings composed of other conscious beings implausible. Block regards consciousness in such entities as "an absurdity" (79), and therefore rejects theories of consciousness that imply it.[7]

Historically, proponents of the Achilles argument also often support their claim that minds cannot have parts by drawing an analogy to groups of people, as in this quotation from Brentano (1987, 293):

> If, when we see and hear, the seeing were the property of one thing and the hearing the property of another, then how could there be a comparison between colours and sounds? (It would be just as impossible as it is for two people, one of whom sees the colour and the other of whom hears the sound.) (cf. Plotinus 1956, 346; De Courcillon and Timoleon 1684; for an example directly targeting panpsychism, see James 1890, 160)

I believe that it is primarily anti-combination that explains this intuitive resistance to the idea of collective consciousness, and in particular the discrepancy in attitudes toward collective intentionality and collective consciousness. People generally want to avoid irreducible, emergent group minds which float above individual minds; such beings seem mysterious, unparsimonious, and even ethically

---

[7] While Block maintains that the compositional aspect of these cases is irrelevant to their force, others disagree: David Barnett (2008, 309) has argued that the best explanation for these intuitive judgments is that "our naïve conception of a conscious being demands that conscious beings be simple" (cf. Montero 2017, 225; Coleman 2017, 259n31).

threatening (Searle 1990, 404; List and Pettit 2011, 9). We can avoid emergent minds while allowing for collective intentionality, as long as that intentionality can be explained through and grounded in that of individual members. But if consciousness in a whole cannot be explained by or grounded in consciousness in its parts, then this anti-emergence attitude rules out collective consciousness. Combinationism dissolves this conflict: social groups can be nothing over and above their members, while still being literally conscious. That is not to say that combinationism entails that collective consciousness is ubiquitous or even actual; it merely shows that the possibility is not absurd.

1.1.3. HUMAN BEINGS WITH IMPAIRED UNITY, AND OTHER UNUSUAL CASES

The anti-combination intuition also constrains the way we think about cases where the unity of a human person is in some way impaired.[8] Consider two complementary cases: the split-brain phenomenon and dissociative identity disorder. Both cases seem somewhat intermediate between what we would normally count as one mind and what we would normally count as many minds, but accepting anti-combination forces us to regard those as the only available options. In the split-brain syndrome, the nervous fibers connecting the two cerebral hemispheres are severed, and although the patient appears normal in everyday situations, very strange results can be produced when stimuli are segregated so as to be processed by only one hemisphere. Simplifying greatly, it seems that, when responding with the motor organs controlled by that hemisphere, the patient shows full awareness of the stimulus, but with the organs controlled by the other hemisphere, they claim not to have seen it. It seems like there are "two people," one for each hemisphere, each with half the body's full set of sensory and motor organs, and each responding rationally to its own sensations but unaware of the other's. Dissociative identity disorder also involves what seem like "partial persons," but in a completely different way: the "alternate personalities," or "alters," are not tied to any particular sensory or motor organs, but instead take sequential or simultaneous control of the whole body. What differentiates them is the memories they can report, the personalities they display, and what they claim about themselves—or, to put it another way, what the patient reports, displays, and claims when exhibiting a particular alter.

---

[8] I will use the term "person" for a certain sort of conscious subject, one possessing intelligence, rationality, and self-consciousness comparable to our own; what counts as a "person" will thus be as vague as what counts as "comparable to." An adult human or an intelligent alien (Vulcan, Kryptonian, or similar) is a person; a dog or a baby is not.

In both of these cases, there is compelling reason to think both in terms of a plurality of individual people and in terms of a single individual showing unusually dissociated behavior. It is very natural to think that the right analysis is somewhere in between—that there are two of *something* person-like, and also one overall unit that they together form. But as long as we hold onto the anti-combination intuition, it will be almost impossible to conceive of any such intermediate option. If there are two people, then there is no single person who subsumes both; if there is a single person, then the constituents or components of that person cannot really be people. This contrasts with how we think about physical things; after all, if we ask how many *brains* the split-brain patient has, any uncertainty as to whether to say "one" or "two" seems merely semantic, because we can always shift away from a language of countable brains and speak in terms of neural parts and their relations. We can say that all the normal parts of a brain are present, but they are no longer interacting as they were before.

Human beings with impaired unity provide one set of cases where nature asks us questions that anti-combination makes it hard to answer. But there are other cases too, such as conjoined twins who share not only parts of the body but also parts of the brain (cf. Langland-Hassan 2015, N.d.), and animals whose nervous systems are less centralized than ours. The most salient example of the latter is the octopus, two-thirds of whose neurons reside in its eight arms, each of which appears to have significant autonomy and responsibility for advanced sensorimotor processing (see, e.g., Sumbre et al. 2001; Gutfreund et al. 2006; Gutnick et al. 2011; Godfrey-Smith 2016; Diamante 2017). Other creatures with decentralized nervous systems, like sea stars and jellyfish, are less clearly conscious at all, but if they are their consciousness presumably will lack the tight integration into a single unit that ours displays (cf. Sterne 1891). Similar things hold for eusocial animals like ants and bees, whose colonies are sometimes regarded as candidates for mentality in their own right: if there is consciousness here, it likely inheres both in individual ants and in the colony, in which case combinationism provides the most natural way to make sense of it. Hypothetical alien hive-minds and futuristic speculation about artificial intelligence provide more scope for envisaging minds which can overlap, contain, and compose one another.

1.1.4. ORDINARY PSYCHOLOGICAL DIVISION

As well as unusual human beings, we all experience what sometimes feels like the beginnings of "internal division," when mental conflicts become so intense as to prompt descriptions like "I am at war with myself" or "I am enslaved by my passions." There is a long history of philosophical psychologies that posit some sort of division of the mind into parts to explain this kind of experience, from Plato's (2000, 111ff.) division into reason, spirit, and appetite to Freud's (1949) division into ego, superego, and id. Other writers, though they do not speak of particular parts, do discuss the importance of avoiding various sorts of "inner division" (Frankfurt 1987; Korsgaard 2009). Cognitive scientists regularly analyze everyday cognitive processes as involving the collaboration of brain systems whose behavior is simpler than ours but still mind-like; examples include the "homunculi" posited in various models of (human and artificial) intelligence (see Selfridge 1959; Dennett 1978b, 1991; Lycan 1995); the informationally encapsulated "modules" suggested to autonomously handle certain domain-specific tasks, from language understanding to face recognition (see, e.g., Fodor 1983; Cosmides and Tooby 1992; cf. Prinz 2006); and the quick-and-dirty "system 1" and slow-and-careful "system 2" distinguished by dual-systems theory (see, e.g., Evans 2003; Frankish 2010; Kahneman 2011). Indeed, one influential conception of how psychological explanation works *in general*, the "neomechanist" approach advocated by Bechtel and Craver (see, e.g., Bechtel 1994; Craver 2015; cf. Rosenberg 1994), identifies as central the decomposition of systems into components, each of which performs parts of the task whose performance by the whole is to be explained. And after considering the split-brain phenomenon, it is hard not to wonder what stops the individual hemispheres of my brain from being conscious in their own right, even in normal cases when they are closely communicating with each other (cf. Nagel 1971, 409; Blackmon 2016).

Of course, it is not clear how much of this talk should be taken as asserting a literal compositeness in human minds, and even if a given statement does assert compositeness, it is not clear what type of entity the parts are meant to be. The Freudian id, for instance, seems to be a mental being of some sort, but should we think of it as a conscious subject with its own phenomenology? And if I fail to achieve some sort of ideal "unity of self," what or who are the things which exist in place of the single self which was aimed for? Indeed, one might worry that treating components of the human mind as mind-like is just a form of anthropomorphism, a "Homuncular fallacy" that inappropriately extends the concepts applicable at one level to another level (Bechtel 1994, 19–20; cf. Bennett and Hacker 2003). But it is only anthropomorphism if those components are not in fact mind-like, and we cannot decide this in advance of examining how they actually work.

Certainly, I do not mean to insist on a literal reading of all such talk, nor to suggest that it is always true, when interpreted literally—just to undermine the confidence often felt that they *cannot* be literally true, because no part of a subject could literally be conscious itself. Combinationism does not say that all parts of subjects, or any particular parts, are themselves subjects: only that we should be open to the possibility. The implications of combinationism for consciousness in parts of the mind are thus rather like the implications, for consciousness in nonhuman animals, of realizing that human beings are not endowed with any special, supernatural soul; we must evaluate each entity for consciousness on its own merits, not prejudge it based on how it relates to us whole human beings.

1.1.5. OVERLAPPING PARTS OF A HUMAN BEING

Finally, we can even set aside all unusual or problematic human conditions and the details of human brain anatomy, and just consider some unremarkable everyday assumptions. Surely a human head is intrinsically capable of supporting consciousness; surely human heads exist; but surely we are not ourselves heads but rather have heads as a part of us. Philosophers have pointed out that it seems to follow that both we and our heads are conscious, so that for every human being there are in fact two different conscious beings—or more, if we also consider such entities as "the top half of a human being," "the brain of a human being," or "all of a human being minus 1 foot" (Merricks 2001, 95; Unger 2006; cf. Burke 1994, 2003; Gilmore 2017). Some philosophers have regarded this as a paradoxical result (a problem of "too-many-minds"),[9] but typically they accept that a parallel result is unproblematic for physical properties: my head and I are two different entities with mass, two different entities which possess eyes, two different entities which fill this region of about a cubic foot of space (Merricks 2001, 106; Unger 2006, 378–379). These results are unproblematic because we accept that one being with mass (for instance) can be part of another, and that then they will both have mass, but the mass of one will include the mass of the other. What makes the parallel result with consciousness seem absurd is the assumption that even when one conscious being is part of another, the one's consciousness cannot *contain* that of the other—i.e., the assumption of anti-combination.

So a successful defense of combinationism would have implications for a variety of debates. We should reject the Achilles argument for substance dualism and should refrain from adding anti-nesting principles to our theories of mind. We should accept the possibility in principle of conscious social groups (and not reject theories just for having that implication), though this leaves open which particular groups might qualify. We should also regard the division, multiplication, and overlap of people as no more theoretically problematic than that of physical objects—and in particular should take seriously models of the split-brain, or of

---

[9] Versions of the same "too-many-minds" objection are also employed in debates over personal persistence, targeting theories on which "we" (persons) are distinct from but share *all* our parts with some other entities (organisms, or bodies).

dissociative identity disorder, or of everyday life, on which there is both a single whole person and also one or more component persons.

Chapter 3 contains a direct answer to "too-many-minds"–style problems about heads and brains, with subsequent chapters considering more complicated cases. In chapters 5 and 6 I discuss the split-brain phenomenon, the consciousness of cerebral hemispheres, homuncular accounts of cognition, and other interesting test cases, as well as sketching how combinationists should think about social groups, both real ones and thought-experimental constructs. And in chapter 7 I discuss how far a theory of experiential combination can support literal or near-literal readings of everyday forms of both "inner division" and dissociative identity disorder.

1.2. Motivating Panpsychism

Although combinationism is relevant to many issues in the metaphysics of mind, it is perhaps *most* relevant to panpsychist theories of consciousness, and in particular "constitutive Russellian panpsychism" (hereafter CRP). Indeed, I have taken the term "combination," as meaning explanatory, nonemergent composition, from the "combination problem" supposed to face CRP (Seager 1995, 280). I am sympathetic to CRP, but my aim in this book is not to argue directly for it: rather, by defending the possibility of composite subjectivity, I hope to solve the combination problem, and thus remove the most serious objection to CRP. So it will be useful to say a bit to acquaint the reader with the view and some reasons for holding it.

Panpsychism (from Greek *pan-* and *psuche*, meaning "all-" and "mind") is the view that consciousness is omnipresent among the fundamental things of the universe: all matter is conscious. If the fundamental things are particles, then every particle of matter has a point of view, an iota of consciousness, which is unimaginably simple but nevertheless differs from our own consciousness only by degree. If the fundamental things are something else—waves, fields, strings, spacetime, or the universe as a whole—then panpsychism says correspondingly that those have some rudimentary glimmer of consciousness. It does not automatically follow that "everything" is conscious, for many things (shoes, ships, sealing wax, etc.) are nonfundamental, built up out of the basic constituents. Whether those composite things are conscious will depend on exactly how consciousness combines.

1.2.1. THE EXPLANATORY ARGUMENT FOR PANPSYCHISM

There are four major arguments in support of panpsychism, which I will call the "explanatory" argument, the "causal exclusion" argument, the "intrinsic natures" argument, and the "continuity" argument. In the following pages I will outline these, as well as distinguishing between constitutive and emergentist panpsychism, with the explanatory, causal exclusion, and continuity arguments favoring the constitutive option, and between Russellian and dualist varieties, with the causal exclusion and intrinsic natures arguments favoring the Russellian option.

The first argument begins with dissatisfaction about "physicalism" as an explanation of consciousness (Nagel 1986; Seager 1995; Chalmers 1995; Strawson 2006), combined with a desire to hold onto "naturalism." By "naturalism" I mean the view that the world contains a single basic type of stuff, whose behavior is governed by a single set of simple, general laws, and that these laws are those revealed by science. The most common version of naturalism among contemporary philosophers is physicalism, the view that the world is entirely made up of matter, and matter is exhaustively described by physics. But some philosophers reject physicalism, even while accepting naturalism, holding that matter is not *exhaustively* described by physics—there are fundamental aspects of matter that physics is blind to. In particular (they tend to say), there are certain things each of us can know about matter, such as that one particular portion of matter (the one between our ears) sometimes feels and thinks and experiences, which go beyond both what physics itself says and what can be deduced from any physical description, no matter how detailed.[10] Because facts about my consciousness are left out by any purely physical descriptions, these "naturalistic anti-physicalists" infer that consciousness must be itself a fundamental feature of reality, no more derivable from physical properties than mass is derivable from charge.[11] Yet consciousness does seem intimately tied to the workings of the physical brain, suggesting that they are linked by *a posteriori* laws of nature (like those saying how much charge electrons have), even if not by *a priori* conceptual necessities (like those saying that a square has four sides). The resultant picture is one on which fundamental "psychophysical" laws bridge the gap, connecting physical and experiential properties just as different physical properties are related by fundamental physical laws.

---

[10] This is a highly abbreviated version of the "hard problem of consciousness," related to the "explanatory gap" (Levine 1983; Chalmers 1995; cf. Nagel 1986), supported by the "conceivability argument" (Chalmers 1996; cf. Kripke 1980; Descartes 1985) the "knowledge argument" (Jackson 1982), and the "structure-and-dynamics" argument (Chalmers 2003a), all of which have been debated and defended at length by others much better than I can do here (e.g., Seager 1995; Lewis 1990; Chalmers 2002, 2009; Dennett 2006).

[11] I use "fundamental" to mean "not grounded in anything else," in the sense of "grounded" explained in section 1.3.

So far this is not necessarily panpsychist; the fundamental psychophysical laws might be "emergence laws," associating consciousness only with certain physical composites (e.g., just with human brains) and not with all matter. The next move is to point out that fundamental laws tend to be simple and general, allowing for a great variety of forms to be built up gradually from a small set of widespread basic elements. They do not attach a fundamental element to a precisely specified sort of rare and complex structure. Moreover, it is arguably this simplicity and generality that makes physics an explanatorily satisfying framework—by contrast, more narrowly applicable "emergence laws" seem unsatisfyingly ad hoc. Consequently, we should expect psychophysical laws to put consciousness more or less everywhere: once naturalistic anti-physicalism is accepted, panpsychism is the natural conclusion.

1.2.2. THE INTRINSIC NATURES ARGUMENT FOR PANPSYCHISM

Next, the intrinsic natures argument tries to show that any alternative to panpsychism is both unparsimonious and obscure (Seager 2006; Strawson 2006; Coleman 2009; Goff 2017a, 139ff.). It works from three premises: that the properties expressed by the language of physics are in some sense "merely structural"; that conscious properties, alone among all the properties we understand, are more than structural; and that all structural properties must be instantiated in something with a nature that goes beyond structure. There is some dispute over how best to define "merely structural" (cf. Stoljar 2013; Mørch 2014),[12] but the rough idea can be brought out by observing that, apart from spatiotemporal terms, all the fundamental properties ascribed by physics—force, energy, mass, charge, etc.—are defined by their place in equations linking them to other such properties. What is it to have charge? It is to have whatever property it is which produces forces when at some distance from another thing with charge. But what is force? It is whatever accelerates mass. What is mass? It is whatever resists acceleration when exposed to force and exerts attractive forces on other things with mass. And so on. All of this still seems to leave unanswered the question of *what* these interdefined properties actually are; physics tells us about the structure that physical properties fit into, but not what those properties actually are. By contrast, it seems as if when we experience some feeling, like sadness or pleasure or the sensation of heat, we *do* know what it is to have that property—perhaps we know this in an inarticulate,

---

[12] If an explicit definition is needed, a good first pass is that a "structural property" is either a relational property, or an intrinsic property which consists entirely in relations among a thing's parts. It contrasts with "absolutely intrinsic"; I take these definitions from Pereboom 2011, 93ff.

hard-to-express way, and perhaps not in all respects, but we are not caught in a network of "whatever it is that . . ." as we are with physical properties.

The intrinsic natures argument then proceeds as follows. Even if physics does not tell us what physical properties really are in themselves—even if it does not tell us their "intrinsic natures"—they must still be something. The structure physics reveals must be implemented in something. So what could this something be—what are the intrinsic natures of physical properties? Experiential properties are one candidate: maybe what we call "mass" is a certain kind of experience, whose characteristic effects and distribution are captured by the equations of physics. Or perhaps the intrinsic natures of physical properties are something completely inconceivable to us, something of which we neither have nor can form any positive conception—call this the "noumenalist" option, borrowing Kant's term for the forever-unknown way things are in themselves (Goff 2017a, 170). The panpsychist claims that these are the only two options, and that we should prefer the first option, which implies panpsychism. Why should we prefer it? Partly, perhaps, because it is unreasonably defeatist to adopt a noumenalist position when a more positive view is available. But also, partly, because noumenalism is unparsimonious. *Some* parts of the material world have conscious experience as their intrinsic nature—namely, human brain processes. So the noumenalist position, which says that some matter has one nature and other matter has a different nature, seems to be needlessly multiplying the number of basic types in the world. Hence Occam's razor cuts against it.

1.2.3. THE CAUSAL EXCLUSION ARGUMENT FOR PANPSYCHISM

Third, the causal exclusion argument for panpsychism (closely analogous to a similarly named argument for physicalism) says that because consciousness seems to have power to affect the physical world, and because events in the physical world seem to be entirely driven by the causal powers of physical things, consciousness must be some part of the physical world (Rosenberg 2004; Chalmers 2015). If consciousness made a causal difference but was separate from physical reality, then its actions would appear as violations of laws of physics—violations which we do not seem to have yet detected and which it seems theoretically unattractive to have to predict. This argument is compatible with some forms of physicalism, but is also compatible with some forms of panpsychism; what it is not compatible with are dualist theories on which consciousness "floats free," independent of the physical world and its causal laws.

1.2.4. THE CONTINUITY ARGUMENT FOR PANPSYCHISM

Finally, the continuity argument (James 1890, 147–148; Clifford 1874/86, 266ff; Goff 2013; Mørch 2014, 153–154; Buchanan and Roelofs 2018) motivates panpsychism by pointing out that scientific progress seems to show that there is nothing supernatural about humanity, nothing in our development as individuals or as a species that marks a genuinely sharp break with the rest of nature. But for panpsychism to be false, there would have to be such a sharp break—a moment when the most "advanced" nonconscious thing was succeeded by the most rudimentary conscious thing, a moment when "the lights turn on." Our evolution was gradual, our fetal development is gradual, and even when there does appear to be a "sudden leap" from a nonconscious stage to a conscious stage, the process always turns out to be resolvable into a gradual sequence of steps when looked at on smaller timescales. As Chalmers (1996, 297) says, panpsychism "avoid[s] the need for consciousness to 'wink in' at a certain level of complexity . . . [because] any specific point seems arbitrary, so a theory that avoids having to make this decision gains a certain simplicity."

1.2.5. VARIETIES OF PANPSYCHISM: CONSTITUTIVE AND EMERGENTIST

Not all panpsychists are combinationists: even if all the basic physical entities are conscious, the consciousness of complex physical entities might not be a mere combination of their parts. There might then be a form of panpsychism on which the experiential properties of human beings are emergent, not mere combinations, generated according to "emergence laws" that directly connect complex consciousness with certain sorts of physical composite.[13] I will use the labels "constitutive" and "emergentist" for combinationist and noncombinationist versions of panpsychism.

This dependence on the challenging idea of composite subjectivity is sometimes used as an argument within the panpsychist camp, against constitutive versions and in support of emergentist versions. But just as often, it is used in attacks on panpsychism as a whole, by critics who assume that the only or best forms of panpsychism must be constitutive. The reason for this assumption is clear when we consider the explanatory argument for panpsychism: for this argument to support

---

[13] Several subtly different distinctions have been drawn here, such as "constitutive" and "emergent" (Chalmers 2015; Goff 2017a, 155), "reductive" and "emergentist" (Goff 2010), "constitutive" and "nonconstitutive" (Mørch 2013), or "constitutive" and "causal" (Mørch 2014). Sometimes this distinction is drawn between different sorts of emergence, such as "weak" and "strong" (Chalmers 2006b), "conservative" and "radical" (Seager 2017), or "weak," "strong," and "brute" (Mørch 2014). Adam Pautz, in unpublished work, also distinguishes "reductive" and "primitivist" versions within the constitutive camp. See also Roelofs 2017b.

panpsychism against physicalist and emergentist alternatives, panpsychism needs to offer an explanatory advantage. But if microexperience does not ground or explain macroexperience, what advantage is there? To put it another way, if human consciousness "emerges" from microexperience, in the strong sense that the latter does not ground and explain the former, why not just say that human consciousness emerges from nonconscious microphysics, in an equally mysterious way?

Another reason to prefer constitutive over emergentist panpsychism is to avoid causal exclusion: emergentist panpsychism risks having microexperience leave macroexperience with no causal work to do. If the relationship between human minds and microminds is closely analogous to that between macrophysical objects and microphysical objects, then it is seems very plausible that the former, like the latter, allows for shared causal efficacy: what the parts do, the whole also counts as doing, but the result is not somehow "caused twice over" (not "overdetermined"). But if macroexperience is emergent relative to microexperience, then it is much harder to see how both can be efficacious without their effects being overdetermined.

1.2.6. VARIETIES OF PANPSYCHISM: RUSSELLIAN AND DUALISTIC

As well as distinguishing constitutive and emergentist versions of panpsychism, we can distinguish Russellian and what I will call "dualistic" versions. Russellian panpsychism uses the conceptual framework developed for the intrinsic natures argument (which is traced to Russell [1927] and Eddington [1929]; cf. Schopenhauer 1969, 97–105) to understand the relationship between physical and experiential properties: the former are just more abstract descriptions of the causal and structural roles played by the latter. This unites the two sets of properties more closely than on non-Russellian versions of panpsychism, on which each physical ultimate simply has two, metaphysically independent sets of properties (hence "dualistic" panpsychism). On the Russellian view, it is not just that each particle has mass, charge, etc. and then *also* has experiential properties, but rather each particle has experiential properties, which ground a set of causal powers whose structure is captured by the equations of physics. Obviously, anyone persuaded by the intrinsic natures argument has reason to prefer Russellian over dualistic panpsychism, since only the former responds to the demand to know the intrinsic natures of physical properties. But the causal exclusion argument also provides reason to prefer Russellianism, since metaphysically independent properties, like the physical and experiential properties posited by dualistic panpsychism, seem to be at risk of causal competition. By analogy, if a particle causes some effect just in virtue of its charge, there seems to be no room left for its mass to also cause that very same effect. But if experiential and physical properties are related as intrinsic basis and structural role, then effects attributed to one can also be attributed to the other.

In summary, the arguments which support panpsychism over non-panpsychist views also seem to favor the constitutive, Russellian, version over other versions—at least if that version is workable at all. But this version is arguably the hardest to spell out, most metaphysically demanding version of panpsychism. What is attractive about it is that it ties together the different facets of the world: it connects micro and macro by being constitutive, physical and experiential by being Russellian. But this simultaneously makes it easier to refute, just by finding any incompatibility between the supposedly tied-together facets.

This is why the combination problem faces CRP especially strongly. Because it is Russellian, it is committed to the fundamental experiential properties being isomorphic with the fundamental physical properties that they are supposed to be the intrinsic natures of. This means that the basic experiential properties will be both quite few in number and also extremely widespread in the universe. And because CRP is constitutive, it is committed to all the diverse and specific forms of consciousness that exist being generated directly out of this basis.

In the previous section I tried to show that the difficulty of conceiving consciousness as composite is not exclusive to panpsychists: some version of the "combination problem" faces a wide range of views in the metaphysics of mind. But CRP implies an especially extreme and thoroughgoing sort of experiential combination, and consequently also faces an especially extreme and thoroughgoing sort of combination problem, with especially constrained resources for solving it (Chalmers [2017, 211] compares it to "trying to juggle seven balls in the air with both hands tied behind one's back"). Yet it is also, if it can be made to work, an enormously appealing and powerful theory, for precisely the same reason it faces this problem over combination: the deep unity it postulates in nature.

1.3. Defining Combination

The definition of combinationism given above employs the following five ideas: "grounding," "explanation," "part," "whole," and "experiential." Combinationism says that a whole's experiential properties can, in some cases, be grounded and explained by those of its parts. In this section I clarify what I mean by these terms.

1.3.1. WHAT IS "GROUNDING"?

By saying that A "is grounded in" B, or equivalently that A is "nothing over and above" B, I mean to capture the, admittedly rough and intuitive, idea that once we have B, that is by itself enough for us to have A.[14] This is, in the first instance, a relation among facts: for one object or property or event to ground another is for all the facts about one to be grounded in facts about the other.

This is compatible with a few different cases: most simply, we can say that A is grounded in B if A is B, for nothing is anything over and above itself. Thus when a physicalist claims that mental events are nothing over and above certain physical brain events, one thing they might mean is that those brain events are identical to mental events: we have two terms ("mental event" and "brain event") referring to one and the same thing.

Identity is symmetrical, so if B grounds A by being A, it will also be true that A grounds B (though see Jenkins 2011). But a second, asymmetrical way for B to ground A is for A to be simply an "abstraction from" B, a less specific or detailed version of B. Thus when someone claims that a certain lizard's being red is nothing over and above its being scarlet, they plausibly mean that being scarlet is a more specific way of being red, so that once something is scarlet nothing more is needed for it to be red.

Other cases are trickier. It seems mistaken to simply *identify* the nation of Canada with its current population (it could endure after they are all dead), or its territory (that existed long before Canada did), or with a certain system of government (it could have a revolution and still be Canada). Yet it seems clear that Canada is nothing over and above certain people implementing a certain institutional structure within a certain territory (cf. Parfit 1999, 17–18). To see why this is so, observe that it seems possible to give logically sufficient conditions for there to be a nation, mentioning only people, institutional structure, and territory, and then also to give logically sufficient conditions for two nations to be the very same nation, in terms of the continuity of those same factors (continuity meaning, roughly, that though any given factor may change, there is only limited, gradual change from one moment to the next). Given all this, and given an initial specification that some nation is Canada (e.g., the nation founded on such-and-such a date at such-and-such a place), we have a complete account of what it would be for Canada to exist at any time—namely that people must implement institutions

---

[14] This requires, but goes beyond, "supervenience": A supervenes on B if any world with B also has A ("no change in A without a change in B"). But supervenience is not enough: if two independent things were both necessitated by the same thing and could not exist otherwise, they would supervene on each other, but neither would ground the other (cf. Schiffer 1987; Horgan 1993; Wilson 2005).

within a territory in such a way that a nation exists, and that a sufficiently continuous history of people implementing institutions within a territory must connect that nation with the nation initially named "Canada." This is grounding, but neither identity nor abstraction.

In cases like this a key role is played by the fact that we can "metaphysically analyze" the grounded entity: thinking about what a nation is reveals a set of conditions for the existence of a nation, and what grounds the nation are the entities (people, territories, etc.) whose activities fulfill those conditions. Goff (2017a, 44ff.) calls this "grounding by analysis," noting the important implication that only entities which admit of metaphysical analysis—only entities whose nature can be analyzed into a set of conditions that other entities could then fulfill—can be grounded in this fashion. If some entities are "primitive" and cannot be analyzed except in a circular way (e.g., "occupying space" is primitive if the only analyses we can give of it are things like "filling space," "having length, breadth, and depth," or "being located somewhere," which are just other ways to say "occupying space"), then facts about them cannot be grounded by analysis (see also Dasgupta 2014, 564–580; cf. Melnyk 2003, 21, 2014).

I will adopt the following rough criterion: A is grounded in B if all it takes for A to exist is for something to be true of B (to use a popular metaphor, all God would have to do to create both is to create B). When A and B are identical, this criterion is clearly satisfied: for A to exist is just for B to exist. When A is a less specific version of B, we can say that for A to exist is just for B to be any of a range of ways. And when A is grounded by analysis, the relevant state of B may be a complex and intricate one, but could in principle be articulated by analyzing the nature of A.

1.3.2. WHAT IS "EXPLANATION"?

What about "explanation"? In many of the above cases of grounding, understanding the grounding thing would allow us to understand the thing grounded—would let us "see why" various facts about it obtain. The difference between explanation and grounding is that one concerns the reality of things, and the other concerns possible states of understanding by us. I will say that A is explained by B when someone who fully understands B is thereby in a position to fully understand A; to put it another way, A is "made intelligible" by B.

This is not by itself a real analysis, since notions like "understanding" and "intelligibility" are little clearer than the notion of "explanation." And not all sorts of "explanation" are relevant here; for instance, I am interested in how components existing at a given moment explain a whole's properties at that very time, not in across-time explanations, where we explain events in terms of separate, earlier events.

Rather, my major point of reference is the supposed explanatory gap between physical properties and consciousness, which contrasts with cases where one set of physical properties intuitively suffices to explain another (see, e.g., Levine 1983; Chalmers 1995; Loar 1990; McGinn 1989). A complete understanding of the microphysical structure and dynamics of a human brain would, in principle, let us "see" why it must have the macroscopic physical features which it in fact has (Levine [1983, 357]: "our knowledge of physics and chemistry makes [such connections] intelligible"), yet would not allow us to "see" why it feels a certain way to be that brain (Levine: it "leaves the connection . . . completely mysterious" [357]). The microphysics explains the macrophysics, but not the phenomenology. So I will index my discussion to the explanatory gap between consciousness and physics: Could there be the kind of connection between mental wholes and mental parts which defenders of the explanatory gap think is missing between consciousness and physics, but accept between physical wholes and physical parts?

Although the relations of grounding and explanation are importantly different, it is natural to regard them as connected. If one thing fully explains another, that is usually a good sign that one grounds the other; conversely, if one thing is nothing over and above another, shouldn't we expect that understanding the latter would let us understand the former? But this cannot always be assumed: it might be that despite some A being fully grounded in some B, there is some stubborn cognitive fact about us that prevents us from understanding the one in light of the other: there might be an explanatory gap even without a real gap, just as it has sometimes been argued that the explanatory gap between consciousness and matter does not betoken any metaphysical difference, but only the presence of two ways to think about the same properties, which we are incapable of intelligibly connecting (e.g., Levine 1983; Loar 1990; Block and Stalnaker 1999; Diaz-Leon 2011).

Even if there are cases where grounding and explanation come apart, the compositional relations between physical properties do not appear to be such a case. If, for instance, we know the present locations of all the parts of a table, it seems clear both that there is no additional reality needed for the table to be located where it is, and that there is no additional mystery for us about why it is located there. This is why I have defined combination in terms of both explanation and grounding: my consciousness is a mere combination of the consciousnesses of my parts if and only if it is *both* grounded in them and their interrelations *and* fully explained by them and their interrelations.

1.3.3. WHAT ARE "PARTS"?

Next, what does it mean to say that something has "parts," or that one thing is "part of" another? Philosophers generally agree that parthood is a transitive relation (parts of a part of me are parts of me), and that two distinct things cannot both be part of the other, and that if I have one part, I must have at least one other part (what is "left over" from removing the first part). Beyond this the notion seems to be primitive: we do not know how to analyze it into terms that do not themselves presuppose a grasp of parthood. But it also seems to be a notion employed in different senses, among which it is important to distinguish.

First, we can distinguish "thick" and "thin" notions of parthood. In the thin sense, any feature or aspect or property of something—anything we can truly ascribe to it—can be called a part of it. We might say, of a dog that is a hybrid of breeds A and B, and which is currently behaving very much like a member of breed A, that it is displaying "the A part of it." We might casually convey that we want two opposed things by saying "part of me wants X, but part of me wants Y." We might perhaps even talk about a red square in terms of its two parts, "redness" and "squareness" (cf. properties as "logical parts" [Paul 2002]). But the "thick" notion marks a contrast with a thing's mere properties: my height, or my build, or my demeanor, are properties of me but not parts of me. The thick notion seems to involve some or all of the following conditions:

1. The parts of something exist simultaneously with the whole.
2. The parts of something are of the same basic category as the whole.
3. The (discrete) parts of something are existentially independent of each other.[15]
4. A thing is existentially dependent on its parts collectively.

The first condition distinguishes parts of something from what goes into making it. To use an example from Bennett (2011, 288), eggs may often be ingredients in cakes, but an egg is only a part of the cake if, even once the cake is complete, there still exists an egg somewhere inside it. When we divide something into parts we are identifying constituents of it that currently exist and currently compose it.

The second condition rules out counting properties of an object as parts of it: parts of an object should themselves be objects, though a property might have other properties as parts (e.g., part of being a bachelor is being male). Similarly, events involving me are not parts of me, and while I may "play a part" in an event

---

[15] I use "discrete" to mean "non-overlapping," "sharing no parts." This is stronger than "distinct," which I use to mean simply "nonidentical," "not the very same thing."

like a hockey game, I am not a part of it in the same sense as its first half or first period (other, shorter events). Obviously parts and wholes need not share all categories—parts of a table need not themselves be tables. But the parts of a table should at least be physical objects.[16]

The third condition says that of any two parts (which do not have a further subpart in common), the one might cease to exist without the other automatically ceasing to exist. They are in this respect like any two things of their kind, considered apart from their composing a whole. The four legs of a table, for instance, are existentially independent things just as much as two unrelated tables are: the existence or nonexistence of the one does not logically imply the existence or nonexistence of the other. This stops things like "the-table-as-square" and "the-table-as-wooden" being parts of the table (cf. Fine 1982, 1999), since doing away with the table-as-square (that is, doing away with the table, considered as a square object) would automatically do away with the table-as-wooden (for it gets rid of the table itself).[17]

The fourth condition says that if the parts all suddenly ceased to exist, the whole would also thereby be gotten rid of. If the four legs and the flat top of the table were to vanish, that would simply be the table vanishing. This rules out treating the causal contributors to something as parts of it. For instance, my parents have had a huge role in forming me, both physically and psychologically. (I might say "they are part of who I am.") But they are not parts of me in the thick sense, because they (and all my other formative influences) could cease to exist without me thereby also vanishing.

Note that this condition does not say that the whole could not exist if the parts did not exist; I have many cells as parts right now, but after a few years most of those cells will not exist while I still do, made of a different set of cells. But this is compatible with me presently depending on those cells in the sense that their

---

[16] I don't know how to rigorously spell out "same basic category," but I can gesture at what seems important. The physical parts of a table can be sensibly compared to the table—we can ask which is bigger, whether they are the same color, what the ratio of their masses is, and so on. We can say how the table leg would have to change to resemble the table more—how it would have to grow, change shape, etc. But it feels like a joke to compare the table with one of its properties—to ask whether it or its shape or its color is larger, or heavier, or harder. And clearly it makes no sense at all to talk about turning one into the other—there is nothing that could be done to a property to "make it into" an object, or vice versa.

[17] Of course two parts of something may overlap. But in this case we can always identify both a part that they have in common and discrete parts of each that are not shared. For instance, a table has as parts a north-facing half and an east-facing half; these are not existentially independent because they share a quadrant. But we can identify that quadrant (the northeast) as another part of the table, and also identify the other, discrete, parts that the two halves do not share (namely the northwest and southeast quadrants). To do this with the table-as-square and the table-as-wooden would require inventing odd entities to be the shared part ("the table without any features") and the unshared parts ("being-square," "being-wooden"). But these would then violate the second condition.

instantaneous and complete disappearance would be my own instantaneous and complete disappearance. Note also that while this means that the existence of a whole is grounded in facts about its parts, it does not follow that all the properties of a whole are grounded in properties of its parts (i.e., are mere combinations); though I suspect the latter is true, it is not true by definition.

So the thick sense of parthood requires that parts and whole exist simultaneously and belong to the same category, that parts are existentially independent, and that the whole existentially depends on the parts. In this book I will generally be operating with the "thick" notion of part, and I intend my definitions of "combination" and "anti-combination" to use this notion. This distinguishes combinationism from certain nearby ideas, namely bundle theory and fusionism. By "bundle theory" I here mean the idea of the subject as a whole comprised of mental states, which are not themselves subjects. Since here the "parts" and "whole" are things of different kinds, bundle theory does not by itself count as combinationism—that would require adding the idea that some or all "sub-bundles" within the mind also qualify as subjects. Fusionism is the idea that two or more subjects can "fuse" into a single, more complex subject—after which they themselves no longer exist. (Seager [2010, 2017] and Mørch [2014] both advance fusionism as a possible solution to panpsychism's combination problem.) Here the "parts" and "wholes" never coexist: there is only first the many and then the one, and so in the thick sense we should not call this a compositional relationship.

1.3.4. WHAT ARE "WHOLES"?

As well as different ways of conceiving of what a thing's parts are, there are different ways of conceiving of wholes. Perhaps the simplest is to think of wholes as just "the many parts counted as one thing" (Baxter 1988, 579). In this sense, to say that two things "compose a whole" is just to group them in thought and name them, to "take them as one" rather than as many. This is the sense of "whole" which fits best with the formal system known as classical extensional mereology (Leonard and Goodman 1940; Lewis 1991, 72–90), with its axioms of unrestricted and unique composition: for any set of things, there is one and only one thing which they compose. Because, after all, for any set of things, we can count them as one thing. Call this very modest sort of "whole" an "aggregate."

Sometimes, however, we seem to think of a "whole" as defined not just by the parts which compose it but by a specific structure they must instantiate, such that it exists only when its parts are structured in that way. A car, for instance, is not simply an aggregate of mechanical parts, because those parts could exist when separated, but the car exists only when they are connected, and connected in the right way (e.g., Fine 1999; Koslicki 2008; cf. Wilson 1999, 2013). Call wholes like this, which exist only when a certain structure is instantiated, "structure-specific wholes."[18]

Whether we think of wholes as aggregates or as structure-specific does not by itself change the plausibility of combination, i.e., of deriving all their properties from the properties of their parts, and the relations among them. But it does change the shape of the derivation. Because aggregates in some sense just *are* their many parts, taken together, they can be expected to have a property corresponding to every property of their parts. Structure-specific wholes, on the other hand, might well be thought to *lack* properties corresponding to those properties of their parts which are irrelevant to their defining structure. That is, structure-specific wholes can have a limited measure of "autonomy" in the sense of being unaffected by all the messy details of their parts. According to Wilson (2010, 2013), it is crucial to the "ontological autonomy" of certain wholes that they have a different set of properties than their parts, and in particular have fewer degrees of freedom, that is, require fewer parameters to fully specify their state. Consider, for example, a whirlpool which forms in water, sucking down fresh water while constantly preserving its vortical structure. It seems to be composed of water molecules, each of which weighs something, but it's not clear that it makes sense for us to ascribe to it any weight at all. Or consider the physical parts of a biological cell, which all have their own specific masses, charges, and locations: the aggregate they compose will correspondingly have a very detailed distribution of mass and charge properties at specific locations. But beyond certain parameters, the details are irrelevant to the preservation of the cell's biological structure, and so we might think of the cell itself as having only the property of "mass and charge distributions being within acceptable parameters," and nothing more detailed than that. But this does not mean that the whole has any properties not derived from its parts.

But there is also a strand of philosophical thinking that separates out "real" wholes much more sharply from "mere" aggregates, which demands that to count as a whole, a thing must have some sort of deep unity, something to make it objectively one and not many (see, e.g., Leibniz 1989, 78–80, 85–90; James 1890, 158–160; cf. Merricks 2001; Shani 2010). Call this sort of whole a "true unit." Whereas for something to be an aggregate is just for us to "take it as one," for something to

---

[18] Note that aggregates do not lack structure (the aggregate of all the parts of my car is, currently, just as structured as my car itself); they are simply not defined by that structure (the aggregate of all the parts of my car could still exist if the parts were disassembled). In this respect I use the term "aggregate" differently from, e.g., Coleman 2012, 139–142, and Morris 2017, 117–120, who apply it only to unstructured wholes like heaps of sand.

be a true unit is for it to be such that we *must* take it as one and *cannot* consider it as a set of parts without losing something crucial to it. A true unit is meant to be "more than the sum of its parts," not just in the innocuous sense that the parts can do different things when working together than when working separately, but in the more demanding sense that the whole should do things that go beyond anything the parts could do, working together or separately. In effect, a true unit should be a strongly emergent whole, a whole whose properties escape any accounting in terms of the properties of its parts.[19]

There is room for lots of metaphysical debate about which of these three types of whole exist, what their relationship is, and which category we ourselves might fall into.[20] Since true units are, almost by definition, not open to a wholly compositional explanation, my defense of combinationism must presuppose that our minds are not true units; conveniently, the scientific progress of the past few centuries seems to have proceeded in large part by abandoning the thought that anything in nature is a true unit, perhaps with the (very questionable) exception of elementary particles. But beyond that, I want to remain neutral about how far we should be thinking of composite subjects as aggregates or as structure-specific wholes, and discuss the combinationist project from both perspectives. After all, part of what motivates combinationism about consciousness is the thoroughgoing compositionality of the physical world, and this involves the explicability of both physical aggregates and physical structure-specific wholes. Chapters 3 and 4 treat subjects as aggregates, while chapters 5–8 treat them as structure-specific wholes. In this way, hopefully, I will catch the right theory somewhere in my net.

1.3.5. WHAT ARE "EXPERIENCES" AND "SUBJECTS OF EXPERIENCE"?

The categories of "experience" and "subject" are hard to define exactly, but easy to gesture at. Whenever there is consciousness (whenever there is "something it is like" for a certain being to be in a certain state, "from the inside"),[21] there is both

---

[19] Strictly, the historically most influential version of this idea is not naturally put in terms of "emergence," since the special unit-making power (sometimes called an "entelechy," "substantial form," or "soul") was not typically thought of as "produced by" simpler things coming together. More likely, it was either divinely bestowed from above or passed on by other true units with the power to "in-form" matter and produce further true units. For my purposes it is harmless to call it "emergent," since I use that term just to mean what is not a mere combination.

[20] Maybe aggregates don't "really exist": our talk of them is just a linguistic shortcut for talking about their parts all together. Maybe structure-specific wholes don't "really exist": our talk of them is just a linguistic shortcut for talking about how aggregates behave when they are structured a certain way ("car" is just what we call a collection of mechanical parts *when they are connected*). What does it even mean to "really exist," as opposed to just "exist"? What kinds of questions are these? (Cf. Lewis 1991, 81; Yi 1999; Fine 2001; Wilson 2014.) Into these thickets I shall not venture.

[21] Philosophers disagree about how much of mental life involves this phenomenological sense of "consciousness"—whether it is only sensations and emotions which have "something it is like" to undergo

some*one* who is having experiences and some*thing* that is happening in or to them. The former might be called a person, soul, self, or, as I will tend to say, a "subject of experience." The latter might be called feelings, mental states, states of consciousness, experiencings, or, as I will tend to say, "experiences."

Going by the way we usually talk about them, subjects are a sort of "thing" or object, which persists through an indefinite period of time, whereas experiences are something like an event, which lasts for some limited duration. Insofar as the one is an object and the other is an event, neither can be a part of the other in the thick sense. Both subjects and experiences, moreover, should be distinguished from experiential properties, properties which are defined by what it is like to instantiate them:[22] on this definition, anything that instantiates experiential properties is a subject, and whenever they instantiate experiential properties they will be "having" some experience or other. But experiences do not seem to be the same things as experiential properties, for the former are particulars (things that occur to specific subjects, at specific times), and the latter are universals (things that can occur to many different individuals on many different occasions). Rather, experiences are particular instances of experiential properties.

The distinction between subjects and experiences is important, because the controversial idea I wish to defend, composite subjectivity, goes beyond the familiar idea that experiences can have other experiences as parts, and even be mere combinations of those parts. It is very natural to think that my "field of experience" (the totality of what I am conscious of at a given moment) can be divided into components, such as my present total visual experience, which is a part distinct from my present auditory or olfactory or emotional experiences. It seems equally unobjectionable to divide my total visual experience into component experiences, like my experience of some particular visible object (e.g., my coffee cup). But while these component experiences might be called "parts of my consciousness," they are not themselves parts of *me*, the subject, because they are not themselves conscious in the way that I am. One can accept the existence of a

---

them, or whether thoughts, beliefs, plans, judgments, intentions, etc. do too. They also debate whether any phenomenology associated with thoughts, etc. is distinctively cognitive or just reheated imagery (Prinz 2011; Horgan and Tienson 2002; Kriegel 2007; Bayne and Montague 2011). I will tend to speak in line with the more "liberal" (Bayne 2010, 5–7) position, that many different mental states have phenomenology, but nothing I say will depend on this.

[22] This is narrower than simply "properties which it is like something to have": if I can desire X both consciously and unconsciously, then there is sometimes something it is like to have the property "desires X," but what it is like does not define that property. Cf. Bayne and Chalmers 2003, 30–31, on "phenomenal states" versus "phenomenally conscious mental states."

component experience of seeing my coffee cup, without accepting the existence of any conscious subject which is conscious of seeing that cup and nothing else.[23]

Although most writers accept that experiences can be composed of other experiences (see Tye 2003, 20–41, for a dissenting view), there is disagreement about how best to individuate experiences, and how to think about their composition. I do not think there is a single right way to individuate experiences: as Bayne (2010, 24) says, "counting experiences is arguably more like counting the number of objects in a room . . . [than] like counting the number of beans in a dish. . . . The idea that there is only one way in which to proceed is somewhat farcical." For simplicity I will adopt the following approach: for each feature of what it is currently like to be me (e.g., I feel sad, and I also feel hot), there is "an experience" (e.g., my sadness-experience and my hotness-experience), and one experience is part of another when my having the one includes and subsumes my having the other (e.g., "I feel hot all over" includes "I feel hot in my feet," so the hotness I feel in my feet is part of my total hotness-experience).

So we can distinguish between experiences composing experiences and subjects composing subjects. But even having subjects composing subjects would not automatically qualify as composite subjectivity in my sense. For there might be a subject that I contain within me somehow—a sentient parasite, a late-term fetus, a second small brain grown in an unusual place—whose consciousness had nothing to do with my consciousness. To rule out this kind of case, I defined combinationism in terms of a part-whole relation where both parts and whole are subjects (because they instantiate experiential properties), and where the experiential properties of the latter are combinations of the experiential properties of the former: a relation between subjects, defined partly in terms of relations between their properties. I will use the terms "component subjects" and "composite subjects" for parts and wholes in this relation. (I will use "they" pronouns for such entities, even when singular; I apologize for the slightly increased ambiguity in some sentences.)

A composite subject might be divided into component subjects along various alternative lines, just as a human body can be divided into many alternative sets of parts. Some divisions ("top-down") might focus on the distinctive, complicated features of the whole, like person-level psychology. Thus if we observe a conflict between two styles of inference someone employs, we might try to distinguish two inferential systems within them and hypothesize that each of them is a component subject. By contrast, other divisions ("bottom-up") might focus on the basic,

---

[23] Similar things can be said for divisions of the mind into "faculties" or "drives" or anything else that is not explicitly itself a conscious subject. I may divide my mind into will, imagination, and intellect, but that does not commit me to thinking that there is anything it is like for my imagination itself to imagine things.

widely shared, more fundamental features of the whole. If the left half of me (or of my brain) and the right half of me (or of my brain) are conscious subjects in their own right, they would be parts in a division of this sort.

The examples of the split-brain phenomenon and dissociative identity disorder (DID), discussed in section 1.1, nicely illustrate this contrast. The two apparent component subjects in the split-brain patient are divided at an anatomical level: one consists of the left hemisphere, the nonhemispheric brain parts, and (roughly) the right half of the body, while the other consists of the right hemisphere, the nonhemispheric brain parts, and (roughly) the left half of the body (since they share major parts, they overlap). This is a more sophisticated form of division than simply carving the body into spatial chunks, but it can be drawn simply in terms of biological tissue, and is to that extent a relatively "bottom-up" division. The alters of a DID patient, by contrast, correspond to a "top-down" division because to divide them from one another we make reference to high-level features like personality and self-identifications. There is no *a priori* reason to expect the two divisions to line up; the alters are unlikely to be exclusively based in distinct brain areas (cf. Rosenberg 1994).

Any *introspective* division of a subject—a division into "whatever underlies *this* experience" and "whatever underlies *that* experience"—will likely be a fairly "top-down" division, and we cannot assume in advance that it will correspond neatly to any natural division of the brain. The same goes for divisions based on felt motives and feelings, including the divisions that become salient in cases of inner conflict. That is not to say that these introspectively defined subjects are not neuron-based: their physical basis is still some assembly of neurons, but those neurons might be spread widely and eccentrically through the brain. Moreover, each of those neurons or clusters of neurons might also play a role in subserving other functions, and to that extent be included in another part (i.e., it may not be introspectively obvious which parts overlap).

I am not presupposing that all these ways of dividing a human subject will yield component subjects; it is possible that some, all, or none do. But if they did, they would not all yield component subjects of the same kind. Indeed, they might seem to yield parts of such different metaphysical status (e.g., a personality cluster and a hemisphere) that they could hardly *both* be conscious subjects. The question of what kind of thing subjects are will be taken up in more depth in chapter 2.

1.4. Plan of This Book

There are three different ways to object to experiential combination: (i) showing it to be inherently impossible; (ii) claiming that it could not work with certain particular sorts of parts and wholes we are interested in, given what we know about them; and (iii) pointing out that we have so far no positive theory of it. Call these internal problems, bridging problems, and lack-of-theory problems (the first two terms taken from Coleman 2017, 250–254).

While the first aim to prove that no sort of composite subjectivity could ever exist, the second instead point either to a particular feature of human consciousness which, they claim, could not be accounted for by any combination of conscious parts, or point to a certain set of putative conscious parts and deny that they are suitable for composing the sort of consciousness that we enjoy. The third sort of objection is that we simply have at present no inkling of how composite subjectivity is supposed to actually work. While this is not in itself an argument against its possibility, it is a reasonable basis for withholding assent from any theory (like CRP) which requires it.

I devote chapter 2 to addressing five internal problems: the subject-combination problem, the unity problem, the privacy problem, the incompatible contexts problem, and the boundary problem. All of these focus, in one way or another, on the metaphysics of the subject and the unity of consciousness, and in chapter 2 I identify the assumptions about subjects and unity that these objections rest on. The rejection of these assumptions provides parameters for a combinationist theory, and the next six chapters then add flesh to the bones. Chapters 3–8 are dedicated to refining, applying, and justifying the abstract claims defended in chapter 2, and thereby to addressing both a number of what I have called "bridging problems" and the more general "lack-of-theory" problem.

Chapters 3–8 actually develop not just one but three theories of mental combination, focused on different issues and tailored to the interests of different constituencies. Combinationism is not in itself a theory of consciousness; rather, it is an idea that can be usefully combined with many different theories. Consequently, I have tried to organize this book so that different parts will be of value to different readers, who can thus skip ahead to the chapters of most interest to them.

First, chapters 3 and 4 present panpsychist combinationism, an account of mental combination addressed to constitutive panpsychists. In these chapters I treat consciousness as a fundamental property, something not explained in terms of anything else but instead baked into the base level of our universe. This means that the most important component subjects will be the microscopic physical parts that make up everything, and in chapter 4 I will consider certain bridging problems arising from the sheer number of microscopic parts we each have.

Second, chapters 5 and 6 present functionalist combinationism, an account of mental combination addressed to philosophers and cognitive scientists interested in the consciousness of intelligent information-processing systems. Whereas panpsychist combinationism is intended as an account of fundamental reality, functionalist combinationism is not: it is a theory of how the processing of information enables the combination of simpler minds into more and more complex and intelligent ones. Chapter 6 applies functionalist combinationism to a number of real and hypothetical examples, sketching out a compositional explanation of the structured consciousness associated with brains (whole ones, half ones, and split ones) and with social organizations.

Finally, chapters 7 and 8 present psychological combinationism, an account of mental combination focused on the special concerns of the most complex and sophisticated sorts of subjects, namely "persons" like ourselves. Persons are not just intelligent subjects; they are subjects with a capacity for rational agency and self-consciousness, and here I will examine bridging problems concerning these capacities, as well as the ways that these capacities can break down into inner conflict or dissociation. Finally, in chapter 8 I draw together the ideas of the preceding chapters through a detailed consideration of a particularly challenging thought experiment, that of two persons fusing into one.

Although these chapters contain multiple theories, these theories are not really rivals; they do not inherently conflict with one another, though they are offered in part to allow different readers with conflicting prior beliefs about consciousness to still accept combinationism. They are instead best seen as aimed at different levels of reality: panpsychist combinationism aims at the fundamental level of nature, functionalist combinationism aims at the level of information-processing systems, and psychological combinationism aims at the level of people, with their agency, their problems, and their self-conceptions. Personally, I think all three theories are true, because consciousness is present at all levels, in interestingly different forms, and all of those forms, though in different ways, can combine.

2 Conscious Subjects, Conscious Unity, and Five Arguments for Anti-Combination

USUALLY WHEN SOMEONE explicitly discusses the idea I've called "composite subjectivity," it's to say that it's demonstrably impossible—that "subjects cannot combine" (Coleman 2012, 1), that "experiences don't sum" (Goff 2006, 53), that "planning for tomorrow or feeling pain are not activities that a lot of simples can perform collectively" (Van Inwagen 1990, 118).

This is held to be something that applies to all forms of composite subjectivity, or at least to all that are of any theoretical interest, and it is held to be knowable *a priori*, by reason alone. To defend the possibility of composite subjectivity, I need to engage and refute the arguments advanced for this extreme denial—the arguments alleging an internal problem with combinationism. So in this chapter I identify five arguments against the possibility of composite subjectivity; in section 2.3 they will be discussed in detail, but they can be briefly outlined as follows:

The subject-summing argument: It seems possible for a whole made of conscious parts not to be conscious itself, not to be a further subject of experience. So how does consciousness in the parts help to explain consciousness in the whole?

The unity argument: Each of us has many experiences, but they seem to all be connected, "unified" in various ways. Experiences spread across many subjects, by contrast, seem separate, "disunified." How can experiences spread across many parts provide the whole with unified consciousness?

The privacy argument: It seems to be an important fact about experiences that each of us can have only our own—others can be aware of ours only indirectly. But then if each experience is "private," available exclusively to a single subject, how can the part's experiences (which are private to those parts) do anything for the whole?

The boundary argument: If minds can combine, what stops my mind and your mind, or even everybody's minds, from combining into some sort of giant mind which would absorb and do away with each of us as individuals? What, in general, stops component minds from "vanishing" into the whole they form?

The incompatible contexts argument: Experiences seem to get much of their character from context, from the other experiences they are unified with. But then any experience shared by part and whole must reflect both the relatively limited context of "what else the part is experiencing" and its larger context of "what else the whole is experiencing"; how can it reflect both?

These arguments are closely related: they all deal either with the metaphysics of the subject or with the unity of consciousness. That is, they all say that composite subjectivity is ruled out either by something about the way that experiences "belong to" certain beings or by something about the way that experiences "hang together." But both of these—conscious subjects and conscious unity—are multifarious notions, often given conflicting definitions and prompting conflicting intuitions. I believe that part of the force of the above arguments comes from this multifariousness: responses that work for one way of conceiving unity, or subjecthood, come across as missing the point on a different conception. Combinationists need multiple responses, reflecting the multiple ways that unity and subjecthood can be conceived, which is why this book contains outlines of three different combinationist theories. Each theory will have to address the five arguments above, though they will do so in different ways. So before evaluating the arguments themselves, and the options for responding to them, I need to examine these two connected notions: the "I" that undergoes experiences and the "unity" that ties all my experiences together.

2.1. What Is a Subject of Experience?

We can define a subject of experience as a being which it is like something to be. If I ask what it is like to be this dog, or this chair, or something else, I am thereby presupposing that the dog, chair, or whatever is a subject. This definition does not tell us much, though it tells us that certain things are subjects (unless we are all very deeply mistaken), such as me, my friends, the people I walk past in the street, etc. And it tells us that whatever subjects are, they are the things we mean when we use personal pronouns, standard human names, and so on. But this does not provide a deep understanding of what subjects are.

Unfortunately, all available philosophical accounts of subjecthood are highly controversial. Indeed, there has been far-reaching disagreement on this topic for centuries. It would be cumbersome in the extreme to discuss every plausible option that is available, but committing to one in particular would inappropriately narrow the interest of my subsequent discussion. Moreover, I am inclined to think (following Rovane 1998, 11, 33ff.; cf. Schechter 2009, 2012a, 583) that no single analysis fully captures our intuitive notion of a subject. However, I do think that two rough clusters of accounts can be distinguished, and that we can be relatively confident that the right account is either somewhere within one cluster or the other, somewhere intermediate between them, or some combination of them. Thus by considering combinationism in terms of both conceptions of subjects, I can perhaps ensure that my arguments will be relevant to almost all reasonable views.

2.1.1. TWO CONCEPTIONS OF SUBJECTS—METAPHYSICAL AND PSYCHOLOGICAL

I will call these two clusters the "psychological" and the "metaphysical" conceptions of subjects. On the psychological conception, a subject is some sort of integrated psychological structure—a self-image, a point of view, a stable personality, an autobiographical narrative, an ongoing stream of causes and effects, or something of that sort. What individuates a subject is usually their distinctive psychological traits, like their episodic memories, their cognitive capacities, or their values and life projects. Crucially, on this conception we have to identify the states of a subject—experiences, beliefs, memories, or whatever—prior to identifying the subject themselves. They are individuated, even constituted, by those states.

By contrast, on the "metaphysical" conception, a subject is whatever being "underlies" those states and their continuities—an immaterial soul, a brain, a human being, or some other kind of enduring concrete substance.[1] Rather that starting from the experiences and constructing something to "have" them, we ask "What entities does the world contain?" and try to identify the one "in which" certain experiences are going on. We may still attend to complex psychological structures, but we look for the entity whose nature and operations *in fact explain* them—whereas on the psychological conception we define subjects to *logically guarantee* them. Even if, like Descartes, we decide that no detectable physical object can be the right thing to have experiences, we are still employing the metaphysical conception if our response is to *add something*, some purely mental substance, to our worldview. For on the psychological conception subjects would be nothing in addition to their experiences, no further thing to be added.

The primary examples of the psychological conception of subjects would include all of what are broadly called "Neo-Lockean" theories of personal identity (e.g., Shoemaker 1970, 1997; Parfit 1984; Noonan 2003; Lewis 1976; Rovane 1998), who trace their intellectual ancestry to John Locke's (1836) "Of Identity and Diversity." There Locke argues that we have the same person at two times wherever consciousness at one time can "reach back" to consciousness at the other; interpreters disagree as to whether this "reaching back" relation is just episodic memory, but Locke's crucial point is that since this relation can connect states of consciousness in different substances (whether brains, souls, or something else), a "person" is not the same thing as any substance. Later writers have often changed the formulation, but the core idea (discussed in more detail in chapter 7) remains: persons are individuated by psychological relations (often grouped under the umbrella term "psychological continuity") that have no essential connection to the substances that underlie thought. Since it is nearly platitudinous that "persons" are conscious subjects, we are clearly dealing here with a psychological analysis of subjects.

One need not be a Neo-Lockean, however, to hold a psychological analysis of subjects. One might be a functionalist, holding that a subject is individuated by the pattern of causal relations that hold among mental states (Shoemaker 1997; Schechter 2015). One might, like Hume (1888, 252), regard the subject as a "bundle," collection, or stream of experiences; one might, like Schechtman (2009), regard it as being, or as constituted by, a series of narratives that are told to oneself; one might, like Nedelsky (2012), regard it as constituted by some kind of social process

---

[1] I take "underlying" to be the sort of grounding that holds between an object and an event or process that "goes on in it"; e.g., a particular organ underlies certain chemical processes if facts about those processes are fully grounded in facts about the organ.

of care or enculturation; or one might, like Dennett (1992) and Bayne (2010, 289), regard it as a sort of fictional character or intentional object, defined by the representations that posit it.[2] Or one might have no specific theory of the subject, and simply be inclined to think that what really defines someone is something about how exactly their mind *works*.

The metaphysical conception of a subject is less unified, since adherents will differ over what a subject is in proportion as they differ over what kind of substance underlies thought and experience. Many contemporary philosophers focus on *biological* substances, in particular human organisms (e.g., Van Inwagen 1990, 142ff.; Olson 1997), and they can with only mild fear of anachronism associate themselves with the views of Aristotle. Others, particularly the earliest critics of Lockean theories, posit nonphysical souls and take subjects of experience to be these (Descartes 1985; Butler 1860; Swinburne 1984). Others say that it is the human body (Williams 1957; Wiggins 1967), or the human brain (Nagel 1986, 39–41), or whatever exact set of physical mechanisms continuously subserves basic experiential capacities (Unger 1990, 139–169). Some philosophers might even identify the subject with the world itself, understood as a single being (Śaṅkara 1994; Schopenhauer 1969). But what unites these views is the idea that the subject of experience is the thing which lies beneath particular experiences, which persists while particular experiences arise and cease, which remains the same even when very different experiences belong to it.[3]

I will make a sequence of claims about these two conceptions of subjecthood. First, both connect to something important in our intuitions about personal survival. Second, both connect to important epistemic interests in our thinking about the world. Third, both connect to important practical interests that the notion of a subject is bound up with. As a result, it would be inappropriate to dismiss either as entirely without merit or significance. And while there might be ways to partially combine or reconcile them, I will in this book remain neutral, talking about subjects according to both the psychological and metaphysical

---

[2] Tye's view (2003, 140–154) is an interesting blend of the two approaches: his notion of the "psychological frameworks" that individuate subjects is clearly an instance of the psychological approach, but the subjects themselves are not the frameworks but whatever physical organ implements them, in line with the metaphysical approach.

[3] Two partial criteria for these conceptions deserve noting. First, if someone thinks that the identities and intrinsic properties of subjects *supervene on* facts about experiences, they almost certainly accept the psychological conception. (But if they deny this, that suggests but does not imply acceptance of the metaphysical conception.) Second, if someone thinks that "subject of experience" is a *phase sortal*, i.e., a term which applies to an entity at some points in its existence but might not apply at other points (like "student" or "adult"; contrast essential kinds like "cat"), then they almost certainly accept the metaphysical conception. (But if they deny this, that suggests but does not imply acceptance of the psychological conception: both Lockeans and Cartesians think that a subject is essentially a subject.)

conceptions without committing to either definitely being the thing we mean to pick out with personal pronouns, human names, and terms like "subject," "self," and "person."

2.1.2. INTUITIVE FOUNDATIONS OF THE TWO CONCEPTIONS

The best way to bring out the resonance of both conceptions with our intuitions is to consider Williams's 1970 paper "The Self and the Future." In this paper, Williams describes the same sequence of events in two ways, generating opposite intuitive reactions. The first description is as follows: two people ("A" and "B") are sent into a futuristic device, which exhaustively scans and records the wiring of their two brains, and then reconfigures each brain in accordance with the model provided by the other. When they come out, they are "switched": there is a person with A's old body, reporting B's old memories, self-identifying with B's name, and in every respect acting like B, and there is another person with B's old body, reporting A's old memories, self-identifying with A's name, and in every respect acting like A. As these two people meet each other, the most natural thing for them to say is "Wow! You have my old body, and I'm in your old body. We have switched bodies—I, A (B), now inhabit B's (A's) body." And it is very tempting, from a third-person point of view, to agree with them—to think that two people have switched bodies. That is just what the psychological conception predicts: all the interesting psychological relations now hold between the present person in one body and the past person in the other body. Yet since no substance has passed between them, the metaphysical conception must disagree.

The second description of these same events, however, makes it seem as though the opposite has happened: two people have retained their bodies but had their psychologies radically altered. This description focuses on the forward-looking perspective of the people involved: before entering the device, each is told in detail about what will be done to them. First, they will have their memories wiped away; then, they will have a series of false memories implanted; then, they will have their temperament systematically altered, and then likewise with all their other personality traits, background knowledge, beliefs, and so on. While this prospect is certainly hugely significant and weighty, perhaps terrifying, each stage seems to be something that the individuals themselves can survive—losing memories, changing temperament, and so on. Indeed, there is no reason in principle why this could not all be done while the person remains awake, enjoying an uninterrupted stream of consciousness even while the contents of that stream change radically. If they are then told that the memories and personality they are to end up with are modeled on another person, what difference does that make? That is a fact about where the instructions came from, but does not change what happens to them, there, in that device, having their brain scrambled.

It seems to me, when considering the case in this way, that the subjects would be perfectly reasonable in thinking of the device as imposing a series of major changes on a single continuous person.[4] But over the course of these changes, all interesting psychological relations between their "new self" and their "old self" are broken, so the psychological conception of subjecthood must deny this. The metaphysical conception, however, can exactly capture what is going on here: a single underlying substance (whether we identify it as the body, the brain, the organism, or something else) is persisting through unusually rapid and radical changes in its properties.

At this point we might start to debate which set of intuitions is stronger, or more reasonable, or better-grounded, or easiest to explain away somehow. But I want to hold onto both, side by side, and think about what kind of function they serve. I think that both serve valid functions, both practical and epistemic. Let me begin with the epistemic functions: How do these conceptions help us to make sense of a perplexing, mutable, world?

2.1.3. FUNCTIONS OF THE TWO CONCEPTIONS

On the one hand, the psychological conception of subjects is epistemically useful because the definition of a psychological subject is inherently so rich in implications: knowing that a person before us is psychologically continuous with a previous person we knew tells us a lot about how that person will behave, far more than knowing any particular psychological trait of theirs. In deploying this concept we can satisfy a general epistemic goal: to identify rich continuities, where much is preserved across time, and deploy concepts to track them.

On the other hand, the metaphysical conception of subjects is epistemically useful for the opposite reason: the definition of a metaphysical subject allows it to undergo extensive changes, and thus can be applied in a greater range of cases (e.g., identifying someone with their brain allows us to make sense of the influence on them of prenatal events, postdementia events, and any other events which affect the brain even when psychological continuity is broken). In deploying

---

[4] This intuition is sometimes harder to elicit than the previous one; that at least has been my experience talking about the paper with undergraduates. What may help to elicit it is Williams's remarks at the end of the paper about easy adjustments that could be made to the procedure, like copying A's psychology into B but leaving A unchanged, or giving A the psychology of B but copying A's psychology into three other people, B, C, and D. No simple switching story can be told about these cases, but the idea that the people remain in their bodies, while their psychology is oddly scrambled, continues to make perfect sense of what is happening.

this concept we can satisfy a different epistemic goal: to identify underlying fundamentals, things which are preserved through many changes, and deploy concepts to track them.

Next, what are the practical functions of "subject" (what Parfit 1971 refers to as "what matters" in survival)? Many of the answers to this question seem to track the psychological conception of subjects, but one, I will argue, better tracks the metaphysical conception.

Here are some of the things that are at stake in asking whether the person before us is identical to a past person P: Are they bound by P's commitments (promises, contracts, debts, etc.)? Are they culpable for P's past crimes, or laudable for P's past heroism? Are they the right person to continue the projects that P started, and carry out the plans that P laid? Do they have the shared history with P's friends and family that gave them their deep emotional relationship to P? Should those friends and family embrace P fondly, or introduce themselves? I think that if we suppose that the person before us is psychologically continuous with P, that will provide a very good reason for treating them "as P" in all of these respects. Since that is what the psychological conception says matters, the prominence of these questions seems to support that conception. Psychological continuity with P at least provides a better reason for treating them as P than would their possession of P's body, brain, or even soul, if there was no psychological continuity. After all, continuity is what would let this person recognize and reciprocate the love of P's friends and family, acknowledge remorsefully or proudly P's past deeds, recall P's commitments and why P took them on, pick up P's plans right where P left off, and so on. Of course, if they did not have P's body or brain, they might react with denial and treat all of this as basically illusory: "I seem to remember doing that awful thing, but it wasn't me! I feel great affection for your familiar face, even though this is the first time we've met!" But for them to embrace the "practical identity" of P would at least feel more natural.

But now consider person P themselves, contemplating a possible future and wondering whether anyone in that future will be *them*. Part of what matters to them may be questions like "Will anyone honor my commitments and repay my debts?," "Will anyone comfort my friends and family?," "Will anyone remember my life and experiences?," or "Will anyone complete the plans I've laid?" But this is surely not the only thing that matters to them; after all, these questions are not wholly different from questions someone can ask about the world after they themselves die, when there is no question of identity. Something else that matters to them is what they can appropriately anticipate—whether they can anticipate pleasant experiences, unpleasant experiences, or no experiences at all. If someone in the future completes my plans, repays my debts, or even remembers my experiences, they are not me if it would be a mistake for me to look forward to their pleasures and dread their suffering. But what determines the appropriateness of anticipation? Presumably I can anticipate any experience that would be part of the same stream as my present experiences. And it seems that I could enjoy a continuous, unbroken stream of consciousness even while my memories, intentions, personality, and so on were radically changed (as Williams's story brings out). Thus it seems that the metaphysical conception is better-placed to capture the relationship between subjects and anticipation than the psychological conception.

None of the intuitive claims that I have made in the past few pages is uncontroversial, but I think that taken together they support the conclusion that we have at least two distinct, and independently attractive, ways of thinking about experiences as "belonging to something." Rather than try to adjudicate which of them best deserves the label "subject" (and the associated status of being referred to by "I"), I will keep both notions in play.

2.1.4. COMBINATION FOR SUBSTRATES AND FOR PERSONAS

We could use the term "metaphysical subject" for the kind of thing that the metaphysical conception is about, if it is true, and the term "psychological subject" for the kind of thing that the psychological conception is about, if it is true. Then it would be an open question which of "metaphysical subjects" or "psychological subjects" exist. I will use the terms "substrate" and "persona" for the things that *would be* metaphysical and psychological subjects, respectively, if any existed. So, given some plausible assumptions about what underlies human experience, the substrate of my experiences is a human brain, and if the metaphysical conception of subjects is correct, then that brain, or the larger bodily or organismic structure that contains and supports it, is a subject, and in fact is *me*. But there is also what we may call "the Luke Roelofs identity," the persona that my experiences fit into (roughly, what would be destroyed if I suffered thoroughgoing retrograde amnesia and massive personality alteration); if the psychological conception of subjects is correct, then that persona is a subject, and in fact is *me*. By formulating things in terms of substrates and personas, we can proceed without deciding which one is really "the subject." We can say that in Williams's thought experiment, two substrates switch personas, and vice versa; we can say that in dissociative identity disorder, and in fictions like that of Jekyll and Hyde, a single substrate may sequentially support two or more personas.[5]

---

[5] Fictional stories of body swaps and so forth are often hard to interpret, because they do not specify the metaphysical mechanisms involved. If the characters in, for example, *Freaky Friday* are wholly material

What is the relationship that holds between the persona that is a candidate referent for a given person's name and the substrate that is a candidate referent for that same name—the relationship between Luke's brain and the Luke Roelofs identity, for example? It is hard to say exactly, but roughly we can say that the substrate, by underlying the experiences which together fit into the persona, also underlies the persona. We might put this in terms of occupying or implementing roles (analogizing it to the relation between brain states and functional states), or in terms of material constitution (analogizing it to the relation between lumps of clay and statues made out of them), or even in terms of performance (analogizing it to the relation between an actor and a character they play, so that the Luke Roelofs identity is something that my brain *does*). However we spell it out, this does not seem to be a relationship between two entities of the same category, in the way that would be needed for either to be a part of the other. Subject-combination could be combination of substrates into substrates, or personas into personas, but not of substrates into personas, or personas into substrates.

Moreover, the distinction between substrates and personas connects with the distinction, drawn in chapter 1, between aggregates and structure-specific wholes. Personas are defined by a certain psychological structure, and so a composite persona must be thought of as a structure-specific whole, not as an aggregate. But a substrate of experience might be either; for example, the brain is a prime candidate for being the substrate of human experiences and could plausibly be regarded as a structure-specific whole, existing only as long as its physical parts remain in certain complex biological relationships. On the other hand, an aggregate of substrates might also be a substrate of experience; indeed, aggregates are in some ways better candidates for substratehood because of their relatively more fundamental, "lower-level" status relative to structure-specific wholes. The existence of a structure-specific whole is grounded in the aggregate of its parts instantiating a certain structure, and in that sense the aggregate underlies the structure-specific whole. If we want to identify the substrate of an experience with what ultimately underlies experience, it might make sense to look "under" the structure-specific whole that underlies an experience, to the aggregate that underlies it in turn. At least, that is one attractive way to think about subjects, and my aim is to have something to say for all the attractive ways to think about subjects.

---

entities, and their body switch involves the rewiring of their two brains, then personas have moved while substrates stayed in place; but if they exchange immaterial *souls*, then personas have in fact remained with the same substrate, and what has happened is that one (mental) substance has come apart from another (material) substance. It is understandable but aggravating how often this is left ambiguous.

So for a systematic defense of combinationism I will have to consider three sorts of entity as candidate subjects: aggregates of substrates (see chapter 3), structure-specific wholes composed of substrates (see chapter 5), and composite personas (see chapter 7).

2.2. What Is the Unity of Consciousness?

If combinationists can address the subject-summing and privacy arguments, perhaps they can show that parts of me having experiences could explain my having those experiences too. And so if many parts of me have various experiences, that might explain why I myself have many experiences. But just as no set of bricks automatically forms a house, no set of experiences automatically forms the kind of unified total experience, the kind of "phenomenal field" of consciousness, that human beings have. After all, these experiences are experiences of many distinct subjects, so shouldn't they be in some sense "isolated" from each other, forming separate fields of experience just as different human beings seem to have separate fields?

We can illuminate this point by considering what it might be like to be a three-headed monster, with three separate brains each having partial control over its body (or alternatively, what it would be like to be a human being who somehow grew fully functional brains in their feet). Surely there is a sense in which, rather than there being any single "something it is like" to be such a being, there are in fact three things it is like. This creature would have its head-one experiences, its head-two experiences, and its head-three experiences, but it would have them separately, not together. So combinationism should be able to explain why, despite our own consciousness arising from many distinct parts of us, we do not find ourselves in the situation of this imagined monster. What "unifies" all the experiences that our brains give rise to?

But maybe I've put the cart before the horse? The above way of putting the problem of unity assumes that we can talk about the three-headed monster as being itself a subject of experience (in addition to its three, or more, smaller conscious parts). We might, however, think that the whole monster is not a subject precisely *because* it lacks unity. That is, we might think that subjects essentially have unified experiences—that unity is part of what it means to be a subject of experience. This would make sense especially if we were thinking of composite subjects as structure-specific wholes rather than as mere aggregates: unity of consciousness is a very natural sort of structure to use for individuating subjects. We would then say: there is a subject of experience for every set of unified experiences, and when not all the experiences associated with a system are unified (as with our three-headed monster), that system is not a subject, though it may contain subjects (the three heads). In chapters 5–8 I explore this idea of subjects individuated by unity, but of course this increases, rather than diminishes, the importance of providing a combinationist account of how experiences get unified.

The problem is, it is far from obvious what "unity" means here. Although both "the unity of consciousness" and "the subject of experience" are philosophical jargon, the latter at least can be anchored to very familiar structural features of language, namely the way that we always ascribe experiences *to* someone and speak of things feeling some way "to" or "for" this someone. It is not as common for us to talk about unity, and so it is not as clear that we should look for one thing that this term "unity" picks out. Whereas different accounts of "the subject" seem to *disagree*, providing rival accounts of the same thing, it is more natural to see different accounts of "conscious unity" as just picking out different things. So in this section I review five things that could be called "conscious unity" and how they relate to unity-based challenges to combinationism.

2.2.1. FIVE SORTS OF UNITY

So, first, we might talk about someone's mind or consciousness being "unified" when it is internally consistent, and conversely speak of it being "split" or "divided" when they harbor inconsistent beliefs, attitudes, or judgments. Schechter (2013) uses the term "coherence unity" for something like this consistency of contents (cf. Korsgaard 1989, 176), and it does seem to be one major part of our normal sense of a subject as having a unified mind. A single subject should not think inconsistent things at the same time, and the occasional exceptions are cause for criticism. For distinct subjects, or even for the disunified experiences in two heads of a three-headed creature, inconsistency would simply be normal, unsurprising disagreement. Call this relation among experiences "global consistency": a set of experiences are "globally consistent" if none of them contradict any of the others.[6]

Second, we might say that two experiences are unified if the present state of each is in part a causal result of the other. For example, suppose I am distracted from my friend's words by a traffic light turning green: my perception of my friend's voice would be different (namely, attended-to) were it not for my more salient perception of the light. And my perception of that green circle would be

---

[6] Since my focus is on the unity of *consciousness*, global consistency here is defined primarily among conscious thoughts and perceptions, not among background beliefs that one is not conscious of on a given occasion. But to the extent that background beliefs heavily inflect the way we perceive and think about things, global consistency in conscious states will tend to require, and ensure, global consistency in standing beliefs.

different were it not for the contrasting black around it, for then I would not see it as a circle specifically. This kind of mutual influence is pervasive in normal human consciousness: you cannot change one experience without its making a difference to many others.[7] Call this relation "causal interdependence."

Causal interdependence seems to be connected to global consistency, in that it is because our many conscious thoughts and perceptions can freely influence each other that they are kept consistent. That is, one form of causal interdependence holds when two experiences, which would otherwise have had conflicting contents, interact to produce a sense of tension or to amend one another, so that we end up with only consistent experiences. Without causal interdependence—with experiences that were "cut off" from affecting each other—global consistency would be unlikely to arise or persist.

One particularly important pattern of causal interconnection is what is called "access-unity" (Bayne and Chalmers 2003, 31). A single state is access-conscious if the subject can use its content to guide their various cognitive activities; for instance, a perception of someone shouting "Fire!" is access-conscious if I can report that I heard it, can remember hearing it later, can form plans and inferences based on the fact that someone shouted "Fire!," and so on. If I cannot do these things, the perception is not access-conscious even if it is like something for me to hear it, and even if it makes a difference to my mood or dispositions. Access-consciousness, thus defined, is a capacity for a particular sort of causal interdependence between the access-conscious state and other mental states. Access-unity is then defined thus: two experiences are access-unified if the subject can use both of them, and the conjunction of their contents together, to guide the same cognitive activities. If, like a split-brain patient, I can respond intelligently to seeing "key" on the left and to seeing "ring" on the right, but not to seeing "keyring," then my visual perceptions are access-disunified.

Access-unity is a particular pattern of causal relations, a particular way that two experiences can interact: we can define any number of other specific such

---

[7] Causal interdependence is hard to characterize if we think of experiences as momentary—as what I am experiencing at a given *instant*, so that two simultaneous experiences are more likely to be influenced by what I states, for then it seems like simultaneous experiences are rarely, if ever, causally interdependent: rather, each will owe its character to certain experiences that happened a moment earlier, but have now passed. To account for this we might say that while conscious unity is usually thought of as a synchronic relation, this particular type is actually diachronic, but holds (stipulatively) only over very short intervals (less than a second, say). Alternatively we might insist that causal interdependence is synchronic, but think of experiences as enduring rather than momentary, with successive, causally connected, qualitatively identical (or very similar) momentary experiences being counted as stages of a single enduring experience. Or, third, we might think of causal interdependence in "common cause" terms, as holding between two experiences which owe their character to (some or all of) the *same* earlier moments of experience. The particular way that we conceptualize the causal web that knits our experiences together is less important that having a label for referring to it.

patterns, and some might be good candidates for being thought of as forms of conscious unity. For example, my various desires interact with my beliefs in such a way that generally, if I desire X and believe that Y will lead to X, I will start to desire Y: this is one sense in which my beliefs and desires are unified. My various feelings of pleasure interact with my perceptions and desires in such a way that if I feel pleasure while perceiving Z, I will generally come to desire Z. And so on. We can refer to these sorts of relations as forms of "functional unity," with access-unity being just one of them.

A fourth way that our experiences are connected is through their representational contents: they present themselves as being about different aspects of the same thing. In perception this primarily takes the form of what is called "feature binding," the relation between experiences of (say) redness and squareness that obtains when we see a red square. But it also involves tying experiences together into, for instance, a single spatially connected visual scene, or an overall sense of a single body with sensations all across its surface. And there are also the relations that knit together elements of thoughts (like the concepts "snorkeling" and "bad idea" in the thought that snorkeling is a bad idea). Call both these relations, and any others that serve to form complex conscious representations out of simpler ones, "representational unity."

Representational unity seems to hold only within the minds of individual human beings. But it does not seem to be pervasive within those minds: sometimes I have unrelated experiences which form no complex representation but which are still had together. So while this relation may be sufficient for two experiences to be "unified" in the sense we are looking for, but it cannot be necessary.[8] Thus some philosophers (e.g., Dainton 2000; Bayne and Chalmers 2003; Bayne 2010) have suggested that there is a further, fifth, sort of unity which is pervasive in ordinary human consciousness: phenomenal unity. The thought is that for two experiences to be representationally unified in any way, they first need to be in some more basic sense experienced together, "there beside each other" ready to be connected. Unless they share a phenomenal field in this basic way, establishing any richer sort of unity will be impossible, like drawing a line to connect items on two different maps.

---

[8] A possible exception is "spatial unity," the type of representational unity that holds between two experiences when their objects are presented as occupying regions of the same space. Spatial unity seems pervasive in our perceptual experiences under normal conditions, but does not obviously extend to our nonperceptual experiences. Moreover, it seems that a subject with multiple distant sense organs would not experience spatial unity, but might nevertheless experience conscious unity if these organs fed information to a single brain (as argued by Tye 2003, 76–78; Dainton 2004, 9–10; Bayne 2010, 262–266; cf. Roelofs 2014b, 91–93).

Phenomenal unity is sometimes said to admit of no further analysis (e.g., Dainton 2000). But other writers (Bayne and Chalmers 2003; Bayne 2010) point out that it does appear to be tied to "phenomenal subsumption": two experiences are phenomenally unified when they are contained as parts within a larger experience, so that there is not only "something it is like" to undergo the first and "something it is like" to undergo the second, but also "something it is like" to undergo both. That is, phenomenal unity is a matter of the composition of experiences into wholes which are also experiences. On this view, the phenomenal unity of everyday human consciousness consists in the fact that all of a given human's experiences are subsumed by their single total experience, but no such total experience subsumes their experiences together with someone else's. And this seems to be the fundamental sense in which a three-headed monster has disunified experiences: there is no *single* thing it is like to be that monster, because there is no single experience that contains as parts all the experiences arising in its three heads.

So "the unity of consciousness" can be resolved into at least five sorts of unity: global consistency, causal interdependence, access-unity and other forms of functional unity, representational unity, and phenomenal unity. When I speak of "unity" in what follows, I will usually mean this cluster of relations: the experiences of one human are "unified" in that they are generally connected to each other in many of these ways.

2.2.2. IS CONSCIOUS UNITY TRANSITIVE?

One debated question about the formal features of unity relations, which will prove important later on, is whether they are *transitive*: Does it follow from one experience being unified with a second, and the second with a third, that the first and third must also be unified? If unity is transitive, then there could not be a system with a "Y-shaped" unity pattern, where two subjects share some but not all of their experiences, and the experiences of each are fully unified with one another, but each one's unshared experiences are not unified with the other's. That is, I could not have two unified experiences, of a sound and a smell, while you share my experience of the smell but not the sound, and also experience a sight, with the sight and smell unified as much as the sound and smell are unified.

The plausibility of transitivity depends on the particular kind of unity being considered. Representational unity seems not to be transitive; to pick a particular variety, predication, there can be a conscious thought that, say, "the archbishop's happiness was fleeting," where fleetingness is predicated of happiness, and happiness of the archbishop, but fleetingness is not predicated of the archbishop, showing that whatever relations are binding together the constituents of that thought are not always transitive. Global consistency is not transitive: consider the sets P, not-Q; not-Q, R; not-P, R. The first two are consistent, the second two are consistent, but the first and third contradict one another. Access-unity and also other forms of functional unity seem not to be transitive: Why couldn't there be a system whose cognitive mechanisms were able to synthesize and employ contents A and B, or contents B and C, but which for whatever engineering reason were not set up to do so with A and C together?

On the other hand, causal interdependence is plausibly transitive, if understood in the weakest possible way: from the fact that A can influence B, and that B can influence C, it does seem to follow that A is capable of having some sort of impact on C, however slight and indirect. But usually we are interested in interactions that reach some minimum of strength, and that sort of interdependence is not transitive: A might have a big impact on B, and B a big impact on C, but A only a small impact on C.

It is for phenomenal unity that the question of transitivity is most controversial. There is no obvious contradiction in the idea of A and B being subsumed within one phenomenal field, and B and C being subsumed within another, so that both pairs are unified but A and C are not. But some writers have felt that this sort of situation is incoherent in some more subtle sense. I am not sure whether phenomenal unity is transitive: when transitivity would matter, I will simply note the relevance of the question. But even if phenomenal unity is not transitive, the other relations discussed above are plausibly not, and consequently "unity" as a whole will be nontransitive even if it has transitive elements.

2.2.3. WHICH SORT OF UNITY IS MOST FUNDAMENTAL?

I have distinguished five different sorts of "unity relations" that experiences can stand in. One important question is how these different relations are related to one another, and in particular how phenomenal unity relates to the other four. Here I think there are broadly two different attitudes that can be taken, which I will call "reductionism" and "primitivism" about phenomenal unity.

"Reductionism" is the idea that phenomenal unity is not really anything over and above the other four sorts of unity (e.g., Shoemaker 2003): all that it is for two experiences to be phenomenally unified is for them to be causally interdependent enough, consistent enough, functionally unified enough, perhaps representationally unified, perhaps access-unified. Since things like causal interdependence or access-unity come in different forms or different degrees, this amounts to thinking that phenomenal unity is a somewhat messily defined thing, a cluster-concept, something which holds when we have "enough" of the other sorts of unity, even though it is very hard, perhaps impossible to say precisely how much is "enough."

By contrast, "primitivism" about phenomenal unity (e.g., Dainton 2000; Bayne 2010) is the view that two experiences being phenomenally unified goes beyond any other form of unity: not only are they interacting, consistent, jointly accessible, and so on, but they are *also* subsumed by a composite experience, and this is not simply a way of summarizing the former facts.

These two views have different implications for the separability of different sorts of unity. If reductionism is true, then any experiences which are phenomenally unified will also be unified in other ways, since that is all phenomenal unity is. But if primitivism is true, then it is at least conceptually possible that two experiences might be phenomenally unified despite not being causally interdependent, jointly accessible, consistent, or representationally unified. Indeed, if primitivism is true, it is not strictly impossible that my experiences and yours are phenomenally unified, despite the lack of any other sorts of unity among them.

The choice among these two views is likely to track views about the fundamentality of consciousness itself. Phenomenal unity involves the subsumption of experiences by a composite experience; to put it another way, it involves a pair of conscious states being itself a conscious state. If consciousness is a fundamental property, so that whether some event or state is conscious is a fundamental fact, then it would be natural to extend that to whether a pair of conscious states is conscious, and conclude that whether two experiences are phenomenally unified is likewise a fundamental fact. That is, primitivism about consciousness and about phenomenal unity go hand in hand. By contrast, reductionism about phenomenal unity goes hand in hand with reductionism about consciousness, since the former implies that whether a pair of experiences is itself an experience depends on whether they are "sufficiently" unified in other ways, which, as noted above, is likely to allow for some vagueness, some borderline cases where there is no good basis for saying that the unity relations involved are sufficient or not. That in turn implies that it might sometimes be indeterminate whether something is an experience, which fits awkwardly with taking consciousness to be a fundamental property.

2.2.4. CAN CONSCIOUS UNITY HOLD BETWEEN DISTINCT SUBJECTS?

The combinationist needs to explain how a composite mind, whose experiences come to it from its many individual parts, can come to be knitted together in all these various ways. More specifically, they need to explain how to understand unity as simultaneously both a within-subject relation, among the experiences of a single whole, and also a between-subjects relation, among the experiences of many parts. We are familiar with the former, but much less so with the latter: How could the relations that tie together all of my experiences hold also between one subject and another?

For some forms of unity, this question is actually fairly easy to answer. In the case of global consistency, for instance, we have a perfectly good grasp of what it is for two people's experiences to not contradict each other, and there is thus no special problem of explaining the consistency of a composite subject's total experience, beyond explaining why particular component experiences tend to be consistent with each other.

Causal interdependence is likewise easily accounted for by purely causal unifying relations: all we need are some causal laws according to which the various parts of the world interact with and affect each other, and we can readily explain how it is that particular experiences come to be causally interdependent.

Moreover, we need not worry that two subjects' experiences being unified in these ways would deprive those subjects of their boundedness, merge them so fully as to no longer be really *two* subjects. Indeed, it might seem that global consistency and causal interdependence are both things that routinely hold between the experiences of different human beings: when two people are talking, their auditory experiences are causally dependent on the other's vocal intentions, which in turn are influenced by their previous auditory experiences. And they might well end up believing very similar things, forming a largely consistent shared worldview.

Of course, it is natural at this point to object by saying that the interactions between two conversational partners' experiences are "indirect," while those among one person's experiences are "direct" (cf. Schechter 2009, 153, 2015, 505). But this distinction, though intuitive, is hard to define exactly (though see Schechter 2018, 95–105); in both cases there is some crucial causal intermediary, whether it is sound waves traveling through the air or nerve impulses traveling down axons. Certainly the causal interactions within one brain are *faster* and harder to interfere with than the causal interactions between two brains, but so what? I think what really lies behind this desire to distinguish direct from indirect interactions is a concern with *phenomenal* unity. The thought is that causal interdependence in the absence of phenomenal unity is just not the same as causal interdependence with phenomenal unity, because phenomenal unity, by linking experiences, putting them "in contact" with each other, allows for a special, "direct" sort of causal interaction. Consequently, the intuition goes, just establishing causal interdependence is not enough to unify two minds, without phenomenal unity.

What about representational unity? We might think that some sorts of social interaction establish a kind of unity of representations. Sometimes I categorize things using concepts that I don't fully understand, relying on other members of my linguistic community to fix their meaning; e.g., when I believe that there are elm trees and beech trees but have no idea what differentiates the two, the meaning of my belief depends not on anything in my mind but on what botanists associate with the two words I use (Putnam 1975; Burge 1979). And sometimes it seems that groups can know things that no individual member knows, through a sort of "distributed knowledge" (Hutchins 1995). It would be nice if we could see this as a sort of primitive representational unity among different subjects (and in chapter 5 I will argue that we can), but at first glance it does not seem to be enough. The connections between two members of a linguistic community or social group seem not to touch their consciousness: even if there is something like a complex thought spread across multiple minds, it is not a complex *conscious* thought. These connections seem to be "indirect" in exactly the same way as I noted above for causal interdependence between subjects: they need phenomenal unity if they are to be a genuine sort of unified consciousness.

Finally, what about functional unity? Considering access-unity as an example, we can observe that access is in large part a matter of causation: if there are two experiences, and they have the power to jointly cause some activity to be performed in a way that reflects the conjunction of their contents, then they are to that extent access-unified; if they have such powers for all the relevant activities that a subject is capable of, they are access-unified for that subject. So can the experiences of two humans be access-unified? There is of course a sense in which we can, and often do, "access" the contents of each other's experiences—by asking each other questions, for instance. And if we count one person's experience as "access-conscious" for the other person when the former tells the latter about it, making it accessible to both, then there is no problem saying that such a state is then access-unified with the other experiences of the second subject. (If I see "key" on the left and you tell me you see "ring" on the right, I can access the joint content "keyring.")

But this is still intuitively different from a single person's access-unity, again because the access here is so "indirect": I can access your experience only because I can access another state that carries information about it (my auditory experience of your words), and you may or may not provide me with that access. The same indirectness can obtain within a single person—we might, for instance, be able to recognize our repressed anger only by reflecting on our memories of how we have acted over the past few days, and this should not make the anger count as access-conscious. The difference in this within-subject case seems to be largely about speed, reliability, automaticity, and similar factors: Can the anger be accessed quickly, reliably, and fully, and does it spontaneously suggest itself when I consider a question to which it is relevant? We can easily imagine making the information-sharing between two people extremely fast, reliable, automatic, etc. (perhaps with futuristic brain technology, as imagined in my chapter 8 thought experiment). Insofar as it still seems as though the between-subjects access is too "indirect" to establish access-unity, I suspect that what really matters is, once again, phenomenal unity.

So can conscious unity hold between subjects? Partly. Most types of unity can sort of hold between subjects, but the lack of one type (phenomenal unity) fundamentally changes their character, making them "indirect," ersatz versions of the relations that hold within a single subject. The combinationist's challenge, then, concerns principally phenomenal unity: How can this crucial relation hold between experiences of different subjects?

This challenge will look very different to primitivists and reductionists about phenomenal unity. Reductionists must think the problem is in a certain sense merely apparent, since phenomenal unity, the key missing ingredient, is really nothing more than the right degree and mixture of the other forms of unity. Our intuition that without phenomenal unity, the other forms are missing a crucial sort of "directness" may be correct in a sense, but only in the sense that without *enough of* the other forms, any particular instance of them will be missing something. The causal interdependence of my experiences and yours when we converse seems like a very different thing to the causal interdependence among my own experiences; the former seems "indirect" in contrast to the latter's "directness." But if reductionism about phenomenal unity is true, then all that it would take to remove this indirectness is to add "more of the same": more causal relations, more mutual access, more transfers of information, between my experiences and yours. By contrast, if primitivism is true, then no amount of strengthening, enriching, or complicating the merely causal relations among two subjects' experiences will be enough to establish phenomenal unity. Phenomenal unity, on such a view, is its own thing, and which experiences it connects are not determined just by how experiences causally and informationally interact.

Because the challenge posed by conscious unity for combinationism is so different for reductionists and primitivists, I will develop two distinct solutions: in chapter 3 I present a primitivist account of phenomenal unity, while from chapter 5 onward I present a reductionist account.

2.3. Five Arguments against Combinationism

Let us return the five arguments that mental combination is impossible. I have drawn them from the existing literature on the combination problem, in particular the work of James, Goff, Chalmers, and Coleman. They do not all appear in quite the forms I have given them; indeed different writers on the combination problem typically differ both in which arguments they regard as the most important and in how they formulate those arguments. Rather than laying out and comparing all these authors' different versions, I have simply presented my own formulations, which I have tried to make clear, concise, and rigorous, and have tailored to bring out the commonalities among the different arguments.[9] In this section I present the arguments and briefly note the options for responding to them; in the next section I consider those options more closely.

2.3.1. THE SUBJECT-SUMMING ARGUMENT

The simplest argument against combinationism is that "subjects don't sum": knowing what it's like to be each of some collection of subjects seems impotent to tell us anything about what it's like to be *someone else*. And since the whole they compose is not any one of them, it seems to be an example of "someone else." A popular way to dramatize this point is inspired by the "philosophical zombie," a being physically and functionally identical to a human being but wholly lacking in consciousness, whose apparent conceivability threatens physicalism. Analogously, the critic of combinationism imagines a "microexperiential zombie" (cf. Carruthers and Schechter 2006, 38; Goff 2009b; Chalmers 2017, 187–188), a physical duplicate of an actual person, each particle of which is conscious but which is itself completely lacking in consciousness. If this creature is conceivable, then premise **3a** is supported and an explanatory gap between subjects is established. A similar point is made by James (1890, 160) and others, who imagine the component subjects as a group of people, and point out that whatever their individual experiences, and whatever their relations to each other, it still seems a further question whether the group they form is itself a conscious subject.

---

[9] The first two arguments, which try to show an "explanatory gap," appear in roughly the below form in Goff 2009a, 2009b; Chalmers 2017, 185–189, and Mendelovici 2018, 4–8; the former also appears less formally in Carruthers and Schechter 2006; and arguably in James 1890, 150–160. The next three are extracted from arguments and suggestions in Goff 2006; Coleman 2012, 2014, 2017; Rosenberg 1998; Dainton 2010; Basile 2010; Tononi 2012; Mørch 2014; Chalmers 2017; Miller 2017; Mendelovici 2018. Rosenberg (1998) and Miller (2017) are especially concerned with the boundary argument, while the incompatible contexts argument appears, in slightly different forms, in Basile 2010, 108ff.; Coleman 2014, 34ff.; and Mørch 2014, 172–175. The privacy argument is presented explicitly in Robinson 2016, 130, and its first premise, in particular, is asserted or assumed in James 1909, 181; Goff 2006, 58–59; Basile 2010, 108; Coleman 2017, 256; Miller 2017, 12).

Premise A1: For there to be composite subjectivity, facts about the intrinsic properties of, and real relations between, a set of subjects must ground and explain the fact that the whole they form is itself a conscious subject.

Premise A2: If one set of facts grounds and explains another, it should be inconceivable that the former obtain but the latter do not.

Premise A3 (Independence): For any set of intrinsic properties of, and real relations between, a set of subjects, it is conceivable that those subjects have those properties and relations, but no other subject exists.

A4 *(from A2 and A3)*: No set of facts about the intrinsic properties of, and real relations between, a set of subjects grounds and explains the fact that the whole they form is itself a conscious subject.

A5 *(from A1 and A4)*: Composite subjectivity is impossible.

Since premise **A1** draws directly from the definition of composite subjectivity, I will set aside the option of denying it. Denying premise **A2** involves insisting that there can be genuine combination even if our efforts at conceptual analysis and understanding will never succeed in grasping the connection—that even though the whole's consciousness is explained by facts about its parts, conceiving of those facts about the parts does not force us also to conceive of the whole as conscious. The remaining option (which I am going to defend) is to deny premise **A3** (the principle I am calling "Independence"): to affirm that there is some set of conditions that component subjects can meet, such that it will become inconceivable that the whole they form is not itself a conscious subject.

2.3.2. THE UNITY ARGUMENT

The idea behind our second argument is that the experiences of a single composite subject must be unified in a way that contrasts with the apparent separateness of experiences had by different subjects. And yet if the whole gets one experience from one part, and another from another part, surely their experiences will be spread out across subjects rather than unified. And on the face of it this will be true whatever the character of those experiences, and however those parts are related. We know conscious unity as a within-subject relation, something connecting the many experiences within one subject's phenomenal field. We do not know how to see it as, or even relate it to, a between-subjects relation, holding between two or more different subjects. Hence we cannot see what relation among component subjects and their experiences could suffice to unify them. Critics of panpsychism could thus imagine another kind of "zombie," a "fragmented zombie" (cf. Goff 2009b, 299–300): a being physically and functionally identical to a human being, made out of conscious particles, and undergoing all the experiences of its parts, but with no unity among them. If this being is conceivable, then we seem to have a second explanatory gap facing experiential combination.

Premise B1: For there to be composite subjectivity, facts about the individual experiences that a composite subject derives from its parts, and the real relations among them, must ground and explain the fact that those experiences are unified.

Premise B2: If one set of facts grounds and explains and entails another, it should be inconceivable that the former obtain but the latter do not.

Premise B3 (Separateness): For any set of experiences deriving from distinct subjects, standing in any real relations, it is conceivable that the whole formed by those subjects not have those experiences in a unified way.

B4 *(from B2 and B3)*: No set of facts about the individual experiences that a composite subject derives from its parts, and the real relations among them, can ground and explain the fact that those experiences are unified.

B5 *(from B1 and B4)*: Composite subjectivity is impossible.

The combinationist's options here are similar to those for the subject-summing argument: denying premise **B1** means abandoning combinationism, and denying premise **B2** means rejecting an attractive model of what "explanation" means; the most interesting option is to deny premise **B3** and try to make sense of conscious unity as something explained by the way that experiences spread among separate subjects are related.

2.3.3. THE PRIVACY ARGUMENT

Philosophers writing about the combination problem often assume, implicitly or explicitly, that for a composite subject's experiences to be fully grounded in those of its parts, there must be particular experiences that are simultaneously undergone by both the whole and some part of it. This is compatible with the whole having some experiences that no single part has, if they are built up out of experiences of different parts. And it is compatible with the parts having some experiences that the whole lacks, which, for whatever reason, are never "incorporated" into the whole. But something, it is often assumed, must be shared. The problem is that a central fact about consciousness, which distinguishes it from physical properties, is that it is "subjective" rather than "objective." Of course these terms have many meanings, but the idea here is that my consciousness is specifically mine, and directly knowable exclusively by me, in a way that contrasts with "public" facts about material things. To know the shape of a table just requires gaining certain evidence, and anyone is in principle equally capable of doing that. But to know my feelings means, in the primary instance, to feel them, and only I can do that: others must hope that those feelings correlate with some observable physical manifestation. And this seems to rule out the kind of "experience sharing" needed for experiential combination.

Premise C1: For there to be composite subjectivity, at least some experiences belonging to a composite subject must also belong to one or more of their component subjects.

Premise C2: Experiences are essentially subjective, tied to a particular perspective.

Premise C3 (Privacy): If experiences are essentially subjective, an experience of one subject cannot belong to any other subject.

C4 *(from C2 and C3)*: Experiences cannot belong to more than one subject.

C5 *(from C1 and C4)*: Composite subjectivity is impossible.

There are three ways for a combinationist to respond to this argument. One is to deny premise **C1**, as Basile (2010, 111) and Goff (2017a, 194ff.) do. Goff puts this by saying that while the experiences of the parts may "constitute" the experiences of the whole, they do not "characterise" it (194): the whole does not itself undergo those experiences. Another option is to deny premise **C2**, and deny that there is any such thing as the special "subjectivity" of experiences. As far as I know, this view is likely to be found only among hard-core physicalists, and moreover it is essentially just a more extreme form of the final option (my preferred one), namely to deny premise **C3** (the principle I am calling "Privacy") and try to make the sharing of particular experiences consistent with their being in some significant way "subjective."

2.3.4. THE BOUNDARY ARGUMENT AND THE INCOMPATIBLE CONTEXTS ARGUMENT

I will present the last two arguments together, because I think they are best viewed in terms of a dilemma arising from a set of shared premises: each argument tries to show that one or the other horn of the dilemma is unacceptable. They both begin by assuming the starting points of the previous two arguments: that experiential combination must involve the sharing of particular experiences and that it must yield conscious unity in the whole.

The arguments then pose a dilemma: consider some pair of experiences belonging to a composite subject, each of which is shared with a different component subject, and which the whole experiences as unified. Must they also be unified "for the component subjects"? That is, is conscious unity subject-invariant, something that holds between two experiences in themselves, and so remains constant whichever subjects we consider them relative to? Or is it subject-relative, something that connects experiences only relative to a particular subject, so that the experiences can be unified relative to one subject, but not unified relative to others?[10] Either supposition is then taken to be unacceptable.

Suppose, for instance, you are now experiencing two things together (e.g., seeing someone's mouth move, while also hearing them sing), and each is also being experienced by one part of you. Clearly these two experiences will color one another: each movement of the mouth will be seen *as* the source of a particular note of the song, and the aesthetic quality of each will be influenced by the presence of the other; the experiences are to some extent interdependent. But what about the part of you that is experiencing just, say, the visual image of the mouth? Do they experience it *as* a musical, noise-producing mouth, or not? If they do, it seems to follow that they are also aware of the sound, and so our initial supposition that they shared only part of your experience collapses. This is the boundary argument: the component subject disappears into the whole. The key assumption (what I will call "Boundedness") is that a subject's consciousness must be "bounded" in the sense that their experiences can be unified only with other experiences *of theirs*.

But suppose my part does not experience the visual image as a noise-producing mouth, but simply as a mouth; then they will be experiencing the visual image differently from me, and surely if they experience it differently, it is a different experience. So our initial supposition that the very same experience is being shared by me and my part collapses. This is the incompatible contexts argument: a single experience is forced to have two incompatible characters, reflecting its unification with two different sets of experiences.

For an even simpler example, consider the experience of seeing blue side by side with red; the red here appears as limited by and contrasting with the blue (and vice versa). If some part of me is experiencing the red alone, does it experience it the same way I do (as limited by and contrasting with another color), or not? If the former, surely that experience implies also experiencing the blue; if the latter, surely that is a different experience of red from the one I am having. Either way,

---

[10] The subject-relative/subject-invariant distinction is obviously connected to the more general distinction between division-relative and division-invariant properties. Given that different divisions of reality can yield different subjects (which combinationists must accept), what is subject-relative will also be division-relative (and vice versa), and what is subject-invariant will also be division-invariant (and vice versa).

we do not get substantive experiential combination into a composite subject with unified consciousness.

As with the unity argument, the difficulty of seeing within-subject and between-subjects relations as two sides of the same coin is at the heart of the problem. If we try to think of two distinct component subjects as having unified consciousness, we run into the boundary argument; if we try to keep conscious unity as a within-subject relation by relativizing it to subjects, we run into the incompatible contexts argument. Something has to give.

The Boundary Argument

Premise D1: For there to be composite subjectivity, at least some experiences belonging to a composite subject must also belong to one or more of their component subjects, which do not also share all the whole's other experiences.

Premise D2: For there to be composite subjectivity, the composite subject must have unified experiences.

Supposition S1 (Invariant Unity): If the experiences which a composite subject shares with its component subjects are unified with each other for the composite subject, they are also unified with each other for those component subjects.

Premise D3 (Boundedness): For any experience e_1 belonging to a subject s, if another experience e_2 is unified with e_1, then e_2 must also be had by s.

D4 *(from D3 and S1):* All component subjects in a unified composite subject will have the same total set of experiences; i.e., there is no genuine combination of experiences going on.

D5 *(from D1 and D4):* Composite subjectivity is impossible.

The Incompatible Contexts Argument

Premise E1: For there to be composite subjectivity, at least some experiences belonging to a composite subject must also belong to one or more of their component subjects, which do not also share all the whole's other experiences.

Premise E2: For there to be composite subjectivity, the composite subject must have unified experiences.

Supposition S2 (Relative Unity): If the experiences which a composite subject shares with its component subjects are unified with each other, they may nevertheless not be unified with each other for those component subjects.

Premise E3 (Interdependence): The phenomenal character of an experience often depends partly on its phenomenal context, i.e., on the set of other experiences it is unified with.

Premise E4: The phenomenal character of an experience is essential to it.

E5 *(from E3 and S2)*: A single experience, shared by part and whole, could have a different phenomenal character relative to the part and to the whole.

E6 *(from E4 and E5)*: If a single experience were shared by part and whole, it could differ from itself in its essential properties, and thus be numerically distinct from itself.

E7 *(from E6, by reductio)*: Composite subjectivity is impossible.

The combinationist has three options here. First, they might try to dodge both arguments, by denying the shared presuppositions that get them started; in particular, they might deny that particular experiences are shared between parts and whole (which was also one option with the privacy argument). Second, they might accept supposition **S1**, that unity is subject-invariant, not subject-relative, and then rebut the boundary argument by denying premise **D3**, "Boundedness." This would mean denying that unity between two subjects' experiences confers all of those experiences on both subjects: even if my experiences are unified with yours, that would not give me your experiences. Third, they might accept supposition **S2**, that unity is subject-relative, and rebut the incompatible contexts argument by denying either premise **E4** or premise **E3**; since premise **E4** seems almost tautological, the more likely option is to deny **E3**, the principle of Interdependence.

2.4. Responses to the Five Arguments

Coleman (2017, 259) aptly summarizes the gist of the above five arguments when he claims, "The self-contained nature of these units [subjects], their phenomenal unity and boundedness, make them singularly unsuitable to the constitution of any further entity." These arguments present internal problems, not bridging problems: they could be made however science revealed the world to be organized, as could the responses I will now evaluate. In the coming chapters I will engage more directly with the empirical facts about the universe, human brains, and human psychology, so as to connect the schematic defense of combinationism given here with concrete cases. But the five arguments of this chapter point to some basic questions all combinationists must answer, and in examining the possible answers, we see the abstract skeleton of any fleshed-out combinationist theory.

2.4.1. SUBJECT-SUMMING AND PRIVACY

I think the best responses to the subject-summing argument and the privacy argument are to deny premise **A3** ("Independence") and premise **C3** ("Privacy"). Let me say briefly why I prefer these to the other options.

One other option for responding to the subject-summing argument is to deny premise **A2**, which says that for *x* to fully explain *y*, it must be possible for a sufficiently ideal reasoner to see, from the conception of *x*, that *y* follows necessarily—i.e., that it is impossible to consistently and fully conceive of *x* in the absence of *y*.

Denying this principle (that explanation requires inconceivability) amounts to relaxing the standards for counting as a good explanation and saying that mental combination can meet those relaxed standards. The problem is that inconceivability does seem like a good standard for explanation and seems to be satisfied in canonical examples of physical combination. For someone who knows the microphysical facts about how water molecules interact at room temperature, their properties and their circumstances and the laws governing them, and who understands what it means to be "liquid," the further conclusion that water is liquid seems to follow entirely *a priori*, simply by deducing that a substance whose parts interact in that sort of way will satisfy the definition of "liquid." The idea of a substance whose molecular parts behave in just that way, but which is nevertheless not liquid, seems self-contradictory and thus inconceivable. Since this seems to be what makes physical combination so explanatory, it is a reasonable standard to hope experiential combination can meet. Consequently in this book I will largely set this form of response aside.[11]

One option for responding to the privacy argument is to deny premise **C2**, the claim that experiences have a special epistemic status called "subjectivity." Relying on this amounts to saying that mental combination is possible only if, as hardcore physicalists sometimes suggest, our most basic intuitions about the nature of consciousness are misleading and unreliable—that even the idea that each of us knows our own experiences in a distinctive, "from the inside" way, which is more direct than how others must know them, is wrong. This will be an unattractive result for many combinationists, especially those attracted to panpsychist views on which our acquaintance with consciousness is taken to provide (at least a glimmer of) insight into the deep nature of reality.

Finally, what about denying premise **C1** and trying to make combinationism compatible with privacy? If a form of combinationism that respects privacy can be

---

[11] Moreover, the appeal to inconceivability is a central part of influential arguments against physicalism, and so for a constitutive panpsychist, who motivates their view by identifying shortcomings in physicalism, it would be dialectically useful to accept premise **A2**.

shown to work, I will have no complaints—but there are several reasons I consider this approach unpromising. Most fundamental is that it radically separates mental combination from physical combination, since the latter has the sharing of property instances as a central feature. Surely physical wholes routinely share physical property instances with their parts: a red surface seems to share, with each of its red subsections, their particular instances of redness; a car may be dented when its roof is dented, and this seems to involve only one instance of the property "being dented." In cases like these it seems natural to say that there is a single instance of the property in question, which can be truly ascribed both the whole and the part. These cases are clearly different from cases where there are two separate and independent instances of the same property (two red things side by side, two distinct dents, etc.).

Second, combinationism that respects privacy will have trouble avoiding causal competition between composite and component subjects. After all, experiences have causal powers, and if there really are two sets of experiences—those of the parts and those of the whole—then both should have separate causal influence. This forces combinationists to either deny any causal efficacy to the whole's experience, or else allow them to intervene in the efficacy of the parts; it would be more appealing to be able to say that the whole has causal efficacy in virtue of its parts having causal efficacy, but this is hard to make out if experiences cannot be shared.

A third worry will come out more clearly in the next chapter, concerning phenomenal unity. To prefigure: given the popular view of phenomenal unity as subsumption by a composite experience, unity between the experiences of distinct subjects turns out to require experience sharing. Privacy thus makes it harder for combinationists to account for phenomenal unity.

Finally, accepting privacy has methodological costs. If experience sharing is possible, then when a composite subject (like, perhaps, one of us) introspects upon their own experiences, they may thereby also be introspecting upon (some of) the experiences of their parts. This means they may be able to discern directly certain things about how component subjects relate, since those relations will be present as structure in the composite's own experience. Privacy rules this out, ensuring that we will only ever have introspective access to one level of experiential reality (our own), never to that which lies below. This inability to introspect onto component subjects is a major reason why Goff (2016, 294; cf. Miller 2018) argues that something crucial to explaining how minds combine is forever hidden from us: since we cannot detect the experiences of our parts introspectively, we have no way to understand how they combine. Insofar as we would like to *understand* combination, if possible, this is another reason to prefer views which deny privacy.

In light of the above considerations, I think combinationists ought to respond to the subject-summing and privacy arguments by denying both independence and privacy:

Premise A3 (Independence): For any set of intrinsic properties of, and real relations between, a set of subjects, it is conceivable that those subjects have those properties and relations, but no other subject exists.

Premise C3 (Privacy): If experiences are essentially subjective, an experience of one subject cannot belong to any other subject.

I do, however, think these premises contain a kernel of truth: each claim would be true if read in terms of discreteness (nonoverlap) instead of in terms of distinctness (nonidentity). That is, they would be true if we read the mention of an "other" subject in either principle as meaning a subject "sharing no parts with the first-mentioned subject," rather than as meaning "not the very same thing as the first-mentioned subject." This would allow for entailments and experience sharing among overlapping subjects, both those who contain each other as parts and those who share a part but do not fully contain each other. Call the claims about nonidentity, which I reject, "Strong Independence" and "Strong Privacy"; call the claims about non-overlap, which I accept, "Weak Independence" and "Weak Privacy."

Strong Independence: For any set of intrinsic properties of, and real relations between, a set of subjects, it is conceivable that those subjects have those properties and relations, but no other subject not identical to a member of that set exists.

Weak Independence: For any set of intrinsic properties of, and real relations between, a set of subjects, it is conceivable that those subjects have those properties and relations, but no other subject not overlapping with a member of that set exists.

Strong Privacy: If experiences are essentially subjective, an experience of one subject cannot belong to any other subject not identical with the first.

Weak Privacy: If experiences are essentially subjective, an experience of one subject cannot belong to any other subject not overlapping with the first.

Let me say a bit to explain the motivation for accepting the weak forms of these theses. The reason to accept weak privacy is that denying privacy across the board, we might lose our grip on a seemingly crucial difference between experiential and physical properties. I can perceive or infer other people's shape and clothes and height and weight in just the same way that they can (such properties are "public" or "objective"), but what they feel and perceive is immediately present to them alone, with a directness that sharply contrasts with the way others must guess about it (such properties are "private" or "subjective"). While it may be debated how exactly to spell out this difference, intuitively we should avoid views which remove the contrast altogether. Fortunately, denying strong privacy need not remove this contrast, for weak privacy still ensures a major contrast between physical and experiential properties. If weak privacy is true, then I have privileged access to someone's experiences if and only if I either am them or overlap with them (sharing a part, or being part of them, or containing them as a part); thus my identity is crucial to my ability to know their experiences. Nothing comparable is true of their physical properties, which are entirely public.

Weak privacy then motivates weak independence, for the easiest way to make sense of explanatory relations among subjects is for those subjects to share experiences, and weak privacy restricts such sharing to overlapping subjects. To put it another way, given weak privacy, all that weak independence rules out is cases where facts about some subjects and their experiences and relations conceptually entail not just that there exists another subject, but also that there is a whole new set of experiences for the other subject to have, entirely distinct from those of the first subjects. And ruling that out seems quite reasonable, since even physical combination generally relies upon property instances being shared between parts and wholes. But strong independence rules out something much more modest and plausible: facts about some subjects and their experiences and relations conceptually entailing that the whole they form is also a subject of (some of) those same experiences. I do not think we should rule this out; I think such entailments can in fact be shown, and I will attempt to do so in the coming chapters. I think failing to distinguish strong from weak versions of independence has allowed the implausibility of explanatory relations between discrete subjects—subjects related like two separate human beings, like you and I—to infect the much more plausible idea of explanatory relations between distinct but overlapping subjects.

I thus deny strong independence and strong privacy, while still accepting weak independence and weak privacy. Subjects can share experiences with other subjects who overlap with them, and when they do thus share experiences, the experiential facts about one can be conceptually entailed by facts about the other.

How exactly this works, however, will depend heavily on what kind of things we take subjects to be, which is why I devoted section 2.1 to disentangling different conceptions of subjecthood. After all, if subjects are personas, analyzable into patterns among experiences, then strong independence does not seem as compelling: personas are nothing over and above properly related experiences, so if we can get the experiences of a group of subjects to stand in the right relations, that provides the right sort of basis for a new subject. (The privacy argument, by contrast, is still pressing for personas.) Strong independence is more compelling on the metaphysical conception of subjects, according to which experiences do not constitute subjects but rather presuppose the prior existence of a subject. When focused on the intuitions which support the metaphysical conception, it is easy to feel that no amount of "shuffling experiences around," contriving the right relations and organization for them, could be enough to generate a new subject: doing psychology is missing the point when we should be doing metaphysics. But then if we shift back to focus on the intuitions supporting the psychological conception, we may feel that any position in basic metaphysics, shorn of detailed psychological structure, is itself missing the point, ignoring what is actually key to subjecthood.

I think part of what has made the subject-summing argument seem so strong to philosophers is that we have these conflicting intuitions about what subjects are, and no consistent theory can do justice to all of them. This is why I think it is necessary to separate different conceptions of subjecthood and develop theories of mental combination tailored to each. In this chapter I have laid out what all these theories will have in common: in the coming chapters I will look at how they will have to differ.

2.4.2. UNITY, BOUNDEDNESS, AND INCOMPATIBLE CONTEXTS

What about the unity argument, the incompatible contexts argument, and the boundary argument? The approach outlined so far already implies certain commitments with regard to these arguments. First, since I accepted premise **A2** of the subject-summing argument, I am bound to similarly accept premise **B2** of the unity argument, which expresses the same idea (that full explanation of y by x requires the inconceivability of x without y). Thus a combinationist who accepts weak independence but denies strong independence will naturally be led to say that the problem with the unity argument is that the following premise is false, and that its falsity can be shown:

Premise B3 (Separateness): For any set of experiences deriving from distinct subjects, standing in any real relations, it is conceivable that the whole formed by those subjects not have those experiences in a unified way.

For the other two arguments, accepting weak privacy in place of strong privacy stops me from taking the first response I noted above, of dodging both arguments by denying that experiences are ever shared by distinct subjects. That leaves two options: accept supposition **S1**, invariant unity, or else accept supposition **S2**, relative unity. Let us consider what these options come to.

The first option is to treat unity as subject-invariant, which means denying boundedness:

Premise D3 (Boundedness): For any experience e_1 belonging to a subject s, if another experience e_2 is unified with e_1, then e_2 must also be had by s.

This means facing down the boundary argument head-on, affirming that a subject's phenomenal field can be "unbounded" in the sense that some or all of its experiences may be unified with other experiences outside its field, which that subject does not itself undergo.

The second option is to relativize unity to a subject, so that even if two experiences are unified for me, they may belong to two distinct parts of me, and be *dis*unified for those parts. It follows from this that we must deny interdependence:

Premise E3 (Interdependence): The phenomenal character of an experience often depends partly on its phenomenal context, i.e., on the set of other experiences it is unified with.

If unity is relative to a subject, then the same experience could be unified with different sets of other experiences relative to different subjects having it; if interdependence were true, that experience would then have two phenomenal characters, reflecting these two sets, and would thus very plausibly be (as premise **E4** says) two different experiences.

We do not have to choose one of these responses to apply to all forms of conscious unity. For different forms of unity, interdependence, boundedness, invariant unity, and relative unity may be more or less plausible, so combinationists should consider "mixing and matching."

In fact, considering some forms of unity immediately suggests that they are better thought of in either invariant or relative terms. Causal interdependence, for example, seems to be a subject-invariant sort of relationship: if A has a certain causal effect on B, it does so whether we look at it with a larger or a smaller context in mind, whether we zoom out or zoom in. But functional unity (including access-unity) and global consistency are just the opposite: what role a certain state plays depends on what system we look at it in. For example, for two states to be access-unified is for them, and the conjunction of them, to be accessible for the guidance of things like action, report, memory, and reasoning. But what are the relevant actions, reports, etc.? If we look at these states relative to a single human being, then we should judge their accessibility according to whether they can guide reports with that person's mouth, actions with that person's hands, reasoning in that person's head, and so on. But if we look at them relative to, say, a large social group, we should judge their accessibility by whether they can guide group-level pronouncements, collective actions, and so on. States might be jointly accessible for my individual uses but have little impact on, or be actively concealed from, the rest of some group I belong to; then we should say that they are accessible, and access-unified, relative to me, but not relative to the group. In light of this, it seems natural to prefer a subject-invariant approach for causal interdependence, which denies boundedness while accepting phenomenal interdependence, while also preferring a subject-relative approach for functional unity and global consistency, perhaps accepting boundedness but denying phenomenal interdependence. With representational and phenomenal unity it is much less clear what to say; different combinationists might treat them either as relative or as invariant. For now the main thing to note is the implications of the choice: if a given form of unity is made division-relative, it must be denied that interdependence holds for that form; if it is made division-invariant, it must be denied that boundedness holds for that form.

In the coming chapters I outline three combinationist theories that develop different approaches to conscious unity. The first, panpsychist combinationism, focuses on phenomenal unity, understood as a primitive and subject-invariant relation; it thus accepts interdependence but denies boundedness for phenomenal unity. The second, functionalist combinationism, focuses on functional unity, which is subject-relative, and treats phenomenal unity as reducible to sufficiently rich forms of functional unity (and thus as also relative to subjects); thus it denies interdependence for both but can accept boundedness. Functionalist combinationism also develops an account of representational unity, treating it as subject-invariant and thus accepting interdependence while rejecting boundedness. Finally, psychological combinationism focuses not on accounting for unity relations themselves, but on the challenges posed when we try to individuate subjects purely according to the pattern of unity relations among experiences. In each case the challenge is to make sense of the various relations from two angles at once: as internal relations structuring a single subject's phenomenal field, and as external relations between the experiences of distinct subjects.

2.4.3. TWO TECHNICAL OBJECTIONS

I think the above arguments all raise deep and interesting objections to combinationism; before proceeding it is necessary to address two objections which are more abstract and technical in character.

The first worry is about individuation. I have defined "experiences" as instances of experiential properties. It's often assumed that instances of properties are individuated by the property instantiated, the object that instantiates it, and the time at which it is instantiated.[12] If so, it will be contradictory for one experience to belong to two distinct subjects, for the experiences of any two subjects must be accounted different experiences just in virtue of their different subjects. But this sort of argument would prove too much—it would show that no property instances, physical or mental, could ever be shared between a whole and a part of that whole, which does not appear to be true. Physical wholes routinely seem to share features with their parts—if my desk is scratched or splotched, and its top is scratched or splotched, it is wrong to say that there are two distinct instantiations of scratchedness or splotchedness, let alone two distinct scratches or splotches. Certainly, this argument could not show that conscious subjects *specifically* are uncombinable, for it has nothing to do with consciousness. Thus I would advise combinationists simply to reject this way of individuating property instances, doing so in some other way, such as by sets of objects that have them, by their causes and effects, or by supervenience bases.[13]

The second technical objection to combinationism is a sort of "semantic competition" among subjects which comes from the "maximality condition" built into the way we speak. Many of our concepts are such that "parts of an F are not themselves Fs, [and are] disqualified as being Fs because they are . . . parts of Fs" (Sider 2001, 357). For instance, we would not call the left half of a rock "a rock," even though it would be a rock were it separated from the right half—or at least, we do not count it in our answers to questions like "How many rocks are there?" or consider it a candidate referent for phrases like "that rock."

It has been claimed that concepts like "subject," "thinker," and "mind" are maximal concepts (e.g., Burke 1994, 136; Sider 2001, 357). If they are, then we might be barred, just by definition, from describing any entity as a subject if it is part of another subject. However, even if our everyday concept of a subject incorporates a

---

[12] For examples of this way of thinking of experiences, and property instances more generally, see Bayne 2010, 24–29; Ehring 1996, 462.

[13] For a defense of the causes-and-effects approach to individuating experiences, see Schechter 2010. For a defense of individuating mental property-instances by their supervenience base, tailored explicitly to allowing overlapping subjects to share particular mental states, see Sutton 2014.

maximality constraint, this is not a genuine objection to composition of subjects. Not all facts about the concepts we use reflect facts about the reality we use them to think about: we have to ask *why* our concept of a subject requires maximality. One possibility is that it is simply a practical simplification: nonmaximal entities are not salient to us in the way that maximal ones are, and we have no need to speak or think about them as such because speaking or thinking about the maximal entities that contain them will suffice for all our practical needs. This seems to be why "rock" is maximal: there is no difference in the intrinsic nature of maximal rocks and "large continuous parts of rocks" we simply get by more efficiently using a word that applies only to the former. Indeed the convenience of such habits of speech is such that in the remainder of this book I will use the terms "person" and "human being" as maximal. But if this is the only reason for the maximality constraint on "subject" and similar terms, then subjects-strictly-so-called, and things that would be subjects were they not contained in larger subjects, are equally interesting from a philosophical perspective.

2.5. Conclusions

Over the next six chapters I will develop three theories of mental combination: panpsychist combinationism, functionalist combinationism, and psychological combinationism. These theories will start from different conceptions of subjects, and of conscious unity, but they will also have certain things in common. All three will deny strong independence and strong privacy while accepting weak independence and weak privacy; that is, all will involve component subjects who, when suitably connected, conceptually necessitate composite subjects because they share their experiences with those composite subjects. And all three will deny separateness and, for each form of conscious unity, either boundedness or interdependence: they will all treat conscious unity as explainable by relations that can hold both within and between distinct subjects.

My main reason for preferring combinationist theories which deny these principles (strong independence, strong privacy, separateness, and boundedness or interdependence) over those that accept them is that I think theories which deny these principles are more ambitious and more interesting, and I think philosophers ought, where possible, to defend the boldest, most ambitious, most interesting claims. Even if those claims turn out to be false, we usually learn more from their failure than from the defense of more timid views. The most interesting question for mental combination, fundamentally, is whether it could work like physical combination, whether it could be intelligible and explanatory in the same way that the combination of physical things is. Most of the alternative options I discussed and set aside in section 2.4 were set aside because they involve retreating from this ambition.

Nevertheless, denying strong independence, strong privacy, separateness, and either boundedness or interdependence is compatible with sharply opposing views on various questions. In particular, it leaves open the following choices:

- Are subjects personas, or substrates of experience?
- Are composite subjects aggregates, or structure-specific wholes?
- Is phenomenal unity reducible to other forms of unity, or primitive?
- Is consciousness fundamental, or explained by some purely physical structure?

The three combinationist theories I will lay out in the coming chapters give different answers to these questions.

Panpsychist combinationism, focused on the simplest and most basic sort of consciousness but treating it as something metaphysically fundamental, will assume that subjects are substrates, not personas, that composites are aggregates, not structure-specific wholes, that phenomenal unity is primitive, and that consciousness is fundamental. It will answer the subject-summing and privacy arguments by taking consciousness to be, like the fundamental properties of physics, division-invariant: the consciousness present in a whole is just the same consciousness as is present in its parts, and it makes no difference how you slice it. And it will address the unity and boundary arguments by taking phenomenal unity to be, like the fundamental relations of physics, pervasive in its distribution, connecting different experiences regardless of how richly unified they are in other respects.

Functionalist combinationism, focused on building up complex conscious systems, also takes subjects as substrates, but treats them as structure-specific wholes rather than aggregates, with the brain as the prototypical structure-specific substrate of experience. Brains are, after all, not metaphysically fundamental (like particles) nor straightforwardly identifiable with sets of fundamental things (like aggregates of particles), but equally they are not mere patterns among experiences (like personas).

Functionalist combinationism addresses the subject-summing and privacy arguments by analyzing subjecthood in terms of functional and informational structure: to be a subject is to be a system that processes information in the right way, so when component subjects process information among themselves in the right way, it necessarily follows that the system they form is also a subject. It likewise addresses the unity and boundary arguments by analyzing conscious unity in information-processing terms: for experiences to be unified, they just need to interact in the right ways.

Functionalist combinationism can be taken in two ways. One, which I will call "pure functionalist combinationism," denies the starting point of panpsychist combinationism by regarding consciousness as entirely a matter of functional structure, and thus not a fundamental property. The other, which I will call "functionalist-panpsychist combinationism" is intended to be compatible with panpsychist combinationism, adding functionalist analyses not to account for consciousness per se but only for the special sort of consciousness that humans and other brainy creatures have. On this second reading, functionalist combinationism is a theory of "complex structured human-like consciousness," which is not the only sort of consciousness but rather just a particularly interesting sort that comes about when information is processed in the right way. (Compare the ecumenical, multilayered version of panpsychism-cum-functionalism offered by Rosenberg [2017].)

Finally, psychological combinationism treats subjects as personas (and therefore as structure-specific wholes). It is largely neutral on questions of metaphysics, including the fundamentality or otherwise of consciousness and of phenomenal unity, since personas are by their nature less metaphysically fundamental than experiences. Thus it largely ignores the subject-summing and unity arguments, presupposing experiences and unity relations rather than trying to explain them. It does, however, face distinctive and interesting issues with privacy and boundedness.

Of these three theories, different readers may find different ones more or less plausible and more or less relevant, and may reject one while accepting another. But my own view is that the theories are not rivals but different views of the same reality—a whole universe of composite subjectivity. I think aggregates exist as well as structure-specific wholes, and substrates of consciousness exist as well as personas, and it can be reasonable in different contexts to refer to different entities as "wholes" or "subjects." The universe is a multilayered thing, which looks very different when viewed through different conceptual lenses. My ambition with these three theories of combination is to show how mental combination runs through the universe in all of these many layers.

2 Combinationism for Panpsychists

3 Composite Subjectivity and Microsubjects

IN THIS CHAPTER I consider combinationism in relation to what the universe is like at the most basic level, independently of the specifics of the human condition. Going by what modern science seems to reveal, the universe consists in a vast number of absolutely tiny things that can be called "particles," possessing a few fundamental physical properties, standing in a few fundamental physical relations, and forming aggregates of various sizes which inherit these physical properties and whose structure is determined by these physical relations.

If constitutive Russellian panpsychism (CRP) is true, conscious experience should somehow fit into this world of particles: like their fundamental physical properties, it should be widely distributed and indifferent to the special features of any earthly ape species. More precisely, the fundamental physical things are conscious subjects ("microsubjects"), the fundamental physical properties and relations correspond with experiential properties and relations, and complex consciousness like ours is explained by the combining of these incredibly simple subjects with their incredibly simple experiences.

In this chapter, I sketch and defend a panpsychist theory on which experiential properties work like fundamental physical properties. As well as assuming the truth of CRP, I will assume that subjects are substrates of experience as opposed to personas, that wholes are aggregates rather than structure-specific, that consciousness is a fundamental property, and that phenomenal unity is a fundamental relation, not reducible to some sufficient density of other sorts of conscious unity. In the coming chapters I will explore different starting points, which generate alternative, complementary theories of mental combination.

The result—panpsychist combinationism—is a combinationist theory that is simple and elegant but deeply counterintuitive in some of its implications. Section 3.1 presents an overview of panpsychist combinationism, identifying how it relates to chapter 2's arguments against combinationism. The two key claims are experience inheritance (the principle that aggregates inherit the experiential properties of their parts) and the micro-unity hypothesis (the suggestion that one of the fundamental physical relations establishes phenomenal unity). Sections 3.2 and 3.3 then clarify, explore, and defend these claims, and section 3.4 presents a further argument in support of experience inheritance, with the micro-unity hypothesis as a premise.

The most controversial claim made in this chapter is that experience inheritance is true *a priori*, and so my final sections explore the reasons for and against accepting its *a priori* status, and some ways to preserve the spirit of panpsychist combinationism if this status is denied. The next chapter then addresses certain additional problems facing CRP, based on the apparent discrepancy in structure between physical reality and human consciousness.

3.1. A Sketch of Panpsychist Combinationism

I begin my sketch of panpsychist combinationism by supposing that microscopic entities have experiences to combine. More specifically, I suppose that all elementary particles are associated with incredibly simple experiences, whose structure is no more complex than the structure of those particles' physical properties. Since they are the metaphysical substrates of these experiences, they will count as conscious subjects according to the metaphysical conception of subjects—they are microsubjects.

Admittedly, it is unclear how far contemporary physics supports the fundamentality of particles. Consider the apparent failure of permutations to differ: in the probabilistic mathematics of quantum physics, the outcomes "particle-A in location 1 with X properties and particle-B in location 2 with Y properties" and "particle-B in location 1 with X properties and particle-A in location 2 with Y properties" must be treated as a single outcome (French and Rickles 2003). Or consider the possibility of indeterminate particle-number: in some cases the number of particles in a system depends, like velocity, on what frame of reference we use to consider it (Domenech and Holik 2007). There are also much older metaphysical questions about the relative fundamentality of particles and space or spacetime. The world might be infinitely divisible, displaying no identifiable "basic parts," or a fundamental whole more basic than any of its parts. For all we know, the fundamental physical entities might be particles, fields, points, spacetime, or something else.

However, these considerations can largely be set aside. They amount to saying that a certain model we are familiar with—of independent, recombinable, countable, more or less solid parts like Lego blocks or the grains of sand in a sandcastle—may not extend all the way down. But that model does extend pretty far down! Cells, molecules, and even atoms are ontologically independent of each other and can be determinately counted, tracked, and recombined, etc. If there is a level where these parts are no longer so "well-behaved," that does not change the fact that human bodies and everything else we encounter are made up of discrete parts on the scales from meters down to nanometers. If subatomic particles are in some sense unreal, my remarks will apply *mutatis mutandis* to whatever the simplest and most basic physical entities are, if any, and moreover will still apply to the comparatively well-behaved atoms, molecules, cells, and so forth.

3.1.1. MICROSUBJECTS AND THEIR EXPERIENCES

What sort of experiences do microsubjects have? There is probably no way to positively answer that question at the current stage of human knowledge. The best we can do is identify constraints on what kind of experiences they *might* have. On the one hand, the physical simplicity of a given microsubject puts a "ceiling" on how far we can attribute complex experiences to it. Partly this is because of Russellianism: if the basic experiential properties are the real inner nature of the basic physical properties, then the two should line up with one another. Partly it is also about making sense of the extremely simple behavior of the basic physical entities: we should not ascribe to them a conscious life which would lead us to expect more intelligent behavior than they display. On the other hand, we can assign a "floor" by reflecting on the explanatory challenge posed by consciousness. Whatever it is about consciousness that cannot be explained in terms of anything else should be recognized as a fundamental feature of matter. Of course, it is a controversial question what it is about consciousness that is hard to explain. A lot of discussion has focused on sensory qualities, like experienced redness or pain, and if we thought that these and nothing else produce an "explanatory gap," we should conclude that microexperiences must involve some sort of sensory quality, but perhaps nothing else. Alternatively, we might think that *meaning*, the capacity to mentally represent things, to be "about" some object, is just as hard to account for in physical terms as sensory qualities are. In that case we should suppose that the basic experiences also have some rudimentary seed of meaning; they are "about something," though that something might be as simple and unspecific as "the world" or "this stuff." If we thought that a sense of the "goodness" and "badness" of certain feelings was likewise primitive, we should include that too at the fundamental level; similarly for will or motivation, or anything else that reflection suggests is not analyzable as some configuration of more basic features.

Some might worry that an expansive conception of the irreducible aspects of consciousness might raise the "floor" so high that no space is left between it and the "ceiling": human consciousness might be explainable only by a sort of experience that is much more complicated than anything a fundamental particle could plausibly undergo. But I do not think this is true. Here is a speculative example of what it might be like to be a fundamental particle, which includes all the above-mentioned basic features but is compatible with extreme simplicity of physical properties and behavior. Suppose the entire content of this phenomenology is a contrast, between a figure and a background, a "something" and a "something else." The former aspect of the experience represents the particle's surroundings insofar as they exert force on it; the latter aspect refers to the rest of the world in general.[1] The particular quality that the "something" is experienced as having will vary depending on the particular way that the particle's surroundings act on it (degree of force, type of force, etc.), but beyond that these representations are maximally unspecific, mere inchoate gesturings outward. This experience is not strictly visual, or tactile, or emotional, or cognitive: it is poorer and less determinate than any of these. But it has an internal motivating power, rather like pleasure or displeasure. It motivates the electron to move blindly toward or away from the source of the force it is feeling, in virtue of the way that it feels.[2] Moreover, because the experience involves a contrast, it contains an implicit sense of negation—that the "something" is not the "something else." And philosophers who think consciousness always inherently involves a special relation of "awareness" or "acquaintance" can add that the subject is, in a very crude way, "aware of" this simple experience, though without the cognitive capacity to reflect on or reason about it.

---

[1] There is thus here a primitive form of the causal theory of reference: experiences refer to whatever causes them, just as we might think human perceptions and perception-based thoughts refer to whatever is causally responsible for them. Note that the particle's experience may refer without having truth-evaluable content—there may be something it is "about" without there being anything it "says" that could be true or false, rather like the primitive "ur-intentionality" posited by some enactivists about cognition (e.g., Hutto and Myin 2017).

[2] This sketch is partly inspired by Mørch's (2014) idea of the basic experiences as indissolubly combining an intrinsic qualitative nature and a causal tendency.

Note that this rudimentary consciousness need include no capacity for shifting attention, for focusing first on one aspect and then on another. Microsubjects need not be able to conceptualize the different aspects or actively distinguish them from each other. Given this, I do not think that the phenomenology sketched out here attributes implausibly complex experience to an electron: there is really no more than a single "bit" of information, this-as-opposed-to-that, motivating one of two responses ("toward" and "away from"), both having a mathematical degree of intensity. And yet it also seems to contain the germs of cognition, volition, affect, and qualitative sensory perception, making it a suitable explanatory base for human consciousness even if those features are all considered primitive.

This is not the only way that it might feel to be a fundamental particle. For instance, maybe the basic motivation is not pleasure or displeasure but a sort of blind love and desire for union with the world that is inarticulately perceived, or a sort of "tension" that is more basic than either pleasure or displeasure (cf. Freud 1961; Schopenhauer 1969; Spinoza 1994). We are not in a good position to decide among these alternatives: positively determining the experiences of the fundamental physical entities is probably beyond current human ability, perhaps requiring a near-completed physics, a near-completed introspective phenomenology, and a near-completed neuroscience (maybe augmented with superhuman powers of reasoning, introspection, and imagination). My goal here is not to decide what microexperience is really like, but to show that there is room for it to be both simple enough to be compatible with our present physics and rich enough that, as long as combination is possible, it provides a sufficient explanatory basis for human experience.

3.1.2. TWO PRINCIPLES FOR COMBINING EXPERIENCES

Supposing that microsubjects have some sort of microexperience, how do they combine? The first and most basic principle of panpsychist combinationism is that experiential properties are inherited: for any collection of microsubjects, the aggregate they compose is a subject of all their experiences.

> **Experience Inheritance (EI):** Whenever a part of aggregate x undergoes an experience (instantiates an experiential property), x undergoes that same experience.

So if one particle is undergoing experience A, and another is undergoing experience B, the aggregate of the two is undergoing experience A and also undergoing experience B. This does not involve any duplication of experiences, but rather a sharing of experiences between part and whole. Thus experiential properties are division-invariant: however we carve up reality, we find the same experiences. In this regard experiential properties work just the same as properties like spatial location, causal power, mass, and charge: wholes have them just in virtue of their parts having them.

The second thesis of panpsychist combinationism concerns the unification of experiences:

> **Micro-Unity Hypothesis (MUH):** The inner nature of one, some, or all of the fundamental physical relations is phenomenal unity; when two microsubjects are related in the relevant way, their experiences become unified, establishing a composite experience that subsumes them.

The phrase "fundamental physical relations" is meant to leave open what these are: the propagation of ripples in fields of force, the exchange of energy-carrying particles, mere spatial distance, or something else. Thus MUH is only schematic: it does not say how exactly phenomenal unity is distributed, only that its distribution matches that of one or more of the basic physical relations. This is already enough, however, to imply that phenomenal unity runs much more widely than we usually think. This is because all the fundamental physical relations we know of, or seem likely to discover, seem to be very extensive in their scope. For instance, gravitational attraction holds between any two particles with mass, whether they are in the same human brain, in different human brains, or one in a brain and one in the corona of the sun.[3] So MUH makes phenomenal unity nearly pervasive, an implication I explore in section 3.3.

While EI is a general metaphysical principle, to be defended *a priori*, MUH is offered as an empirical postulate: it aims to describe how the fundamental laws of our universe in fact work, not how they necessarily must work. MUH says that when two microsubjects do not stand in whichever of the fundamental physical relations is important, then even if they compose a composite subject, they compose one with disunified consciousness. Adopting the above suggestion that microsubjects are conscious of "this-against-the-background-of-that," a composite

---

[3] In relativistic physics no interaction is instantaneous, so for any time period t, there will be a sphere around an object beyond whose perimeter it cannot have any causal effect within time t. (This zone of interaction is sometimes called a "light-cone," since it is conical in four dimensions.) But clearly phenomenal unity does arise, so if all interactions take some amount of time, then either phenomenal unity must take some amount of time to establish, or else the physical relation which is phenomenal unity is just spatial distance, not any kind of interaction.

formed out of causally unrelated microsubjects would experience two "thises" against two backgrounds, each with its respective quality and motivation. But despite being conscious of A and being conscious of B, it would not yet be conscious of "A and B": A and B do not appear as contrasting with or connected with each other in any way. When they enter into the relevant relation, however, whatever that involves, their experiences become connected, so that they form a single experience which subsumes each and is undergone not by either microsubject but by the composite subject they form.

That concludes my sketch of panpsychist combinationism. How does it address the five internal problems considered in chapter 2? First, EI conflicts with strong independence, since the (*a priori*) truth of EI implies that when we consider a whole made of conscious parts, we cannot consistently conceive of it as lacking consciousness of its own—because it is just them, considered together. Since it is just them, it has the consciousness they have, just like it has the mass they have, the volume they have, and so on. Moreover, EI contradicts strong privacy but supports weak privacy: it implies that particular experiences can be shared between wholes and parts, but not that they can be shared by discrete subjects. Next, MUH answers the unity argument by treating phenomenal unity as one of the fundamental relations knitting together our universe, holding not just within a single subject's experience but between the experiences of distinct subjects. But MUH does not imply—and panpsychist combinationism denies—the key premise of the boundary argument, that unity between two subjects dissolves their distinctness; rather, each undergoes an experience unified with another experience they do not undergo. And the incompatible contexts argument is dodged by not relativizing unity to subjects. Of course, both experience inheritance and the micro-unity hypothesis demand further explication and defense, which I seek to provide in the next three sections.

3.2. Why Are Experiential Properties Inherited?

The most basic objection to combinationism is that consciousness in a thing's parts tells us nothing about consciousness in that thing itself—that part and whole, being different subjects, are too "metaphysically insulated" for any property of the one to be a mere combination of properties of the other. In chapter 2 I called this principle "strong independence," and according to panpsychist combinationism, strong independence is false because the following principle is true:

Experience Inheritance (EI): Whenever a part of aggregate *x* undergoes an experience (instantiates an experiential property), *x* undergoes that same experience.[4]

But why should EI be true? Not all properties are inherited, after all; a heap of beans is not itself a bean, nor even bean-shaped. My primary answer (section 3.4 provides a supplementary answer) is that experiential properties are primitive properties and that primitive properties are inherited.[5]

Thus I appeal not to anything specific about experience but to the general nature of the part-whole relation. Previous writers on the subject-summing problem (Goff 2009a, 2009b, 2017c; Coleman 2014, 33–34, 2017, 256–258) have tended to proceed by scrutinizing consciousness and subjecthood, looking for a distinctively experiential way to "hook" wholes and parts together. I instead claim that they are automatically hooked together, just because of what aggregation *is*. In a slogan, aggregates inherit the primitive properties of their parts because they are simply those parts considered as one thing rather than as many. More precisely, I will defend a principle of the "substantive indiscernibility of parts and aggregate," which entails EI, and which I argue is the best explanation of why many physical properties are inherited.

I should first clarify that when I say that aggregates undergo the same experiences as their parts, I mean "undergo" in the most minimal way. Recall the simplicity of microsubjects and the correspondingly rudimentary way in which they undergo experiences. When a human being experiences something, that generally lets them reflect on it, report it, remember it, focus attention on it, form a concept to name and categorize it, and so on. It is hard to imagine undergoing an experience but not being able to do any of these things with it—we might even be reluctant to call that "consciousness." Yet microsubjects cannot do any of these things, so the sense in which they have experiences lacks all of these usual connotations, stripped down to nothing but the "raw feeling" itself. I claim that wholes inherit experiences in this same rudimentary way: a whole undergoes the

---

[4] It might be worried that this gives wholes experiential properties "only in a derivative sense," not in the proper and primary sense in which we ourselves have them. But this is an equivocation on "derivative": while it is true that wholes have their properties in virtue of other things doing so, they still literally have those properties just as their parts do: a ten-ton weight that inherits its mass from its parts still literally weighs ten ton.

[5] By a "primitive property" I mean a property, the most revealing concept of which is primitive. A primitive concept is one that cannot be defined in terms of any other concepts, except those that are reciprocally definitionally dependent on it. I say "the most revealing concept of which" because one property might be represented by multiple concepts, including some which aren't at all revealing of its nature (e.g., "the property I just thought of" is not a very revealing concept; it tells us nothing about the property it represents).

same "raw feeling" as its parts but may not be able to attend to, reflect on, or otherwise actively think about its experiences. This kind of very simple and un-impressive consciousness is division-invariant, equally present however we divide up the stuff that instantiates it, even though more cognitively complex sorts of consciousness may not be.

Moreover, the "wholes" which inherit experiences are here thought of simply as aggregates, not as structure-specific wholes. In chapter 5 I will discuss what it takes for a structure-specific whole to inherit experiences; that discussion will turn out to be closely connected to the question of what it takes for something to "undergo" an experience in the richer sense. In this chapter I focus on getting a basic kind of experience for a basic kind of whole, hoping that this more basic task will provide the foundation upon which the more sophisticated task may be accomplished.

3.2.1. THE SUBSTANTIVE INDISCERNIBILITY OF PARTS AND WHOLE

Why do aggregates inherit experiential properties from their parts? Begin by considering the "indiscernibility of identicals," the principle (sometimes known as "Leibniz's Law") by which, if two things are identical, every property of one is a property of the other. This principle lets us infer, from the premises that Bob is Robert, and that Bob is eighteen, that Robert is eighteen. This principle is explained just by what identity is: if two things are one and the same, it is contra-dictory to describe that thing one way under one label, and a conflicting way under another label.

The relation between an aggregate and its many parts is similar to the identity relation in certain salient ways. David Lewis (1991) identifies several similarities, such as the fact that an aggregate and its parts can share the very same locations, and the fact that if you "describe the character of the parts [and] describe their in-terrelation . . . you have ipso facto described the [aggregate]" (81), which he takes to motivate "the thesis of Composition-as-Identity" (82; cf. Baxter 1988; Cotnoir 2013; Baxter and Cotnoir 2014). This thesis does not quite say that composition and identity are the very same relation, but merely that they are "strikingly anal-ogous" (Lewis 1991, 84). Part of the reason why they are not the very same rela-tion is that the "indiscernibility of parts and aggregate" is clearly false: aggregates often have properties that their parts lack, and vice versa. For example, an ag-gregate that weighs 10 kilograms can have parts that weigh 1 kilogram; a square aggregate can have triangular parts; an aggregate that contains arsenic can have parts that are arsenic-free. But rather than abandoning the analogy between iden-tity and composition, we should qualify the indiscernibility of parts and aggregate.

As Lewis (1991, 87) says, "It does matter how you slice it—not to the character of what's described . . . but to the form of the description." To try to capture the way that the "character of what's described" remains the same, however we slice it, I propose:

> **Substantive Indiscernibility of Parts and Aggregate (SI):** For every property had by some part of an aggregate, that aggregate has a corresponding property, and for every property had by an aggregate, one or more of its parts have (individually or collectively) a corresponding property.

The idea is that the properties of the aggregate and the parts do not differ "substantively," in that facts about the whole and the parts involve the same portion of reality. Their differences are just differences in the appropriate way to describe that reality: the properties of one may not be strictly the same properties as those of the other, but they are still "corresponding." Going along with this, it is natural to think of the fact of an aggregate having the one property as *grounded in* the fact of one or more parts having corresponding properties, and vice versa; that is, there seems to be symmetrical grounding here, just as grounding by identity is symmetrical.

But what are "corresponding properties"? I do not have a precise definition, unfortunately. The idea is that the aggregate having the one property and the part(s) having the other are not really two distinct facts, but the same fact described in two ways. But how do we tell which property corresponds to which? For some properties, analysis of what that property is—what it takes for an object to instantiate it—will by itself reveal the other properties that would correspond to it under various circumstances. In such cases the corresponding property to X is one that either grounds X by analysis or is grounded in X by analysis.[6] But for primitive properties, which do not admit of any analysis, we cannot identify corresponding properties by this method. For such properties, I claim, their only corresponding properties are themselves, and so when they belong to the parts the aggregate must also have them. To put it another way, SI says that for each property of the parts, the whole either has the same property, one grounded in it by analysis, or one that grounds it by analysis. All properties of aggregates will thus be either division-invariant or intelligibly division-relative.

Because experience is irreducible to anything nonexperiential (or so say panpsychists), at least some experiential properties are primitive. Of course

---

[6] Or both—it may be that neither the whole's property nor the parts' property is more fundamental than the other.

there might be analyses of some experiences in terms of others (e.g., to feel Schadenfreude is analyzed as feeling pleased as a result of consciously thinking that someone else is unhappy), but the process of analysis must come to an end somewhere. Whichever experiential properties are primitive will be inherited if substantive indiscernibility is true, and if they are inherited, the other experiential properties that are constructed from them will also be inherited (e.g., if I inherit the pleasure and the thought of another's sadness, properly connected, then I inherit Schadenfreude). Thus if SI is true, EI follows: it is impossible for an aggregate to be made of conscious matter and yet not be conscious, just as much as it is impossible for Robert to be eighteen and Bob twenty-three, if Robert is Bob.

I will try to clarify the idea of "corresponding" properties through examples, and thereby also make my main argument in support of SI. To some extent SI is intuitive by itself: if a change is made to part of something, surely it follows that the whole thing will have been changed in some fashion. But a stronger justification for SI is indirect: it best explains the behavior of physical properties.

3.2.2. EXAMPLES OF PHYSICAL PROPERTIES OBEYING SUBSTANTIVE INDISCERNIBILITY

Begin with spatial location: the following principle is affirmed as obviously true by Van Inwagen (1990, 44), Lewis (1991, 85), Sider (2007b, 52 and throughout), Bennett (2015, 266), and McQueen (2015):

> **Location Inheritance:** An aggregate is located at a given point or region of space whenever one or more of its parts is, simply in virtue of the part being located there.

Of course, there is an obvious sense in which I am located in a different (larger) area than, say, my foot. But there are two senses of "located" (cf. Sider 2007b, 52n4): it can mean "wholly located," and this is not inherited, but this sense can be defined in terms of the other, more noncommittal sense, which is inherited. To be "wholly located" in some region is to be "located," in this noncommittal sense, at all and only the points in that region.[7]

Another plausible example of an inherited property is causal responsibility: what an aggregate does is just all the things which its parts do.

---

[7] This is a general pattern with many terms: compare the two readings of "fills this cup," either as "fills this cup exactly" (which tells us the thing's volume) or as "fills this cup and possibly more" (which tells us only a lower bound on its volume), or of "ate some of the cake" either as "ate a small portion of the cake and no more" or as "ate at least a small portion of the cake."

Power Inheritance: An aggregate exercises a given causal power whenever any of its parts do, simply in virtue of the part exercising that power.

To use an example from Merricks (2001, 111), when a baseball shatters a window, each of its atoms causes something (e.g., a slight increase in the energy of one part of the window), and what the baseball causes is just all of these many small effects, which add up to shattering the window.[8]

A good example of correspondence without inheritance is shape. Say a table has a certain shape—roughly, a flattened cuboid with four elongated cuboids attached at its corners. None of the particles that compose it has this shape, yet they clearly display properties that correspond to it: it could not be *shaped* that way unless the parts were *arranged* a certain way. In some discussions of composition, philosophers have used the phrase "arranged tablewise," meaning "arranged in one of the ways that corresponds to the kind of shape a table can have" (Van Inwagen 1990, 109ff.; Sider 2007a, 1; Thomasson 2009, 256). Nobody tries to spell out what exactly it means for things to be arranged tablewise, but they do not need to: our grasp of "table-shaped-ness" (a property of the whole) is quite sufficient for us to grasp "arranged-tablewise-ness" (a property of the parts).[9] The very casualness with which terms like "tablewise" can be introduced shows how readily we can translate between the properties of the parts and the properties of the whole. And the difference between shape and location is simply that shape properties can be analyzed, and their analyses will identify distinct ways of describing the same fact—either as many things being arranged or as one thing being shaped. Understanding what it takes for a single thing to be, say, cubic, reveals also what it takes for a set of things to be arranged cubewise.

Of course, being arranged tablewise is not the kind of property that science talks much about. So consider "having a dipole moment": a water molecule has a dipole moment; i.e., it is relatively negatively charged on one side, and relatively positively charged on the other. This corresponds directly to certain charge-properties and relative-position-properties of its parts. It would be impossible for the atoms to have those properties, and the molecule not have a dipole moment,

---

[8] It is necessary to formulate causal powers here in ways that make no reference to their bearer as such. For instance, the power "to attract negatively charged particles" is implicitly the power to attract them to *oneself*, and so will mean different things when ascribed to a proton and to a building that proton is a part of. So we should instead specify this power in terms that do not make any reference to its bearer (e.g., "to subject negatively charged particles to a force of magnitude x and direction y").

[9] Being arranged tablewise is a collective property: the parts (plural) are thus arranged, but no individual part could be said to be thus arranged by itself. But just as it is clear how the whole being table-shaped corresponds to the parts together being arranged tablewise, it is also clear how the latter fact requires that individual parts have certain (locational and relational) properties.

or vice versa, and this is something we can see just from analyzing what having a dipole is.[10] Similar things hold for properties like solidity (Jackson 1998, 3–4) and liquidity (Horgan 1993, 379).

A case that has received some debate is the additivity of certain basic physical properties, such as mass and charge. If something is composed of five discrete parts, each weighing 1 kilogram, then it weighs 5 kilograms: its total-mass property corresponds to their component-mass properties. This seems like a paradigmatic case of an aggregate having a property that is a mere combination of the properties of its parts. But some philosophers have denied that the correlation between the values of component masses and total masses is an *a priori* matter: it is rather a contingent fact that we have discovered empirically (e.g., McLaughlin 1997, 38–39; cf. Broad 1925, 63). If it is a contingent fact that mass is additive, it is hard to see it as conforming to any such abstract metaphysical requirement as SI. But in fact I believe that although mass additivity is not *a priori*, something close enough to support SI is.

McQueen (2013, 2015) points out that matters are complicated here because in relativistic physics, mass additivity is actually *false*: an aggregate's mass depends not just on the masses of its parts but on their velocities. Insofar as we discovered empirically that relativity theory, and not Newtonian mechanics, is correct, we have thereby discovered that mass is not additive, but rather is a function of component masses and velocities. However, physicists do not generally take the composition of masses, following whatever formula, to be itself one of the fundamental laws; it is not something to be included alongside Newton's or Einstein's laws of motion and gravitation. Rather, it is derivable from those laws. The lesson is that while mass additivity is not *a priori*, what is true *a priori* is that if Newtonian mechanics were the whole truth about the microscopic behavior of matter, then mass would be additive. Likewise, it is true *a priori* that if Einsteinian relativity were the whole truth about the microscopic behavior of matter, then mass would be a certain function of component masses and velocities.

But how exactly does mass additivity, or an alternative formula, follow *a priori* from the laws of microphysical behavior? McQueen (2013, 2015) offers a detailed philosophical examination of several derivations presented in physics textbooks (e.g., Kibble and Berkshire 2004, 12; Lindsay 1961, 19–21); in the space available I can only briefly summarize the general pattern of these derivations. They appeal

---

[10] At least, that is impossible as long as we hold everything else fixed: the molecule might lack a dipole moment simply because it has some other atomic parts whose charges and positions allow them to cancel out those of the others, or the molecule might have a dipole moment while the normal parts were not charged, if some other parts were. The point is that we cannot change things at either level without some corresponding change at the other level.

to the laws connecting force and acceleration, with "mass" defined as the objective feature of things which accounts for their resistance to acceleration given a force on them. An aggregate's acceleration is then defined, in terms of the acceleration of its parts, and the force acting on it is likewise defined, as equal and opposite to the force it exerts, which in turn is defined by the forces its parts exert. With figures for the aggregate's acceleration under a given force, we can compute its mass. The key physical premises are the relationship between mass, force, and acceleration, and the law that to each force exerted there is an equal and opposite force. The key metaphysical premises are location inheritance and power inheritance, which are implicitly required to specify, respectively, the acceleration of (McQueen 2013, 53–54) and force on (54–55) the aggregate. This fits neatly into my account of corresponding properties, because the derivation rests on an analysis of our most revealing concept of mass—namely, that it is the objective feature of things that mediates between force and acceleration, according to a certain set of empirically discovered equations. Reflection on that analysis is what reveals the exact mathematical structure of correspondence between mass in the aggregate and mass in the parts.

Even if many physical properties obey substantive indiscernibility, are there others that do not? Can we find either properties of wholes that correspond to nothing about their parts, or properties of parts that correspond to nothing about the wholes they form? Both sorts of example have been discussed by metaphysicians, but I believe neither really threatens SI.

First, what about wholes which *lack* properties corresponding to some of those of their parts? There do seem to be cases that could readily be analyzed this way, like the whirlpool or biological cell mentioned in chapter 1, section 1.3. But these are clearly examples of what in chapter 1 I called structure-specific wholes, and so do not threaten SI as a principle applying to aggregates.

For properties of wholes corresponding to nothing about the parts, we might consider emergent properties, appearing only in certain wholes and not predictable in advance even from the most complete knowledge of the individual parts. There are currently no generally accepted examples of such emergent properties, but for a period in the nineteenth and early twentieth century many philosophers thought, apparently quite reasonably, that both chemical compounds and biological organisms had causal powers that could not be predicted from the most complete knowledge of their parts (e.g., Mill 1882; Broad 1925). While the progress of science seems to have refuted these ideas, I follow McLaughlin (1992) in thinking that the emergentist's views were not *a priori* false: nature could have turned out to work the way they thought it did.

Does SI conflict with the apparently reasonable, though seemingly false, empirical hypothesis of emergence? Not necessarily. First, SI is about aggregates, and it might be that emergence is possible only for structure-specific wholes, or even true units. Second, although emergence is usually discussed in part-whole terms, the scientific implications of traditional scientific emergentism can be equally well cashed out in terms of general and specific conditions. On emergentist scientific theories, matter has some powers that manifest only under very specific circumstances, while on nonemergentist theories, matter displays all its powers under a wide range of circumstances. This contrast can be expressed entirely in terms of properties belonging to the smallest particles of matter. For example, Broad (1925, 65) suggests that the properties of silver chloride are "emergent" relative to those of silver and of chlorine. This amounts to saying that atoms of silver and chlorine (the parts) have certain powers that manifest only in the very specific case where they are bonded together—hence those powers "cannot . . . be deduced from the most complete knowledge of [silver and chlorine] *in isolation or in other wholes*" (63, emphasis added).[11] This does not threaten SI: when the special powers are manifest, they are manifested both by whole and by part, and when they are merely latent, we can ascribe them both to the parts and to the impotent wholes they then form. If silver chloride has the "emergent" powers, we should both ascribe these powers, when they are manifested, to the silver atoms and the chlorine atoms, and also ascribe these powers, when they are latent, to any aggregate containing silver or chlorine not bonded to each other.

3.2.3. WHY DO PHYSICAL PROPERTIES OBEY SUBSTANTIVE INDISCERNIBILITY?

So physical properties seem to obey substantive indiscernibility. Why? The explanation I prefer is that substantive indiscernibility is true across the board, about physical and mental properties alike. Sider (2007b) draws a similar conclusion: the best explanation for things like the inheritance of location is something about the composition relation itself, namely that it is akin to the identity relation. This seems to me the simplest and most satisfying account, and it implies that SI holds for experiential properties, thereby supporting EI.

One alternative explanation would be that SI holds for physical properties because of something about matter specifically: not all things show this intimacy of whole and part, but only the physical stuff that happens to make up our universe. This explanation still supports EI, given the sort of universe we appear to inhabit:

---

[11] Shoemaker (2002) calls these "micro-latent" causal powers, as opposed to "micro-manifest" ones.

a universe composed entirely of matter, some or all of which is conscious. For in such a universe, all the experiential properties that occur will belong to matter, and so obey SI.[12]

An explanation that was genuinely problematic for combinationism would be if SI held for various physical properties for disparate reasons, with no general unifying theme or principle behind it. If location was inherited for one reason, causal effects for another, charge and mass for some other unrelated reason, and so on, then there would be no basis for drawing any conclusion about experiential properties. However, it is implausible on the face of it that so many different properties should show such similar behavior for completely different reasons: it seems more reasonable to prefer a more systematic explanation for their behavior given above.

It would also be a problem for combinationism if physical properties obeyed SI specifically because they are physical *properties*, rather than because they are properties of a certain stuff. In particular, Russellian panpsychists hold that physical properties are, ultimately, "structural" properties, abstract descriptions of the ways that some nonstructural properties are related, while experiential properties are the underlying nonstructural properties that do that relating. A critic might claim (and from conversation I believe this is Goff's position) that structural properties are inherited, because the roles which define them can be played equally well by a thing's own properties and by the properties of its parts. In particular, a structural property's defining roles might be played equally well by the property of *experiencing X* and by the property of *having a part that experiences X*. Then a whole could have the structural properties implemented by the experiences of its parts, without itself experiencing anything. I do not have a decisive objection to this account, though it seems to me still to leave something unexplained: Why is the part-whole relation such that wholes can have structural properties in virtue of the nonstructural properties of their parts? Other relations (being larger than, being fond of, being genetically related to, being earlier than) do not work like this: I cannot instantiate structural properties in virtue of the properties of my relatives, or things larger than me, or things I am fond of. The most satisfying explanation for this special feature of the part-whole relation is that wholes in some sense *are* their parts, and not a genuinely distinct thing related to them. But

---

[12] EI would then be nomologically necessary but not metaphysically necessary, though it would still be metaphysically necessitated by more basic facts about our universe, namely that it is exclusively composed of a kind of stuff for which SI holds.

that is not a knock-down argument for accepting SI, and critics might think that the apparent conceivability of a nonconscious whole made of conscious parts (like the microexperiential zombie) counts against it; in section 3.5 I will consider in more detail what panpsychist combinationism can say about the microexperiential zombie and the threat it seems to pose to EI.

3.3. How Do Microexperiences Become Phenomenally Unified?

Whereas the previous section's case for experience inheritance was pure metaphysics (parts and wholes necessarily share properties), the relations among experiences depend on the contingent laws of our universe. In chapter 2 I distinguished "primitivism" from "reductionism" about phenomenal unity: Is phenomenal unity just a matter of being sufficiently richly connected in various other ways (causally, representationally, functionally, etc.), or is it a distinct and more basic relation? If reductionism is true, then the challenge of explaining phenomenal unity is nothing beyond the task of explaining those other relations, which are better tackled in chapter 5 as part of functionalist combinationism, not here. But let us suppose that primitivism is true. In that case I propose that phenomenal unity is the inner nature of one or more of the fundamental physical relations:

> **Micro-Unity Hypothesis (MUH):** The inner nature of one, some, or all of the fundamental physical relations is phenomenal unity; when two microsubjects are related in the relevant way, their experiences become unified, establishing a composite experience that subsumes them.

This postulate could be attacked in a number of ways, so in this section I will defend it against the following three objections:

1. Why think that phenomenal unity corresponds to one of the fundamental physical relations (and not to some relation that holds only within animal brains)?
2. Doesn't MUH, by extending phenomenal unity beyond the bounds of human brains, dissolve individual subjects into an all-encompassing cosmic consciousness?
3. Doesn't MUH, by extending phenomenal unity beyond the bounds of human brains, contradict the starting assumptions that gave us a grip on the very idea of phenomenal unity?

3.3.1. WHY UNITY IS PROBABLY EVERYWHERE

The most obvious objection to MUH is simply a question: Why on earth think that phenomenal unity is coextensive with one of the fundamental physical interactions?

Since we ourselves enjoy unified experiences, we know that many microexperiences do in fact stand in the relevant unifying relation: the laws of nature dictate that microexperiences, at least sometimes, form composite experiences. MUH goes beyond this, to claim that the laws of nature associate phenomenal unity with one of the fundamental physical relations (or with several of them). Perhaps, for instance, the situation we describe mathematically in terms of two particles imposing electromagnetic forces on one another, or the situation of their imposing any forces on each other, or even the situation of their being at some spatial distance, is simply the situation of two microsubjects' experiences becoming phenomenally unified. Of course we cannot at present have much idea of *which* relation; like the question of what experiences microsubjects have, this question could likely be answered only at some future time when we have advanced considerably in physics, in phenomenology, and in neuroscience.

But why shouldn't phenomenal unity be associated with a nonfundamental physical relation, or even with no physical relation at all? After all, that would allow us to vindicate the natural assumption that phenomenal unity holds within, but not between, human brains, by defining some nonfundamental relation such that it holds only between particles in a human brain. We could then say that only when particles are related in *that* way—only when they interact in the right kinds of patterns, with the right degree of strength, in the right kinds of materials—do their experiences come to mutually co-present. Of course we would need to do a lot more neuroscience to know exactly how to define this relation, but there are problems with this approach that can be recognized in advance of such work. I believe that any theory on which unity is associated with a nonfundamental physical relation will lose out, in a comparison of theoretical elegance and simplicity, to a theory which associated it with a fundamental physical relation.

To see this, suppose we have identified some relation R which holds between particles in a human brain (and perhaps some other sorts of brain), but not between particles in different brains, and we hypothesize that it is *this* relation which correlates with phenomenal unity. Now consider a hypothetical sequence of steps, as gradual as we like, between a set of particles in a brain, related by R, and a set of particles spread across two brains, not related by R, such that at each point in the sequence the particles are interacting *slightly* more strongly than before in whatever ways are relevant to R. We want to say that at one end of this sequence there is no phenomenal unity, while at the other there is, but from the perspective of fundamental physics there is no point where any fundamental break occurs: it is all just particles and forces.[13]

Things might not have turned out this way—we might have found that certain fundamental forces kick into action only within the boundaries of human heads, so that no such gradual sequence could be constructed. Indeed, we might have found that consciousness depends on immaterial souls, interacting with but separate from the material brain. In that case there would be a clear, sharp, nonarbitrary boundary between the kind of interactions that take place between two of my experiences (within a soul, with no physical steps at all), and between mine and yours (a soul-state causes a physical state, which causes another physical state, which causes a state in a different soul). In such a world, the intuitive distinction noted in chapter 2 between the "direct" relations that my experiences seem to bear to each other and the "indirect" relations they seem to bear to your experiences would be real. But scientific investigation has not revealed a world like that; it has revealed a world where the interactions within one mind and the interactions between minds differ only in degree—in strength, sensitivity, reliability, speed, and so on. In such a world, for any proposed R, we can construct a sequence as above, where each one of the many tiny steps is, from a physical perspective, as trivial and unimportant as any other, and none of them seems like it could make the difference between unity and disunity.

Do we really want to say that phenomenal unity is something that "kicks in" only when a certain *precise* degree of physical relatedness is present? Can we believe that, to put it crudely, there is no unity when two distant particles exert a force of 24-trillionths of a Newton on each other, nor when they get a little closer and exert a force of 25-trillionths of a Newton, or 26-, but as they grow nearer and the force between them increases—perhaps when they reach 1,301-trillionths of a Newton, perhaps 2,753-, who knows—there is suddenly unity?

It is deeply unappealing to think that a change of 1-trillionth of a Newton should make such a big difference. For one thing, it seems completely arbitrary that it should be 2,753 rather than 2,752 or 2,754. For another thing, it seems to make phenomenal unity basically epiphenomenal: there is virtually no difference in the causal behavior of two things that exert 2,753- rather than 2,752-trillions of a Newton on each other, so it becomes hard to understand how phenomenal unity could play any significant role in what causes what.

---

[13] An argument very like this one is made at greater length in Goff (2013). This argument closely resembles the "continuity argument" for panpsychism itself, outlined in chapter 1, as well as the "vagueness argument" for unrestricted composition given by Lewis (1986, 212) and Sider (1997), and certain arguments concerning human subjects made by Parfit (1984, 231–243) and Unger (1979, 1990, 191–206).

Of course this is just one more version of the ancient "sorites paradox": no tiny step can suddenly produce unity (just as no single-hair-removal can make someone bald), but a transition from disunity to unity must occur at some point (just as progressive removal of hair must eventually make someone bald). Analyses of the sorites paradox abound, but broadly speaking, most solutions involve the idea that the word being applied can be applied in a variety of fractionally different ways. For instance, the vagueness of "bald" lies in the fact that any of a range of maximum numbers of hairs is an equally good candidate for the meaning of "bald."[14] When someone has little enough hair to be bald by one standard, but too much by another standard, it is semantically indeterminate whether they are bald.

A solution like this works well for concepts like "bald," whose meaning can be specified in more basic terms (number of hairs). The different acceptable ranges of application can be understood as different precise descriptions in these more basic terms. But this requires an analysis of the vague concept in terms of degrees on an underlying spectrum. Being indeterminately bald just means having a number of hairs we are unsure how to classify, but what is it to be indeterminately unified? After all, when experiences are unified they are parts of a composite experience, so if it is semantically indeterminate whether two experiences are unified, it will be semantically indeterminate whether there is a subsuming experience or not. If consciousness were analyzable into some complex of physical facts, and phenomenal unity into a complex of physical relations, then we could make sense of indeterminacy as a matter of most but not quite all of those complex physical conditions being present. But if consciousness is a fundamental property, as panpsychist combinationism supposes, then there is no in-between possibility which our label "conscious experience" indeterminately applies to. Either a state is a conscious experience or it is not; either there is something it is like to be in that state (even if something incredibly simple, dim, and faint), or there is nothing it is like. But then the boundaries of unity could not be vague.

So I find myself driven to a surprising conclusion: since the only nonarbitrary physical boundaries lie between not interacting at all and interacting a bit, even a tiny bit, there is probably phenomenal unity whenever two experiences are physically related at all, regardless of how strongly.

---

[14] On "epistemicist" approaches (Williamson 1994), some particular one of these meanings is in fact the true meaning of "bald," but we are unable to know which; other analyses differ in the role of contexts (e.g., Graff 2000), in whether the multiplicity of acceptable ranges of application is simply a failure of specification or a positive specification built into the meaning of the words (Fine 1975; Raffman 1994, 2013), and on other points. But the plurality of acceptable ranges of application is common ground.

3.3.2. HOW TO ADDRESS THE BOUNDARY PROBLEM

MUH implies that the phenomenal fields in the world are of vast size, limited only by the reach of the fundamental physical relations. Each of these fields will extend far beyond a human being, on the scale of light-seconds or light-years. And perhaps (especially if phenomenal unity is transitive, so that wherever the fields overlap they form a single larger field) subsuming all of these fields is the single huge field of the universe. In either case, we are dealing with fields on a scale far larger than the human individual.

Indeed, the transitivity of phenomenal unity may provide an alternative route to the same worrying conclusion. Dainton (2011, 255), for instance, argues that given transitivity, and given that "every particle composing the planet Earth is linked (directly or indirectly) to every other by a chain of physical connections (or interactions)—a by no means implausible assumption—then the entire planet will consist of a single fully unified consciousness." Here the point is that even if the interactions which establish unity are quite local and small-scale, the existence of long connecting chains will still generate large, suprahuman, phenomenal fields. Consequently, avoiding this kind of result is hard for the combinationist panpsychist: they must *both* deny the transitivity of phenomenal unity *and* associate it with a sufficiently specific and rare sort of interaction. Rather than contorting the view to make it fit commonsense intuition, I prefer to embrace the counterintuitive consequences of allowing fundamental experiential relations to behave like fundamental physical relations.

But isn't this result disastrous? The idea that all the experiences in the universe are phenomenally unified, subsumed by the vast phenomenal field of the whole cosmos, is precisely what was worrying proponents of the boundary argument. Even if they sympathize with the motivations for MUH, they might feel that its implications are so patently false as to make it a nonstarter. After all, MUH seems to imply that all of my experiences are unified with all of yours, and those of everyone else on earth, as though we all formed some kind of vast supraconsciousness. But (these critics might say) of course we don't. Rosenberg (2004, 88) suggests that "this view . . . banishes middle-level individuals from existence."

But does the presence of this larger unified mind, containing us as parts, really conflict with our existing and having the kind of consciousness that we do? No. Wholes do not in general "banish their parts from existence," even if the same relations that hold within the whole also hold between it and other things. A table leg is not banished from existence by the table, even if the same molecular bonding relations that connect its parts to one another also connect them to the rest of the table.

Of course, if we thought that phenomenal unity between two experiences confers both on the subject of either, then we would have a problem, for then my experiences being unified with yours would imply that I was having your experiences, and you were having mine, and everyone was having all the experiences; there would then be no subjects who, like us, undergo only some and not all of the world's experiences. But we should not think that unity has this effect—the idea that it does is what in chapter 2 I called "boundedness":

> **Premise D3 (Boundedness):** For any experience e_1 belonging to a subject s, if another experience e_2 is unified with e_1, then e_2 must also be had by s.

Panpsychist combinationism denies boundedness for phenomenal unity and claims that my experiences are unified with yours even though I am not undergoing yours. Whenever two human brains exert (say) a minuscule gravitational attraction on each other, this suffices to establish a composite experience that subsumes the experiences of each but leaves each still only undergoing their own experiences, not those of the other.

Why might someone think boundedness is true? One reason might be that they are impressed by the thesis that I called interdependence—the way that when two experiences become unified it changes the character of each:

> **Premise E3 (Interdependence):** The phenomenal character of an experience often depends partly on its phenomenal context, i.e., on the set of other experiences it is unified with.

If interdependence is true, then we might reason as follows: if my experiences were unified with yours, they would to some extent reflect the character of yours. When you started to feel sad or happy, that would impact the way I felt—we would have a kind of telepathy. Avicenna (1952, 5.3.7–8) seems to express this thought when he rejects the idea of a single continuous soul in all bodies because then "it would have knowledge or ignorance in all [the bodies] and it would not be hidden for Zayd what is in the soul of Amr" (cf. James 1909, 201–203; Goff 2012).

That would be a reason to think that MUH is incompatible with the actual degree of mutual ignorance that we humans experience. The further step to thinking that boundedness is true across the board might go as follows: if each of two unified experiences makes its subject aware of the other, then the subject is introspectively aware of both, and this seems tantamount to having them both. After all, the subject is being made aware, consciously, of what that experience is like. Isn't that just what having an experience is? I am not sure exactly how plausible such an inference is; I am to some extent trying to reconstruct what is motivating those who affirm a principle I deny. (In Roelofs [2016] I examine in more detail what reasons might be given for affirming boundedness for phenomenal unity.) Here I will simply say why MUH, with its implication of unity between my experiences and yours, is neither necessarily false (due to boundedness) nor empirically false (due to our obvious ignorance of each other's experiences).

Let us grant that unified experiences affect each other's character; this does not stop us from saying that they may do so more or less strongly. Maybe when I see someone's dancing at the same time as I hear the music, the two experiences interact deeply, allowing me to see their movements as synchronized with and expressing the music. But I am also having plenty of other experiences at the same time (the feel of my clothes on my arms, an idle thought, a vague nagging feeling of having forgotten something), with far less impact on either how I see the other person or how I hear the music. Indeed, some unified experiences (e.g., my current feeling of my socks and the visual image of a lampshade beside me) are phenomenally unified but seem to make virtually no interesting difference to one another. Perhaps a strong supporter of interdependence will insist that there is still some sort of mutual influence (see, e.g., Dainton 2010; Chudnoff 2013), but it must be so mild as to be easy to miss. Plausibly, the strength of this mutual influence is linked to the strength of the causal interactions between the experiences; if this is the case, then the mutual influence established by phenomenal unity between my experiences and yours will be fainter even than that between two mutually irrelevant experiences of mine, like those of my socks and the lampshade.

The objector might press the point as follows: Doesn't MUH still imply some sort of phenomenal influence of my experiences on yours, however faint? I reply: Sure! But such an influence will (1) be so faint that we will not be able to use it to learn anything specific about each other's experiences, (2) will blur together with the influence of everything else in the universe, and (3) will have been present constantly throughout our lives, so that we have no idea what it would be like to live without it. Given this, what evidence do we have that this influence is not actually being exerted? How do we know that in a world of fundamentally separate minds, like the world envisaged by Descartes, we would not have lived all our lives with a slightly different "background feel" to our experiences, though without ever being able to identify it because we never had anything to contrast it with?

The objector might push their objection a slightly different way: Surely MUH still implies the possibility of some kind of strange supernatural telepathy? After all, if we simply made it so that our brains exchanged more information, then the mutual phenomenal influence they have in virtue of being phenomenally unified would become stronger and more distinctive, allowing each of us to know, just from the character of our own experiences, what the other was experiencing. I reply: Sure! That is called communication, and we do it regularly. When I talk to my friend, or gesture at them, or smile at them, I am manipulating the physical relations between us (whose inner nature, we are supposing, involves phenomenal unity) so that their experiences will give them knowledge of mine. MUH simply says that what I am doing to my friend is not fundamentally different from what my left hemisphere does to my right hemisphere when it transmits nerve signals down the corpus callosum: both involve physical transfers of information; both involve phenomenal unity. A more detailed examination of this sort of process will have to wait until chapters 5 and 6, but for now I will simply say that according to MUH, it is a mistake to speak, as the objection does, of "supernatural" telepathy: telepathy is the most natural thing in the world.

3.3.3. WHY CONSCIOUSNESS SEEMS BOUNDED

A final objection would allege that MUH is stretching the very idea of phenomenal unity past the breaking point. Didn't we introduce phenomenal unity as a relation that characteristically holds within, but not between, the consciousness of different humans? And so if we start to think that my experiences actually are phenomenally unified with yours after all, don't we lose our grip on what phenomenal unity was meant to be?

It sometimes happens that we initially form a concept to refer to something based on its evident presence in some cases, and apparent absence in others, only to later find that it is actually present in both cases. For example, the concept of "gravity" was originally introduced for the downward tendency of stones, water, and other bodies that fall downward, while air and fire were ascribed a corresponding property of "levity," a natural tendency upward. As it turns out, air and fire have gravity (weight) as much as earth and water, and the upward force on them is a result of gravity: denser substances around them jostle them out of the way. So gravity turned out to be present even in the cases it was initially contrasted with. This did not undermine the original meaning of the concept, because gravity was still *evident* in earth and water in a way that it was not in air and fire, so that its evident presence in heavy substances could be used to fix reference to it.

Something similar applies to phenomenal unity, if MUH is true. Each human being enjoys overall unified experiences, and moreover this unity is evident to their introspective self-awareness; even if pairs of human beings enjoy overall unified experiences, neither the pair nor either individual has introspective awareness of that fact. This pattern of introspective impressions was our original datum, and we need not violate it by extending phenomenal unity more widely: we simply replace one explanation of the lack of an introspective impression of unity in the pair (viz. that there is no unity) with a different explanation (viz. that there is unity, but no capacity to introspect it).

The evidentness of phenomenal unity in reflective beings here plays the same role as the evidentness of gravity/weight in objects heavier than air. Each of us can report a rough summary of all the many experiences we are having right now—I can "cast my inner eye about" and tell you that I am seeing certain things, feeling and hearing others, with my mind on a certain topic, and so on—and that I am experiencing all these things together. You can tell me similar things: each of us thus reports the content of a single complex experience which subsumes many others. But this is not enabled simply because those complex experiences exist and subsume their parts: it is enabled because of the human brain's capacity to do this kind of introspective survey, to synthesize an overall impression of a conscious field.[15] According to MUH, there is another, even more complex experience, which subsumes both of ours (at least as long as we are close enough for our brains to be exerting forces on one another). This experience has a subject—it is being undergone by a pair of people, the composite that you and I are parts of. But this subject is not integrated enough to survey its field of consciousness and report a summary. Equivalently, the composite experience which mine and yours form together is not in a position to produce an introspective summary; it is not poised for that kind of access. To that extent, it could be misleading to describe it as a conscious state (in a sense nobody is "conscious of it," i.e., nobody is "access-conscious" of it), even though it is phenomenally conscious in the sense that there is something it is like to undergo this state.

The situation is rather as though we are standing under two different streetlights, which reveal circular areas of an unbroken, continuous street surface. Introspection is the light, and phenomenal unity is the continuity of the surface that it reveals. It is compatible with what we are seeing that the continuity of the surface stops where light stops, so that we stand upon separate pedestals with no link between them. But it is also compatible with what we are seeing that the surfaces extend beyond where the light stops, and in fact are just one big surface. I think our default assumption, if we ever consider the question, is that we in the first situation—standing on "separate pedestals," unified minds with no unity out beyond them. It's an easy, intuitive, idea, and it might have been true: we might have inhabited a world where every mind was a true unit, with a precise and

---

[15] In the case of animals which lack the concept of "an experience," and so cannot reflect on their total experience as such, there at least remains a capacity to survey all the different things they are conscious of—all the smells, sights, sounds, and so on—so as to access an overarching sense of their manifest environment as a whole.

objective boundary between itself and the rest of the world. Plenty of philosophers have defended such a view, and it is arguably implicit in the very widespread view that for each human being, there is a distinct entity, a "soul," which can and hopefully will survive the dissolution of the body. I think the seeming bizarreness of MUH partly reflects that such a view is baked into how most of us think about the world, whether or not we would on reflection accept the metaphysics it implies.

But that world of sharply bounded minds does not seem to be the world we inhabit. Insofar as scientific investigation of the world has revealed no fundamental physical breaks in the fields of matter and energy whose perturbations make up human brains and bodies and everything else, scientific investigation gives us reason to prefer the rival hypothesis, that there is just "one big surface," one big phenomenal field. Our two lights illuminate different sections of the same surface; our two brains enable introspective awareness of different subfields of the same phenomenal field.

What enables the formation of a second-order thought about the totality of my current experiences is that each of these experiences broadcasts enough information to the rest of my mind. This broadcasting of information changes and enriches each experience, so that each reflects and carries information about the others. This interweaving of experiences into more complex wholes is examined in detail in chapter 5; the key thing to note here is that, unlike phenomenal unity itself, this sort of access-unity does come in degrees. One part of my brain can send out more or less information, or better or worse information, or information that is harder or easier to detect, to other parts. And between the within-brain information transfers enabled by synapses and nerve fibers, and the minuscule gravitational attraction that any two brains exert on each other, there is a smooth continuum of intermediate degrees of communication.

Consequently the form of access-unity involved in the capacity for introspective survey and summation, unlike phenomenal unity itself, can be semantically vague. Recall that it can be neither determinately true nor determinately false that a man is bald, because our concept "bald" does not specify precisely how much hair is "enough" hair not to be bald is. Likewise a set of experiences can be neither determinately unified nor determinately disunified, because being unified requires "enough" information to be shared between experiences and synthesized by various mental systems, and our intuitive conception of unity does not specify how much information is "enough." This lets us say, as we were inclined to, that experiences are unified within the confines of organized structures like the human brain, disunified between disparate objects like two people lying on a beach, and in in-between cases, like perhaps split-brain patients, semantically indeterminate between unity and disunity.

3.4. The Subsumption Argument from Micro-Unity to Inheritance

In the previous two sections I defended experience inheritance as an *a priori* necessity and the micro-unity hypothesis as an *a posteriori* conjecture. There is, however, also an argument in support of experience inheritance (or something close to it) which takes MUH as a premise, and thus establishes only that EI is true in the actual world if MUH is. That argument can be summarized quite readily: If every set of parts is connected by the fundamental physical relations, then MUH implies that every set of parts has unified experiences; this means that their experiences are subsumed by a composite experience; but since experience implies a subject, this means there must be a composite subject to undergo the composite experience. Call this "the subsumption argument."

3.4.1. THE SUBSUMPTION ARGUMENT LAID OUT

Formally the argument goes like this:

Premise 1: The deep nature of one of the fundamental physical relations is phenomenal unity (the micro-unity hypothesis).

Premise 2: All of the fundamental physical relations hold either universally or nearly universally.

Premise 3: When a set of experiences is phenomenally unified, there is a composite experience which subsumes them.

Premise 4: For any experience, there must be a subject.

Premise 5: To undergo a composite experience involves undergoing all the experiences it subsumes.

6 *(from 1 and 2)*: For all, or almost all, aggregates in our universe, the experiences belonging to its parts are all phenomenally unified.

7 *(from 3 and 6)*: For all, or almost all, aggregates in our universe, there is a composite experience that subsumes all the experiences of its parts.

8 *(from 4 and 7)*: For all, or almost all, aggregates in our universe, there is a composite subject that is undergoing a composite experience which subsumes all the experiences of its parts.

9 *(from 5 and 8)*: For all, or almost all, aggregates in our universe, there is a composite subject that is undergoing all the experiences of its parts.

Let me first say a bit about the premises of this argument, and then comment on the conclusion, which is not quite EI but comes very close.

The first premise is, of course, simply MUH, defended in the previous section. The second premise is an observation about how nature appears to be organized, again discussed in the previous section. "Nearly universally" here means over large enough scales to connect all sets of things whose consciousness might be of interest to humans—not just "the parts of my brain" but also "my brain and your brain," or "all the brains on earth," or "all the toenails and cactuses on earth." And if phenomenal unity is transitive, "nearly universally" will likely imply "universally," because even things too distant to stand in some fundamental physical relation are probably connected indirectly by a chain of such relations.

Premises 3 and 5 are just articulating the plausible Bayne-Chalmers analysis of phenomenal unity: for two experiences to be unified is for there to be something it's like to undergo both together. The key new claim is premise 4, that experiences require subjects. We might call this the "ownership principle":

> **Ownership Principle:** For any experience, there must be a subject who experiences it.

I think the ownership principle is very plausible, as long as it is kept in mind that we are operating with a distinctly unimpressive sort of subjecthood: if panpsychism is true, then it must be possible for subjects to be as unintelligent as an electron is. If we took "being a subject" to imply intelligence, self-awareness, and so on, then the ownership principle might be much more doubtful, but readers who demand such things of anything called a "subject" will probably find functionalist combinationism, outlined in chapter 5, more congenial. According to panpsychist combinationism, a subject is simply any entity that it is like something to be, however simple, and experiences are instances of properties defined by what it is like to instantiate them. Given these definitions, the ownership principle is more or less tautologous.

Suppose we accept the premises: What about the conclusion, item 9? This stops short of saying that all aggregates undergo the experiences of their parts: instead it says that "all or almost all" aggregates are associated with a subject which undergoes the experiences of their parts. The first difference—all versus "all or almost all"—is one that, by definition, matters little for any human purpose. Even if mental combination occurs only in "almost all" aggregates, that is more than enough to account for the formation of human-scale subjects and to generate the same counterintuitive profusion of subjects that EI does.

What about the second difference? The subsumption argument establishes only that for each aggregate, there is a subject sharing all the experiences of its parts—not that this subject *is* the aggregate. But this difference too is not of very great significance, because in this chapter I am assuming the metaphysical conception of subjects. If this conception is correct, then an experience's subject is the entity which metaphysically underlies an experience; the aggregate in question has a very good claim to being that entity, and so plausibly this difference from EI vanishes. On the psychological conception of subjects, we might instead say that the subject is the composite experience itself, or that it is a distinct being constituted by that experience but nothing over and above it (cf. the discussion of "thin" subjects explained by unity in Mendelovici 2018). I do not think the difference between such a view and panpsychist combinationism, as I have defended it so far, is a huge one.[16]

Interestingly, the subsumption argument could have been used as an argument *against* combinationism, if we accepted the principle of strong privacy. The argument shows that one thing combinationists might want (unifying relations among distinct subjects) implies experience sharing. The composite subject undergoes the subsuming experience, and thus also undergoes the experiences subsumed: each part's experience is thus shared by the composite. I take this to support my decision in chapter 2 to deny strong privacy (cf. Roelofs 2016, 6–11).

3.4.2. IS THIS PHENOMENAL BONDING?

It is worthwhile here to compare panpsychist combinationism, particularly as it comes out of MUH and the subsumption argument, with the "phenomenal bonding" account offered by Goff (2017a, b). On the latter account, we posit a "phenomenal bonding relation," about which we cannot know anything except that when subjects stand in this relation, they form a composite subject with unified consciousness. Goff (2017a, 183–186) moreover postulates that this unknown relation is most likely the deep nature of the relation of spatial distance, and that consequently it will bond microsubjects into composite subjects more or less indiscriminately.

---

[16] There is the following wrinkle: for all the subsumption argument shows, the subject undergoing the composite experience associated with one aggregate need not be distinct from the subject undergoing that associated with another aggregate. There might thus be fewer composite subjects than aggregates. But the principle of avoiding arbitrariness tells against this possibility: what precise, nonarbitrary principle could determine which aggregates are subjects and which aren't *while ensuring* that every nonconscious aggregate is contained within at least one conscious aggregate? The only nonarbitrary view I can see here is the very extreme one that there is, in addition to the microsubjects, only *one* further subject, associated with the whole universe and undergoing all the composite experiences associated with any aggregate at all. Such a view implies that there is no such thing as me or you, unless both of us are identified with this one cosmic subject, and thus with each other. But even if this—incredibly radical—view is correct, there must be some sort of "figure of speech" by which we can make sensible claims about "Luke Roelofs" and other people, and their differing properties. After all, even if ultimately there is just the one cosmic mind, we want to capture the difference between "true" statements like "Luke Roelofs believes in combinationism" and "false" statements like "Everyone believes in combinationism." Given that there must be such figures of speech available, all my talk of aggregates should be reinterpreted as involving such figures of speech.

There are some important similarities between my theory and Goff's. We both posit that one of the fundamental physical relations has a phenomenal deep nature, and that this relation accounts for the combination of microsubjects into composite subjects with unified experiences. We both are inclined to think that such mental combination probably occurs universally or nearly universally, on the grounds that any restriction would have to be arbitrary. I have no objection to calling the relation I posit among microsubjects a "phenomenal bonding" relation. But there is an important difference between my theory and Goff's (even setting aside my *a priori* defense of EI): the bonding relation I posit is an introspectively familiar one, not a mysterious one we have no conception of. The relation I posit is simply phenomenal unity among experiences, the same basic relation we are each acquainted with among our own experiences.[17] In this way my theory avoids what Goff calls the "mysterianism" of his theory, the need to postulate something unknown so as to make combination work. While such a claim is (by its nature) hard to decisively refute, it is also somewhat unsatisfying, not only because it posits something whose nature is permanently opaque to us, but also because this posit makes it harder to see what explanatory role is played by the parts themselves being subjects (cf. Coleman 2017, 256–258). After all, we could just as easily posit an unknown "relation X," which forms subjects out of parts which are *not* themselves subjects. Without understanding the nature of either mystery relation, and how it connects with the subjecthood of the component subjects, there is little obvious advantage in postulating phenomenal bonding rather than X.

This difference between my theory and Goff's flows directly from our different attitudes toward experience sharing. Because I think that wholes undergo the same experiences as their parts, I can say that the relation which bonds their parts together into a subject is simply a relation among those experiences. And we are already acquainted with relations among experiences, in particular with phenomenal unity. Goff, by contrast, denies experience sharing, holding that the experiences of the parts "constitute" but do not "characterize" the experiences of the whole. Consequently, the relation which bonds the parts together into a whole is not any relation which we wholes might be acquainted with among our parts. Indeed, Goff argues for precisely this reason that we will never be able to form any positive conception of the phenomenal aspect of this relation.

---

[17] Chalmers (2017, 200–201) briefly suggests the possibility of developing a view like Goff's in this direction, with phenomenal unity as the bonding relation, but considers the boundary argument (which I discussed in sections 3.3.2 and 3.3.3) especially pressing against such a view. Cf. Miller 2018.

Overall, I am not sure if it is embarrassing or reassuring to have two completely different justifications for the same principle (EI), one entirely *a priori* and one deriving it from a posited contingent fact about our universe. On the one hand it may seem a bit like having two completely independent accounts of how one came into legitimate legal possession of certain goods: each story casts suspicion on the other. But on the other hand, it does reinforce my feeling that even if I have taken a wrong turn somewhere, the basic ideas of panpsychist combinationism—unity and subjecthood pretty much everywhere, experiences shared between parts and wholes—are along the right lines, at least if constitutive Russellian panpsychism is true.

3.5. Why Do Microexperiential Zombies *Seem* Conceivable?

In section 3.2 I made a case for the *a priori* truth of experience inheritance, the claim that experiential properties are division-invariant, present in a given portion of reality regardless of whether we see it as one whole or many parts. This implies the impossibility—indeed the inconceivability—of a nonconscious whole made of conscious parts, like the "microexperiential zombie" envisaged by many critics of constitutive Russellian panpsychism. And yet such a scenario has seemed conceivable to many philosophers; indeed, most people probably think it is not only conceivable, and possible, but also *actual*. (The solar system has me as a part, and I am conscious, but it is not.) Indeed, it sometimes seems conceivable to me, when I think about it the right way. So even if we thought that the argument given in section 3.2 is sound, we still need some account of what mistake explains the apparent conceivability of nonconscious wholes with conscious parts, and why smart people make that mistake.

What has gone wrong? I think there are two distinct conceptual confusions at work, one concerning wholes and one concerning consciousness, both of which are hard to avoid. In short: it is easy to overinflate what wholes are, so as to give a spurious appearance of conceivability to scenarios where their properties diverge from those of their parts. It is also easy to conflate phenomenal consciousness with access consciousness, and thus to mistake a scenario where a whole with conscious parts lacks access consciousness for a scenario where it lacks phenomenal consciousness. When considering something like the macroexperiential zombie, these two confusions work together in a mutually reinforcing way. In this section I try to motivate this view, that the conceivability of nonconscious wholes with conscious parts is only apparent. But I will also, in the next section, try to show that much or all of panpsychist combinationism can survive even if this claim for *a priori* status is abandoned.

3.5.1. CONFUSION ABOUT WHOLES, AND THE APPARENT CONCEIVABILITY
OF COMPOSITIONAL NIHILISM

Let me first describe the confusion I think is possible regarding parts and wholes. The best way to start is by observing that some philosophers have thought it conceivable that physical combination could fail, because I think it is more intuitively obvious in this case that some sort of mistake must have been made. Back in section 3.2 I mentioned Merricks's discussion of what a baseball smashing a window causes (namely, just what its parts cause). But in fact, strictly Merricks denies that the baseball causes whatever its parts cause, because he denies the baseball exists. He thinks that if there were such physical composites, they would have the same causal powers as their parts, but he employs this as a premise in an argument that believing in the existence of wholes like baseballs is unnecessary. He reasons as follows: Baseballs, and other physical wholes, might or might not exist in addition to their microscopic parts. Whether they do exist or not makes no difference to what happens (since anything they would do, their parts are doing already), and since we should not posit things which make no difference to what happens, we should eliminate physical wholes from our theories (Merricks 2001). We should conclude that, strictly, there are no tables, no planets, no houses, no rocks, but just atoms "arranged tablewise," "arranged planetwise," etc.

Merricks, and other "nihilists" or "eliminativists" about ordinary physical wholes (e.g., Van Inwagen 1990; Unger 2006), clearly take it to be conceivable that the atoms composing a baseball exist, but no whole composed of them exists. (Indeed, they take it to be actually true.) But their arguments, it seems to me, are in fact an excellent reason for thinking that this situation is *inconceivable*. For the conclusion of their arguments—that tables, planets, houses, rocks, etc. do not exist—is highly implausible, and yet follows fairly reasonably from that claim of conceivability. If it is genuinely conceivable that there could exist atoms arranged tablewise but no tables, that would suggest it was a real possibility. But then we have to ask: What evidence can we find to tell us whether that possibility is actual? And the way the choice has been set up, we will of course be able to find no evidence: because wholes do the same things that their parts are already doing, they are not the kind of thing whose existence would produce detectable evidence. I conclude, though, that the choice is badly set up: the nonexistence of tables despite the existence of atoms arranged tablewise is *not* an option, and to think of it as an option is to misunderstand the relation between parts and wholes. At least, it seems far more likely to me that these philosophers have misunderstood this relation in some way, than that there are no tables.

To summarize my argument here: it seems obviously reasonable to believe in tables, but there is no empirical evidence in support of their existence. I conclude that the reasonableness of believing in them is not evidence-based, because their nonexistence is not a genuine option: when there are atoms arranged tablewise, *of course* there is a table, since it is just those atoms considered together.[18] If it were consistently conceivable that a table not exist, despite there being atoms arranged tablewise, that would support thinking that such a thing was possible, a genuine option. Since it is not a genuine option, we should suppose that it is not consistently conceivable.

Why is it not conceivable? Where is the contradiction? The contradiction lies in violating substantive indiscernibility, which is a special case of the contradiction involved in violating the indiscernibility of identicals. It is contradictory to say that Bob exists, and Robert is Bob, and yet Robert does not exist. Likewise, I maintain, it is contradictory to say that atoms arranged tablewise exist, and that a "table" is a whole composed of atoms arranged tablewise, and yet no table exists. But then the question recurs as: Why does it seem conceivable—to Merricks, to Van Inwagen, perhaps to you the reader, even to me when I get myself into the right mindset—that there could be atoms arranged tablewise, but no table?

I think it is because of an inflated idea of what wholes are supposed to be. I think atoms arranged tablewise logically entail the existence of tables because I think tables are (with a few caveats) just those atoms taken together: they are aggregates. But (as discussed in chapter 1, section 1.3.4) some philosophers have felt that there is a major difference between a "mere" aggregate and a "true unit," and that only the latter really deserves the title of "whole" (since aggregates, after all, are just their parts taken together!). If, when we talk about "wholes," we are really looking for true units, then aggregates will not really count. Aggregates, after all, are meant to be just their parts taken together, and so by the standards of a seeker for true units, calling them "wholes" is like a sleight of hand, a sneaky attempt to "launder" many into one. By the standards of a seeker for true units, views like panpsychist combinationism are perhaps better seen as nihilist about wholes: on such views there are no wholes, only parts (or, even better, only uncountable "stuff" that is neither singular nor plural). After all, such views take human beings to be basically equal in their metaphysical status to tables, or any other sort of physical aggregate, and so if tables don't exist, neither do we. But to

---

[18] This is a slight oversimplification: plausibly tables are structure-specific wholes, not aggregates. But, as I argue in chapter 5, structure-specific wholes derive their existence from aggregates instantiating the right structural properties.

my mind it is more reasonable to say that both we and tables exist, though neither of us is, ultimately, anything over and above a bunch of particles interestingly arranged.[19]

The conceivability of particles arranged tablewise without tables makes sense, if "tables" must be true units or nothing, since true units by definition have features that are not derived from their parts, and so will not be conceptually entailed by their parts. But I think it is a mistake to think this applies also to "tables" understood as aggregates; at least, it seems that going down this road even for aggregates has seemingly absurd conclusions, such as the nonexistence of tables. An inflated idea of what wholes should be makes it seem coherent to vary their existence and properties independently of those of their parts.

I think the same inflation is at work in the apparent conceivability of nonconscious wholes with conscious parts, like the microexperiential zombie. To conceive of such a scenario, we first assign some properties to the parts (including consciousness), and then introduce a further entity, the whole, to which we assign a different and independent set of properties. We construct, so to speak, separate files for the many parts and for the one whole, and what we write in one file need not also be written in the other. But if the whole involved is just an aggregate, then it is a mistake to construct two separate files. There is just one file, read by different programs; one reality, differently described. To construct a second file is implicitly to treat the whole as something emergent, a true unit of the sort that Merricks, Leibniz, and others are looking for.

But what separates the microexperiential zombie from things like tables is that a second confusion, over the nature of consciousness, is working to reinforce this first confusion, by connecting it to a real and important possibility which is easy to misdescribe, namely that of a non-access-conscious whole with access-conscious parts.

---

[19] There is no need to dig in our heels over how to use the word "whole." I can happily accept the result that panpsychist combinationism says there are no wholes. Since there are no true units, there are no wholes by the standards of those who want their wholes to be true units. What we thought were wholes, including our own selves, are not single things at all: they are just many, many particles arranged in various ways. And what we each thought of as "my" stream of consciousness is in fact a stream of consciousness undergone collectively by these particles. The principle of experience inheritance, which I presented as connecting experiences in a whole and in its parts, should instead be understood as connecting experiences undergone by many things collectively with experiences undergone by many things individually: it says that whatever experiences one member of a group undergoes individually, the group members undergo collectively. Whether we refer to a group of particles experiencing things together as a composite subject is, in the end, a matter of semantics.

3.5.2. DIVISION-INVARIANT PHENOMENAL CONSCIOUSNESS AND DIVISION-
RELATIVE ACCESS-CONSCIOUSNESS

Here is something that is certainly true: just from some part of me undergoing an experience, it does not follow that I as a whole have cognitive access to that experience, or that it is informationally integrated with my other experiences, or that it will make a difference to my behavior. And in everyday talk this is precisely what would lead us to call it "unconscious": even though it is going on in me, I have no idea about it, and it makes no difference to what I do. In an important sense it is not conscious: it is not access-conscious.

According to many philosophers, that is all there is to consciousness: if some event in me is not cognitively accessible, if it does not play the right functional role in how I work and how I behave, then it is not a conscious experience (in chapter 5 I call this "pure functionalism"). If these philosophers are right, then experience inheritance is false: since what plays the right functional role in some part of me may not play that role for me as a whole, consciousness is not division-invariant. On the plus side, though, a functional analysis of consciousness would allow for consciousness to be *intelligibly* division-relative, and thus would still be compatible with a form of combinationism. But that form will not be panpsychist combinationism: it will be either functionalist combinationism or psychological combinationism, laid out in chapters 5–8.

Panpsychist combinationism is a form of constitutive Russellian panpsychism, which rejects any functional analysis of consciousness. No complicated organizational structure is, by itself, sufficient for consciousness; while it may make a difference to the structure of consciousness, it does not account for raw experientiality, for phenomenal consciousness. And, according to panpsychism, phenomenal consciousness can exist in very very simple forms, without cognitive access, behavioral complexity, or any of the others things we usually associate with it. But this distinction between phenomenal consciousness and access-consciousness is in some ways a hard distinction to keep clear—because whenever we try to focus on the phenomenality of some experience we are having, we must do so by cognitively accessing it!

I think the conflation between these two senses of "consciousness" is partly responsible for the apparent conceivability of nonconscious wholes made of conscious parts. We intuitively recognize that a whole with conscious parts may not be *access*-conscious of their experiences, and indeed may not be access-conscious of *any* experiences. It may be entirely without anything we would want to call cognition. Indeed, most wholes containing conscious parts are like this: for any of a million different random assemblages of things we might consider, which happen to include me, almost none will be consistently organized so that their overall functioning is sensitive to my individual experiences. To inherit access-consciousness from me, the whole needs to be organized in the right way, to give my experiences the same functional role in the whole as they have in me.

But that does not mean that these wholes lack phenomenal consciousness of my experiences. And if substantive indiscernibility, as I have interpreted it, is right, then they cannot lack that, because they are just me and some other things taken together. And phenomenal consciousness (we are assuming in this chapter) is not susceptible to any kind of analysis that would reveal that it means different things relative to different divisions (in the way that access-consciousness is susceptible), so there is no difference between the aggregate having that experience, considered as one, and its having that experience, considered as many things including me.

So what explains the apparent conceivability of nonconscious wholes with conscious parts is the interaction of the phenomenal/access confusion with the aggregate/true unit confusion discussed in the previous section. When I ask myself whether wholes containing me might lack consciousness, I first find myself struck by the very salient possibility of wholes containing me which lack access-consciousness of my experiences. And, second, because it is hard to keep phenomenal consciousness and access-conscious apart in imagination, this pushes me toward imagining that the wholes in question lack phenomenal consciousness of my experiences as well. And then, third, because of the ease of thinking of wholes as true units, floating free of their parts, I find myself easily able to keep simultaneously in mind the thought that the whole entirely lacks phenomenal consciousness while its parts do not, without feeling that the two are contradictory. But in fact both the second and third steps in this mental construction are mistaken.

3.5.3. INTUITIVE CASES OF MENTAL COMBINATION

I think it will help to illustrate and motivate these claims if I discuss a particular type of mental combination which is much more familiar than the sort panpsychists posit. It is an instance of what in chapter 1 I called "trivial combination," where a composite subject's consciousness is fully accounted for by the consciousness of just one part (and that part's relations to the others). Consider, for instance, your own brain. Suppose that we were willing to say that the brain itself is conscious—there is something it is like to be a brain. Suppose, in fact, that the brain's consciousness is just the sort of consciousness we typically ascribe to people; after all, it is widely accepted that all the conscious states we ascribe to people are in some sense based in the brain. Now consider the whole human being—the thing which has the brain, and all other organs—as parts. Could that composite thing lack consciousness, given that it contains this conscious brain as a part? (A precisely analogous question can be asked of substance dualists: If the soul is a part of the whole human being, and the soul is conscious, could it be that the whole human being fails to be conscious?) It seems to me that the most plausible answer is no: the whole human being cannot fail to be conscious, because it automatically "picks up" or "inherits" the consciousness of its brain.

This is just how the fundamental physical properties work: the whole human being cannot fail to occupy the space its brain occupies (as well as that occupied by its other parts), to have the mass its brain has (as well as that of its other parts). To conceive of the whole human being as having parts with a certain mass, or location, but as itself lacking those features, is incoherent: it is to both affirm and deny certain properties of a single entity—because the whole human being just is its brain and other parts, considered together.[20]

Let us consider a few ways that someone might reject this account of the brain-person relationship. They might simply deny that whole human beings, of the sort I have described (which have organs as literal parts), are ever conscious. One way to do this is to say that such things are just human *bodies*, things with biological persistence conditions: conscious beings have psychological or phenomenal persistence conditions. But this is just to reject the metaphysical conception of subjects, which I am supposing here. (They would then, presumably, deny that brains are the right kind of thing to be conscious either.) Fortunately, denying strong independence is considerably *easier* on the psychological conception of subjects, as I discuss in chapter 7.

Another response would be to say that whole human beings are conscious "only in a derivative sense": brains are properly conscious, and whole people merely by courtesy (cf. Dainton 1998, 681–682; Bailey 2015). But surely the most natural thing to say, on first reflection, is that I myself am a whole human being, and that I myself am literally conscious, not "conscious" by some sort of polite or convenient fiction. So this move, though possible, is itself counterintuitive.

Might an objector insist that, even if human beings inherit the consciousness of their brains, it is at least still conceivable that they not do so? But this opens them up to some very unnerving consequences. If we cannot establish this inheritance *a priori*, then surely we would need to find some empirical evidence that human beings really are conscious (and not just unconscious vehicles for conscious brains). And even if we assured ourselves that they are, we would then need

---

[20] As with the table, this is oversimplifying a bit: the human being is not *exactly* just the parts taken together, because it would cease to exist were they to be widely separated. It is a structure-specific whole constituted by the aggregate of those parts—it is them, taken together, arranged in a particular way. See chapter 5 for a fuller discussion.

to explain that: Why are human beings conscious? Could some be conscious and others not? It seems to me that these are not serious questions we need to empirically investigate (any more than we need to empirically investigate whether, in addition to particles arranged tablewise, there are tables); whatever the right answer is, it must be one that we settle on *a priori*.

Finally, an objector might say that the privacy of experiences breaks the analogy between experiential and physical properties. The reason I inherit the physical properties of my brain is that doing so requires no multiplication of property-instances, but merely their sharing between part and whole. Yet strong privacy rules out an analogous sharing of experiences. But we have already rejected strong privacy, while proposing weak privacy in its place. Indeed, the case of a human being and their brain intuitively supports denying strong privacy: if both are conscious, surely they do not have two streams of experience proceeding independently, but rather share a single stream of experience.[21]

Sutton (2014) analyzes cases like this as involving two beings that "share a supervenience base for" the relevant properties (622): if the part of something whose intrinsic features are sufficient for a given property to be instantiated is shared by another whole, then both wholes will instantiate that property in a "non-summative" way (622). "Non-summative" means that though two beings instantiate the property, the total amount of that property is not thereby increased: there is just one instance of the property, but it belongs to multiple beings. Sutton offers this analysis, which explicitly allows for "two non-identical beings that think the same thoughts" (622) as not only plausible on its merits, but also as the best way to resolve the "too-many-minds" problem (mentioned in chapter 1). This problem faces any view that distinguishes a person from the living organism or material body that constitutes them at a given time, or which distinguishes the latter two objects: since all appear to be capable of thinking (they "share the equipment"), these theories seem to imply "too many minds." But the problem also faces any view which recognizes the existence of both humans and their heads.

---

[21] Another case that works to undermine strong privacy is that of conjoined twins fused at the skull. Such twins can have nerve tissue connecting their brains, and there is no reason in principle that there could not be shared brain parts, connected with and fully integrated into both brains. Would it not then seem reasonable for there to be a single experience, arising from this shared brain area, belonging simultaneously to both twins? An actual case does exist in which a "bridge" of nerve tissue connects the thalami of two twins, and anecdotal evidence indicates that this allows some sharing of perceptual information. Relatively little study has been done on this case because the twins, Krista and Tatiana Hogan, are still so young (Dominus 2011; Langland-Hassan 2015; cf. Montero 2017, 220). Since this case may involve more of a "bridge" between two brains than a fully shared brain structure, it is not clear whether we should think of the Hogan twins as literally sharing particular experiences; nevertheless, an extrapolated case where that would seem the right thing to say, on both anatomical and functional grounds, is not hard to imagine.

According to Sutton, there are not too many minds because person, animal, and body all share the same mind. I take no stand on the proper analysis of persons, animals, and bodies, but I agree with Sutton that many beings can share the very same thoughts and experiences, if they overlap.

Finally, of course, an objector might point out that if the brain were isolated from the other organs—unable to control them, unable to receive sensory inputs from them, just sitting there like a tumor—we might not think that the whole human being shares the consciousness of the brain. And this is completely right: if the brain was differently connected to the rest of the body, the whole human being would not be access-conscious of the brain's experiences, just as the solar system is not access-conscious of my experiences. It may well be that access-consciousness and phenomenal consciousness are intimately connected, so that nothing can be phenomenally conscious if it is not access-conscious of at least some things, but in this chapter I am assuming the opposite: that phenomenal consciousness can and does exist without access-consciousness. In light of that, the fact that the whole human being is not always access-conscious of the brain's experiences does not entail that it is not phenomenally conscious of them.

3.6. What If Experience Inheritance Isn't *A Priori*?

I do not expect that the previous sections' arguments will convince everyone who worries that violations of EI are conceivable, and that EI is thus not *a priori* true. It is worthwhile, therefore, to say a bit about what follows if EI's *a priori* status is denied.

I think that the theory I have sketched (EI and MUH), or something like it, is what best follows through on the ambition of constitutive Russellian panpsychism, of placing consciousness at the base level of reality and treating it like other fundamental properties. And it does so most fully and most satisfyingly if EI is an *a priori* truth, grounded in the substantive indiscernibility of parts and wholes. But even if we give up on EI being *a priori*, we could retain the core and spirit of panpsychist combinationism, in at least two major ways: through a form of pan*proto*psychism on which something analogous to EI is *a priori* true, or through a version of panpsychism in which EI is an *a posteriori* truth about our universe.

Both of these "fallback" options retain the idea that something about consciousness is fundamental. Someone obviously might reject EI's *a priori* status because they think it is simply a mistake to treat any aspect of consciousness as fundamental. In particular, if physicalism is true, and the only fundamental facts are those stable by physics, then all facts about consciousness are, ultimately, facts about some very complicated sort of structure in the brain: all that it means for consciousness to exist is for nonconscious matter to be arranged the right way. In that case, though, panpsychist combinationism was wrong from the get-go, so its failure is not particularly surprising. Combinationism may still be true, but it will have little to say about the fundamental architecture of reality. Readers convinced of this kind of view should simply skip this chapter and the next one, and proceed immediately to chapter 5.

What would be more worrying would be for EI to not be *a priori*, even though something about consciousness is fundamental; this is the more pressing sort of objection, which I have encountered from several philosophers sympathetic to panpsychist combinationism. It is for them that I offer the following fallback options, tailored to two different sorts of critics. One sort thinks not only that EI is not *a priori* true, but that it is definitely false, because it implies conscious subjectivity in things which are *clearly* not conscious subjects. The other sort thinks EI might be true of our world, but is not a necessary truth.

3.6.1. TRADING EXPERIENCE INHERITANCE FOR PROTO-EXPERIENCE INHERITANCE

Consider first the critic who thinks EI is definitely false. They might say something like the following:

> If EI were true, then piles of sand, clouds of dust, and even such widely scattered aggregates as "the sum of all the left toes in the Milky Way" are conscious subjects: it is like something to be them. But this is absurd; we know a priori *that to be a conscious subject requires more complexity, or more integration, or more of something, than is possessed by random aggregates.*

Back in section 3.2, I noted that EI made sense only as a principle governing "bare" experiential properties, ones which do not presuppose self-awareness, unity, intelligence, and so on. In effect, this first sort of critic is saying that such properties are not really any sort of experiential property: once you subtract those things, what is left is not really conscious experience, and instantiating such "stripped-down" properties is not enough to be a conscious subject. This sort of critic may well be skeptical of panpsychism in the first place, since anything as simple as an electron would likely not qualify as a subject by these standards. If they were nevertheless persuaded by the arguments usually taken to support panpsychism (e.g., that consciousness is not fully explained merely by physical structure), they might naturally gravitate toward "panprotopsychism," the idea that all the fundamental physical entities are endowed with something "proto-experiential" but are not themselves conscious in the strict sense.

The fallback position I would suggest for critics inclined to think EI is definitely false is panprotopsychist combinationism. It is like panpsychist combinationism, but is panprotopsychist instead of being panpsychist, replacing EI with an analogous principle for proto-experiential qualities:[22]

Proto-Experience Inheritance: Whenever a part of x instantiates a proto-experiential property (e.g., unexperienced qualities), x also shares that instance of the proto-experiential property.

The notion of "proto-experience" is admittedly rather obscure. Sometimes it is taken to be something completely unknown, but such that if we *did* understand it, we would be able to deduce from its nature that consciousness must arise from it under certain conditions (see Chalmers 1996, 2015). Less mysterian versions might say that the proto-experiential is something which we are acquainted with in consciousness, even though at the base level of reality is exists without consciousness. The most developed form of this is Coleman's (2013, 2015, 2017) constitutive Russellian panqualityism. Coleman analyzes consciousness as involving two key components: qualities and awareness. Qualities characterize the distinctive "what it is like" of each different experience, but without awareness there is no consciousness because there is nothing the experience is like *for* anyone. Coleman thus splits the task of explaining consciousness into two subtasks: explaining why there are qualities, and explaining why there are subjects who are aware of them. The latter subtask he attempts to address structurally: a subject exists whenever there is a complex system set up in the right way to represent its own states (an analysis borrowed from physicalists like Rosenthal [2005]). It is only qualities, he thinks, that are fundamental and inherent in matter.

Panpsychist combinationism already has much in common with Coleman's view. We agree that what is simplest and most basic in consciousness is inherent in matter, and that humanlike subjects arise when these raw materials are embedded in the right kind of sophisticated information-processing structure. We agree that the raw materials inherent in matter generate the experiences we have in a wholly constitutive way—complex but not in principle mysterious. Our disagreement

---

[22] Panprotopsychist combinationism also, of course, needs to replace MUH with an analogous principle holding that one of the fundamental physical relations somehow functions to "unify" proto-experiential properties, where the relevant sort of "unity" is simply whatever is needed to allow distinct proto-experiential properties to generate a unified consciousness. (Coleman [2017, 261–262] at one point suggests quantum entanglement as the best physical relation to play this role.)

is simply about whether these raw materials—"what is simplest and most basic in consciousness"—are something that deserves to be called "consciousness," or whether that label should belong only to the sophisticated humanlike form.

Whatever protoexperiential properties are, proto-experience inheritance is meant to be derived, like EI, from the substantive indiscernibility of parts and wholes, together with the idea that proto-experiential properties are fundamental. It says that these properties are pervasive in nature, and moreover that for a whole to instantiate them is nothing over and above its parts instantiating them. But consciousness itself requires that these raw materials be organized into some sort of richer structure—most likely some minimum degree of causal interdependence, representational unity, access-unity, and global coherence, perhaps accompanied by such capacities as attention, introspection, memory, and so on. In chapter 5 I lay out functionalist combinationism, which examines precisely this process of constructing and then combining complex, intelligent conscious systems: those who find EI absurd may find that theory more amenable.

3.6.2. TREATING EXPERIENCE INHERITANCE AS AN *A POSTERIORI* TRUTH

Above we considered critics who say not only that EI is not *a priori* true, but that it is definitely false—and who thereby commit themselves to some sort of substantive *a priori* preconditions for being a conscious subject. A very different style of critic might say the following:

> We cannot decide anything about EI a priori: *it might conceivably be true, it might conceivably be false. There is nothing intrinsically absurd about the idea that, in the universe we inhabit, every composite thing, including widely scattered aggregates, is a conscious subject. Consciousness is a fundamental property of nature, and could in principle exist in any sort of distribution, with or without intelligence or unity. Nothing about either the nature of consciousness or the nature of composition can tell us whether composites of conscious parts are themselves conscious.*

To these critics I would suggest that, even if EI is not true *a priori* and necessarily, it is probably true contingently. That is, I would accept the possibility of microexperiential zombie worlds, where functional duplicates of us exist, made of the same conscious parts, yet entirely lacking in consciousness themselves. But this world is not such a world: in this world, wholes inherit consciousness from their parts.

This invites two questions: If EI is not true *a priori*, what justifies us in believing it to be true? And if it is not true necessarily, what explains its being true in the actual universe we inhabit? I have one answer to the first question, and three alternative answers to the second. The answer to the first question is, in short, that EI is the simplest explanation of the fact that we are conscious. We know that we human beings are conscious, and everything we learn empirically about the way the world works seems to show that we are neither fundamental (we are just grand assemblages or configurations of matter) nor fundamentally different from our surroundings (the way that matter is organized in a human being differs only by degree from the way it is organized in a water droplet, or a table, or a frog). The simplest hypothesis consistent with all of this (if we accept that physicalist reductions of consciousness fail) is that matter itself is conscious, and that assemblages of matter are conscious in virtue of this. More precisely, EI has the following virtues:

1. It is very simple to state: like the fundamental equations of physics, it could be "written on a T-shirt" (Lederman 1993, 21–22).
2. It is uniform: it applies to human beings no more or less than any other organism, and to organisms no more or less than to any other sort of system.
3. It is compatible with the continuity of nature: it does not try to draw any sharp boundaries onto the messy smear of reality, between systems that strike us as "integrated enough to be conscious" and those that do not.
4. It closely parallels the behavior of the fundamental physical properties, rather than diverging from them.
5. It is ontologically nonadditive: it does not require that putting together conscious parts generate anything "over and above" those parts, anything in addition to them; it simply says that their aggregate (i.e., them considered as one) is related to their experiences the same way they are.
6. And in virtue of being nonadditive, it avoids causal exclusion: since wholes have the very same experiences as their parts, when those experiences make a causal difference we can say that both parts and whole are simultaneously causally responsible.

I cannot say in advance that no better principle than EI could be devised, that would outdo it in these respects; if such a principle can be shown, that will only strengthen combinationism. And of course EI does not all by itself explain why humans experience things in the particular way that they do; that requires an account of how the multitude of simple experiences they inherit from their parts can add together into a recognizably human sort of experience, which the remainder of this book explores. But considering the subject-summing problem by itself, apart from those other problems, I think EI is the most theoretically elegant principle by which to get conscious wholes out of conscious parts.

But what explains EI's being actually true in this world, if it is not true necessarily? Consider three suggestions. First, in section 3.4 I presented an argument that the widespread phenomenal unity posited by MUH implies composite subjects for every set of conscious parts. Perhaps it is the fact that phenomenal unity pervades the cosmos that explains EI. Or (second) perhaps Goff is right to be "mysterian," and what explains the existence of composite subjects is something about matter, or the relations among pieces of matter, which we do not have any positive conception of. On either of these two hypotheses, composite subjects are explained by a fundamental but contingent fact about our universe. Just as our universe happens to be a spatial universe, or a universe suffused with electromagnetic force, or a universe containing neutrinos, though there is no logical necessity to its being any of these things, so also it happens to be a universe tied together by some form of phenomenal bonding.

The third possible explanation of why EI is contingently true would be that it follows from the contingent truth of "cosmopsychism," a version of panpsychism on which the universe as a whole is the most fundamental thing. As I noted back in section 3.1, it is still not clear what the fundamental physical entities are, and in particular whether they are very very small and numerous, or very very large and unique. (This question has some affinity with philosophical debates stretching from the ancient Greeks to the present day [cf. Schaffer 2010] about whether the universe is fundamentally many, forming one whole, or fundamentally one, refracting into many parts.) Different versions of panpsychism have been distinguished based on this question: "micropsychism" (which takes the fundamental conscious entities to be very very small and numerous) and "cosmopsychism" (which takes the fundamental conscious entity to be the universe as a whole).

I said in section 3.1 that this question actually matters little for evaluating panpsychist combinationism. This is for two reasons: firstly, empirically it seems as though all the physical facts about, e.g., a human body, can be traced to facts about particles and their interactions—even if those particles are in turn explained by facts about the universe as a whole. That is, micro-level entities still have explanatory priority over macro-level entities, so it makes sense to focus on how that micro-to-macro explanation works. Second, I think that in a certain sense the whole question of micropsychism versus cosmopsychism is mis-posed. That question is often framed as whether wholes are more fundamental than their parts, or parts more fundamental than their wholes. But it seems to me that opposing parts and wholes like this, as though they are in competition for priority, misses the key point, namely that neither is more fundamental than the other because they are not really distinct. The whole is neither prior to, nor posterior to, its parts: it just is them. Whether we take them together or divide it into parts, it is the same reality; the difference is in our ways of conceiving and describing it. So in that sense panpsychist combinationism, deriving from the substantive indiscernibility of parts and whole, is neither micropsychist nor comospsychist.

But perhaps I am wrong. Perhaps it really does matter whether we start with a conscious universe and try to extract human-size subjects from it, or start with conscious particles and try to compose human-size subjects from them. In particular, there seems to be a feeling animating many contemporary cosmopsychists that the former is somehow easier than the latter, because it allows the human-size subjects to be genuinely real and yet be nothing in addition to the whole. By contrast, cosmopsychists suggest, if a human-size subject were formed out of conscious parts, it would either be strongly emergent, or it would not be genuinely real, but just a sort of convenient fiction (e.g., Goff 2017a, 209ff.; 2015; Nagasawa and Wager 2017; cf. Miller 2017; Albahari 2018; Shani and Keppler Forthcoming).

If it is true that middle-size subjects can be adequately explained by cosmopsychism but not by micropsychism, then panpsychist combinationism should be replaced by "cosmopsychist combinationism." As with the other fallback options considered so far, this is not as great a change as it might seem. Even though I have spoken in "micropsychist" style so far, building up larger wholes out of smaller parts, I have been led to recognize principles that entail a universal subject: the cosmos itself inherits the experiences of all its inhabitants, and there is extensive unity among these experiences. In this sense the psychic cosmos is already implied by panpsychist combinationism; the only change to turn this into cosmopsychist combinationism concerns the metaphysical priority of this cosmic subject over other things. This is compatible with EI and MUH: EI simply says that when parts have experiences, so do wholes, while MUH says that when experiences stand in certain relations, their sum is an experience. Although it is natural to assume that the former clauses (parts having experiences, experiences standing in certain relations) express the more fundamental facts, this is not required; the more fundamental facts might instead be expressed in the latter clauses (wholes having experiences, composite experiences existing), which identify the grounds for the former.

3.7. Conclusions

The universe described by panpsychist combinationism, and its two key theses, experience inheritance and the micro-unity hypothesis, is in many ways a strange one. The starting point—that all fundamental physical entities are conscious—was strange enough. Because of EI, all aggregates of these fundamental entities will also be conscious, sharing the experiences of their parts: this is a 'universalist' form of panpsychism (cf. Buchanan and Roelofs 2018). And because of MUH, all aggregates whose parts physically interact will have composite experiences which unify those many simple experiences. Indeed, overlapping aggregates with interacting parts will share these composite experiences with each other. In short, consciousness works just like other basic physical properties. Every fundamental physical entity has some degree of, say, energy or location, and aggregates of these entities share the energy and location of their parts. Overlapping aggregates share some of their accumulated properties with each other. If we wish to measure the total energy of a system, it does not matter whether we count it as one whole, as many tiny parts, or as two large parts: it is the same reality, with the same energy, however we carve it. Similarly, it has the same consciousness however we carve it. And just as the basic physical relations run indiscriminately throughout the universe, not respecting the boundaries of organisms or anything else of interest to humans, so does the basic phenomenal relation. The world that physics seems to reveal is one in which it is hard to recognize ourselves: a great endless stretch of mass/energy, with each of us just a complicated ripple in this sea, and no privileged way to divide it up into macroscopic parts. According to panpsychist combinationism, this world is also a world of consciousness, and its consciousness is structured in just the same way: an endless phenomenal field, with each of us just a complicated ripple in this sea, and no privileged way to divide it up into macroscopic subjects.

4 The Problems of Structural Discrepancy

CHAPTER 3 OUTLINED panpsychist combinationism, a combinationist panpsychist theory on which every fundamental physical thing is conscious, the fundamental physical relations unify their experiences, and composites inherit consciousness from their parts. I tried to defend this theory against the fundamental internal problems for combinationism discussed in chapter 2, but it needs defending also against a cluster of "bridging problems," which do not apply to all combinationist theories but only to panpsychist ones.

These problems stem from the apparent discrepancy between the structure of microphysics and the structure of human consciousness, a discrepancy that seems to tell against identifying our brain processes with our consciousness. Here is a representative statement of this supposed discrepancy from Maxwell (1979, 398):

> How is it that the occurrence of a smooth, continuous expanse of red in our visual experience can . . . involve particulate, discontinuous affairs such as transfers of or interactions among large numbers of electrons, ions, or the like? Surely being smooth or continuous is a *structural* property, and being

particulate or discontinuous is also a structural property . . . incompatible with being smooth and continuous.

For a more detailed statement, I am indebted to Lockwood (1993), who distinguishes three specific strands of the problem:

- Our experience is relatively *coarse-grained*, while any plausible composite basis is very *fine-grained*.
- Our experience is *qualitatively diverse*, while any plausible composite basis has only a *few qualitative ingredients*.
- The *type* of structure found in experience "seems not to match, even in coarse-grained fashion, that of the underlying physiology." (274)

Following Chalmers (2017), I will call these the "revelation problem" (190): how does fine-grained structure *disappear* from the whole's perspective; the "palette problem" (189): how does qualitative diversity *appear* in the whole's perspective; and the "mismatch problem" (191): why do the *types* of structure diverge?

Let me say a bit more to convey the force of these problems. The revelation problem concerns the apparent absence from our experience of the sheer degree of detail that physics tells us is present in our brains. Consider someone smelling a simple odor or hearing an unchanging pure tone. From the subject's point of view, these events may appear pure and structureless, but we know that they arise from the simultaneous activity of a great number of different neurons, each with billions of billions of parts. So we may wonder, "How do all these microstructural discontinuities and inhomogeneities come to be glossed over?" (Lockwood 1993, 274). This problem is particularly pressing for panpsychists because they usually think that undergoing an experience provides at least some direct insight into its nature; physicalists who think experience is a superficial feature of reality, or even an illusion, need not be so worried. But panpsychists seem committed to the thought that if our experience really is immensely fine-grained, then that richness "couldn't help but be manifest to consciousness" (Coleman 2012, 144).

To set up the palette problem, I will quote again from Lockwood (1993, 276):

There is nothing qualitatively distinctive about a neuron in the auditory cortex, or the corresponding action potential, to mark it out from a neuron, or the firing of a neuron, in the visual cortex. So how, on this basis, is one to account, say, for the fundamental phenomenological difference between a sound and a flash? . . . It seems inconceivable in much the same way, and for much the same reasons, that it is inconceivable that an artist, however skilled, should conjure the simulacrum of a Turner sunset from a palette containing only black and white paints.

Consciousness seems qualitatively rich, but any structure isomorphic with the physical brain would be qualitatively homogeneous, with the same basic ingredients present throughout, albeit in varied structures. Combinationists must explain how the diversity of qualities we experience arises from the qualities experienced by our smallest parts.

The mismatch problem is expressed by Chalmers (2017, 183) thus:

> Our macroexperience has a rich structure, involving the complex spatial structure of visual and auditory fields, a division into many different modalities, and so on. . . . Macrophysical structure (in the brain, say) seems entirely different. . . . Microexperiences presumably have structure closely corresponding to microphysical structure, and we might expect a combination of them to yield something akin to macrophysical structure. How do these combine to yield macrophenomenal structure instead?

Consider, for instance, that the division of the human brain into two hemispheres is a very noticeable feature of its physical structure, but this large-scale feature seems not to show up in consciousness at all and was discovered not by introspection but by visually inspecting human brains. By contrast, the division of consciousness into distinct sensory modalities is vividly obvious from the inside but very hard to discern from an outside inspection of the brain. This last problem is the most open-ended, since it touches on all the particular structures we find in consciousness. It will not be fully addressed in this chapter: rather, I will attempt here to show how, in general, panpsychist combinationism allows for conscious structure to match information-processing structure rather than gross physical structure. In the next chapter I explore in more detail the specifics of conscious structure.

4.1. Enriching Panpsychist Combinationism

The problems of structural discrepancy, and in particular the revelation problem, seem very forceful if we allow ourselves to assume that experiences of what I will call "phenomenal contrast," where we are presented with two distinct elements that each present themselves as not-the-other, is the default and automatic consequence of inheriting two distinct experiences from different parts of ourselves. By rejecting this assumption, we can make the problems much more tractable.

4.1.1. PHENOMENAL CONTRAST AND PHENOMENAL BLENDING

Consider the experience of seeing a red patch next to a yellow patch. Not only are you experiencing red, and experiencing yellow, and experiencing them together— you are also experiencing them as two distinct things. This feature of your experience is what I am calling "phenomenal contrast," and it goes along with (but is not simply the same as) various cognitive abilities, to do things like focus on the red but not the yellow, judge how sharply they contrast with one another, remember each color distinctly so as to recognize each if you see it by itself elsewhere, and so on. Phenomenal contrast is a feature of the composite experience's phenomenal character, and it comes in many forms. (Compare the experiences of red above yellow, red below yellow, red on a yellow background, etc.) These are different ways to experience red and yellow together.

My claim is that not all ways to experience red and yellow together—i.e., not all composite experiences which subsume an experience of red and an experience of yellow—involve phenomenal contrast. Some present red and yellow to the subject, without presenting them as distinct, and thus without the subject's being able to attend to one or the other, to judge their contrast, to remember each individually, and so on. I will call these composite experiences "phenomenal blends" of red and yellow; their subjects experience red and yellow together in a blended way, not as two distinct things. Moreover, I cautiously suggest that sighted human beings sometimes undergo blended experiences of red and yellow when they experience the color orange, though this specific example is not essential to my case.

I suggest the possibility of blending as an *a priori* truth about the nature of experience. If blending is possible, then the metaphysical distinctness of two or more elements in human experience—the fact that they in fact arise from separate parts of that human being—need not correspond to their phenomenal distinctness, i.e., to the experience of phenomenal contrast.

More specifically, I suggest that whether a composite experience involves phenomenal blending or phenomenal contrast, and what sort of phenomenal contrast it involves, depends on the informational structure in which it is embedded, on the way its different elements relate to the rest of the subject of that composite experience. Experiences are blended, I claim, whenever they form a composite experience (i.e., are phenomenally unified), but the composite's subject is unable to recognize the presence of this complexity, to distinguish its elements, or to direct attention onto one or the other of them. The elements are, I will say, "radically confused with one another" relative to that subject. Phenomenal contrast between elements requires that information about those elements be separately accessible by their subject.

4.1.2. THREE MORE HYPOTHESES

The final three claims of panpsychist combinationism address the problems of structural discrepancy by appeal to the above claims about the possibility of, and requirements for, blending and confusion.

> **Radical confusion hypothesis (RCH):** What makes human experience seem to be relatively coarse-grained is not an actual lack of fine-grained detail, but rather the fact that all of its component microexperiences are radically confused with one another.
>
> **Small palette hypothesis (SPH):** All the phenomenal qualities experienced by humans and other beings arise from blending different combinations of the small range of basic phenomenal qualities experienced by microsubjects.
>
> **Informational structure hypothesis (ISH):** The overall structure manifest in human consciousness corresponds to the structure of information-processing in the human brain, not to its gross physical structure.

The first two hypotheses are two sides of the same coin, describing a single process by which structural complexity in a composite experience is manifest to its subject as a particular quality rather than as a multiplicity of distinguishable elements. They thus aim to address the palette problem and the revelation problem together. A human brain inherits the vast array of experiences going on in its parts, but most of them are radically confused; this is why human experience seems so much less fine-grained than the brain's physical structure. But while the fine-grained details are not available for distinct awareness, they are preserved in the form of an increased diversity of qualities: phenomenal blending builds new qualities for experience to display, and thereby allows human brains to experience a range of qualities far outstripping those experienced by its microscopic parts.

For unified experiences not to blend, they must be distinguishable rather than confused. This requires that the system experiencing them have a capacity to respond to them differentially, to treat them as distinct. Fundamentally, this requires that information about them be separately accessible, that changes in one part have different effects on the rest of the system than changes in the other. There is a lot of this kind of information-processing in the nervous systems of animals, and very little in inanimate objects (with the possible exception of computers). It follows that our best guess about the experience of ordinary inanimate objects—tables, chairs, rocks, sand grains—is that they have completely blended experiences: they experience many many things, but experience them as a single homogeneous quality.

The third hypothesis, ISH, then appeals to the confusion and distinguishability of different brain processes to address the mismatch problem. Consider, for instance, the fact that human experience is divided into distinct sensory modalities, some involving spatial fields like the visual field. It is a familiar fact that we cannot experience a phenomenal contrast between two different colors at the very same point in the visual field. To experience two colors at the same point seems to be possible only by experiencing them as a blend. The visual field is thus in a sense constructed out of possibilities of phenomenal contrast, with each point defined by the impossibility of such contrast at that point and the enforcement of blending. If I am right that phenomenal blending reflects confusion and phenomenal contrast reflects distinguishability, then the explanation of this structural feature of our consciousness will lie in informational structure, namely the pattern of systematic distinguishability and confusion.

Chapter 5 explores how informational structure determines conscious structure in more detail; in this chapter I focus on substantiating the claim that the radical confusion hypothesis and the small palette hypothesis solve the revelation problem and the palette problem, respectively. But first I need to lay out more precisely and more clearly the informational notions (confusion and distinguishability) that correspond to the phenomenal notions (blending and contrast) that I employ.

4.2. What Is Confusion?

I will explain the notion of radical confusion by first introducing a very broad notion of confusion, and then defining radical confusion as a specific variety. I take the label "confusion" from the early modern rationalists, some of whom faced their own versions of the revelation problem. In particular, Spinoza and Leibniz are both committed to the claim that every event occurring in the human body has a corresponding mental event in the human mind.[1] How is this fantastic level of mental detail to be reconciled with our apparent ignorance of the processes occurring in our bodies? For both authors, the solution appears to rest upon the idea of *confusion*: bodily sensations are always confused, and thus while the mind

---

[1] Leibniz's problem is even more radical, since each mind represents not only its own body but the whole universe.

perceives them in some sense, it is in another sense unaware of them.[2] Consider a famous passage from Leibniz (2012, 96):

> The perceptions of our senses even when they are clear must necessarily contain certain confused elements . . . [for] while our senses respond to everything, our soul cannot pay attention to every particular. . . . It is almost like the confused murmuring which is heard by those who approach the shore of a sea. It comes from the continual beatings of innumerable waves.

And here is one from Spinoza (1994, 140):

> The human body, being limited, is only capable of distinctly forming a certain number of images within itself at the same time. . . . If this number is exceeded, the images will begin to be confused, and if the number . . . is largely exceeded, they will all be completely confused with one another. . . . When the images become quite confused in the body, the mind also imagines all bodies confusedly without any distinction, and will comprehend them, as it were, under one attribute.

Both passages seem to present the same idea: the finite capacities of the human mind ensure that many of its ideas will be "confused" in that it will be unable to distinguish them. Michael Della Rocca (2008, 113) helpfully offers the following definition: "For Spinoza, an idea is confused when it represents . . . two separate things and yet the mind is unable to distinguish these things by having an idea that is just of one of the objects and an idea that is just of the other of the objects."

4.2.1. VARIETIES OF CONFUSION

I define confusion thus: two mental elements are confused with each other, relative to a subject and a mental operation, when that subject can perform that mental operation on both at once, but not on either separately. They are distinguishable insofar as they are not confused. I intend the phrases "mental elements" and "mental operations" to cover any kind of mental thing which can be the object of any kind of mental process: the notion of confusion is neutral among different accounts of how the mind is organized. Prominent examples of mental operations might include "thinking" or "entertaining," "introspecting" or "being aware

---

[2] Leibniz appears to recognize and respond to the challenge of blurring much more explicitly than Spinoza does. Developing a Spinozistic response to the blurring problem is thus more of an exegetical task; see M. Wilson (1999) for a discussion of some attempts and their shortcomings.

of," "attending," "imagining," or "recognizing" in the sense of categorizing under concepts or of judging distinct from or identical with something else. Mental elements might be "experiences," "ideas," "contents," or "phenomenal qualities" understood as the things, awareness of which constitutes the having of an experience. In the primary instance these elements will be particulars, but we can easily define a secondary sense in which two types are confused for a subject when any particular instance of those types onto which a given subject could direct a given operation would be confused with an instance of the other type.[3]

Note also that since confusion is subject-relative, the same element might belong to both part and whole but be confused for one but not for the other. Indeed, for small enough parts confusion might disappear simply because the parts each experience only one thing, and can thus trivially be said to be able to "distinguish" it from what they are not experiencing. It follows also that phenomenal blending is subject-relative: when I experience red and yellow blended into orange, parts of me may experience the same yellow and red unblended.

Let us draw three distinctions among types of confusion. First, since confusion is relative to a mental operation, elements might be confused relative to *all* the mental operations a subject is capable of; call this "strong confusion," and call the contrasting case, where elements are confused only relative to some operations, "weak confusion." For instance, we might be unable to call to mind the flavor of coffee without at the same time calling to mind the bitterness of its taste, yet nevertheless be able to attend (and apply concepts, like "bitter") to them separately. Then the experiences of flavor and bitterness would be confused relative to some mental operations (like "calling to mind"), but not relative to others (like "attending"), and so would be weakly, not strongly, confused.

Second, confusion may be symmetric or asymmetric. Suppose I can think of two things together, and think of the first without the second, but cannot think of the second without the first. Then there would be a sort of confusion involved regarding the one but not regarding the other: they are "asymmetrically confused." For example, perhaps we can never experience certain bodily sensations (e.g., pain, itching, discomfort, or nausea) without also experiencing displeasure, and cannot even attend to the distinctive sensory element of the sensation without attending also to that displeasure. Nevertheless we can experience and think about displeasure independently of the sensory element; hence there are two distinct

---

[3] Note that confusion is different from indiscriminability, the relation between two items which "appear the same" to a subject. Indiscriminability involves two things seeming qualitatively equivalent to a subject even while they are recognized by that subject to be numerically distinct, and thus distinguished.

elements present here which are asymmetrically confused relative to some mental operations.

Third, confusion may depend on circumstances. Someone who is tired, distracted, drunk, or having to respond quickly may be unable to distinguish things which they would be able to distinguish given better conditions: that is, their experiences may qualify as confused only relative to those circumstances. Confusion may also be relative to a subject's conceptual repertoire; it might be that they cannot distinguish two ideas using their present concepts, but would be able to if they refined their concepts or learned new ones. Indeed, a common activity of philosophers is to claim to have identified a confusion of this sort in our everyday concepts, which requires the introduction of technical concepts to remove. Call confusion which can be removed by adjusting the subject's bodily surroundings or condition, or improving their conceptual repertoire, or in some similarly mild way, "shallow confusion." By contrast, call confusion which persists even into ideal conditions, "robust confusion."

There is also an important intermediate case: confusion which persists until the subject becomes distinctly acquainted with an element of the same type as the confused elements. For example, suppose the sensory component of pain is robustly confused with the unpleasant affect pain involves, except for subjects who have experienced "pain asymbolia," the rare condition of feeling pain without finding it at all unpleasant (cf. Grahek 2007; Klein 2015). If they regain normal pain experiences, they might find themselves newly able to attend to (or imagine, recognize, etc.) its sensory element in isolation. If this were to happen, we might say that their original confusion was "nearly robust": removable only by somehow acquainting them with (an instance of the same type as) one of the confused elements on its own.

I define "radical confusion" as confusion which is strong, symmetrical, and either robust or nearly robust. The radical confusion hypothesis says that the microexperiences we inherit from our smallest parts are all radically confused with one another in this sense.

4.2.2. KNOWING ABOUT AND EXPLAINING OUR CONFUSION

We can often tell that we are suffering from confusion, *if* that confusion is weak, asymmetric, or shallow. The easy way to identify shallow confusion is to remove it and contrast the resulting distinction with the earlier confusion. With robust confusion, that is impossible, but we might notice the confusion if it was only weak, for we would then be able to distinguish the elements in one fashion while noting our inability to do so in another fashion. For example, if we could not imagine one sensation without another arising alongside it, but could still attend to the two separately (and go on to name and conceptualize them independently), the possibility of two attentive acts would be a sign of two mental elements. Finally, if confusion is asymmetrical, we can distinguish the confused pair from at least one element, and thereby infer the existence of a contrasting element which we cannot distinguish from the pair.

What if we suffered from confusion that was strong, symmetric, and robust? Lacking all three of the above means of recognizing confusion, we could not tell that we were confused. Similarly, if we suffered from confusion that was strong, symmetric, and nearly robust, it would be undetectable, except by means of independent acquaintance with elements of the same type as the confused ones: call such confusion "nearly undetectable." Thus radical confusion will be either undetectable or nearly undetectable.[4]

According to the radical confusion hypothesis, all the experiences of our microparts are shared by us, but they are radically confused relative to us, which leads us to misinterpret them as coarse-grained. That is not to say that each microexperience is confused with every single other one, taken pairwise, but that each element is radically confused with a great many other elements.[5] But why?

The explanation for this confusion is provided by the simple fact that the human brain is not constructed so as to be able to individually register and distinguish all the trillions of events in its neurons, nor to direct attention onto them, report them verbally, encode them in memory, or otherwise access them. This lack of sensitivity to minute internal fluctuations is not surprising; any physically plausible mechanisms would display it. For two things to be distinguishable for a

---

[4] What about "cacophonous" noises? For instance, if we enter a bar and are overwhelmed by the combined noise of many voices, chair movements, music, and so on, we seem to perceive that there are multiple sounds present but cannot focus on any one of them individually (cf. discussions of the "problem of the speckled hen": Ayer 1940; Tye 2009). Is this radical confusion that we can detect? I think this is actually better analyzed as a case of shallow confusion exacerbated by the brevity and equal salience of the elements. The component noises *could* be separately attended with time and effort but are so short in duration that we cannot focus on them before they are gone and so similar in salience that we cannot select one to devote the necessary effort to. In such a situation, if we do decide to arbitrarily seize upon one component and focus on it, we usually succeed if it persists for more than a few moments. So this is not a case of radical confusion.

[5] This might mean that there are a number of clusters of experiences, all members of each of which are pairwise confused with each other, but not with the members of other clusters. Alternatively, it might involve continuous chains of confusion, with the end-points distinguishable but each pair of steps confused. The latter version would be ruled out if confusion were transitive, and as defined it appears so: if A cannot be thought without B being thought, and B cannot be thought without C being thought, then A cannot be thought without C being thought. However, this transitivity disappears if we allow for the "cannot" to assert only very low probability: that is, if A is thought then B will *almost* certainly be thought, with a probability close to 1, but might not be. The probability of C being thought will be slightly less, and so on, until we fall below the (likely vague) threshold for "cannot." (Cf. discussions of the nontransitivity of phenomenal indiscriminability, such as Goodman 1951; Hellie 2005; Raffman 2012.)

subject is for that subject to be able to direct mental acts onto them separately, which presupposes the capacity for mental acts like "attending to," "reflecting on," "inferring from," "coming to believe," etc. Plausibly, to count as performing any such activity on some item requires that facts about that item impact the other states of the subject. Differences in that item must make a difference to the rest of the system: the system must extract information about the item, must be receiving some sort of "signal" from it and be able to discern that signal from background noise. In a sense all the tiny parts of the brain send "signals" to the rest of the brain, through the chemical, electromagnetic, and even gravitational effects they have on their surroundings. But these signals will be very weak and stand out from background noise very little. Consequently, for small enough elements, the resources required to distinguish them are greater than the brain can muster, even under ideal circumstances, and hence they will be radically confused. To use a social analogy, it is hard for everyone in a room to hear everyone else, especially if some have weak voices. In a room of a trillion people, no individual's voice would be distinctly audible, because the others would produce so much noise (both literal and statistical), even though their voice is part of the audible roar.

Phenomenal blending involves radical confusion together with phenomenal unity. In at least some cases the confusion among ingredients is only *nearly* robust, and the same experience types occur separately on other occasions; this is what allowed us to grasp the blending relation, by comparison of qualities like red, yellow, and orange. Note that in cases like this it is particular instances, not types, that are confused: "reddish experience" and "yellowish experience," as types, are not confused at all, for a normal human, but when they have an orangish experience they have reddish and yellowish experiences which are radically confused with one another, and which they would not be able to distinguish at all had they never experienced red or yellow separately.

So, to sum up: when the components of an experience are distinguishable by the subject, they are phenomenally presented as discernible, separate, parts—in an experience of phenomenal contrast. Their subject has an impression of their multiplicity. When they are radically confused, by contrast, they are present qualitatively, as contributions to the total quality of the experience they blend into, which can only be grasped as distinct by a subject who already knows what to look for. A subject who lacks any distinct acquaintance with the ingredients will not be able to distinguish the elements, and they may as a result misinterpret their experience as lacking any such elements. That is, they may mistake the lack of any impression of multiplicity for a positive impression of simplicity and thereby misinterpret their experience as coarse-grained in a way that it is not.

4.3. Radical Confusion and the Revelation Problem

In the previous section I tried to motivate the idea that if we inherited trillions of microexperiences from our microscopic parts, they would be radically confused with one another, and we would be unable to tell that there were trillions of them. The radical confusion hypothesis says that this explains why our experience appears to be so much more coarse-grained than our brains are, and in particular why we do not experience phenomenal contrast among these many microexperiences:

> **Radical confusion hypothesis (RCH):** What makes human experience seem to be relatively coarse-grained is not an actual lack of fine-grained detail, but rather the fact that all of its component microexperiences are radically confused with one another.

4.3.1. THREE VERSIONS OF THE REVELATION THESIS

Does this really solve the revelation problem? I will consider three objections, each in a different way claiming that my proposal conflicts with the sort of direct knowledge each of us has of our own consciousness. This direct knowledge is often formulated in terms of a "revelation" thesis, saying that the nature of a conscious experience is always "revealed" to subjects who have it. There are actually three different sorts of revelation principle,[6] which generate three sorts of objection to my proposal:

---

[6] This "revelation principle" was first given that name in Johnston (1992), who held it to apply to color properties insofar as they are manifested in visual experience; subsequent authors have discussed it specifically with regard to experiential properties (Stoljar 2006b, 221ff., Byrne and Hilbert 2006; Chalmers 2017; Goff 2017a, 85ff.). The most perspicuous formulation is the following:

> **Revelation Principle:** [In having] a concept of a conscious state the content of which is wholly based on attending that state . . . the complete nature of the conscious state being attended to is directly revealed to the concept user. (Goff 2017a, 107)

A principle along these lines has been considered by some to reflect a deep and self-evident truth about the very idea of an experiential property (Strawson 1989; Johnston 1992), or as the best explanation for the kinds of judgments we seem able to make about experiences and their differences and similarities (Chalmers 2002; Goff 2017a, 109–113). Moreover, revelation or something like it plays a role in prominent arguments against physicalism (Chalmers 2009; Goff 2017a, 74ff.); insofar as panpsychists often rely on such arguments, they have special reason to make sure that their proposals are compatible with revelation. Chalmers's key premise is that the "primary intension" and "secondary intension" of phenomenal concepts coincide; this, like the revelation principle, says that we grasp experiential properties not by some accidental feature but by their essence: when we think of an experiential property, we know what it is that we are thinking of. This "coincidence of intensions" is, like the revelation principle, only apparently in tension with RCH, for the same reasons as are given below.

1. A "no illusions" thesis: It is incoherent for us to fall victim to an illusion about our own consciousness. The objection is then that the RCH requires an "illusion of simplicity," i.e., for our experience to seem simple or coarse-grained and yet not actually be that way.

2. A "revealed essence" thesis: When a subject focuses on and scrutinizes an experience they are having, they are in a position to learn the whole essence of the experiential property they thereby instantiate. The objection is that if the RCH were true, scrutiny of our experiences ought to reveal to us that they are formed out of a huge number of microexperiences, but in fact we are completely unaware of this fact.

3. A "self-presentation" thesis: When a subject has an experience, they are automatically in a position to know that they are having it. The objection is that according to the RCH we are having many experiences (the microexperiences that are parts of our composite experiences), which we have no way of detecting or knowing about.

The "no illusions" thesis differs from the "revealed essence" and "self-presentation" theses in that the former infers from appearance to reality (if consciousness seems a certain way, it must actually be that way), while the latter two infer from reality to appearance (if consciousness were a certain way, it would have to appear that way). For each argument, I will show that the revelation thesis in question, when rightly understood, does not rule out the RCH.

4.3.2. THE "NO ILLUSIONS" ARGUMENT

So first, what of the objection that RCH posits an "illusion in consciousness"? If this was true, it would be problematic, for the idea of an illusion in consciousness is arguably incoherent. Illusions are when something seems one way but is not that way, but consciousness just is how things seem, so this discrepancy cannot arise; the seeming itself cannot be false.

But radical confusion is not an "illusion of simplicity": an illusion is where our experience tells us something false—as when a straight stick placed in water looks bent. Our experiences do not "seem simple" in this sense; they do not feel some way that only simple experiences feel. Rather, their character is like the apparent motion of the sun—a veridical impression prone to an easy misinterpretation. The sun's motion is not an illusion: that is how stationary objects look to a rotating observer. But we very readily infer from it something mistaken, namely that the sun orbits a stationary earth. Similarly, says the panpsychist combinationist, our experiences feel exactly how massively complex but radically confused experiences feel. What they are "telling us" is true: that we cannot distinguish details within them.

Is it really plausible that we should systematically misinterpret the manifest structure of consciousness? Here are three reasons to think so. First, the misinterpretation has no bearing on any practical interest, and indeed may be made by only a handful of theorists; after all, most people have no particular opinion about the structure of consciousness. Second, when we take lack of distinguishable elements for lack of elements, the sort of inference we make (taking absence of evidence for evidence of absence) is easy and tempting, and often quite reasonable; indeed, it might be justifiable if we had no independent reason to think that experience arises from the massively composite brain. This corresponds, in the case of the sun's apparent motion, to the error of neglecting to account for the motion of our own point of view, which is also an easy and tempting heuristic, and often appropriate: usually when we see something move it is not because we are standing on something that is rotating relative to it.

Finally, we make this error in an unsupportive context, where our normal presuppositions do not hold and it is hard to acquire information to correct them. In the case of the sun's apparent motion, we cannot leave our earth-bound position to look from a third point of view (and when we do, on a shuttle or satellite, the mistake vanishes). Moreover, we lack the usual cues that our own standpoint is moving (e.g., air resistance). Similarly, when we interpret the "smoothness" of our experiences, not only do we lack the usual indications that our experiences are confused, but we are also profoundly limited by the fact that if our experiences *are* all massively complex, then we have no idea what a simple experience would be like.

It bears emphasizing that we are not in the position of one who has experienced both massively complex but radically confused experiences and also genuinely simple experiences, who could then observe the character of both. Rather, if our parts' experiences really are radically confused relative to us, we are in the position of someone experiencing one or the other of these and trying to determine which without any basis for comparison. In such an unsupportive context, we might easily go wrong.

4.3.3. THE "REVEALED ESSENCE" ARGUMENT

Second, consider the objection that according to RCH, one of the key features of our experiences is that they are composed of a trillion little parts, and that if this were true, we'd be able to tell by reflection on our experiences.

But in fact RCH implies no violation of revelation regarding composite experiential properties, because what we are ignorant of in this case is not something essential to the *property* in question. As Chalmers (2017, 190) puts it, "It is . . . coherent to hold that the nature of a phenomenal property is revealed by introspection although the grounds of a specific instance are not." Consider: there is no contradiction in orange-experience being a blend of red-experience and yellow-experience for humans, but also existing in some other world, with different laws of nature, as one of the fundamental properties or as a blend of two qualities we cannot imagine (but whose suitability to blend into orange-experience would be evident to us if we could). If those possibilities are real, then being blended out of red-experience and yellow-experience is not essential to orange-experience, and revelation does not require that its blendedness be revealed to human introspection. The presence of particular ingredients necessitates the particular quality that is their resultant, but the reverse necessitation need not hold.[7]

Goff (2017a, 198) objects to my account of confusion on this score, holding that "we have direct phenomenal concepts of many . . . experiences, and hence if they were identical with complex micro-experiential states, our direct phenomenal concepts of those states would reveal this to us." This objection turns on the relationship between what is essential to an experiential *property* and what is essential to a particular *experience*. Goff attributes to me the view that "each [macro]experiential property is identical with the property of having a large number of specific micro-experiential properties (perhaps standing in certain relations to one another)," but in fact my considered view is only that each *particular macroexperience* is identical to a composite of many microexperiences in certain relations. The general property that a given macroexperience is an instance of— the phenomenal character that it has in common with all other experiences, however constituted, that feel that specific way—is not identical to the various sets of microexperiential properties whose instances might constitute instances of it on various occasions. In previous work (Roelofs 2014a), I was not as clear on this point as I should have been, and Goff has my gratitude for pushing me to refine my position.

---

[7] Note that nothing said here undermines conceivability arguments against physicalism. Those arguments rely on the idea that our acquaintance with consciousness lets us know whether a given situation we conceive of would be sufficient to underlie consciousness. That does not imply that acquaintance with particular experiences lets us know what specific situation underlies them. For a fuller defense of the compatibility of the RCH with the conceivability arguments against physicalism, see Roelofs (n.d).

4.3.4. THE "SELF-PRESENTATION" ARGUMENT

Finally, consider the objection that, according to RCH, we are each currently having trillions of experiences about which we are completely ignorant, and that this is incompatible with the "self-presenting" nature of experience.

But RCH implies no violation of the self-presentation principle because that principle needs to be qualified. It is not about subjects being struck with automatic knowledge, but about their being put in a position to know, and taking advantage of that position requires meeting various other conditions. One obvious condition is conceptual: a subject that lacks the concepts of "experience" or "essence" (e.g., a fish, probably) cannot come to know anything about the essence of an experiential property. But another condition is attentional: subjects come to know the essence of a particular experiential property only when they focus on that property, which various factors (e.g., distraction, intoxication, tiredness) may interfere with (cf. Brogaard 2017, 148). Radically confused experiences cannot be attended to (distinctly) and so their subject cannot know about them or their essences, even though the experiences do "present themselves" in the sense that *if* their subject could attend to them (and met the other conditions, like conceptual competence) they could know introspectively both that they were having those experiences and the essences of the experiential properties they were instantiating.

Note moreover that the radical confusion hypothesis does allow for a limited sense in which microexperiences *are* accessible and *can* be attended: namely that they can be accessed, and attended, but only by acts which are also accessing and attending many other microexperiences at the same time. They cannot be *individually* accessed or attended, but they can be accessed or attended *collectively*.

The objector might continue to object, as follows: "It is all very well to say that we know of our experiences only if we can attend to them, and that various internal and external factors can make this easier or harder. But even when things make it very very hard to distinctly attend to an experience of ours, they cannot make it impossible: if I am having an experience, it must be at least *possible* to distinctly attend to it!"

I reply that distinctly attending to microexperiences *is* possible, in principle. They are, so to speak, "right there" in our consciousness. They are incredibly difficult to pick out, however—as difficult as it is for the large-scale dynamics of our brain to be sensitive to a change in a single particle somewhere in our brain. But there is no in-principle impossibility in there being such sensitivity, anymore than there is any in-principle impossibility in a human being jumping and, by a fantastic coincidence of repeated perfectly timed gusts of wind, flying to the top of a mountain. In any realistic sense we cannot do this, but that is simply to say that the odds of its happening by chance are so minuscule as to not be worth considering.

There may in the future be ways to make this kind of in-principle possibility into a more practical possibility. Neurosurgery may allow for an enhancement of the human brain's self-monitoring powers; perhaps so too can lower-tech methods like meditation. Perhaps some combination of the two might be refined to the point where a brain could make itself distinctly sensitive to what is going on in a particular neuron, or even to certain structures within that neuron, and in the limit even to what is going on in a single particle (though of course being able to do this for each individual particle does not imply being able to do it for all of them at once). Perhaps we will instead build AI which possesses this capacity for fine-tuned inner sensitivity from the beginning. It is hard to speculate about what that experience would be like, because consciousness is not like a slide under a microscope, which remains stable while we change how closely we scrutinize it: these enhancements of self-awareness would be changes in the brain and thus would involve changes in our conscious state itself. The most we can say is that if there is a spectrum of skill at self-monitoring, with thoughtless or sleep-deprived people at one end and (perhaps) expert meditators at the other, then in the future it may become possible to create beings further advanced along that spectrum than any currently existing.

4.4. Phenomenal Blending and the Palette Problem

In section 4.1, I proposed that, whenever a composite is not sufficiently sophisticated to distinguish the elements of its unified total experience, it will be aware of them simply as a "phenomenal blend." This claim by itself does not say anything about the qualitative diversity or homogeneity of the microexperiences themselves. One view that panpsychists could take (what Chalmers [2017, 205] calls the "large palette" approach) is that all the vast range of qualities experienced by humans and other animals are already possessed at the fundamental level. But this is implausible, since it seems unlikely that such simple minds could share all the diversity of qualities that human minds have, especially if Russellianism is true and the basic experiential properties correspond to basic physical properties, of which there do not seem to be that many.

The far more attractive alternative is what Chalmers (2017, 205) calls the "small palette" approach, on which "all macroqualities can be generated from just a few microqualities, if we find the right underlying microqualities." I formulated this as:

Small palette hypothesis (SPH): All the phenomenal qualities experienced by humans and other beings arise from blending different combinations of the small range of basic phenomenal qualities experienced by microsubjects.

Let us define the required sort of "blending" more precisely. It involves a composite experience which, merely in virtue of two (or more) parts of it displaying certain phenomenal qualities, and not being distinguishable by its subject, displays a single phenomenal quality, distinct from either but reflecting both in such a way that its dependence on them is intelligible. Call the former qualities the "ingredients" and the latter the "resultant." Note that the ingredients are still there: they do not go away when they form the resultant so as to no longer be instantiated. Yet nor is the resultant mere appearance: the resultant and ingredients are both genuinely present. Moreover, we have phenomenal blending only when it is intelligible why *that* resultant comprises *those* ingredients. One way to capture this relation would be in terms of resemblance:

Blending-resemblance principle: Every ingredient in a phenomenal blend makes the resultant quality resemble that ingredient a bit more, i.e., a component experience with quality X makes the composite experience's quality "more X-ish."

For instance, we can capture the intelligibility of orange being a blend of red and yellow by noting that orange is both somewhat reddish and somewhat yellowish, and taking this to reflect the qualitative contributions made by a red component and a yellow component. Note that the blending-resemblance principle does not say that the *only* way that a quality can become X-ish is by having X as an ingredient, nor that there is only one way to generate a particular resultant. This is important for the position defended in section 4.3.3, that it is not essential to the qualities we experience that they arise out of any specific set of ingredients; in another world other minds might experience the very same qualities as us, as a result of blending different ingredients or without any blending at all.

I will defend SMH, involving phenomenal blending so defined, against three objections: that phenomenal blending is completely impossible; that even if some qualities could be blends, many of the qualities humans experience could not be resultants of blending; and that even if all the qualities humans experience could be resultants of blending, they could not arise from blending the same set of ingredients.

4.4.1. IS THERE SUCH A THING AS "PHENOMENAL BLENDING"?

The possibility of phenomenal blending is controversial. William James (1890, 157), for example, insists that "we cannot mix feelings as such, though we may mix the objects we feel, and from *their* mixture get new feelings." Yet there do seem to be cases where we are distinctly acquainted, on different occasions, with both ingredients and resultant and can "just see" that the one is a combination of the others.

The examples most often appealed to involve colors. Lewtas (2013) suggests that orange experiences result from blending red experiences with yellow experiences; in a similar vein Chalmers (2016, 205) writes, "If the same entity simultaneously is aware of a degree of redness and aware of a degree of whiteness (at the same location), it is plausibly aware of pinkness (at that location)." This accords with the historical popularity of what Mizrahi (2009, 2) calls a "'phenomenalist' view of colour composition," on which "binary" colors like orange and pink appear different to us from "unitary" colors like red and blue. Another candidate is aromas, tastes, and flavors—the flavor of a given food or drink being a blend of tastes and aromas provided by its ingredients.[8]

Of course the examples are not conclusive; it remains possible to deny that they involve any actual blending of experiences. Here is a representative passage from James (1890, 158):

> I find in my students an almost irresistible tendency to think that we can immediately perceive that feelings do combine. "What!" they say, "is not the taste of lemonade compounded of that of lemon *plus* that of sugar?" This is taking the combining of objects for that of feelings. The physical lemonade contains both the lemon and the sugar, but its taste does not contain their tastes, for if there are any two things which are certainly *not* present in the taste of lemonade, those are the lemon-sour on the one hand and the sugar-sweet on the other. These tastes are absent utterly.

Combinationists can agree with James that the mere fact that stimuli (sugar and lemon) have blended does not guarantee that the corresponding experiences have.

---

[8] Psychologists, following McBurney (1986), have distinguished three ways for sensations to combine: analysis, when "two stimuli mixed in a solution keep their individual qualities of sensation"; synthesis, when "when two stimuli that have been mixed in a solution lose their individual qualities in order to form a new (third) sensation" (Auvray and Spence 2008, 1019–1020); and fusion, when "sensations [are] combined to form a single percept [which] . . . remains analyzable into its constituent elements even when otherwise perceived as a whole" (Prescott 2012, 79). The sort of cases that I have in mind are both what these schemes call "synthesis" and what they call "fusion."

But it seems phenomenologically right to say that, in at least some cases, the experiences do blend. So why is James so sure that they do not?

Perhaps James means that because the sourness of lemon is subtly changed by being mixed with the sweetness of sugar, it is not strictly present in the blend. In most contexts this would be fallacious, since part-whole relations often involve the parts affecting each other, but there may be a special reason for objecting to such mutual adjustment in the phenomenal case, namely the principle of *phenomenal essentialism*, which appeared as premise **E4** in chapter 2. If how a quality is experienced is essential to it, and it is experienced differently in different contexts, then it is numerically distinct in those different contexts (Cf. Mørch 2014, 154n19). Hence though parts are often changed by being in a certain whole, phenomenal qualities cannot be, because any phenomenal change makes them a different quality.

If we grant this argument from phenomenal essentialism, and suppose that in tasting lemonade the sweetness and sourness are phenomenally altered in some subtle fashion, then the taste of lemonade cannot be a blend *of the very same qualities* as are experienced in other circumstances. But the taste of lemonade may still be a blend; its ingredients may be the subtly different "counterparts" of the sweetness and sourness experienced in other circumstances. Nobody can deny that we often experience phenomenal qualities, in different contexts, which are at least similar enough to warrant us calling them "the same." And this same near-identity can be used to make sense of what James's students thought: that "the same" qualities are present in the lemonade blend and in isolated experiences. Thus even if this argument succeeds, it does not rule out blending in general.

Alternatively, perhaps James is saying that because it would not be true to say that "I am experiencing the sourness of lemon," it follows that my experience does not contain the sourness of lemon. But this equivocates between two senses of "experiencing the sourness of lemon." This might be an overall characterization of my experience, and thus mean "has an experience of lemony-sourness as their sole taste experience," or it might simply characterize an element of my experience, and thus mean "has a taste experience of lemony-sourness, perhaps among others." But since the latter clearly does not imply the former, the falsity of the former is no argument for the falsity of the latter.[9]

---

[9] Similar remarks apply to the apparent truism that nothing can display two colors at once to the same observer: nothing could both look red and look white at once. In one sense of "look red" and "look white," nothing can do both, but this is because to "look red" in this sense definitionally precludes displaying any other visual qualities. But in another sense, looking both red and white might just be "looking pink." Pink things look red, but unlike the things we tend to call "red-looking," they also look white. This is analogous to the point made in chapter 3, section 3.2.2. about two meanings of "located at."

4.4.2. DO WE EXPERIENCE EVIDENTLY SIMPLE QUALITIES?

Perhaps some of the qualities we experience are blends of others, but an objector might insist it is only some—those with a "phenomenologically composite" character (like orange). They might maintain that others (like red) display a "phenomenologically simple" character, and these could never arise from blending.

I cannot directly refute this objection, but I think it is at least as plausible that "phenomenologically simple" character is simply our having no acquaintance with the ingredients in a blend. Often a quality initially seems simple and unanalyzable—until further experience lets us discern the components within it. Dennett (1991, 73–74) describes an auditory example of this phenomenon, in which the sound of a chord played on a guitar appears simple and pure to the untrained ear, but comes to seem composed of distinct notes when one is familiar enough with the notes individually to recognize them in the mixture. In a similar vein, wine tasters often say that with practice, one learns to discriminate the different components of a wine's taste. And research showing that, e.g., untrained subjects frequently construe certain odors as increasing the sweetness of a taste, while trained subjects do not (Bingham et al. 1990), reinforces the point that we are often fallible in distinguishing different sensations (cf. Chuard 2007). These cases make it plausible to suppose that all qualities seem phenomenologically simple until we can discern their ingredients—so that the apparent simplicity of a given quality does not warrant denying that it has ingredients.

It should be emphasized that neither the idea of phenomenal blending in general, nor the SPH in particular, is committed to any account of the specifics of *colors*. It is very possible that our sense of which particular colors are blends of which particular others is contaminated by our experiences with mixing paints or mixing light. The SPH does not say whether the qualities that blend into different colors are red, blue, and yellow (the primary colors of pigment), red, blue, and green (the colors our three types of retinal cone cell are most sensitive to), qualities corresponding to "luminosity," "saturation," and "hue," or something else. That is ultimately a question for psychology, neuroscience, and phenomenology to jointly answer. The utility of color experience is to give us insight into the general capacity of phenomenal qualities to blend into others, but systematizing this insight is no trivial task.

4.4.3. DO WE EXPERIENCE QUALITIES TOO DISSIMILAR TO COME FROM THE SAME INGREDIENTS?

A final objection is that even if all the phenomenal qualities which we experience are such that they might be the resultants of blending, there still do not appear to be any known qualities that could plausibly be the ingredients for all of them. McGinn (2006, 96) expresses this concern when he writes:

> We cannot . . . envisage a small number of experiential primitives yielding a rich variety of phenomenologies . . . [for] you cannot derive one sort of experience from another: you cannot get pains from experiences of colours, or emotions from thoughts, or thoughts from acts of will. There are a large number of phenomenal primitives.

McGinn is probably right that we cannot reasonably hope to get all qualities from any small set of *known* qualities, but the combinationist need not think that the basic ingredients are known to us. Instead, the basic ingredients may be "alien qualities," unimaginable but not inconceivable. It is a commonplace that there are such qualities: just as a human born anosmic cannot imagine olfactory qualities, we are all similarly limited regarding the qualities of the many sensory modalities that humans lack. We can entertain and accept the existence of such qualities, but we cannot "know what they are like."

Presumably, if familiar qualities can blend, so can alien ones. But can they blend *into familiar qualities?* For instance, might the familiar phenomenal quality of redness be a blend of two alien phenomenal qualities (call them AQ1 and AQ2)? If so, maybe all our phenomenal qualities result from blending, even when we cannot identify their ingredients. (Of course, in one sense we *can* imagine AQ1 and AQ2, just by imagining redness. But when we do so, we cannot *separate* AQ1 from AQ2. They are imaginable together but not *distinctly* imaginable.)

However, even accepting the possibility of phenomenal blending among alien qualities, it may still seem that the different qualities we experience are too radically heterogeneous to be blends of the same ingredients. This problem is particularly pressing when considered in conjunction with the previous section's defense of the "revealed essence" thesis, that undergoing an experiential property puts us in a position to know its entire essence. In that section I noted that having a property's essence revealed to us is compatible with not knowing certain things that would follow from its essence, if we were also acquainted with other essences. In particular, knowing the essence of a quality does not by itself reveal all the different qualities which might blend together to make it: it only allows us to tell whether a given set of qualities, whose essences we must first already know, are suitable to blend together into it.

But when it comes to comparing two qualities that we do experience distinctly, this defense is unavailable. If both of their essences are revealed to us, surely we should be able, in principle, to discern every necessary truth about how those qualities relate, and that should include their resemblance or lack thereof. According to the SPH, all the qualities we experience have elements in common, and to that extent surely ought to resemble each other at least somewhat. But then the "revealed essence" thesis implies that we should be in a position to discern those resemblances.

Indeed, this objection to my combination of the RCH and the SPH has been raised by Goff (2017a, 195–197), who offers the sight of red and the taste of mint as an example of two qualities which seem completely dissimilar, having no element in common. This is a serious objection, which demands a careful response. One might block it by simply denying the "revealed essence" thesis, but that would have the dialectical cost of undermining the case for panpsychism over physicalism (though perhaps not fatally). I would prefer to keep the "revealed essence" thesis and accept what it entails in this connection: that all the phenomenal qualities we experience must be *discernibly* similar to each other. And it is not clear to me that this is false—that redness and mintiness really have nothing in common. After all, our ability to recognize two things as akin to one another is usually enhanced by our ability to recognize and attend to the features they share, and if we cannot pick out their shared features we may wrongly feel that they are entirely unlike. Since we cannot recognize or attend to the basic ingredients, we may hastily form false impression of radical heterogeneity.

Of course, inability to pick out shared features does not always stop us registering similarities. Sometimes two things "seem alike" in some way, without our being able to say how. And this kind of inarticulate resemblance is in fact commonly encountered among experiential qualities: we frequently describe qualities of one modality using terms drawn from another (warm, harsh, sweet, soft, loud, etc.) or use sensory terminology to describe emotional or cognitive phenomenology. The SPH implies that, if fully and ideally scrutinized and analyzed, these inarticulately felt kinships would slowly reveal an edifice of systematically connected qualities covering our entire range of experience. This is the position taken by Coleman (2016, 264, emphasis in original), who writes:

> Just as it's possible to move across the colour spectrum in tiny, almost undetectable steps, it must be possible to move from tastes to sounds, sounds to colors, and so on, via equally tiny steps. Tiptoeing between modalities already seems *conceivable* in certain cases, perhaps even actual. We know that what we experience as 'taste' is really some kind of fusion of qualia sourced from the nose and from the tongue. . . . It even strikes me as plausible that tactile qualia are just (qualitatively) more 'forceful' or 'solid' counterparts of 'thinner' auditory qualia. To address qualitative incommensurability we

must stretch to conceiving of such continuities as the rule rather than the exception. (cf. Hartshorne 1934, 35ff.; Coleman 2015)

Coleman suggests in particular that we may be mistakenly taking some of our qualities as completely dissimilar because we lack the contrast required to see the respects in which they are similar. After all, if the SPH is correct, the respects in which all our phenomenal qualities are similar are precisely those respects in which they differ from the qualities we would experience if we existed in another world made of different fundamental constituents, and those qualities are by hypothesis so dissimilar from everything we know as to be completely unimaginable. Coleman (2016, 265) analogizes us to a hypothetical being which only experienced color qualities, but experienced different clusters of them in response to different sorts of stimuli: "This creature's tactile sensations are all varying shades of red, vision presents only blues, smell the greens, and so on, with the places where these qualities (for us) overlap conveniently screened out by the organism's evolution." Such a being would likely think of these different color qualities as completely unrelated quality spaces, but we with our full visual range see them as portions of a single quality space; "perhaps a being with a qualia-space correspondingly greater than ours as ours is greater than the color-only creature, would conceive of human qualia as belonging to a single 'modality'" (265). I find this claim about the ultimate, though nonobvious, continuity of all the qualities we experience plausible, but it is a substantial phenomenological commitment, and may well be false. Consequently, the revealed essence thesis may be most threatening to constitutive panpsychists not through the revelation problem itself, but through intensifying the palette problem.

4.5. Conclusions

Letting consciousness work like physical properties is necessary to vindicate the promise of constitutive Russellian panpsychism as nonphysicalist but still naturalist. But it will not profit us if we lose any hope of explaining human consciousness in this dizzying vortex of endless, mindless experience. The proposals in this chapter—the radical confusion hypothesis, small palette hypothesis, and informational structure hypothesis—lay the groundwork for this explanation. They show that our consciousness's genuine qualitative diversity, and apparent coarse-grainedness, are two sides of the same coin, and no objection to its being a combination of trillions of trillions of the same sort of part. They also tell us something about the consciousness of inanimate things, things with consciousness but without intelligence. If our experiences are blends because of our limited powers of discrimination, inanimate things must have even more thoroughly blended experiences. The answer to "What is it like to be a table?" is roughly: it is like experiencing a single quality, though not one that any human has ever experienced. We higher animals are different, in that we can differentiate our experiences from each other. This gives us a form of consciousness that is highly structured compared to that of inanimate things; the next chapter explores how this structure is constructed.

3 Combinationism for Functionalists

5 Composite Subjectivity and Intelligent Subjects

THE HUMAN BRAIN is often called the most complex object in the universe. In this and the next chapter I develop a theory of the role this complexity plays in mental combination. I have called this theory "functionalist combinationism" because it focuses particularly on "functional structure," the set of ways that different states of a system are caused by, and cause, other states of that system. One popular view in the philosophy of mind is that consciousness itself, and indeed all mental phenomena, are ultimately explained by functional structure; call this "pure functionalism" (e.g., Putnam 2003; Dennett 1991; Shoemaker 2000, 2003). According to pure functionalism, the way to get minds is simply to take some material, which may be in itself completely mindless, and organize it to implement the right functional structure, to work the right way. Readers attracted to pure functionalism should take functionalist combinationism as an independent and complete theory of mental combination, a rival to and replacement of the panpsychist combinationism of chapters 3 and 4. (Call this version of the theory "pure functionalist combinationism"). Pure functionalism implies that chapters 3 and 4, which treat consciousness as a fundamental property, were misguided right from the start.

But many philosophers who are not pure functionalists still think that functional structure is of vital importance in a full understanding of the mind, even if it is not the whole story: call this "impure functionalism" (Lewis 1980; Chalmers 1996, 274ff.). In particular, I think readers attracted to panpsychist combinationism would do well to also accept functionalist combinationism as a supplementary theory, a theory specifically dealing with how the sort of consciousness possessed by human beings and other animals differs from but depends on the more basic consciousness that is fundamental and pervasive in nature. (Call this version "functionalist-panpsychist combinationism.") In this chapter I will lay out functionalist combinationism in a form that is, as much as possible, neutral between pure and impure functionalism, but will at times note how the theory's implications differ between the two.

Like in chapter 3, and unlike in chapter 7, I will think of subjects as substrates of experience rather than personas; that is, I identify the subject of some experiences with the system within which they arise, rather than with any sort of construct out of those experiences. But unlike in chapter 3, and like in chapter 7, I will think of composite subjects as structure-specific wholes, not as aggregates. Subjects which are made of parts are not just those specific parts, considered as one; they are defined by the particular way their parts are put together, and exist only as long as those relations are maintained.

To put a name to this crucial "way their parts are put together," I will use the term "intelligent subject" for conscious beings with the kind of complex functional organization displayed by humans and many other animals. The aim of functionalist combinationism is to understand how there could be intelligent subjects composed of other intelligent subjects, and how in such cases we could relate facts about consciousness in the whole to facts about consciousness in the parts. The next chapter examines four case studies where intelligent subjects seem to combine into other intelligent subjects. The entities concerned include biological organisms, organs, and parts of organs (i.e., human beings, human brains, and subsystems within human brains), as well as social groups made up of such organisms; functionalist combinationism is also intended to cover artificial conscious systems like hypothetical future AIs or cyborgs, and conscious nonhuman organisms, although I do not discuss any such cases in detail.

Panpsychist combinationists have a special reason for interest in functional structure. As well as understanding how intelligent subjects can compose other intelligent subjects, they need to explain how intelligent subjects could be composed by the simpler, *un*intelligent subjects they postulate. This challenge is particularly urgent because panpsychist combinationism implies such a widespread distribution of both subjecthood and phenomenal unity. By defending experience inheritance, the combinationist may solve the subject-summing problem, but they seem to obliterate the distinction between physical systems which are, and which are not, subjects of experience. Yet our notion of what it means to be a subject of experience is surely partly defined by the fact that it applies to human beings, some animals, and perhaps other creatures (aliens, spirits, robots) that operate in similar ways, but does not apply to clouds, ovens, or trees, and certainly not to arbitrary aggregates like "all the toasters in Norway." Similarly, considerations of elegance and nonarbitrariness may support the view that phenomenal unity holds among all causally connected sets of experience, but this seems to violate the very contrast—between how one person's many experiences are related and how different people's experiences are related—that initially prompted us to formulate the idea of phenomenal unity.

So the functionalist-panpsychist combinationist, having accepted the metaphysical foundations laid out in chapter 3, is under a special pressure to show that our intuitive distinctions can be "reconstructed" upon that counterintuitive, but theoretically elegant, foundation. This is part of a general difficulty for panpsychists that chapter 4 called the "mismatch problem": the world as physics sees it looks to be structured along very different lines from human consciousness. In chapter 4 I offered the informational structure hypothesis as a schematic solution to this problem:

> **Informational structure hypothesis (ISH):** The overall structure manifest in human consciousness corresponds to the structure of information-processing in the human brain, not to its gross physical structure.

For panpsychists, functionalist combinationism serves to flesh out and substantiate the ISH, to explain how we get human consciousness out of the vast expanse of rudimentary consciousness postulated by panpsychist combinationism.

5.1. Defining Intelligent Subjects

Functionalist combinationism focuses on "intelligent subjects," a type of conscious system that is more recognizable as a subject than the panpsychist's microsubjects. In order to have an at least somewhat definite idea of what systems these are, and what is required from a compositional explanation of one, I offer the following rough and tentative definition:

> An intelligent subject $=_{def}$ A conscious subject whose consciousness is structured and whose experiences play the functional roles characteristic of

intelligence in virtue of their phenomenal character, conscious structure, and representational content.

This definition is intended to actually apply to all the sorts of creatures which we are intuitively inclined to regard as conscious subjects (human beings and some or most animals), to not apply to all the sorts of creatures which we are intuitively inclined to regard as definitely not conscious subjects (most inanimate objects), and to be indeterminate in application to the sorts of creatures which we are intuitively uncertain whether to regard as conscious subjects (e.g., snails, worms). Pure functionalist combinationists can fully endorse these intuitions and regard "intelligent subject" as equivalent to "subject": there are no nonintelligent subjects. Functionalist-panpsychist combinationists will reject these intuitions as applied to consciousness per se, because they regard many nonintelligent things (indeed, all material things in the universe) as conscious subjects. But they can still explain and vindicate these intuitions if they can explain why only some systems are intelligent subjects.

The above definition involves four key components: phenomenal consciousness, consciousness being "structured," the functional roles characteristic of intelligence, and experiences playing roles in virtue of their character, structure, and content. Call these "consciousness," "structured consciousness," "intelligent functioning," and "coherence" between consciousness and functioning. Pure functionalists hold, in essence, that intelligent functioning is all there is to explain; consciousness and structured consciousness are themselves explained by intelligent functioning, and this guarantees their coherence with it. Thus by their lights the definition given above is somewhat redundant. Because of the primary importance of intelligent functioning, I will spend most of this section elaborating and exploring this notion; in the next section I ask what it would take to ground and explain some system's being an intelligent subject. But first let me say a little to clarify my notions of "structured consciousness" and "coherence."

5.1.1. STRUCTURED AND COHERENT CONSCIOUSNESS

I draw the term "coherence" from Chalmers's (1996, 220) discussion of "the coherence between consciousness and awareness," where "awareness" means essentially "access-consciousness," i.e., the "psychological correlate of [phenomenal] consciousness . . . wherein some information is directly accessible, and available for the deliberate control of behavior and for verbal report."

Coherence: Any state of a subject which is phenomenally conscious will also
be access-conscious, and vice versa.

As Chalmers observes, general conformity to coherence is a striking feature of everyday experience for creatures like us: the information that guides our behavior
and internal processing is generally the same as the content of our conscious experience, even if exceptions are possible. (For possible exceptions or qualifications,
see Chalmers 1996, 221–229.) Thus I have defined intelligent subjects in such a way
as to make it partly definitional of them: their experiences must play certain functional roles in virtue of their experiential features.

Note that coherence presupposes a certain sort of consciousness: consciousness
comprising multiple distinguishable experiences which differ from each other but
interact in sufficiently varied ways to play functional roles, including the role of
being access-conscious. This is what I mean by saying that intelligent subjects must
have "structured consciousness": if they simply undergo one big undifferentiated
blur, or a million distinct but qualitatively identical experiences, or anything like
that, then coherence cannot hold them and they cannot be intelligent subjects.

This still does not tell us exactly what it is for consciousness to be "structured."
A first attempt might be that consciousness is structured when it is divisible into
parts which are then related to one another. But "divisible into parts" is importantly ambiguous. In chapter 4 I argued that we should not assume that just because an experience is metaphysically divisible (i.e., it has elements grounded in
different substrates) it will display "phenomenal contrast" (i.e., be experienced by
its subject as presenting distinct elements). What I called "phenomenal blending"
involved metaphysically divisible experiences that lack phenomenal contrast,
where different qualitative elements are seamlessly incorporated into a new
quality. For consciousness to be structured requires not metaphysical distinctness
but phenomenal contrast; thus a subject whose experiences are all phenomenally
blended together lacks structured consciousness.

Moreover, "related to one another" is too weak a criterion. (All my experiences
bear to one another the relation "occurring later than wooly mammoths who lived
earlier than," but that is not part of the structure of my consciousness.) The sorts
of relations that matter are those that make a phenomenal difference to the subject, that are manifest in consciousness. Most obviously, they include two of the
"unity" relations distinguished in chapter 2, phenomenal unity and representational unity, but they may well include others. I do not think I can offer a complete
account of what these relations are, beyond encouraging the reader to consider
their own present experience, and the various ways that its elements hang

together. Of course not all intelligent subjects need have consciousness structured in exactly the way that human consciousness is structured; they need only have enough conscious structure for their consciousness to be capable of coherence with intelligent functioning.

5.1.2. DEFINING INTELLIGENT FUNCTIONING

But what exactly is intelligent functioning? Let me first note, and set aside, the question of how exactly "functional roles" and "functional structure" can be rigorously described. Early functionalists were much enamored with computational formulations, which characterized functional structures as something like computer programs (e.g., Turing 1950; Putnam 2003). But other functionalists have objected to this approach, often preferring models based more closely on the structure of the brain (e.g., Smolensky 1987), or explicitly saying that our ways of formulating functional descriptions will have to evolve in tandem with our understanding of the workings of the mind (cf. Block 1992, 71–74). I have no stake in these debates; what I will say about functional roles is rough enough not to depend on how exactly they are defined.

Whatever functional roles are, which are the ones characteristic of intelligence? I will follow tradition in being somewhat vague on this score. These roles are the sort of thing that we all know on some level—they are what we are noticing and responding to when some creature "seems conscious" to us. But, like the rules of grammar, they are extremely hard to articulate. I will just gesture at a few examples; note that in each case it is required that the interactions in question be stable and reliable across time:

- Intelligent subjects have a set of states (which we might call "beliefs") which interact with each other so as to ensure that they remain generally "consistent."
- Intelligent subjects have states of two kinds (which we might call "desires" and "beliefs") and a set of capacities for action which interact with each other so that whenever the beliefs entail that an action would satisfy a desire, and only then, that action is likely to be taken.
- Intelligent subjects have mechanisms (which we might call "decision-making") that connect all tendencies toward action (driven by different desires) and prevent multiple conflicting actions from being taken by prioritizing some desires over others.
- Intelligent subjects have a set of states (which we might call "pleasures and displeasures" or "happiness and sadness") which are set up so as to

automatically give rise to desires either to pursue or to avoid them, and which tend to be produced when it is believed that a desire has been met or frustrated.

- Intelligent subjects have a set of states (which we might call "sensations") which correlate well with conditions in the external world, which are largely independent of their desires and decision-making, and which tend to influence the formation of new beliefs.

Obviously many refinements, clarifications, and additions are necessary for a full account, but the above is sufficient for my purposes.[1]

Note that to the extent that a system functions intelligently, we can usefully and meaningfully talk about that system's "perspective" or "point of view." Because there are states playing the role of sensations and beliefs, we can use them to characterize "how the world seems" to the system; because there are states playing the role of desires and pleasures, we can use them to characterize "what is important" in that apparent world; because there are a specific set of actions available under a decision-making mechanism, we can make sense of asking what the system "should do," what actions are "called for" by important features of the apparent world.

I point out the special applicability of the term "perspective" to intelligent subjects because I suspect it plays a role in our intuitive willingness to ascribe consciousness to them. Subjects with a perspective in this sense are ones which we can imagine being, and moreover ones whose behavior we can usefully predict by imagining being them (for further discussion see Buchanan and Roelofs 2018). That is, only with intelligent subjects does imaginative simulation start to get a grip, and it seems likely that our impression of a thing's consciousness depends importantly on our ability to perform such simulations—to put ourselves "in its shoes."

5.1.3. THE VAGUENESS OF INTELLIGENT FUNCTIONING

A key feature of intelligent functioning is that it is *vague*; that is, it admits of borderline cases which neither clearly qualify as intelligent functioning, nor clearly fail to. The reason it is vague is that none of our states plays its functional role infallibly: sometimes I fail to pursue my desires given my beliefs, sometimes my perceptions are biased by my desires, sometimes all my representations fail to be

---

[1] Note that I have not included capacities like language use or reflective self-consciousness, nor have I made any special mention of reasoning, problem-solving, or abstract thought, all of which are prominent in some definitions of the word "intelligent." My aim is to capture what is distinctive about a wide range of animals, not what is distinctive about humans or any subset of humans.

consistent with one another, and so on. Since we are still intelligent subjects, the phrase "play its role" in the above definition must be read as "usually plays its role." But what counts as "usually"? After all, in some pathological cases people seem to suffer from major failures of intelligent functioning on a daily basis (in psychosis, delusion, hallucination, etc.). But at the same time, there must be some minimum reliability, for otherwise almost anything could be said to be "unreliably intelligent": we could interpret any system's internal states as being "desires" and "beliefs" of various sorts, and as long as it "acted appropriately" on at least one occasion we could then chalk up the ninety-nine other occasions to the system's fallibility. Somewhere in between the ideal of 100% reliability that we never reach and the absurdity of 1% reliability, it begins to be reasonable to call a system intelligent, but plausibly there is no sharp boundary.

There is also vagueness that derives from a requirement of complexity. Some people might have more desires, or more beliefs, or more capacities for sensation than others; this does not mean that they are intelligent subjects and the others are not. But again, there must be some minimum, or everything will count. Consider a rock which tends to fall downward when not supported. We could interpret it as having the desire to reach the earth's center, the belief that moving downward will accomplish this, and very simple capacities for action (move downward) and perception (detect which direction is down). But surely we do not want to count it as an intelligent subject just because its functioning conforms to the above principles when interpreted in these terms. (After all, we could equally well interpret it as desiring to rest on some hard surface and moving downward in desperate hope of finding one.) So some minimum degree of complication seems necessary, but again there seems no way to draw a sharp boundary.

I regard this vagueness in what counts as an intelligent subject as a welcome implication, for it provides the most plausible way of handling a broad range of beings which fall in between what intuition would judge "clearly conscious" and "clearly unconscious"—creatures like worms, insects, jellyfish, plants, and even cells. While there is plenty of scope for genuine discoveries about how such creatures operate, even with complete knowledge of their physiology and behavior it may be impossible to definitively put each of them either in the same category as rocks or in the same category as monkeys. And it doesn't seem plausible that some particular small enhancement or quirk of neurology should "turn on the lights"—that one species of worm, say, should be strictly nonconscious and another, almost identical species be dimly conscious. Thus it seems the most reasonable thing is to admit that for some or all of these creatures, it is semantically indeterminate how to categorize them, just as there are men whose heads are borderline cases of baldness, neither definitely bald nor definitely not bald but somewhere in between.[2]

(The functionalist-panpsychist combinationist, of course, will here rehearse the arguments from section 3.3 of chapter 3, against the idea that worms and their ilk are borderline cases of phenomenal consciousness per se, for [they will say] consciousness does not admit of analysis into some vague degree on an underlying spectrum. Consciousness is a fundamental property, so either there is something it is like to be X, or there is not. So functionalist-panpsychist combinationists should take a somewhat nuanced view here: everything is conscious, including rocks and worms and monkeys and us, but not all conscious things function intelligently. We and monkeys do, while rocks don't. And because intelligent functioning can be analyzed into various matters of degree [viz., complexity and reliability], there will be intermediate cases which could equally well be counted as the very feeblest sort of intelligent subject, or as almost an intelligent subject but not quite. There is no sharp boundary: the clear but imperfect coherence of a human perspective shades imperceptibly into the useless, inert, confusion of what-it-is-like-to-be-a-rock, and in between goes through stages that we have no decisive reason to classify on the one side or the other.)

5.1.4. INTERNAL AND EXTERNAL FUNCTIONING, AND BLOCKHEADS

A final important note about intelligent functioning is that we can distinguish "external" functioning (what outward responses the system makes to various stimuli) from "internal" functioning (how the system is organized, how its different inner states relate to one another). Our intuitive appreciation of a system's functional structure is, inevitably, primarily driven by its external functioning, since that is what we are most used to seeing. But internal functioning is also important, as we see when we consider a hypothetical system which has the same external functioning as one of us, but a very different, and much simpler, sort of internal functioning. Block (1981) imagines such a being, which has come to be called the "Blockhead." It is a humanoid device controlled by a rudimentary mechanism searching a vast lookup table which contains every possible one-hour-long

---

[2] Note that it may often be useful, in thinking about these intermediate cases, to treat "intelligent functioning" as gradable, so that functioning can be more or less intelligent. This removes some of the vagueness of "functions intelligently," construed as a predicate that does or does not apply, just as we can remove the fuzzy boundary between "is bald" and "is not bald" by simply rating each head on a scale of "degrees of hairiness." But this will not remove all vagueness, since there are many different factors involved (in both intelligent functioning and baldness). Any particular scale will depend on picking a particular way to weight these factors, out of many equally valid weightings, giving rise to indeterminacy about the ordering of certain cases (e.g., is the man with fewer but thicker hairs "balder" than the man with more but thinner hairs?).

intelligent-seeming English conversation. If allowed to search this galaxy-spanning list at superluminal speeds, the device could simulate intelligent conversation (for an hour) merely by finding on its list a "canned" conversation which matches its present one up to the last-received utterance. Here there is intelligent-seeming external functioning without intelligent internal functioning. There are no internal representations that can be combined to form more complex representations, or used for inferences, or stored for later access, or anything like that. There are no goal-states, no process for mediating between conflicting desires or selecting the right means to an end; there is precisely one process, of moving down a list and checking for exact matches. Block thinks, and I agree, that this device is obviously not intelligent; its appearance of intelligence derives from "canned" intelligence, the intelligence exercised by its designers in exhaustively distinguishing the sensible from the nonsensical canned conversations (cf. Jackson 1993).

Functionalist combinationists should not regard creatures like this (let us call them all "Blockheads") as intelligent subjects—they should require both internal and external intelligent functioning. For pure functionalists this makes it natural to say that Blockheads just aren't conscious at all, but panpsychist combinationists cannot say this (since for them, everything is conscious). What I think they should say instead is that while Blockheads have consciousness, they lack structured consciousness and coherence; even if they have some experiences, and behave outwardly like a conscious being, their behavior is not lined up with or governed by particular features of their consciousness, like ours is. Because they lack the right internal structure, what they do is divorced from what it is like to be them, and they are not intelligent subjects.

5.2. Explaining Intelligent Subjects

If intelligent subjects can be composites, they are plausibly structure-specific wholes, not aggregates. They are defined by their parts exhibiting the right features and the right organization, not just by being those parts considered as one. Moreover, the persistence conditions we intuitively ascribe to them seem to make special reference to their structure. My brain and body right now as I write, for instance, are probably made up of less than half the same atoms as they will be by the time you read this, when most of the atoms that now compose them will be spread through the environment as dust and water vapor. So if we thought I was an aggregate of atoms we would seem pushed toward saying that I will then be a widely dispersed cloud of dust and water vapor, and that some new person has taken my place. But we refuse to say this, insisting instead that I continue to exist, and continue to be an intelligent subject, as long as *some* collection of atoms is continuously instantiating the structure of my brain and body. Thus it looks like we are thinking of me as a structure-specific whole. At each moment, an aggregate of atoms *constitutes* me, but I am not identical to it, since I am constituted by a different aggregate of atoms a moment later. And similar things go for other intelligent subjects, like you, your parents, or your cat.

Combinationists need to show how one intelligent subject could be grounded and explained by others which compose it; functionalist-panpsychist combinationists need moreover to show how intelligent subjects could be grounded and explained by unintelligent microsubjects. So let us first ask: How, in general, does one ground and explain the existence and properties of a structure-specific whole?

5.2.1. EXPLAINING STRUCTURE-SPECIFIC WHOLES IN GENERAL

Let us start with a nonmental example. Consider a tower made of wooden blocks. All that it takes for this tower to exist is for the wooden blocks to be related a certain way ("arranged towerwise," i.e., on top of one another). This flows from the "essence" of the tower: towers are essentially tall and thin. This is not itself something to explain; this is just what we mean by "tower." All that needs to be explained is why the relevant properties are instantiated, and we can explain that without mentioning the tower itself. Because structure-specific wholes are defined by a particular structure, they admit of metaphysical analysis and can be grounded by analysis in whatever accounts for the instantiation of their defining structure.

But note that the tower's essential property is not "being arranged towerwise," since it is not thus arranged; rather, it is tower-shaped. And the property of being tower-shaped is not instantiated by any of the blocks. Is this a problem? Of course not, since the tower's essential property is instantiated by the aggregate of the blocks: it is a corresponding property to their collective property of being arranged towerwise. The something-like-identity between the aggregate and its parts (what in chapter 3 I called SI, the substantive indiscernibility of parts and aggregate) ensures that the defining property of a tower is instantiated, and the existence of the tower follows. Other properties of the tower, like its color, are likewise explained by the aggregate that constitutes the tower having those properties.

But not all properties of the aggregate are shared by the structure-specific whole. The aggregate, presumably, began to exist when the bricks did—in a factory, made by some workers. But the tower's history is much shorter: it was not made in a factory by workers; it was made on the floor by a child. This history is of course still explained by something about the aggregate, namely the fact that the aggregate came to be tower-shaped on the floor, by the action of a child. But to know which of the properties "offered up" by the aggregate will belong to the structure-specific whole, we need to attend to its essence, its defining structure. And properties of the aggregate that have nothing to do with this structure, like its history prior to becoming tower-shaped, make no difference to the structure-specific whole. This is why we could not use SI to directly explain the existence and properties of the tower: the tower and the aggregate of blocks that constitutes it at a particular moment are not substantively indiscernible, since there are facts about the aggregate that do not correspond to anything about the tower.

So in general we might say that structure-specific wholes can be explained in two steps: the aggregates that constitute them inherit properties from their parts in virtue of being simply those parts considered as one, and their essence specifies a set of requirements, a "filter," determining both which properties must be instantiated by the aggregates in order for the structure-specific whole to exist, and also which properties of the aggregates are shared by the structure-specific whole and which are not.[3] Moreover, when the structure-specific whole shares properties with the aggregates that constitute it, this is not plausibly regarded as the property being instantiated twice; rather, the two entities share the same token property instance, just as (according to the arguments of chapter 3) the aggregate can share property instances with its parts. For instance, the tower occupies a certain part of space; so does the aggregate; so does one of the blocks, which is part of both; but this part of space is occupied only once, and the instance of the property of occupying it is shared by all three entities.

Suppose we try to apply the same procedure to intelligent subjects, as defined in the previous section. We would need to consider the essential properties of intelligent subjects (which I am taking to be consciousness, intelligent functioning, and structured consciousness, connected so as to secure coherence), and then explain how it comes about that aggregates of matter instantiate those properties.[4]

---

[3] Is the structure-specific whole really a distinct thing from the aggregate of blocks? Wouldn't that have the strange result that two distinct physical objects occupied the very same space? Yet it seems contradictory for them to be the same thing, since one came into existence earlier than the other. These paradoxical puzzles have been discussed extensively (see, e.g., Geach 1967; Gibbard 1975; Bennett 2004), and I make no attempt to solve them here. I hope simply to show how experiential combination is no *more* problematic than physical combination. Readers are welcome to regard either the structure-specific whole or the aggregate as a mere linguistic fiction, not a real entity.

In particular, readers might want to "cut out the middleman," dispensing with the aggregate and saying simply that a structure-specific whole exists when a set of parts collectively instantiate a corresponding property to its defining properties (e.g., a tower exists when some objects collectively instantiate "being arranged towerwise," because that is a corresponding property to the tower's defining property of "being tower-shaped"). But this is not a substantive change, since the whole point of SI is that the aggregate is just the parts considered as one. To drop it from the explanation in favor of the parts collectively is just to drop it and replace it with itself.

[4] There is an ambiguity in "the essential properties of intelligent subjects." I mean the properties which are essential to something's being an intelligent subject; these might not be the same as the properties which are essential to a certain intelligent subject's being itself. The two might come apart if an intelligent

5.2.2. EXPLAINING CONSCIOUSNESS

Explaining why an aggregate of material parts might instantiate consciousness is, obviously, a big challenge. It is famously difficult to explain why anything at all is conscious, and I will not here attempt to do so. If constitutive panpsychism is true, then things are conscious because they are built out of conscious matter. If pure functionalism is true, then things are conscious because they are organized so as to function intelligently. If theistic dualism is true, then things are conscious because God chose to implant immaterial souls into certain physical bodies. If some other theory of consciousness is true, then its posits explain why things are conscious.

We can, however, ask a more precise question: What role can consciousness in a thing's parts play in grounding and explaining consciousness in that thing? According to panpsychist combinationism, consciousness in the parts very directly grounds and explains consciousness in the whole: wholes (or at least aggregates) share all the experiential properties of their parts. But if pure functionalism is true, then things are more complicated. For the whole to be conscious is for it to exhibit intelligent functioning; for the parts to be conscious is for them to exhibit intelligent functioning. So to see the relationship between consciousness in the whole and in the parts we will need to first consider the relationship between intelligent functioning in the whole and in the parts.

5.2.3. EXPLAINING INTELLIGENT FUNCTIONING—DIVISION RELATIVITY

Intelligent functioning, unlike phenomenal consciousness, is in principle very easy to explain. Aggregates inherit the causal powers of their parts (or so I argued in chapter 3), and specific causal structures can then be explained by the relevant theories in physics, chemistry, and biology: intelligent subjects exist because gravity caused planets to coalesce, because carbon can form such long and complex molecules, because evolution selected for greater intelligence in certain environments, and so on. While this part of the explanation is far from easy, it is proceeding apace, and the combinationist can happily rely on it.

What role is played, in this complicated but unmysterious explanation of functional structure, by intelligent functioning in parts of the thing? Certainly it is nothing so simple as automatic inheritance; a whole with parts which function intelligently may not itself function intelligently (consider the solar system and its human parts, for instance). This is because, whereas causal powers are plausibly division-invariant, functional structure is division-relative.

---

subject could cease to be an intelligent subject while remaining itself, as we might think is the plight of a patient in a persistent vegetative state.

Functional structure is division-relative because the functional role played by a particular state is defined in terms of the other states which it interacts with. My beliefs are disposed to mutual-adjustment-to-ensure-consistency with all of my other beliefs, but not with your beliefs. Thus we will see intelligent functioning when we look at all of my beliefs together, but not when we look at all of yours and mine together.

In the previous section I noted that we could think of intelligent functioning as coming in degrees; we could then say that different levels show different degrees of intelligent functioning. The more you and I share information and cooperate, the closer we come to functioning intelligently as a pair (equivalently, the closer the pair comes to functioning intelligently as a pair). And plausibly I function more intelligently than any of my neurons does considered as a neuron, although perhaps neurons themselves function more intelligently than, say, pebbles, or atoms. Looking at different scales will reveal different degrees of intelligent functioning, some of which will be sufficient to call units on that scale "intelligent subjects" and some of which will not.

5.2.4. EXPLAINING INTELLIGENT FUNCTIONING—SENSITIVITY, CONTROL, AND COORDINATION

In light of this division relativity, intelligent functioning in a thing's parts will contribute to intelligent functioning in the whole only if the relevant parts are "hooked up" to the rest of the whole in such a way that their states can play the same or similar functional roles for the whole as they do for the parts. The simplest such case would be "trivial" combination, where a single part is entirely responsible for the intelligent functioning of the whole. Consider the relationship between a human brain and a human being: the whole functions intelligently largely because the brain, a particular part of it, does so.[5] For example, sometimes the whole human being wants food, detects the presence of pizza nearby using sight, recalls that pizza is food, and walks toward the pizza as a result. When this happens, the brain is performing essentially the same functions: it wants food, detects the presence of pizza nearby using the inputs received from the eyes by the occipital lobe, recalls that pizza is food, and initiates walking toward the pizza by sending signals down the spinal cord as a result. What allows for the functioning of the brain to be shared by the whole human being is that the brain's states both *control* the rest

---

[5] "Largely" here does not mean "entirely": much of the brain's processing is influenced by features of and feedback from the body, in such a way that assigning sole responsibility for intelligence to the brain is arguably a distortion. Nevertheless an oversimplified idea of the brain-body relationship is a useful illustration of the point being made here.

of the body (there are brain states that can initiate or prevent contractions of the body's muscles) and are *sensitive* to the rest of the body (there are brain states that are reliably caused by stimulation of the body's sense organs). This control and sensitivity allows the brain's intelligent functioning to be simultaneously the intelligent functioning of the whole body.

Control and sensitivity are still key when we move beyond trivial combination and consider wholes with multiple, intelligently functioning parts. To the extent that the states of each part have some measure of control of, and sensitivity to, the rest of the whole, their intelligent functioning belongs also to the whole. Consider here a team of people working together on some cooperative project, like sailing a ship or building a house. Insofar as the perceptions of each are somewhat sensitive to the situation of the whole group, and the voluntary actions of each have some control over what the whole group does, their individual states can play the functional roles characteristic of intelligence not just for each of them but for all of them.

Control and sensitivity are not quite enough all by themselves, however; there must also be coordination between the different intelligent parts. If they control the whole's behavior but do so independently of one another, for instance, then one is likely to undo what another does, and the whole will display paralysis or self-defeating behavior rather than intelligent functioning. (Consider an army with ten generals who never talk to each other.) The parts must coordinate their activities somehow, whether through a "division of labor" (different parts have primary control of different aspects of the whole's behavior), a "majority vote" (different parts sum or synthesize their respective impulses to determine the whole's behavior), or some other method. We can boil this down to the following principle:

> **Conditional functional inheritance:** If a part of X has an experience which plays a certain functional role, then that experience plays the same or a similar functional role for X to the extent that the part in question is connected to the rest of X such that its experience has sensitivity to, control over, and coordination with other events occurring in X.

The notion of "the same or a similar functional role" is rough and intuitive, like so much else in this chapter. Consider some examples: if a subsystem of my brain works to determine the colors in a visual image and construct a visual color map, then the "map experience" it generates does not play quite the same role in its functioning as it does in mine (e.g., for me it prompts revisions in my beliefs about fruit in my immediate environment, while the subsystem has no beliefs about fruit), but clearly the roles it plays for the subsystem and for me are systematically connected. Likewise, when someone reports what they think to the other members of their institution to influence an ongoing debate, what is reported does not play quite the same role for them and for the institution: for them perhaps it is a belief, a settled view that they will unhesitatingly act on, while for the group it is one thought among others, perhaps entertained but not yet endorsed. Yet clearly there is something important in common between the two roles. The particular sorts of control, sensitivity, and coordination that a part's experience has will determine how similar the functional roles it plays at the two levels are, as will the roles played by states of the whole's other parts.

5.2.5. EXPLAINING STRUCTURED CONSCIOUSNESS AND COHERENCE

Finally, what about explaining the last two components of my definition, structured consciousness and coherence? After all, it is not enough to have both consciousness and intelligent functioning: a subject is an intelligent subject, like one of us, only if its experiences are the states which play the relevant functional roles, in virtue of their experiential features—only if it functions intelligently *because of* its experiences. This requires that its experiences be diverse and powerful: it must be capable of many distinct sorts of experiences, which can affect each other differently and can give rise to different behavioral expressions.

Pure functionalists have a ready explanation of coherence: consciousness is nothing over and above the right kind of functioning, so coherence could not fail to be true. But according to panpsychist combinationism, consciousness is in principle separable from any functional notion, including awareness/access-consciousness. Coherence could thus completely fail for some sorts of subjects, even though it is in fact generally true of us, and functionalist-panpsychist combinationists need to give some idea of what explains this. (In section 5.4 I suggest that coherence holds for us because our consciousness gets its structure from *information integration*, which also underlies functional structure.)

What about structured consciousness? As with consciousness itself, I will not attempt the daunting task of providing a general-purpose explanation of how any subject ever comes to have structured consciousness. What I will examine, though, is the more specific question of how a thing's conscious parts can contribute to the structure and coherence of its consciousness. As with intelligent functioning, the easiest case is trivial combination, where a single part does all the work. If a whole has a single conscious part, which controls its overall functioning (as is roughly the case with a human being and their brain), then the structure and coherence of that part's consciousness will also belong to the whole's. The whole inherits all the experiences of the part, and so its consciousness is structured however the part's consciousness is structured.

But what is much more perplexing is how the whole's consciousness will be structured if it inherits experiences from multiple parts. If a group inherits its members' experiences, or a brain inherits the experiences of its subsystems, how do these "fit together" for the whole? This is, I think, the most challenging question for functionalist combinationism to answer, and so addressing it will occupy the next two sections.

5.3. Structured and Unstructured Consciousness

An intelligent subject with a single conscious part that controls and is sensitive to its overall functioning will have consciousness that is structured the same way as that part's, and which displays the same coherence between consciousness and function. An intelligent subject with no conscious parts will have to get its conscious structure in some noncombinationist way, which goes beyond the scope of this book. But what if an intelligent subject has two or more conscious parts, both of which have structured consciousness that coheres with their own intelligent functioning, and both of which have a significant degree of control over and sensitivity to its overall functioning? Since it inherits their experiences, the structure of its consciousness must in some way depend on the structure of theirs, but how? That is what this section and the next try to outline.

First, a note on terminology. I said earlier that "structured consciousness" could be understood as "enough conscious structure for consciousness to be capable of coherence with intelligent functioning." I employed the notion of "conscious structure," whose relationship to "structured consciousness" should be made clear. In short, conscious structure covers all the relations among elements of consciousness which, when there are enough of them, count as structured consciousness. So unintelligent wholes with intelligent conscious parts, like the solar system, lack structured consciousness but still contain a lot of conscious structure, namely, that exhibited by its various intelligent conscious parts, like me or you.[6]

---

[6] Here is an analogy. A cell can be said to be "biologically organized," meaning something like "organized in the way characteristic of biological organisms." But a compost heap that contains that cell is not biologically organized (showing that "being biologically organized" is division-relative). Nevertheless, there is something we can say of the compost heap: it contains biological organization (namely, it contains that of the cell and its other biologically organized parts). After all, someone looking to study biological organization could do much worse than looking at a compost heap. So we can distinguish something division-invariant ("biological organization") from something division-relative ("biological organizedness"). My distinction between "structured consciousness" (division-relative) and "conscious structure" (division-invariant) is analogous.

5.3.1. EXPLAINING PHENOMENAL UNITY

The first question about explaining conscious structure is what explains phenomenal unity, and to this question we have already seen one answer. Panpsychist combinationists, appealing to the arguments of chapter 3, can say that phenomenal unity is irreducible to, and separable from, other relations like access-unity or global consistency. And this irreducible, division-invariant relation pervades the universe: the experiences of any two intelligent subjects are already unified regardless of how exactly they are interacting, but by itself this phenomenal unity does not guarantee representational unity, causal interdependence, or anything like that. What remains to be explained is thus principally representational unity.

Pure functionalist combinationists, by contrast, will want to explain phenomenal unity by reference to the holding of "enough" other relations, in particular functional relations. Phenomenal unity between two experiences means that the composite they form is itself an experience, and according to pure functionalism, whether a state is an experience depends on whether it plays the right functional role. So for pure functionalists, the explanation of phenomenal unity will "piggyback" on the explanation of functional unity given in the previous section, and phenomenal unity will share the division-relativity of functional unity.

So on both versions of functionalist combinationism, the key aspect of conscious structure that still needs to be explained is representational unity, and it is this that the rest of this section focuses on.

5.3.2. THE CANVAS MODEL AND THE SUPERIMPOSITION MODEL

It will be useful to start by reflecting on two somewhat metaphorical models of how conscious structure might arise from combining multiple structured consciousnesses. Both presuppose phenomenal unity among the combining experiences, since without that there will be no single consciousness that they combine into, but only a number of distinct and separate consciousnesses in one system. But beyond that assumption they diverge.

One, which is very easy and tempting but ultimately unhelpful, is what I call the "canvas" model. Here we imagine each component experience being "placed" at a certain point in a preexisting space. From my parts I inherit, say, a red-experience and a blue-experience, and so I experience red-here-and-blue-there, like two paint splotches on a canvas. Coleman (2012, 157–158) is the most explicit advocate of this approach, saying "to take us toward the combination of the panpsychic ultimates . . . the metaphor-model I will appeal to is that of paint patches on a canvas" (157).[7]

The canvas model makes a lot of sense if we assume a correspondence between metaphysical distinctness and phenomenal contrast—between there being two or more elements of our consciousness which are grounded in distinct parts of us, and the experience of being presented with two distinguishable elements. In chapter 4 I identified, and rejected, this assumption: the fact that two elements of my consciousness come from different parts of me does not imply that I will experience them as two distinct things contrasting with each other. On the contrary, I proposed that the default state for a composite experience subsuming two experiential parts grounded in distinct parts of the subject is not phenomenal contrast but phenomenal blending: by default the two subsumed experiences will be present only as contributions to the quality of the composite experience. This proposal, and the rejection of a correspondence between metaphysical distinctness and phenomenal contrast, was crucial to chapter 4's solutions to the palette problem and revelation problem.

A more basic problem with the canvas model is that when we combine paint patches into a picture by putting them at certain locations on our "canvas," a crucial role is played by the canvas itself—but where does the canvas come from? Why does it have particular locations available, arranged in the particular dimensions that it has? This kind of metaphor makes combination seem easy, but only by smuggling something in that does most of the work for us. An adequate model of combination should be one on which the "space" is actually constructed by the components themselves: the paint patches must build the canvas.

For this reason, I prefer to think of the composition of consciousness in terms of the superimposition of layers—less like painting, more like animation using multiple transparent celluloid sheets (cf. Lee N.d., 21–22). Each component, just like the composite, has its own conscious "space," divided and organized in its own way. Insofar as human consciousness is appropriately described as a "phenomenal field," something within which different elements are laid out, some central and some peripheral, some nearer to each other and some further apart, we should regard the component subjects composing humans as having their own such fields, not as contributing elements which are somehow "fitted into" the whole's.[8]

---

[7] If we are more interested in propositional representations, the analogue might be to imagine a great list of propositions, or (perhaps equivalently) an extremely long conjunction: if part of me thinks "it's hot" and part of me thinks "I'm excited," I end up thinking "it's hot and I'm excited." (Cf. the idea of phenomenal unity as closure under conjunction: Tye 2003, 36–40; Bayne 2010, 47–72).

[8] It is a tricky question what literal sense can be made of the popular phrase "phenomenal field." In Roelofs (2014b) I defend one interpretation, where "distances" correspond to degrees of causal interdependence.

Philosophers have debated whether human consciousness is "holistic" or "atomistic," i.e., whether the whole phenomenal field comes first, with particular experiences as merely abstracted aspects of it, or the parts come first, with the whole being merely a bunch of them woven together (Gurwitsch 1964; Searle 2000; Dainton 2010; Bayne 2010; Chudnoff 2013; Koksvik 2014). One effect of accepting the superimposition model in place of the canvas model is that even though combinationists are committed to a metaphysically "atomistic" view where independent component experiences come together to form the phenomenal field, they can combine this with "holism" in the following sense: none (or not all) of the experiential elements that we can introspectively distinguish are metaphysically independent of the whole field. The different "layers," different component fields, are more fundamental than the total field, but the elements appearing in the total field need not be—they can be mere abstracted aspects, because they each represent intricately combined contributions from many component fields.

5.3.3. PHENOMENAL BLENDING AND INDETERMINACY

This "superimposition" model immediately raises the question of how the layers are "aligned." Because each component subject has its own conscious field, but there is no preexisting composite field to organize them, there seems to be nothing to decide how the internal structure of one field should map onto that of the others. Does the attentional focus of one component map onto the attentional periphery of another? Does the visual field of one component map onto the auditory experiences of another? Even if two visual fields are lined up, should the top of one map onto the top of the other, or onto its bottom, or onto its left side or center? It seems that unless something can fix the component fields into particular relations, the composite's field will be underdetermined; we have no reason to suppose it to be one way rather than another, out of all the ways that its component fields might be aligned.

Rather than treating this underdetermination of conscious structure as a problem, however, I propose to embrace it. It is a virtue of the superimposition model that it predicts such underdetermination as the default outcome, because this allows it to make sense of conscious *un*structuredness. In chapter 4 I hypothesized the correlative processes of radical confusion and phenomenal blending, whereby multiple conscious elements appear as an undifferentiated quality that incorporates its ingredients qualitatively without their appearing distinctly. Here I can present the same idea in a new connection: phenomenal blending is what you get when multiple fields of consciousness are superimposed without anything to fix their alignment. In such a situation, composite experience is equally well envisioned as any of the possible ways to superimpose its component fields, and so is not well described by any of them alone. Because there is no basis for singling out one of these patterns, the composite's actual experience must be undifferentiated. If functionalist-panpsychist combinationism is true, then the composite does undergo this undifferentiated experience, despite its undifferentiatedness; if pure functionalist combinationism is true, then the composite lacks consciousness altogether, since according to pure functionalism entirely unstructured consciousness is no consciousness at all.

Note in particular that phenomenal blending and phenomenal contrast are, on this account, division-relative. The parts might experience a phenomenal contrast between two or more distinct elements in their conscious fields, but the composite experience of the whole blurs these together so thoroughly that the whole experiences no phenomenal contrast. Or, more precisely, the whole experiences those various contrasts undergone by the parts, but in a confused fashion, so that it cannot discern either.

Experiences often have representational content; they are about something. So it is worth noting what this undifferentiated mode of combination might mean for representation. I think the most natural thing to say is that the content of the consciousness of unstructured composites is "indeterminate" among all the many ways to relate its components' contents, although this demands two qualifications. First, this kind of "indeterminate consciousness" is very different from the status I earlier ascribed to creatures like worms and bacteria, of being "indeterminately" intelligent subjects. In that earlier case, the point was that a representation applied from outside (our concept of an "intelligent subject") is not fully and precisely defined, and so when applied to certain conscious beings will not yield a determinate truth-value. But the point now is that if the conscious state itself has content, that content will not only fail to be fully and precisely defined, but massively fails even to approximate precision.[9]

The other key qualification is that we should not describe the consciousness of unstructured composites as "indeterminate" with respect to its phenomenal character. There is a particular, objective way that it feels to be such a composite

---

[9] Indeterminate reference is a better model for the indeterminacy I am ascribing to unstructured composites, rather than indeterminate application of predicates. For example, many people have thoughts about "the outback," but as Lewis (1986, 212) notes, "it's vague where the outback begins . . . because there are many things [precise regions of desert], with different borders, and nobody has been fool enough to try to enforce a choice of one of them as the official referent of the word 'outback.'" Does a given person's thought that "the outback is hot" refer to outback$_{4356}$? Does it refer to outback$_{4876}$? There is no way to say that it refers to one but not the others, so the most reasonable thing to say is that it refers indeterminately to all of them: its content is indeterminate between "outback$_{4356}$ is hot," "outback$_{4876}$ is hot," and all the others. In something like this way, it seems to me, we must suppose that unstructured composites, if they represent anything, indeterminately represent a baffling array of different contents.

(namely, a blend of all its components' experiences), and to call its phenomenal character indeterminate would seem to deny this. To put it another way, I follow the common opinion among philosophers that indeterminacy is an essentially representational phenomenon, and so can pertain to how we represent something or to how it represents the world, but not to how it feels.

5.3.4. THE ROLE OF PHENOMENAL BINDING

In order to get structured consciousness with contrasting elements, instead of simply a blend, something must serve to fix the alignment of the superimposed layers, so that particular elements in one component field are experienced by the whole as connected with particular elements in another. On the canvas model this role is taken by the canvas, the "space" into which component experiences are placed, but I have rejected any such canvas. So instead what fixes the relations between elements must be some sort of relation between the component fields themselves. We might metaphorically speak of this relation as "pinning" two layers together at a certain point; to have a label for the relation which accomplishes this, I will call it "phenomenal binding" (taking the term from Woodward [2015, 151ff.], drawing on the extensive literature in psychology on the "binding problem"). Phenomenal binding both makes the content of the composite experience more determinate and gives it a "structured" phenomenal character, in which distinct and contrasting elements are available to be distinguished by the subject.

Plausibly neither of these is accomplished all at once, though; for most creatures, indeterminacy in content is somewhat reduced, but only somewhat,[10] and patterns remain somewhat "blurry." When we are tired, disoriented, or in the first half-second of being startled, our experience is blurrier than normal in the sense I have in mind. It is not quite homogeneous, for there is still a sense of many specific possibilities, but our lack of a sense of which one is actual gives it a relatively un-differentiated character. For example, when we are disoriented and do not know which direction is the one we had been heading, it seems to me that our experience of our surroundings blurs together all the live possibilities (that it was *this* direction, that it was *that* direction, etc.) to produce an overall experience which "feels indefinite." The more unstructured a composite is, I suggested, the blurrier

---

[10] This fits with the metaphor of "pinning": putting a pin through two layers ensures that the two elements the pin goes through are co-located in the composite field, but since the two layers can still move relative to each other, the alignment of other elements remains indeterminate. Of course, if the layers were imagined as two-dimensional and perfectly rigid, then all indeterminacy could be removed by just two pins. But we should probably not imagine them as two-dimensional and rigid. (Indeed we should be agnostic about how far any such metaphorical picture matches the actual features of microexperience.) In Roelofs (2014b) I argue that the human phenomenal field is a deforming one, with an open-ended number of dimensions.

is its experience on average, and thus the closer it is to experiencing a single big blend. And even our most highly structured experiences, when we are maximally alert and confident, confidently monitoring many complex tasks and stimuli, retain some small measure of blurriness "at the edges." When we scrutinize them closely enough, virtually all of our everyday thoughts and words turn out to have some degree of indeterminacy in their content; functionalist combinationism says that this is not surprising, because radical indeterminacy is the default condition of all composite subjects.

5.4. What Is Phenomenal Binding?

But what is this relation I have called "phenomenal binding"? I do not know exactly, and will not try to deduce it from first principles. But if I am right that the default outcome of combining phenomenal fields is an undifferentiated blur, and that no preexisting "canvas" can "slot" them into a structure, then there must be some relation among phenomenal fields which gives rise to conscious structure in the composite experience they form.

Whatever exactly it is, this "phenomenal binding" needs to be considered under three aspects: its objective aspect, how it is manifest externally, detectable by the objective methods of natural science; its within-subject aspect, how it is manifest in the consciousness of the whole, who undergoes multiple phenomenally bound experiences; and its between-subjects aspect, how it is manifest in the consciousness of each part, who undergoes an experience that is bound with another experience which they do not undergo. In this section I consider what seems plausible to conjecture about these three aspects of phenomenal binding.

Note that these aspects may well not be such that each of them strictly necessitates the others; for instance, whatever the objective aspect is, we might imagine a zombie world, devoid of consciousness, where objectively equivalent physical relations obtain. And whatever the between-subjects aspect, we can imagine a Cartesian world, populated with sharply separate immaterial souls, where individuals have experiences with just the same character as those which, in our world, are phenomenally bound, but which are not bound because of the utter separateness of the Cartesian souls. I do not pretend to have a full grasp of how to think about and relate the different aspects of the phenomenal binding relation whose existence is implied by the theory developed so far, and so the following section is best taken less as the presentation of a completed account and more as an attempt to work through what we can reasonably say about phenomenal binding's three aspects, and to identify and resolve some of the tensions that arise in doing so.

5.4.1. PHENOMENAL BINDING AS INTEGRATED INFORMATION

We can start with the objective aspect: What observable differences between physical systems might correspond to the presence or absence of phenomenal binding structure? I think the most attractive proposal is that phenomenal binding correlates with *integration of information*.

I am far from the first to suggest that informational structure is crucial to complex consciousness (see, e.g., Baars 1988; Chalmers 1996, 284–292, 2017, 209–210; Gabora 2002); it seems empirically obvious that the processing of information in the brain is systematically connected to the structure of consciousness. That was chapter 4's "informational structure hypothesis," and this link between conscious structure and informational structure seems particularly important to explaining the coherence between conscious structure and functional structure. For me to be access-conscious of something, it is clearly a requirement that information about it be broadcast widely to different subsystems of my mind, so that it can guide various cognitive and behavioral tasks. So to understand why conscious structure is coherent with access-consciousness, and more broadly with intelligent functioning, it makes sense to look at the structure of information.

For the idea of *integrated* information I am specifically indebted to Giulio Tononi's (2004, 2008, 2012; Tononi and Koch 2014; Oizumi et al. 2014) "integrated information theory" (IIT) of consciousness. The key insight is that information as usually defined is unsuitable to account for consciousness, because a system's consciousness is intrinsic to it: each of us experiences what we do independently of what anyone else thinks about it. Yet the traditional mathematical conception of information (drawn from Shannon 1948) as "differences that make a difference" makes information dependent on an observer, and thus extrinsic. That conception says that one entity carries information about another when knowing the state of the first allows an observer to deduce the particular states of the second, or at least to reduce their uncertainty about it somewhat: more information means a greater reduction in uncertainty. Considering integrated information, however, allows us to characterize a system's *intrinsic* informational properties. A system integrates information to the extent that differences in one part make a difference to the other parts, so that the system is effectively its own observer.

More precisely, information is integrated to the extent that differences in one part not only make a difference to other parts, but make *different* differences from what other differences, or differences in other parts, would make—particularly when these influences run mutually, with each part both affecting and being affected by the others. Tononi nicely illustrates the idea by contrast with cases where there is information but a lack of integration of it. A photograph, for instance, stores a large amount of information, allowing that information to flow from the photographed object to whoever looks at it. But each point in the photograph is indifferent to the other points, so the information in the photograph is not integrated at all (Tononi 2012, 57–59). Likewise, a pair of books contains the information in the one book and that in the other, but neither book's contents make any difference to the other's, so that although having two books means more information, it does not mean any extra integration of that information. For the information to be integrated would require something like each book's being updated, edited, filled with citations or corrections, based on the content of the other; only then does each page reflect the influence of, and thus integrate information from, both books.

When information is integrated, an investigator examining one part of a system could, in principle, deduce significant things about the state of many other parts; after all, we routinely do this by listening to verbal reports, which reflect activity all across the brain even though they are proximally produced by particular parts of the motor cortex. Moreover, the system acts as its own investigator; it will proceed differently based on these subtly different results, where each particular event both reflects a distinctive set of causes and also produces a distinctive set of effects. Consider in particular that a particular brain event (e.g., that which initiates my voluntarily raising my arm) typically reflects a huge number of other brain events: all the perceptions, emotions, memories, beliefs, desires, etc. that either did make or could have made a difference to whether and how I performed it. Moreover, this decision then feeds back to all those others, potentially making a difference to them.

Information integration underlies intelligent functioning, but it is not the same thing. To function intelligently, a system must integrate at least a fair amount of information (with the exception of "Blockheads," which have only external, not internal, intelligent functioning), but a system might integrate information without functioning anything like an intelligent subject. A device might be built, for instance, that takes in and organizes vast amounts of information, but has nothing remotely like desires, beliefs, decision-making, perception, etc. If pure functionalism is true, then all this information integration would involve no consciousness of any sort; by contrast, functionalist-panpsychist combinationism implies that such a system would have a richly structured consciousness that was nevertheless utterly alien to ours, and consequently impossible for us to intuitively recognize as conscious (cf. Aaronson 2014; Tononi 2014; Buchanan and Roelofs 2018). On either view, information integration is a necessary but not sufficient condition for intelligent functioning, and thus for intelligent subjecthood. It follows that if information integration is also phenomenal binding—i.e., is also what accounts for the specific structure of our consciousness—then we should expect a general congruence between functional structure and conscious structure: thus we have (at least the beginnings of) an explanation for coherence.

Tononi attempts a rigorous mathematical quantification of information integration as "phi," but I will not tie myself to this way of developing the above ideas. Phi is calculated based on the "cause-effect information" of particular parts of a system relative to other parts, where a part has greater cause-effect information when both the set of possible states of the other parts which might have caused it and the set which might result from it are more selective (i.e., differ more from the maximum-entropy set of possible states, where we are maximally uncertain of which state the other parts are in). A system generates more "conceptual information" the more cause-effect information its parts have relative to each other, and phi is then the degree to which a system generates "irreducible" conceptual information, in the sense of generating more than any two parts we divided it into would generate if modeled as independent of each other.[11]

While the attempt at precise quantification is valuable for empirical purposes, there is no need for functionalist combinationism to commit to it. Indeed on a theoretical level it introduces new puzzles about its meaning: it is simply not clear what it means to have a higher or lower "quantity of consciousness" or "degree of conscious structure" (cf. Pautz 2015). How structured is your consciousness right now? Perhaps you can say "very," and perhaps you can roughly compare it to other occasions, but it would be faintly comic to think there is a precise numerical answer. (Compare questions like "How structured is this car?")

Another reason for combinationists not to buy IIT wholesale is that it is sharply anti-combinationist, due to its "exclusion postulate," according to which, within any hierarchy of nested systems and subsystems, only one layer can be conscious (see Tononi 2012, 59–68; Tononi and Koch 2014, 6; Oizumi et al. 2014, 3, 9–10). Whichever entity has the highest value of phi is conscious, and any system which contains it as a part, or is contained within it, lacks consciousness entirely even if it has significant phi. By this principle, a neuron kept alive in a petri dish would be conscious, but neurons in a living human brain are not conscious simply because they are part of a higher-phi system, the brain, whose consciousness excludes theirs. And if a human society ever became sufficiently integrated that its phi value exceeded that of an individual human, all the members of that society would

---

[11] This is a deliberately simplified summary of an intricate mathematical structure, which admits of multiple subtly different types of "phi" and has evolved through multiple versions. I have tried to capture the core idea that remains constant through all versions; interested readers should consult Tononi 2004, 2008, 2012; Tononi and Koch 2014; Oizumi et al. 2014; and the website www.integratedinformationtheory.org.

be instantly but undetectably zombified, deprived of consciousness just by being part of a conscious whole.[12]

For both the above reasons (the lack of need for precise quantification, and the exclusion postulate), I wish to take on what I see as the guiding insight behind IIT, not the theory itself. Functionalist combinationism needs only the key idea that systems which integrate information do so intrinsically, not relative to an observer, because they function as their own observer. Instead of following Tononi's method of calculating a phi-value and equating it with something like "quantity of consciousness" or "quantity of conscious structure," I prefer to say simply: each interaction among a whole's conscious parts, in proportion as it integrates information, effects some degree of some form of phenomenal binding among the phenomenal fields of those parts. This very loose claim obviously leaves a lot of room for further investigation, elaboration, and refinement: after all, functionalist combinationism is more a sketch of a theory than a theory.

Similarly, I depart from Tononi in that, instead of privileging the particular level where a maximum of integrated information might be found, functionalist combinationism treats information integration as determining conscious structure wherever it occurs. This allows me to use "information integration" for something division-invariant, even though Tononi's notion is very division-relative. In Tononi's sense, for instance, a pair of noninteracting human beings has zero phi, because it is not a maximum of integrated information: it integrates no information at all compared to one division of it into parts (namely, into person-1 and person-2), since no information would be lost by treating those parts as independent (since the state of one carries no information about the state of the other). But a combinationist need not say that the pair has "zero information integration." Combinationists need not care about *maxima* specifically, because they have no need to identify one specific level as the right level for consciousness to the exclusion of all others. They can instead point to the fact that as well as one division into parts that carry no information about one another, the pair also has a great many divisions into parts which carry lots of information about one another (e.g., into "left-half-of-person-1+left-half-of-person-2" and "right-half-of-person-1+right-half-of-person-2"). Even though the two-person system is not integrating

---

[12] The stated motivation for the exclusion postulate is Ockham's razor: given consciousness at one level, it would be superfluous to also postulate consciousness at other levels. But this reasoning makes sense only if consciousness at the other levels was something over and above consciousness at the highest-phi level, which is precisely what combinationism denies: the whole is conscious, but its consciousness is not something new in addition to the consciousness of the parts. By analogy (and recalling section 3.5 of chapter 3) I think it would be absurd to deny that composite objects have any mass, on the basis that mass for the composite would be a superfluous addition to the mass of its parts: its mass is nothing over and above theirs, and so "comes for free."

more information than certain of its parts, it is nevertheless a system within which a great deal of information is being integrated. It contains that information integration without being itself a maximum of integrated information in the same way that it contains the conscious structure of its parts without itself having structured consciousness.

5.4.2. PHENOMENAL BINDING AS MUTUAL CO-PRESENTATION

So I suggest that the externally observable aspect of phenomenal binding is most likely information integration. But what is trickier to understand is what phenomenal binding means for the component subjects involved—to understand its between-subjects aspect. In particular, here we face in particularly strong form the dilemma posed by the boundary argument and the incompatible contexts argument from chapter 2. That dilemma, recall, was roughly this: either we think of conscious unity as relative to subjects, so that two experiences belonging to different component subjects can be unified relative to the whole, but disunified relative to those two parts ("relative unity"), or else we think of it as a relation among experiences independently of what subjects they belong to, connecting two experiences whether we focus on the composite subject that experiences them both or on the component subjects that experience only one each ("absolute unity").

In the first case we must deny "interdependence" (the idea that being unified by itself changes the phenomenal character of experiences), on pain of a single experience ending up with multiple incompatible phenomenal characters from being unified simultaneously with different sets of experiences relative to different subjects. In the second case we must deny "boundedness" (the idea that my experiences can be unified only with other experiences of mine, not with experiences I do not have).

So far we have seen that different options make more sense for different sorts of unity. Causal interdependence is an absolute relation, so for it combinationists should deny boundedness, but functional unity and global consistency are subject-relative, so for them combinationists should deny interdependence. In chapter 3 I argued that phenomenal unity, if it is taken to be a fundamental relation, should also be absolute, like the fundamental physical relations, and so for it functionalist-panpsychist combinationists should deny boundedness. Pure functionalist combinationists, since they take phenomenal unity to depend on some sort of functional unity, should instead take it as subject-relative and thus deny interdependence.

What about representational unity? Unfortunately, both boundedness and interdependence seem *most* compelling when we are considering representational unity. When I try to focus on the representational unity between some of my experiences, to identify what it is about their unity that goes beyond their merely being experienced together, what I end up with is that each experience in some sense "connotes" or "references" the others. What I mean by this is that in undergoing one of them, I am made aware of the presence of the others and how those others are related to it, and when I focus attention on one of them, it already "points me on" to the others as potential foci for attention. Each has the others in its background; by having one experience, the subject is already given an inkling of the others.

For example, when I see a cat, I can distinguish visual experiences of its various parts, can distinguish the colors from the shapes, can distinguish these from the emotional experience of affection it evokes in me, or the conceptual experience of recognizing it as an animal of a certain type. Yet the distinguishing seems in a certain sense artificial: scrutinizing any part for its individual content seems to reveal not a self-contained atom of meaning but things like "affection—*for the thing I see*," "orangeness—*of that shape there*," "a leg—*of that body*." Each contains a reference to the other experiences.

This is why it seems unpalatable to deny interdependence. The problem for the combinationist is that they must either deny interdependence or boundedness, and boundedness is *also* very compelling for representational unity. How can the sort of mutual indication, the sort of internal pointing-to each other, that representationally unified experiences display, be made sense of as a relation that might hold between the experiences of distinct subjects? How can a subject have an experience that stands in this relation to an experience they do not have?

I do not think, however, that these two intuitively plausible principles are actually on a par. I think that the intuitive appeal of boundedness is largely illusory, and that reflection on certain common experiences can undermine it very effectively. By contrast, I do not see an equally good way to deny interdependence: even if not all pairs of representationally unified experiences exhibit the sort of "interpenetration" that interdependence claims, it seems that many do. For this reason, I think combinationists should deny boundedness for representational unity.

The appeal of boundedness is that it can at first seem hard to make sense of one subject's experiences reflecting the specific character of some other experiences in the way described just above, without it following that those other experiences belonged to that subject. This would seem to require that the experiences of the one subject convey to them, just in being experienced, the presence of the other experiences, but do so without actually providing the full character of those other experiences. This would seem to require that the first experience have, baked right into it, not just the positive sense that the other experience exists and has certain features, but also the negative sense that the other experience has other features, that its character goes beyond what the first experience conveys. There must be a sort of "negative" phenomenology, a sense of the other experience as having a nature that is *not* fully captured in the first experience's indicating it.

Fortunately, this sort of experience—being aware of something, and thereby aware of the presence of other things that we are *not* aware of—is actually a pervasive feature of everyday human consciousness. It is most obviously present in visual perception: our visual experience of a three-dimensional object is always an experience of it *as* having concealed sides and a concealed interior that we cannot presently see (Clarke 1965; Noë 2005; Nanay 2010; Briscoe 2011). It is also present, I believe, in mind-perception: our immediate awareness of another person's expressive behavior is an experience of that behavior *as* expressing something that is not fully revealed to us, namely their mental state (Smith 2010, 2015; Church 2016; Roelofs 2018; Chudnoff 2018; cf. Krueger 2012). And similar phenomenology is arguably present also in cognitive experience (Jorba 2016) and in the experience of trying to remember something (James 1890, 251ff.). This intermingling of positive and negative, whereby we are aware of one thing as continuous with something else we are aware of not being aware of, and thus as indicating that something else without fully revealing it, has been given a plethora of labels: "adumbration," "amodal perception," "horizon(tality)." But I will adopt the term "co-presentation" (see Michotte et al. 1991; Husserl 1970, 1982, 2001; Merleau-Ponty 1962; cf. Kelly 2004).

I think mutual co-presentation is the best tool for letting us deny boundedness while accommodating the intuitions that support it, allowing representationally unified experiences to convey each other's presence to their subjects without thereby fully providing each other's character.

To see more clearly how this would work, consider the structure of an ordinary case of perceptual co-presentation, e.g., me looking at a table. Here the front of the table co-presents the back: that is, I have an experience which directly presents one thing (the front) as part of a larger whole (the table), which is presented as having aspects that are not directly presented (the back). The proposal defended in different forms by myself, Smith, Church, and Chudnoff is that when I interact with someone and, as we might say, "read" their mental states in their bodily actions, I likewise have an experience which directly presents one thing (their bodily movements) as part of a larger whole (the process of them having a mental state and expressing it), which is presented as having aspects that are not directly presented (the mental state itself). The suggestion I am making now is that representationally unified experiences each directly present themselves, to their subject, as parts of a larger whole (the composite experience), which is presented as having aspects that are not directly presented (the other experience).[13]

Co-presentation can be more or less informative about what is co-presented, and it seems natural to relate this to information integration. So let us suppose that the more information is integrated between two component subjects, the more specific is the "something more" which each experiences some element of their own experience as continuous with. This is like the progression from seeing a distant black blob as "the visible portion of some object" to seeing it as "the head of some creature"—independently of what is actually revealed (still a black blob), it comes to tell us more about what is concealed (that it is a creature with a head) through a richer understanding of how the two relate (as head-to-creature, not just part-to-whole).

For instance, to have an experience representing P-or-Q might perhaps involve having one experience representing P and another representing Q, each of which co-presents the other as "an alternative." The experience representing P need not be so informative as to indicate *what* the other represents; it might only demonstratively refer to it as "that alternative to P," just as my visual experience might not indicate what the rear side of the coffee cup looks like, but only that it is "the opposite side of what I directly see." An experience can be informative by indicating only how what it co-presents relates to what it presents.

Which forms of informative co-presentation, among which simpler contents, correspond to which representational relations, is obviously a huge topic. But I am not trying to give a systematic account of human representational capacities, only to sketch out how combinationists might think about them.[14] The key thing is that informative co-presentation allows a subject to incorporate references to another's experiential content into their own, without fully grasping or deploying that content themselves. We might use another metaphor, namely that of citation: when one text cites another, its content is enriched without what does that enriching being actually in the text. Many authors citing each other may lack the skills or even the concepts to understand what the others do, but can still jointly create an intellectual edifice richer than any could create alone.

---

[13] Unlike in the perceptual case, of course, they do not present themselves through a distinct experience that represents them (that would obviously lead to an infinite regress of experiences presenting experiences); rather, they are presented to the subject just by themselves. That is, this suggestion assumes that it makes sense to see experiences as "self-representing" (or "self-presenting," if one prefers), i.e., the idea that whenever we have an experience (e.g., seeing a green plant) we are simultaneously made aware of two different things: the external object which the experience represents (the plant) and the experience itself. For defenses of this idea see Strawson 2015; MacKenzie 2007; Zahavi and Kriegel 2015; for some critical evaluation see Schear 2009.

[14] See Mendelovici (2018) for a similar point: the challenge of explaining the mind's various forms of structure should not be seen as a special problem just for panpsychists (or other combinationists).

5.4.3. PHENOMENAL BINDING AS REPRESENTATIONAL UNITY

So the objective aspect of phenomenal binding seems likely to be something like information integration, and the between-subjects aspect seems likely to be something like mutual co-presentation. Finally, the within-subject aspect is just the familiar relation of representational unity. That is, we already know something about phenomenal binding for the whole, because we enjoy structured consciousness. Of course there are many ways that experience can have structure, and so there must be many variants of phenomenal binding. This is not surprising, given how we have characterized it: it connects elements in different phenomenal fields to one another, and so may take on as many different particular forms as there are different kinds of elements in phenomenal fields.

But the most prominent sort of structure exhibited by human consciousness is representational unity of various forms. In vision, for instance, there has been extensive empirical investigation of "feature binding," which relates our independently processed impressions of color, shape, and motion.[15] In linguistic thought there is the link that connects predicates to their subjects, and clauses in complex sentences to each other.[16] In both cases we see a relation which welds two representations, of "something F" and "something G," into a representation of "something F and G." It seems likely that the particular forms it takes (e.g., visual feature-binding and predication) reflect its conditioning by different complex systems (the human visual and linguistic systems); in simpler subjects it presumably takes a less sophisticated form, though we should not expect to be able to form a positive idea of its specific features.[17]

It is very plausible that representational unity presupposes phenomenal unity: two experiences cannot together form an experience with complex representational content if they do not even form an experience. This means that what combinationists say about phenomenal unity will ramify into what they say about representational unity, and thus into what they say about phenomenal binding.

---

[15] See, e.g., Treisman and Gelade 1980; Duncan and Humphreys 1989, 1992; Treisman and Sato 1990; cf. the problems raised for adverbial theories of intentionality in Jackson 1975.

[16] See particularly Soames 2010, where a mental act of predicating is appealed to in order to solve the long-running debate on the "unity of the proposition."

[17] I am assuming for the sake of argument that at least some conscious states have representational content intrinsically; if this is false, and conscious states either lack content or get it entirely in virtue of factors or processes (e.g., functional organization or evolutionary functions) which have nothing specifically to do with consciousness, then the explanatory burden on the combinationist is correspondingly lightened. Note that this implies that I am primarily discussing "narrow" rather than "broad" content: if the content of a state depends partly on extrinsic factors (like causal history), then a theory of consciousness will account only for those aspects of content that are independent of those extrinsic factors.

Consider first the (somewhat simpler) position of functionalist-panpsychist combinationists. They take phenomenal unity to be a fundamental relation, and thus treat it as division-invariant (and pervasive in nature). This is convenient, if I was right in the previous two subsections to treat both information integration and mutual co-presentation as division-invariant relations. For then the functionalist-panpsychist combinationist can say that, in the actual world at least, phenomenal binding is a division-invariant relation manifest in three ways: physically as information-integration, for component subjects as mutual co-presentation, and for composite subjects as representational unity. Although these three things might come apart in zombie worlds, Cartesian worlds, and other strange worlds, that fact is fairly inconsequential for what happens in this world.

Pure functionalist combinationists are in a more complicated situation. They tie phenomenal unity (like consciousness itself) to functional unity, and functional unity is division-relative: what roles states play in a given system may diverge from what roles they play in parts of that system or in a more encompassing system. Consequently phenomenal unity is also division-relative: two experiences might form a composite experience relative to one system but not another. Since phenomenal unity is a precondition for representational unity, this also applies to representational unity. But the intuitive plausibility of interdependence militates in favor of seeing representational unity as division-invariant. How can this tension be resolved? I am not entirely sure, but here is a suggestion.

I think pure functionalist combinationists ought to address this tension by distinguishing two relations: a division-invariant relation involving information integration and mutual co-presentation, and a division-relative relation which consists in the former relation plus phenomenal unity, yielding representational unity. Let us call the former "pre-phenomenal binding" and the latter "phenomenal binding": pre-phenomenal binding is a matter of how two experiences affect each other, both physically and phenomenally, while phenomenal binding is just that same interaction considered relative to a system in which the two experiences together have the right functional profile to form a single composite experience.

That implies that we get representational unity relative to a given subject when (1) two experiences are integrating information and mutually co-presenting (both division-invariant facts), and (2) those two experiences are phenomenally unified relative to that subject. Strictly, interdependence is denied, and boundedness accepted, for representational unity, but only in the sense that making two pre-phenomenally bound experiences into representationally unified experiences (by considering them relative to a subject for whom they play the right functional role to be phenomenally unified) does not change the individual phenomenal character of each. The spirit of interdependence is vindicated, because making two experiences pre-phenomenally bound in the first place (i.e., having them integrate information so as to mutually co-present) *does* change their phenomenal character, and whenever we undergo two representationally unified experiences, we can recognize this interdependence, this interpenetration, between them.

5.5. So How *Do* Intelligent Subjects Combine?

The foregoing discussion, particularly in section 5.4, got decidedly complicated, and the reader has my apologies for that. So let me try to summarize the key proposals made in this chapter, so as to generate a few principles that might make up the working core of functionalist combinationism.

Functionalist combinationism is concerned with "intelligent subjects," which are characterized in both functional and phenomenal terms:

> An intelligent subject $=_{def}$ A conscious subject whose consciousness is structured and whose experiences play the functional roles characteristic of intelligence in virtue of their phenomenal character, conscious structure, and representational content.

Because this analysis of intelligent subjecthood is available, we can ground and explain the existence of an intelligent subject just by showing how the key features (consciousness, conscious structure, intelligent functioning, and coherence between the last two) come to be instantiated. Functionalist combinationism is concerned not with the general question of what explains and grounds the existence of intelligent subjects but with the much more limited question of what role in that explanation and grounding could be played by the consciousness of component subjects.

Functionalist combinationism is compatible both with pure functionalism, which says that once intelligent functioning is in place all the rest follows (guaranteeing also the coherence between conscious structure and intelligent functioning), and with impure functionalism, which accepts the importance of intelligent functioning but takes something else to be necessary in order to add consciousness to the mix. In particular, panpsychists may accept panpsychist combinationism, from chapters 3 and 4, as their ultimate account of consciousness, but add functionalist combinationism as a "second layer" accounting for the special features of intelligent subjects.

5.5.1. CONDITIONAL EXPERIENCE INHERITANCE

There is enormous disagreement about how consciousness and conscious structure can be explained, while the explanation of intelligent functioning is pretty simple in principle, though extremely complex in practice. So let us start with that:

> **Conditional functional inheritance:** If a part of X has an experience which plays a certain functional role, then that experience plays the same or a similar functional role for X, to the extent that the part in question is connected to the rest of X such that its experience has sensitivity to, control over, and coordination with other events occurring in X.

This does not yet say that the whole system is conscious, just that it has a state playing (something close to) the functional role of a conscious state. The two versions of functionalist combinationism then add different further principles to explain consciousness: pure functionalists can say that consciousness is reducible to having states playing the right functional roles, while panpsychists can say that systems inherit consciousness from being made of conscious matter. Either option allows us to move from conditional functional inheritance to conditional experience inheritance:

> **Conditional experience inheritance:** If a part of *X* has an experience which plays a certain functional role, then X shares that experience, with the same or similar functional role, to the extent that the part in question is connected to the rest of X such that its experience has sensitivity to, control over, and coordination with other events occurring in X.

This principle applies most straightforwardly to cases of trivial combination, when a single intelligent subject guides the overall functioning of a system that contains it. In such a case, CEI says that the system is also the subject of that part's experiences—that, for example, my brain and I share our consciousness. The more interesting case is when multiple parts of a system are conscious, and their experiences share control over, and sensitivity to, its overall workings, and their experiences are sufficiently integrated with one another. In this case, the system inherits all their experiences, subsumed in a composite experience which each of them experiences only part of.

Note that conditional experience inheritance does not require that the conscious parts whose experiences are inherited are *intelligent* subjects; if unintelligent subjects are possible, then as long as their experiences play some functional role, however simple, those experiences could be inherited by the whole given the right functional embedding. A whole with experiences that play simple roles for its parts might connect them in such a way that they can play *more* complex roles in its overall functioning; that is, an intelligent subject might inherit experiences from unintelligent parts, as panpsychists say we do.[18]

5.5.2. THE THREE FACES OF PHENOMENAL BINDING

The structure of the whole's consciousness reflects the structure of, and relations among, the consciousness of its parts. My preferred metaphor for this is to think of each part's phenomenal field superimposed on the others, with points in the fields (i.e., experiences) sometimes pinned to each other (phenomenally bound), and the fields indeterminately lined up otherwise. In the limiting case of zero information integration (in a being which would not qualify as an intelligent subject at all) the composite experience is simply a phenomenal blend, a single quality involving no phenomenal contrast, no discernible structure. Metaphorically, the fields are completely unfixed in their alignment, as though spinning around over one another so that the structure of one simply blurs out the structure of the other.

I labeled the relation which brings the parts' experiences into a definite structure "phenomenal binding"; I have suggested that this relationship's within-subject manifestation in representational unity, that its between-subjects manifestation is mutual co-presentation, and that its objective aspect is information integration. But pure functionalist combinationists face a specific difficulty in trying to understand this relation. If pure functionalism is true, then phenomenal unity requires functional unity, which is division-relative, even though representational unity seems to make a genuine difference to the unified experiences, seemingly requiring it to be division-invariant (at least if the incompatible contexts argument is valid). This tension pushed me, in the previous section, to suggest that if pure functionalist combinationism is true, then although representational unity itself (which requires phenomenal unity) is division-relative, there is a division-invariant relation (provisionally labeled "pre-phenomenal binding") which involves information integration and mutual co-presentation, and which yields representational unity (relative to a particular division) as soon as phenomenal unity (relative to that division) is present.

---

[18] Compare Lycan (1995, 40) on homuncular functionalism: "We explain the successful activity of one homunculus, not by idly positing a second homunculus within it that successfully performs that activity, but by positing *a team* consisting of several smaller, individually less talented and more specialized homunculi—and detailing the ways in which the team members cooperate in order to produce their joint or corporate output."

We can put these complications aside if we focus on cases where two experiences are functionally integrated enough for phenomenal unity relative to both parts and whole. In such cases, both sorts of functionalist combinationist can say the following: for the whole which experiences both, there is a representationally unified complex of experiences; for the parts which undergo only one or the other, there is an experience which co-presents another, by presenting its given content as one aspect of something not-fully-given. Corresponding to the increasing definiteness of the composite field is the increasing informativeness of the co-presentation present in the component fields. The parts' richer impression of each other's state, the whole's experience of one thing characterized by multiple aspects, and the integration of physical information across the system are, so to speak, three sides of the same coin.

5.5.3. INCLUSIONARY AND EXCLUSIONARY APPROACHES

Pure functionalist combinationists can leave matters there: composites inherit those experiences that are embedded in the right functional relations, but no others. Their phenomenal fields comprise only experiences that are both phenomenally conscious and access-conscious. Call this the "exclusionary" model of combination: any experiences in the parts that are not causally connected so as to be access-conscious are not inherited, and so not phenomenally conscious for the whole at all. This agrees with the spirit of Kant's (1997, B131-2) famous remark that "the 'I think . . .' must be able to accompany all my representations; for otherwise . . . the representation would either be impossible or else at least would be nothing for me."[19]

Functionalist-panpsychist combinationists face one last puzzle, however, which they might resolve in a similarly "exclusionary" way, or in a contrasting "inclusionary" way. The puzzle concerns the relationship between the consciousness of intelligent subjects and the consciousness of the aggregates that constitute them. The latter is governed not by conditional experience inheritance but by chapter 3's simpler principle of experience inheritance: it comprises all the experiences of the aggregate's parts, regardless of their functional role, and hence regardless of their accessibility. Does the intelligent subject too undergo all these inaccessible experiences?

---

[19] Other sentiments in this ballpark include Rosenthal's (1986, 329) principle that "conscious states are simply mental states we are conscious of being in" and Chalmers's (1995, 202) "detectability principle," that "where there is an experience, we generally have the capacity to form a second-order judgment about it."

One option for functionalist-panpsychist combinationists is to say no, to insist that since the intelligent subject is not identical to the aggregate, it need not undergo the same set of experiences. The intelligent subject undergoes only the access-conscious experiences, and no others; the aggregate undergoes both the access-conscious experiences and also the rest. This view of the intelligent subject's consciousness could be called "exclusionary," just like the pure functionalist's view.

But this response might seem to rest too much weight on the distinctness of the intelligent subject and the aggregate. Structure-specific wholes are not strictly identical to what constitutes them, sure, but they're not truly distinct either. The tower of blocks is not quite the same thing as the mass of blocks, but it's also not quite another thing.

So it is worth noting another option for functionalist-panpsychist combinationists: the "inclusionary" approach. This would say that experience inheritance holds for intelligent subjects, implying that many intelligent subjects (those with conscious parts whose experiences are not functionally integrated into the whole's intelligence) experience a sort of "phenomenal overflow" (Block 1995, 2005, 2011; Rosenthal 2007): they are phenomenally conscious of things that they cannot cognitively access.

What would it be like to be such a subject, with many more phenomenally conscious experiences than one is access-conscious of? I think the claims made so far in this section suggest that these isolated experiences will form a sort of unattended, inarticulate "background consciousness," which all structured consciousness appears against.[20] This is because they are, almost by definition, not integrating information with the rest of our experiences, and so not phenomenally bound to any of our other experiences. In our metaphor of superimposing layers, these elements are not tied down enough to have any determinate place in the composite field—they are present, but equally present everywhere, and to that extent make little difference anywhere in particular. If two or more experiences were both isolated in this way, they would both occupy the background and moreover would blend together, as though to put a very faint lens filter onto our view of the world.

The inclusionary option is an extension of the radical confusion hypothesis from chapter 4. There I argued that there could be phenomenal overflow with respect to the internal structure of each access-conscious experience. Your feeling of pain when you prick yourself is certainly access-conscious: according to panpsychist combinationism this feeling is in fact composed of trillions of components

---

[20] There is some affinity here with the *alayavijñana*, "background consciousness" or "storehouse consciousness," posited by certain Buddhist philosophers in the Yogacara school (Asanga 1992).

(the experiences associated with the microscopic brain events that add up to that macroscopic brain event), which are not access-conscious individually though they can be accessed as a mass.

Even an exclusionary approach would not deny that the pain is experienced by the whole (since it meets the right functional criteria), and experiencing the pain means experiencing the microexperiences that compose it. What is now at stake is experiences in the parts of something that are not, even in mass, access-conscious for the whole. For instance, consider the microexperiences associated (according to panpsychism) with all the events in my body that are not part of brain functioning (like events in blood cells, skin cells, the fluid in the brain's ventricles, and so on). The exclusionary option is to say that these experiences make no contribution to the consciousness of the whole. The inclusionary option is to extend the radical confusion hypothesis to say that these experiences are confused with the whole's entire phenomenal field.

This raises the phenomenological question: Do we experience such a "background consciousness"? I cannot be sure: at times it sounds like an accurate description of my experience, but at other times I am doubtful. And by definition, it will be all but impossible to conclusively detect, since it makes so little functional difference. Rather than come down on one side or the other, I will simply note various places in the next chapter that certain experiences will be informationally and functionally isolated, and will thus either not belong to the composite subject, or form an inarticulate conscious background for it.

Panpsychist combinationism aimed to be a theory of fundamental reality, subject to the standards appropriate to such theories: parsimony and uniformity of ultimate laws and *a priori* entailment of other laws. Functionalist combinationism does not aim for fundamentality: functional structure is by definition nonfundamental. Consequently the standards of success are somewhat different. It is still important to seek simple, elegant principles that are not needlessly complex or arbitrary. But nonfundamental principles can achieve elegance in ways that would be unacceptable for fundamental principles: they can include "other things being equal" clauses, to allow for an open-ended range of exceptions to a given generalization; they can restrict themselves to applying only under specific conditions, and employ simplifying concepts, even if those conditions or those concepts are themselves very hard to specify simply in fundamental terms.[21]

---

[21] For example, an elegant biological principle might be something to the effect that "species that produce large numbers of offspring invest less care in each one, and tend to prosper in unstable environments, while species that produce small numbers of offspring invest more care in each one, and tend to prosper in stable environments" (cf. MacArthur and Wilson 1967; Pianka 1970). But this principle would not fare well by the standards applied to fundamental theories, because there are numerous large or small exceptions, and because the conditions under which it applies (e.g., ones where populations of

Consequently, I will make use of ideas (like "intelligent functioning," "information integration," and "conscious structure") that I cannot give explicit, reductive definitions: all we should demand is that these ideas should be no less clear, intuitive, and illuminating than familiar psychological and philosophical ideas (like "sensory modality," "instrumental reasoning," "propositional content") that we already use to think about human minds. That is, my hope is not that functionalist combinationism will be a complete account of intelligent subjects, but only that it can be usefully incorporated into our ongoing, slow but steady efforts in understanding them.

---

reproducing organisms can exist) and the concepts it employs (e.g., "parental investment") would be very hard to specify simply in fundamental terms.

6 Composite Subjectivity in Organisms, Organs, and Organizations

CHAPTER 5 OUTLINED functionalist combinationism, but fully fleshing it out is well beyond the scope of this book. The functional and informational relations that play central roles in the theory are complex and multifarious and must be simultaneously viewed under three aspects: as objective physical structures, as structures experienced by a single composite subject, and as external relations between subjects. I do not claim to have rigorously defined or exhaustively analyzed these structures under any of their three aspects. I have simply tried to connect together the rough understanding we already have of those aspects—of information integration from observing physical systems, of conscious structure from our own consciousness, and of mutual co-presentation from our interactions with other people.

The best way to enrich the theory is to apply it to some cases studies, in the hope of showing how functionalist combinationism can illuminate some of the most perplexing debates in philosophy of mind. For this chapter I have chosen four case studies:

1. Ned Block's Nation-Brain thought experiment.
2. Actual human nations considered as candidates for consciousness.
3. The split-brain phenomenon.
4. The ordinary human brain understood as comprising multiple parallel processes determining conscious content partly independently of each other.

The first two involve a set of discrete parts, each uncontroversially an intelligent subject, together forming a system that shows some indications of subjecthood. The second two involve a system which is uncontroversially, or at least plausibly, an intelligent subject, composed of (overlapping) parts which individually show some indications of subjecthood.

6.1. Composite Subjectivity in the Nation-Brain

My first case study is the "Nation-Brain" thought experiment described by Block (1992) as an argument against functionalism. This is a best-case scenario for composite subjectivity, for it is stipulated to have conscious parts and yet be functionally identical to a human brain. This functional structure is realized not by neurons but by people: we have somehow persuaded the citizens and government of some sufficiently populous country to simulate a particular human brain using radios.

Each citizen is given a device which can send and receive signals to and from the other citizens' devices and given detailed instructions of the form "If you receive signals from such-and-such devices, send out signals to such-and-such other devices," for as many pairings of input and output as are needed to perfectly simulate the chosen brain. An appropriate human-like robot body is then wired up to be controlled by the citizens in a way that parallels the sensory and motor connections between body and brain. This body (call it the system's "avatar") walks around, responds to its environment, and expresses complex thoughts just like a human would, in virtue of several billion people pressing buttons.

Block thinks it counterintuitive that this vast group of button-pressing citizens must *itself* be conscious just like a human being. He concludes that pure functionalism is false, since the Nation-Brain and a normal brain could differ in consciousness but have all the same functional states. I am neutral on the truth of pure functionalism, but even if it is false, I do not think the Nation-Brain shows this.[1]

---

[1] If functionalist-panpsychist combinationism is true, then there is no contradiction in a nonconscious, "zombified" version of the Nation-Brain. But even then, given that the psychophysical laws of the actual

I think some versions of the Nation-Brain would be conscious, and the intuitive rejection of consciousness in the Nation-Brain stems from tacit acceptance of anti-combination. In this section I try to show how a combinationist can overcome that intuitive rejection.

The reason I say "some versions" of the Nation-Brain would be intelligent subjects is that some versions probably would not be, for reasons unrelated to anti-combination. Block distinguishes two forms of functionalism, according to how they formulate functional descriptions: capital-F "Functionalism" (which I will call "machine-functionalism") and "psychofunctionalism." The first identifies mental states with states of a certain kind of Turing machine,[2] while the second identifies mental states with whatever functional states are posited by a projected complete psychology. That is, one understands "functional state" in terms of a certain, well-defined sort of abstract system, while the other understands "functional state" as a place-holder for whatever the best scientific models of human psychology turn out to talk about.

We can accordingly distinguish two versions of the Nation-Brain: machine-functional and psychofunctional. The former matches a human brain just in those respects which would be captured by a Turing-machine table, the latter in any respects that psychology might have cause to appeal to. Since a Turing-machine table identifies its states solely by the output and state-changes they produce for any given input, the machine-functional Nation-Brain can be set up to give each citizen a very simple job:

> On one [giant satellite] is a bulletin board on which is posted a state card, i.e., a card that bears a symbol designating one of the states specified in the machine table. . . . Suppose the posted card has a "G" on it. This alerts the [citizens] who implement G squares—"'G-men" they call themselves. Suppose the light representing input I17 goes on. One of the G-men has the following as his sole task: when the card reads "G" and the I17 light goes on, he presses output button O191 and changes the state card to "M." This G-man is called upon to exercise his task only rarely. (Block 1992, 70)

Clearly this is not how the human brain is organized: there is no single "bulletin board" which all neurons monitor, nor is there a single list of inputs such that

---

world make human intelligent subjects, those laws will likewise make some versions of the Nation-Brain intelligent subjects.

[2] A Turing-machine table is a sort of very abstract program defined by a set of inputs, a set of outputs, and a set of internal states, along with exhaustive rules for what outputs should be generated, and what state moved to, when a given input is received while in a given state.

at any time there is one and only one input. A psychofunctional Nation-Brain would have to more accurately mirror the brain's setup, for instance by having many citizens active in parallel, and by having each citizen communicate with a great many others—up to several thousand, if citizens are to play the role of neurons.

The reason for distinguishing these two forms is that even a functionalist combinationist could think that the machine-functional Nation-Brain is not an intelligent subject, on the basis that there is no intelligent *internal* functioning and very little integration of information. Each citizen need only detect two things (the input and the state) and need never learn anything of the doings of the other citizens. Changing the instructions given to one citizen makes no difference to the other citizens, except via changing what state is displayed on the "bulletin board." Without integrated information, there would not be enough conscious structure for the Nation-Brain's states to play their roles in intelligent functioning *in virtue of* their phenomenal character and representational content. Without conscious structure or coherence, the system would be what in chapter 5 I called a "Blockhead."

So let us focus on the psychofunctional Nation-Brain. Many people find it deeply implausible that this collection of button-pressing people should be conscious. Why? To some extent it may just be sheer weirdness, combined with the sense of vertigo elicited by supposing any visible, tangible object to literally be a conscious subject. (As Huebner [2014, 120] says, "It is hard to imagine that collectivities can be conscious; but, it is just as hard to imagine that a mass of neurons, skin, blood, bones, and chemicals can be . . . conscious.") But intuitive resistance to Nation-Brain consciousness seems to go beyond this (see, e.g., Knobe and Prinz 2008; Huebner et al. 2010), and I believe the reason is that the Nation-Brain is made of conscious citizens. This opposition to Nation-Brain consciousness based on its parts being conscious can be articulated into at least four distinct objections:

1. If the Nation-Brain is conscious, its consciousness must be distinct from the consciousness of each citizen, so where is this "extra" consciousness?
2. The citizen's experiences are not unified with one another, so the Nation-Brain's consciousness is massively disunified, and thus nothing like ours.
3. The citizens can report their experiences; if the Nation-Brain shares their experiences, why can't it report them too?
4. Consciousness in the Nation-Brain would be explanatorily redundant.

Defending combinationism therefore means defending the consciousness of the Nation-Brain, and in the remainder of this section I will consider and rebut the above four objections.

6.1.1. WHERE DOES THE EXTRA CONSCIOUSNESS FIT?

Consider first the following sort of objection:

> *The Nation-Brain is nothing over and above the citizens, so it cannot have an extra consciousness in addition to theirs. Yet its consciousness is not identical to any of theirs, so it is not conscious at all.* (See, e.g., Searle 1990, 404; List and Pettit 2011, 9)

This objection could be summed up by saying that consciousness belonging to the whole system has "nowhere left to fit." Its experiences are not those of any particular citizen, since it may feel and think very different things from any of them. Yet it also cannot be somewhere "outside" them, since it is simply them and nothing more.[3] If the Nation-Brain were conscious, it would be a mysterious emergent mind somehow floating free above those of the citizens, or else it would be one of them. But the combinationist theory developed over the past few chapters shows that this need not be the case: the consciousness of the Nation-Brain is entirely grounded in and explained by that of its citizens, and all of its experiences are composed of subsets of their experiences.

Which of their experiences? To answer this question we must look primarily at what information is integrated across the Nation-Brain, which means looking at what information from each citizen is broadcast to others. What is primarily broadcast is the citizen's motor experiences of pressing buttons; these in turn carry information about their causes, namely the signals that citizen had received (i.e., certain perceptual experiences, seeing the lights flash or similar), and whatever mediated between the two (i.e., certain thoughts, memories, and decisions, such as "Ah, the gamma pattern—that means I need to signal to devices, um, let me see, 2435, 5784, and 2049!"). Call these three things together—the perceptions, the mediating thoughts, and the resultant actions—the citizen's "radio experiences." My first claim about the psychofunctional Nation-Brain is that those of its experiences which play a role in its intelligent functioning are composed exclusively out of the citizen's radio experiences.

---

[3] Strictly, of course, the system also includes various radio devices, but to pose our question most sharply we should keep their information-processing role to a minimum: the citizens must choose the right buttons to press, not allow any automatic programming in the radios to do it for them.

This excludes most of the experiences the citizens have (everything they think and feel and perceive that is unrelated to this zany scheme we have somehow compelled them to participate in) because information about them is not integrated and they consequently cannot be accessed by the whole for any cognitive purpose. Whether these informationally isolated experiences nevertheless still belong to the Nation-Brain depends on the choice discussed in section 5.5 of chapter 5, between "inclusionary" and "exclusionary" approaches to combinationism, divided by whether being an intelligent subject precludes having inaccessible experiences. If it does, then the Nation-Brain shares only the citizens' radio experiences, and no others. If it does not, then the Nation-Brain's experiences are simply all of those of its parts: a few billion consciousnesses experienced all at once.

Let us dwell on the inclusionary option a bit. This description seems ludicrous at first. Surely, someone might object, there is no coherent experience answering to the description "experiencing the full mental life of a few billion different people at once." In a sense this objection is correct: there is no *coherent* experience here, because there is not enough information integration among these billions of conscious fields to make them align in any definite way. For the most part, they blend together, their joint content massively indeterminate, their joint quality nothing more than a constant inarticulate background blur. Only a few of these experiences are informationally integrated (the radio experiences), and so only a few of them combine in determinate ways so as to "line up" and reinforce each other. These experiences, and only they, coalesce out of the haze: the architecture of the system manages to bring a particular pattern into stable clarity, and the one it brings to clarity is the only one that can subserve intelligent functioning. And if the exclusionary approach is right, then this stable clear pattern is the entirety of the whole's consciousness.

6.1.2. HOW CAN THE WHOLE HAVE UNIFIED EXPERIENCES?

Consider next the following sort of objection:

> *The radio experiences of the citizens are not unified, since they belong to many different people. Thus if the Nation-Brain shared them, its consciousness would be massively disunified, and thus nothing like our own.*

What is true is that the informational interactions among different citizens' radio experiences subserve intelligent functioning only at the Nation-scale, not at the citizen-scale. But the pure functionalist and the panpsychist will likely have different ideas of what this means. The panpsychist, appealing to the arguments of chapter 3, can say that we need to distinguish phenomenal unity (i.e., subsumption by a state that is phenomenally conscious—a division-invariant relation) from richer relations like access-unity or global consistency (which are division-relative). Regarding phenomenal unity, the experiences of the citizens were already unified even before the Nation-Brain was established, just on account of their being interacting parts of a fundamentally conscious world. But the interactions among them were so information-poor that this unity did not enable access-unity (which is needed for an introspective impression of unity) at any scale above that of a single citizen: hence no subject was able to report the unity between different citizens' experiences. And this is still the case for the citizen's non-radio-related experiences. But with the radio devices being used, the citizen's many experiences are now subsumed by a state which is able to subserve intelligent functioning, and in particular produce introspective impressions of itself as a single state, at the nation-scale.

The pure functionalist, by contrast, will want to explain phenomenal unity by reference to division-relative relations like access-unity, and so for them phenomenal unity will also be division-relative. Since the radio experiences are functionally related in the right ways at the nation-scale but not at the citizen-scale, this view implies that the experiences will be phenomenally unified relative to the one scale but not the other. Since the radio connections are integrating information, they will still be "pre-phenomenally bound" relative to all scales, but only at the scale of the whole Nation-Brain is this accompanied by phenomenal unity, and so only at this scale does this constitute representational unity.

What does this mean at the level of the individual citizens? If phenomenal binding involves informative mutual co-presentation, then my proposals in chapter 5 suggest that each citizen's radio experiences will co-present the others', which it seems plausible they will. Each citizen experiences the flashing lights and pressed buttons as manifestations of something larger, namely the radio cascades that cause or result from them. Each citizen, that is, will have some degree of awareness of the "thoughts" flowing through the system, so that their radio experiences are all mutually referential. This awareness of context will likely not be very informative, and may fall well short of what the citizens would be capable of if they dedicated themselves to understanding each other's participation in the Nation-Brain in detail. (This would be analogous to some of my neurons dedicating themselves to studying neuroscience, if that were possible.) Indeed, measured by degree of information shared, the unity between the radio experiences of one citizen and the next will be significantly less than that between the radio experiences of one citizen and other experiences of that citizen. But this does not impugn the relative unity of the Nation-Brain's consciousness, because the information integration between two citizens' radio experiences is equal (by stipulation) to that between the experiential contributions of two neuron firings in a single citizen's brain. And since there are as many citizens as neurons, this is the relevant comparison.

6.1.3. WHY CAN'T THE WHOLE REPORT ITS PARTS' EXPERIENCES?

A third objection might go as follows:

> *If the Nation-Brain were undergoing its citizens' radio experiences, then it would be able to report them, and we could ask it what lights particular citizens were seeing or what buttons they were pressing. But since it is functionally equivalent to a human being, we know it cannot tell us.*

All of the Nation-Brain's experiences that subserve intelligent functioning are composed of experiences of seeing some lights flash, recalling some instructions, deciding to follow them, and pressing some buttons. Yet if we ask it, via its robotic avatar, whether it feels as though it is seeing lights flash and pressing buttons, it will usually say no, just as the human being it is modeled after would usually say no.[4] Yet the radio experiences have their phenomenal character essentially: what it is like to undergo each of them cannot vary between the distinct subjects who undergo it. So it might seem that the Nation-Brain must both feel like it is seeing lights and pressing buttons, and not.

The solution to this seeming paradox comes from the doctrines of confusion and blending laid out in chapter 4. Just as each distinguishable experience of ours corresponds to a great many synaptic firings, which we cannot distinguish from one another and which consequently are experienced together as a single blended quality, so the Nation-Brain experiences cascades of many radio experiences as phenomenal blends, unable to distinguish different citizens' experiences from one another (and certainly unable to discern their internal components—particular seeings-of-this-light and pressings-of-this-button) and thus unable to discern or report that they have the character of visually perceiving something and pressing buttons in response.

But the Nation-Brain's sensation is not just any confused blur: it is a blur with a specific quality, based on the quality of the radio experiences and the particular ways they cause one another. Whatever a particular distinguishable sensation feels like for the Nation-Brain, it feels that way because of what the radio experiences

---

[4] It will say yes when we have given the avatar a radio device of its own, but this is no more relevant to the metaphysics of its consciousness than giving a normal human some brain matter to feel with their fingers.

feel like, filtered and blended based on the way information is integrated among the relevant citizens. Most likely, none of its sensations will feel quite the same as our sensations do; in particular, if panpsychism is true, then our experiences are blended out of whatever experiences a neuron has when it fires, while its experiences are blended out of light-seeing and button-pushing experiences. Yet because the informational structure is the same in both cases, there will be structural similarities in the number of qualities that can be distinguished, in which qualities are similar to which, and so on.

6.1.4. WHY BOTHER WITH CONSCIOUSNESS IN THE WHOLE?

A final objection might run as follows:

> *The consciousness of the Nation-Brain is superfluous: it does no causal or explanatory work that is not already done by the consciousness of its component citizens.*

This objection takes the possibility of reduction (deducing every fact about the Nation-Brain from facts about its citizens and their relations) as a reason for elimination (denying that the Nation-Brain is conscious). If this sort of reasoning were valid, however, the possibility of deducing every fact about, say, an organism from facts about its component molecules would be a reason for denying that organisms exist (cf. Huebner 2014, 126–182). I take it that such a deduction is possible in principle, but that organisms obviously exist, and conclude that reduction is not enough for elimination.

This objection would be well-motivated if the Nation-Brain's consciousness were not fully grounded in that of the citizens; if they were metaphysically independent things then we would have to ask which of the two was causally responsible for any given result. But in fact this question makes no more sense for the Nation-Brain and its citizens than it does for a brain and its neurons. Of course there may remain some questions of "whole or parts" that do make sense, such as whether an explanation pitched at one level is more illuminating or more efficient or more satisfying than an explanation pitched at another level. But in this sense it is clear that the Nation-Brain will sometimes be the right level at which to explain things, since explanations that mention only the citizens will be swamped with irrelevant detail, just like explanations of human action that mention only neurons. Answering "Why did the avatar ask for my phone number?" with "Well, citizen 2567348 pressed buttons 32, 3, and 75, and that sent signals to citizens 5543, 890897, and 43455, who then . . ." may be a strictly true answer, but it is not a useful or satisfying explanation compared to "Because the Nation-Brain wants to date you."

In summary, functionalist combinationism suggests that there is indeed something it is like to be the (psychofunctional) Nation-Brain. It is either like being billions of different people all at once (the inclusionary option), or it is only the determinately structured aspects of the latter (the exclusionary option). Either is hard to make sense of, because simply superimposing billions of streams of consciousness will, by default, have the effect of blurring out every interesting detail of each. What gives the Nation-Brain experiences with complex determinate content is that out of this vast tissue of overlain experiences, certain patterns coalesce because of the way that certain of the billions of streams are aligned with one another. The form of these coalescing patterns depends on how information is integrated, but what fills out the pattern is the consciousness inherent in the system's parts, namely the citizens who compose it.

6.2. Composite Subjectivity in Social Groups

The Nation-Brain is a thought experiment, but we can also ask about composite subjectivity in actual nations, and more broadly in social groups like corporations, communities, and couples.[5] We can begin by asking how such entities, considered as putative conscious subjects, differ from the Nation-Brain.

6.2.1. INFORMATION INTEGRATION IN NATION-BRAINS AND NATIONS

First, the Nation-Brain plausibly integrates more information as a whole. By stipulation, it integrates as much information on the nation-scale as a human brain does on the brain-scale, while most actual nations arguably integrate significantly less. Consider: if we made some arbitrary intervention on one individual or small group, how much would the behavior of a randomly chosen other citizen be affected, and how much would the way it was affected depend on the particular sort of intervention we made? Some interventions would produce noticeable effects (e.g., a particularly gruesome mass murder might cause news reports), but most would not—most changes to the mind or body of most individuals would make only a negligible difference to the lives of most other individuals. In pre-twentieth-century societies this would be even more true, and in a random large group of people (as opposed to a nation) even more.

---

[5] I will focus on nations for simplicity, but any large group whose members interact frequently would do as well (corporations, provinces, cities, or even arbitrary chunks like "everyone in Southern England but not in London").

At the same time, actual nations make much more use of the cognitive capacities of their parts than the Nation-Brain. The Nation-Brain, as befits a hyperbolic thought experiment, treats its members as mere button-pushers, following mechanical rules and responding only to lights flashing on their handheld devices. In effect, it tries to make them behave like neurons, and thus ignores all the ways that their capacities exceed those of neurons. Actual nations can afford no such wastefulness. In real groups, more of the information in each individual's brain can *potentially* be integrated into the system's functioning, because the channels of information transfer between citizens are richer and more flexible than the button-pushing that the Nation-Brain relies on. In fact these channels are simply our familiar modes of human communication, chief among them language and the kind of face-to-face interaction in which we "read" the moods, intentions, and other mental states in someone's expression, body, voice, etc. Although our everyday lives often acquaint us with the limitations of these methods, they are really remarkable compared to virtually anything else known to exist. As Schwitzgebel (2015, 1707) says:

> People exchange a lot of information. How much? We might begin by considering how much information flows from one person to another via stimulation of the retina. The human eye contains about 10^8 photoreceptor cells. Most people in the United States spend most of their time in visual environments that are largely created by the actions of people (including their own past selves). If we count even 1/300 of this visual neuronal stimulation as the relevant sort of person-to-person information exchange, then the quantity of visual connectedness among [the USA's 3×10^8 citizens] is similar to the neuronal connectedness within the human brain (10^{14} connections). Very little of the exchanged information will make it past attentional filters for further processing, but analogous considerations apply to information exchange among neurons.

The familiar consequence of these connections is that humans living in societies can develop an incredibly rich idea of each other's experiences, and of how their own experiences relate to theirs. We can have experiences like, for example, competitive gameplay, in which every step of our strategic thinking and feeling is inflected by our awareness of what our opponent is thinking and feeling, based both on past experience with them and on ongoing observation of their moves and demeanor. As a result, the experiences of a small set of people interacting in a real society could potentially form a complex experience with a more complex determinate content than the same people could in the Nation-Brain, where each knows the others only as the anonymous receivers of the signals they send, and the anonymous senders of the signals they receive.

Because of their capacity to make fuller use of the information-processing and information-sharing capacities of individual citizens, actual groups could in principle come to have a composite subjectivity that far exceeds an individual's in complexity and power (and which consequently also exceeds the Nation-Brain's). But in practice this potential is largely unrealized, for at least the following two reasons. First, while humans are very good at integrating information with individual others, their methods of doing so don't scale up very well. While two people might readily establish a detailed shared understanding of an environment, task, or topic, it is much harder for ten people, even harder for a hundred, and so on (cf. Shapiro 2014). By contrast, that Nation-Brain's mechanisms, which seem less impressive at small scales, are better at coordinating functions and integrating information across the entire system. (They are, in fact, precisely as good at that as our neural mechanisms.) Second, humans largely serve their own, individual goals, which only sometimes require integrating information with others, and often strongly tell against doing so. Our brains work very differently: neurons do not decide on each occasion whether signaling to others is "worth it" for that neuron.[6] So the kind of superhuman mega-intelligence which could in principle arise from human social groups would require radical transformations both in the mechanisms by which members interact (they would need to scale better) and in the incentives for which members act (they would have to secure patterns of behavior that prioritized system-scale over individual functioning). Perhaps the future of neuroscience, information technology, or social science will yield developments that might effect such transformations. I take no stand here on whether such a speculative "collectivization" of the human mind deserves to be seen as utopian, as dystopian, or as a mix of both; I intend simply to throw our actual situation into sharper relief by comparison.

6.2.2. WHAT IS IT LIKE TO BE A NATION?

What does the generally low level of information integration in human societies mean for their collective consciousness? It may well mean that they are not

---

[6] Of course, each individual neuron's interests are inextricably bound up with the functioning of the whole; they do not have the option of living independently and cannot procure food, oxygen, or anything else beneficial to them except by procuring them for the whole organism. This just illustrates the point being made: human nations do not act like human brains, because humans do not act like neurons, because they *are* capable of (more or less) independent existence, or at least of ditching one set of cooperators for another. The establishment of such identity of interests at the *genetic* level seems to play a crucial role in the establishment of large-scale biological systems, such as multicellular organisms, eusocial insect colonies, and even the eukaryotic cell (see Godfrey-Smith 2012).

conscious at all: if pure functionalism is true, there is a (vague) minimum level of functional organization and complexity required for any kind of consciousness, and it may well be that no human groups currently meet that level (though see Schwitzgebel [2015] for an argument that they do). To put the same point differently, individual experiences may never meet conditional experience inheritance's standards of control, sensitivity, and coordination relative to any actual social groups. But even then, there remains the possibility of a group becoming sufficiently better organized than our present-day groups—and if panpsychist combinationism is true, then even present-day nations will be conscious, though perhaps they do not qualify as intelligent subjects. So let us just ask: If a human nation were conscious, what would it be like to be it?

Start with the many consciousnesses of the citizens, considered as undergone by a single entity at once. For simplicity, let us first consider just two citizens' fields of consciousness, undergone together. Each is structured in the usual way: senses which disclose a continuous surrounding space, attention focused either on some aspect of this perceived world, or on some inner thought or mental image, and so on. If we try to imagine these undergone together—"superimposed" on one another, according to my favored metaphor—how should we line them up? Is the attentional focus of one phenomenally bound with the focus of the other? Do we superimpose their visual fields so that "up" and "down" coincide, or so that one is upside-down relative to the other? Or do we superimpose the visual field of one onto the bodily sensations of the other, so that each colored object seen by one is phenomenally bound to some portion of the other's skin? Questions like this abound and cannot be given any *a priori* answer. By default, the two fields blur together, so that the content of the total field is massively indeterminate and experienced as a blend of all the qualities of the experiences of both.

When the two people are actually interacting, they begin to somewhat integrate information about their minds, and this indeterminacy is correspondingly somewhat reduced. This involves each experiencing a form of co-presentation whereby their visual and auditory perceptions of the words or behavior of the other appear as revealed aspects of something with other experiences as its concealed aspect. Functionalist combinationism says that because their experiences integrate information and mutually co-present, they are pre-phenomenally bound; if they are also phenomenally unified they will be phenomenally bound, and thus representationally unified. Under normal circumstances two people's experiences are surely never sufficiently functionally unified to count as phenomenally unified by the standards of pure functionalist combinationism, though according to functionalist-panpsychist combinationism they are in fact phenomenally unified from the very beginning (like all experiences). If the latter is correct, then they do form a composite experience, with a somewhat determinate representational content. But since the average level of information integration in human societies is not very high, a great deal of indeterminacy remains. The composite experience might be compared to the feeling of looking around a foggy environment, with faint, confusing images appearing and disappearing out of the haze. (Of course it is not a visual image, so this analogy is quite limited.)

To make a nation an intelligent subject would require that it display intelligent functioning at the nation-level, which is arguably still a futuristic dream. But sometimes the mental states of members of some groups do inch a bit closer to group-level intelligent functioning, by guiding the activities of other individuals in unison with their individual subjects' activities, giving rise to a range of phenomena which have been studied under the heading of "collective intentionality."

6.2.3. COLLECTIVE INTENTIONALITY

The study of collective intentionality starts from the observation that in everyday life we routinely speak of, for example, a crowd trying to topple a statue, a company trying to maximize its profits, or an army trying to find out where its enemies are hidden. Obviously some of this everyday talk is simply anthropomorphism, or self-serving ideological blather (e.g., a politician attributing their popularity to having "tapped a reserve of almost-forgotten hope in the nation soul"), but recent philosophers have devoted considerable effort to defining conditions under which it is well-motivated and rigorously defensible. I will review three particular forms of collective intentionality which are studied in this literature, noting briefly how functionalist combinationists might think about the consciousness involved: I will label them "joint intentionality," "authority relations," and "joint commitment."

By "joint intentionality" I mean cases where multiple people all have mental states of the same sort with the same content, and stand in relations which allow the set of their matching states to play the same role in guiding behavior for all of them as it does for each of them. This has been discussed most fully in relation to joint intentions and their role in joint action. Intuitively, there is a difference between people doing something together and their doing the same thing independently, even if the bodily movements involved are identical. Even in simple cases, we can tell the difference between two people walking somewhere together and their merely walking to the same location beside each other (Gilbert 1990).[7]

---

[7] The step from joint action to joint intention is motivated by the fact that the joint/nonjoint distinction seems to apply only to intentional actions (no similar difference seems to exist between, say, falling together and falling individually).

Several rival accounts of joint intention have been offered,[8] but the one I prefer is Bratman's (1997, 2009, 2014), on which for people to jointly intend to do something is (roughly) for them each to intend that they all do it, for them each to intend this *because* the others do, and for each to know all this of the others. In short, a joint intention is a set of corresponding interdependent intentions. For our purposes the significant thing is that joint intentions involve information integration: since each must know that the others intend, and base their own intention on this knowledge, the mental state of each must reflect (carry information about) the mental state of the others. Each individual's experience accordingly features a highly informative form of co-presentation: they are indirectly aware of the others' intentions, as things-I-am-not-directly-aware-of, yet also have a fairly specific idea of the nature of those intentions, and base their own intentions on them.

According to the theory laid out in chapter 5, this means that from the whole's perspective, the experiences that relate to this joint intention (experiences of hoping, acting, monitoring progress, etc.) will connect in a relatively determinate way, potentially giving rise to a composite experience that is not simply a blend. Moreover, these interdependent experiences of the participants then serve a recognizable cognitive function, namely guiding action. So in cases of joint action, the massively confused experience of the group whose members act together begins to resolve itself a little. To put it very roughly, the more people who are involved, and the more sensitive each is to the others' progress, the more reasonable it becomes to say that the whole system (a nation, or whatever social group we are considering) consciously intends their goal and acts to achieve it.

What about states other than intentions? There is less work on this, and it is harder to identify a plausible set of sufficient or necessary conditions (but see Gilbert 2002; List 2018). Indeed joint intentions are likely to be the most common joint mental states, since intentions are the most directly action-guiding states, so people will most easily converge there when they need to work together. But people can also potentially be regarded as having, say, joint beliefs and desires, maybe even joint emotions, when people's individual instances of these states are connected in a way that lets them play the cognitive role typical of belief (or desire, emotions, etc.) for the whole group.

The second form of collective intentionality involves some individuals acting in a way that is guided by the mental states of other individuals, independently

---

[8] The views of Bratman and Gilbert (1990, 2000, 2002, 2009) receive the most discussion here, though I treat their accounts as accurate descriptions of two slightly different phenomena rather than rival accounts of a single phenomenon. Other approaches include those of Searle (1990), Tuomela (2007), and Tollefsen (2014).

of whether they themselves have a corresponding mental state of that sort. For instance, if A will obey any instruction B gives them, then B's intentions can guide both of their actions, independently of what intentions A has.[9] At the extreme, a whole nation might come to behave in a consistent, intelligent way because everyone there follows without question the instructions of a single dictator.[10]

Such "authority relations" allow the experiences of individuals to play cognitive roles in large-scale social systems. Yet the information integration involved might nevertheless be very modest, because those who obey get only the information about their particular tasks, and those who command get only the information of assent. The co-presentation involved is less informative: each knows that the other has some hidden inner life, but knows less of the content of this inner life.

A composite subject whose component subjects coordinate in this manner might consequently have a different sort of consciousness than one whose parts relied on joint intentionality. The former might be "phenomenally impoverished" relative to the latter, rather like if we sometimes had perceptions or emotions which felt "faint," dull, and affectless, but which still had the same effect on what we did and thought. In the extreme case of dictatorship described above, the nation would think and act on the basis of states it barely felt. That is not to say that these states are not conscious—the dictator is conscious, after all, and their experiences are inherited by the whole, so that the nation thinks and acts based on them. But the phenomenology of these experiences is not in proportion to their role. Thus even if a nation were to bend to the dictator's will perfectly, ensuring intelligent functioning, it would arguably not be an intelligent subject (or perhaps would be only a borderline case of one) for the same reason that the machine-functional Nation-Brain is not: its intelligent functioning is not based on conscious structure. It would be somewhere in between an intelligent subject and a "Blockhead."

A third form of collective intentionality arises when people jointly undertake to "act on" states that they all understand but which they may not individually feel. For instance, a committee might resolve that, when acting and speaking in their capacity as members of that committee, they will act and speak as though some proposition P is true, independently of whether most or any of them think that P is actually true. I will call this "joint commitment," borrowing the phrase

---

[9] It is not quite true that this is independent of A's intentions: A must still intend to follow B's instructions, and when B says "do X," A must form an intention to do X. The point is that A need not intend, or even know about, the whole structure and ultimate goal of B's plan.

[10] In saying that this would make the nation "behave intelligently" I mean simply that we could interpret it as doing things in order to accomplish a single set of goals, according to a single set of beliefs. Its behavior might nevertheless be ruinously stupid, either because the dictator was an idiot or because, lacking active contributions from any of the other individuals, they could not monitor national events or formulate national plans in adequate detail.

from Gilbert (1990, 2000, 2002, 2009), though applying it somewhat more narrowly than she does. On her account, any collective intentional state (a belief, an
intention, even an emotion) exists when two or more people jointly commit to
acting in accord with that state. I do not know if this is a good way of thinking
about collective intentionality in general, but it does seem a good model for cases
like the committee.

Joint commitments fit better than either joint intentionality or authority relations for interpreting things like laws, charters, contracts, and other written
documents which coordinate people's thoughts and action. If a number of people
have committed to a document which mandates that certain steps be taken to accomplish a certain goal, that can explain their acting to accomplish that goal by
means of those steps, even if none of them particularly care about that goal for its
own sake.

The component experiences involved in joint commitment are in some respects
not that different from those involved in authority relations: the individuals allow
their behavior to be guided by a certain mental state, while relating to it as something external and not their own. The difference is that these "other-directed"
states do not have any individual's mental state as their focus: there is no one who
commands, only many who obey. What was said above about collective intentionality based on authority applies even more here: the system functions intelligently
but may have impoverished phenomenology.

6.2.4. THE INSTABILITY OF REAL-WORLD GROUP MINDS

These three forms of collective intentionality are often combined (e.g., a
committee might act jointly to write a charter to direct the many other
individuals over whom it has authority). Ordinary human societies are a patchwork built up from diverse forms of social interaction, and so if a nation were
conscious it would have some degree of conscious structure, though a very different sort of structure from our own. In some cases particular institutions or
communities may even be engineered to have a sufficiently stable and consistent
set of dispositions that it makes sense to describe them as rational agents with a
single set of beliefs and desires which they consistently act on (cf. List and Pettit
2011; Tollefsen 2014).

But the extent of collective intentionality should not be overstated. In particular, episodes of collective intentionality tend to be less stable the larger in scale
they are, and so insofar as a nation could be said to have "thoughts," they will
often be too unpredictable and unstable for us to speak of stable dispositions like
beliefs or desires. Because the arising and subsiding of particular episodes of collective intentionality depends so heavily on the interplay of unpredictable factors

that the whole has no cognitive access to (i.e., the private decisions of individuals about how to interact with each other), the whole's stream of consciousness will lack coherence and stability. Moreover, even if a given collective state managed to persist for a long time, the *role* it could play would depend on its relation to other collective states; even if one institution, say, manages to retain a stable and cohesive plan of action for years, they will get little done except insofar as they can persuade, compel, or manipulate other parts of society. It is as though a person, even when they did manage to hold a single idea in mind for some length of time, then found that at different times this idea might or might not be reportable, or usable for planning, or suitable for recording into memory, or might be able to guide only behavior involving the left half of their body.

The resulting degree of instability, in both the arising and subsiding of thoughts and experiences and in the roles they play, makes the structure of any possible nation-consciousness barely imaginable to compulsively coherent beings like us humans. Perhaps the best analogy is with "lowered modes" of consciousness, such as delirium, dreaming, epilepsy, or coma. Bayne and Hohwy (2016) discuss the challenges of defining and distinguishing such modes, proposing to do so by a mixture of whether complex contents can be represented, whether attention is controlled and distributed normally, and whether the contents of consciousness are available for the normal range of cognitive and behavioral uses (cf. Bhat and Rockwood 2007). A social group's consciousness, considered as a whole, will likely count as radically deficient on all three scores.

I said in chapter 1 that I think the widespread intuitive resistance to the very possibility of collective consciousness is partly driven by anti-combination, and thus mistaken. But I think resistance to the idea that actual human societies could be conscious has another, more correct basis. Even if human societies are, in the strict and fundamental sense, conscious (as functionalist-panpsychist combinationism says), their consciousness is rarely useful to think about. To explain why any particular event happens, it will almost always be more useful to appeal to facts about individuals. The instability of the "nation-mind" means that there are few useful generalizations that can be made about its cognitive functioning: whether it will have a certain thought, and what role that thought will play, depend too heavily on the unpredictable complexities of individuals or small groups and their alliances, friendships, feuds, moods, and estimations of personal cost and benefit from any given collective act. And if we need to make reference to the details of individuals and smaller groups anyway, we might as well just use them as our explanation.

Yet this lack of explanatory usefulness is not a reason to deny the *existence* of collective consciousness; it is only a lack of one sort of reason to posit it. If the existence or possibility of collective consciousness follows from the best meta-physics of consciousness—in particular, if it follows from the best explanation of what makes *us* conscious—then we should shrug and observe that many things exist which it is rarely useful to talk about.

6.3. Composite Subjectivity in the Split-Brain Patient

The results of severing the corpus callosum, which connects the two cere-bral hemispheres, are among the most perplexing phenomena in the study of the brain: a person who seems most of the time perfectly normal but at other times operates as though two quite separate agents lived in their head, responding to inputs from different subsets of the body's sense organs, using different subsets of the body's motor capacities. Since its first descrip-tion, this phenomenon has prompted philosophical discussion: the options canvassed include:

1. The two hemispheres are distinct subjects, with two separate streams of consciousness, who somehow coordinate their activities perfectly almost all the time (call this the two-subjects view, with the other seven being different one-subject views; see, e.g., Puccetti 1973, 1981; Schechter 2009, 2015).

2. There is one subject, who undergoes two distinct streams of consciousness, such that all the elements of each stream are unified with each other but not with those of the other stream (call this the two-streams view; see, e.g., Tye 2003; Bayne 2010).

3. There is one subject, who undergoes a single unified stream of consciousness but has an impaired ability to access all its contents together (call this the one-stream view; see, e.g., Bayne and Chalmers 2003; cf. Schechter 2010).

4. There is one subject, whose consciousness is partially unified, so that experiences based in different hemispheres, though not unified with each other, are both unified with certain core experiences possibly based in subcortical structures (call this the partial-unity view; see, e.g., Lockwood 1989, 1994; Hurley 1998).

5. There is one subject, who has two simultaneous streams of mental processing, of which one is conscious and the other unconscious at each moment, with consciousness switching between the two (call this the switch view; see, e.g., Levy 1990; Bayne 2008, 2010; cf. Schechter 2012b).

6. There is one subject, who has two streams of consciousness under experimental conditions when stimuli are carefully segregated between sense organs, but one stream the rest of the time (call this the contextualist view; see, e.g., Marks 1980; Tye 2003).

7. The left hemisphere (or more precisely, whichever one has language capacities) is a conscious subject, and the other hemisphere is an unconscious automaton (for discussion see Nagel 1971, 402–404; Tye 2003, 117).

8. The left (language-using) hemisphere is a conscious subject, and the other hemisphere, though conscious, does not have sufficiently unified experiences to qualify as a subject (for discussion see Nagel 1971, 403–405).

Functionalist combinationism does not by itself support one of these interpretations over the others; rather, it partially dissolves the seeming incompatibility between them, allowing us to see them as alternative ways of describing the same facts.

The upshot of combinationism is that we should think of the questions "How many subjects?" and "How many streams of consciousness?," posed about the split-brain case, in something like the way that we think of the question "How many brains?" This question is not easy to answer, but it is easy to leave unanswered: it does not demand a single definite answer because when we recognize the respects in which it is appropriate to describe the situation as involving one brain, and also recognize the respects in which it is appropriate to describe the situation as involving two brains, we have understood how things stand. It would be a mistake to insist on seeking for some further, objective fact—the number of brains. We can see that this would be misguided because we can see that there is a single physical system here which has many of the features associated with our concept "brain," and that it has two (overlapping) physical parts which each have many of the features associated with our concept "brain," and that this is all there is to the system. The fact that brain-like things can be parts of other brain-like things is crucial to this equanimity: combinationism allows us to take the same attitude toward subjects.

More precisely, I believe that views 1–5 of the above all contain important elements of truth, and that functionalist combinationism lets us affirm these all together. In this section I will first summarize the experimental results pertaining to split-brain patients, then review the ways that a functionalist combinationist could partly agree with each of the five noted views.

6.3.1. A QUICK OVERVIEW OF THE SPLIT BRAIN

First, the known facts. The cerebral hemispheres are connected by a bundle of nerve fibers called the corpus callosum, as well as by certain other connections, and most fundamentally by their both being linked to the nonhemispheric parts of the brain. The "split brain" results from severing the front part of the corpus callosum (with or without cutting certain other connecting areas), but leaves much of the subcortical brain intact; we have no evidence that the entire brain can be bisected without killing the patient. Thus there is an important sense in which it is misleading to think of the split-brain patient as having two complete and separate half-brains: what they have two of is what I will call "hemisphere systems," each consisting of the unsplit nonhemispheric parts and one or other cerebral hemisphere. Since the hemisphere systems both contain the nonhemispheric parts, they overlap and are not discrete from each other.

From cases where an entire hemisphere is destroyed or removed, we know that what remains—a single "hemisphere system"—can support more or less normal human consciousness by itself (albeit with various incapacities relating to, for instance, controlling both sides of the body). This is important, because it means that even non-panpsychists have good reason to regard hemisphere systems as themselves candidates for being (intelligent) conscious subjects. Hemispheres by themselves, without the nonhemispheric parts, seem incapable of doing anything interesting, and so we might doubt that they are conscious subjects (unless we are panpsychists and prepared to ascribe some form of subjecthood very widely).

Most of the time split-brain patients show few abnormalities in thought or action: the experiments that make the split-brain patient so perplexing involve making efforts to present different stimuli to the sensory channels which primarily feed to each hemisphere; for the left hemisphere this includes touch over most of the right side of the body, the right ear, the right half of the visual field, and the left nostril; for the right hemisphere, the reverse. Under these circumstances, we find striking dissociations, in particular failures of access and representational unity. Access-unity fails in the sense that certain contents are unavailable for guiding the same processes as other contents; for example, when we show the word "key" to the right hemisphere, it cannot be verbally reported (because the left hemisphere controls language), but if we ask the patient to pick up the object they saw the word for, and let them use their left hand (controlled by the right hemisphere), they will readily pick out a key. Representational disunity here means the apparent lack of any consciousness of conjoint contents spread across both hemispheres; for example, if the patient is shown the word "keyring," with "key" going to the right hemisphere and "ring" going to the left, they will pick out a key (with their left hand) and a ring (with their right hand), but not a keyring. They will even report having seen only the word "ring," and deny having seen either "key" or "keyring." What are we to make of this?

6.3.2. THE TRUTH IN THE TWO-SUBJECTS VIEW

Let us begin with the two-subjects view. On this account there are two conscious beings at work in any given split-brain case: one which undergoes the experiences corresponding to neural activity across the left hemisphere and the nonhemispheric parts (call it "Lefty"), and one which undergoes the experiences corresponding to neural activity across the right hemisphere and the nonhemispheric parts (call it "Righty"), with any experiences corresponding to activity just across the nonhemispheric parts being shared by both subjects. Let us use the term "hemisphere subjects" for the type of thing that Lefty and Righty are. Lefty perceives everything coming into the right-hand set of sense organs, and responds as best it can using the right-hand set of motor organs, while Righty does the same with the left-hand sets.

We can tell that Lefty and Right are distinct, on the two-subjects view, because under experimental conditions we can in effect address "questions" (stimuli) to them independently and receive different sets of "answers" (responses). But most of the time their distinctness is hidden by the near-perfect synchronization of their activities, accomplished by some mixture of subcortical connections (that allow the activity in one hemisphere to affect that in the other), subcortical processing (neural activity in their shared part, which likely plays a significant role in integrating things like motor control and emotion), and detection of peripheral sensory cues (e.g., Lefty picks up on what Righty is doing, by seeing the left hand's movements in the right visual field). Nagel (1971, 406) considers this view, pointing out that sometimes two people do seem to work "as one," as in "pairs of individuals engaged in a performance requiring exact behavioral coordination, like using a two-handed saw, or playing a duet." Perhaps the two hemispheres are like this? But Nagel worries that this position is unstable: "If we decided that they definitely had two minds, then [why not] conclude on anatomical grounds that everyone has two minds, but that we don't notice it except in these odd cases because most pairs of minds in a single body run in perfect parallel" (409). I think Nagel's worry here is cogent (though for criticism see Schechter 2018): if we accept that there can be two distinct subjects despite its appearing for all the world as though there was only one, we seem to lose any basis for confidence that the same thing is not happening in other cases. He continues:

In case anyone is inclined to embrace the conclusion that we all have two minds, let me suggest that the trouble will not end there. For the mental operations of a single hemisphere, such as vision, hearing, speech, writing, verbal comprehension, etc. can to a great extent be separated from one another by suitable cortical deconnections; why then should we not regard each hemisphere as inhabited by several cooperating minds with specialized capacities? Where is one to stop? (Nagel 1971n11)

Where indeed? For a noncombinationist, the postulate of two minds is an alternative to the postulate of one mind, and the postulate of a dozen minds is an alternative to the postulate of two. And so the noncombinationist has to choose one specific number, while having just given up any basis for being confident in their choice. But while this is a problematic result for noncombinationists, it is no problem at all for the combinationist, whose ontology already allows for multiple distinct subjects making up larger composite subjects. The combinationist has no problem saying that the split-brain patient is two, or more, subjects because they have no problem saying that each of us is two, or more, subjects. That adds to, rather than replacing, the knowledge that each human being as a whole is a subject, just as our learning that our cells are to all intents and purposes organisms can add to, rather than replacing, the knowledge that each human being as a whole is an organism.

The presence of two subjects in the split-brain case is thus changed from a uniquely paradoxical fact into part of the unremarkable background. What is distinctive about the split-brain case, relative to the normal case, is not the presence of two subjects, but the change in their mode of interaction. Where before they accomplished a remarkable degree of information integration through multiple mechanisms including, in particular, the corpus callosum, now they must rely on fewer of those mechanisms and correspondingly integrate information less completely and less reliably, with more dependence on external feedback (like seeing the left hand in the right visual field) and redundancies of information in their environment (like a scene which looks the same way when it falls in the right visual field at one moment as it does when it falls in the left visual field a moment later). In experimental contexts, they are deprived of these environmental feedbacks and redundancies, and we observe the resulting failures of integration.[11]

---

[11] It is rather as though we had two identical twins (the hemisphere subjects) pretending to be a single mind directly controlling two bodies, but in fact using a combination of discreet mobile phones and a well-developed ability to read the other's body language. Cutting the corpus callosum is like taking away their phones, and stimulus-segregating experiments are like putting a screen between them to stop them from watching each other's body language: neither by itself will impair their ability to accurately report the other's experiences, but doing both will. (The analogy is poor, of course, in that the twins

6.3.3. THE TRUTH IN THE ONE-SUBJECT VIEW

But one-subject views are not for this reason mistaken. There is a good basis for calling the split-brain patient a single subject, and for talking about what "he" or "she" is experiencing—just as there is a good basis for calling someone with an un-split brain a single subject. The most direct argument for a single subject is that this is overwhelmingly how both the patients themselves and all those who interact with them think of the case. That is a relevant consideration not because what people spontaneously think is always right, but because it reflects the explanatory and predictive usefulness of thinking of them as a single subject—as a single planner, a single rememberer, a single holder of beliefs and desires, and so on. In particular, when we count people (in a vote, say, or to apportion resources), it will not be a good idea to count the split-brain patient as two, or three, or any greater number. The fact that "one subject" is the most explanatorily and predictively useful form of description is a powerful, though defeasible, reason to think that it captures something about reality.

Once again, the combinationist has no problem making sense of this. Although the loss of the corpus callosum impairs the hemisphere subjects' ability to integrate information between them, it still leaves them with plenty of channels for doing so, and so there is still a composite subject composed of them whose experiences have highly complex, determinate content. Moreover, for some reason yet to be fully understood, the cognitive uses made of this content are still largely cross-hemisphere; for example, the patient makes plans that will be carried out with both of their hands, and thus presumably with some involvement by both hemispheres, and things they have learned are available to guide the actions of both hemispheres. The main reason not to regard the whole system as a single conscious subject is simply that there are also good reasons to regard it as two subjects, and for a combinationist that is no reason at all, since the two subjects can compose a third, sharing their experiences.

6.3.4. ONE-STREAM, TWO-STREAMS, AND PARTIAL-UNITY VIEWS

But what about the unity of consciousness? Even if we have answered the question "One subject or two?" with "Both!," there is still the question of whether the streams of consciousness associated with the two hemispheres are unified with one another (as the one-stream view holds), not unified with one another (as the two-streams view holds), or somewhere in between (as the partial-unity view holds).

---

must be imagined as knowingly seeking to deceive, while hemisphere subjects seem oblivious to their multiplicity—the reasons for this failure of self-knowledge will need to wait for chapter 7.)

There are compelling arguments that seem to point in all three directions. First, there is evidence of disunity that seems to tell against the one-stream view: the above-mentioned phenomena of functional and representational disunity. The argument against the one-stream view is simply this: surely if experiences in the two hemispheres were phenomenally unified, they would also be representationally unified and access-unified? If phenomenal unity doesn't secure such connections, what is the point of it (Bayne 2008, 286, 2010, 197–199)?

On the other hand, many functions do seem to remain representationally and behaviorally integrated in split-brain patients, though the details vary among individuals (Bayne 2008, 287–290; Schechter 2015; Pinto et al. 2017). Some can compare stimuli presented to the two hands, but not to the two halves of the visual field; that is, they can indicate whether their two hands are feeling similar things, but not whether the same images are appearing on both sides of their visual field (Gazzaniga and Freedman 1973). Since they can also indicate whether the right hand is feeling something similar to what is seen in the right visual field (and the same on the left), this seems to show an intransitive pattern of comparative capacities. There is also the fact that some sensory information is not hemisphere-specific, such as the sense of touch in the head and neck. This poses a challenge to the two-streams model, since if the best explanation for representational and access-disunity is phenomenal disunity, it seems that the best explanation for representational and access-unity is phenomenal unity. When normal people judge whether two stimuli are similar, they do it by having experiences of each, and having a subsuming experience that unifies both. Why think that split-brain patients do it in a different way?[12]

The upshot of these two sets of evidence seems to be that some experiences of the split-brain patient are phenomenally unified, and others phenomenally disunified, as the partial-unity view says. But the partial-unity view is vulnerable to its own "objection from inconceivability," based on its treating phenomenal unity as nontransitive (Bayne 2010, 43–45). What is it like to be the split-brain subject, on the partial unity view? Suppose there are three experiences, A, B, and C, where A and B are unified, and B and C are unified, but not A and C. If the split-brain patient has one phenomenal field that contains A and B, that field cannot also contain C (since A and C are not unified). Yet if they have another phenomenal

---

[12] It should be recognized that there are various cases in which split-brain patients have displayed apparently unified thought or action, but later been found to have accomplished this integration by indirect means, such as by having one hemisphere direct the eyes to a certain target based on information it possesses, and the other infer that information from observing where its eyes are pointed. But there are also many displays of unity that remain even after care is taken to prevent such cross-cuing. See Schechter (2015) for fuller discussion.

field that contains only B and C, we leave out A, and moreover they seem to be experiencing B twice over. (How would their consciousness be different if B were two distinct experiences with the same character, one unified with A and one unified with C?) In short, there is no set of experiences that can be identified as "what it is like to be" that subject. The set {A, B, C} is not fully unified, and so has no overall phenomenal character, while both {A, B} and {B, C} leave something out. So there appears to be no coherent way to conceive of this subject's experience from the inside.

The choice among these three views largely depends on the question of how phenomenal unity relates to other unity relations, and combinationism is compatible with different answers to this question. Phenomenal unity might be distinct from, and dissociable from, other unity relations; panpsychist combinationism takes this view, and concludes that phenomenal unity is likely pervasive in the material world. This suggests the following view: all the split-brain patient's experiences are phenomenally unified (just as all experiences are), but richer unity relations (access-unity, representational unity) hold only in the "Y-shaped" pattern claimed by the partial unity account. Experiences based in the nonhemispheric parts are richly unified with those based in the right hemisphere and with those based on the left hemisphere, but the latter two are not richly unified with one another (though they would be in an intact brain).

The view suggested by functionalist-panpsychist combinationism is technically a "one-stream" view, since it affirms phenomenal unity between the hemisphere subjects, but it is in some ways more like a partial-unity view. Phenomenal unity in the split-brain seems less significant if such unity is everywhere, and the more significant sorts of unity are admitted to hold only within a hemisphere, or between a hemisphere and the nonhemispheric brain areas.

Considered as a partial-unity view, functionalist-panpsychist combinationism provides a distinctive answer to the objection from inconceivability, concerning what it is like to be the split-brain patient as a whole. They experience the whole set of experiences belonging to both hemispheres, but in such a way that the hemisphere-specific experiences are only weakly, if at all, phenomenally bound. Since they are are not "lined up" with one another, they have no determinate conjoint content. Of course, some information is integrated across the hemispheres, and some experiences may be primarily dependent on subcortical structures; these will have definite content and structure from the whole's perspective, and so can be unproblematically ascribed to them. But even though these are continuous with the experiences specific to the hemispheres, the latter are blurred out by their low-information interactions, so that to the extent that the experiences based in the two hemispheres differ, the split-brain patient undergoes neither with any distinctness.

What if phenomenal unity is not a distinct, primitive relation but instead more tightly bound up with functional and representational relations (as pure functionalist combinationism says)? Then whether the split-brain patient has unified consciousness depends on the details of those relations—what kinds of interaction, what kinds of information transfer, what kinds of mutual accessibility are required to set up phenomenal unity? Are they transitive or not? Is there a single set of necessary relations, or are there many different ways to get phenomenal unity? To these questions of detail pure functionalist combinationism offers no specific answer, and so it does not by itself decide among one-stream, two-streams, and partial-unity accounts.

What combinationism adds to the debate is that it treats conscious unity as both a between-subjects relation and a within-subject relation. This means that one-stream and partial-unity views become compatible with two-subjects views as well as one-subject views (and, indeed, with three-subjects views). Each hemisphere system might be a conscious subject and nevertheless have all or some of their experiences phenomenally, functionally, or representationally unified with those of the other hemisphere system.

What is this like—what is it like to be a hemisphere subject in (say) a phenomenally unified split brain? Functionalist combinationism suggests that it is like undergoing a set of experiences all richly unified with one another (experiences based in that one hemisphere and in the nonhemispheric parts), but also having an unusual sort of co-presentation, reflecting the impact of the other hemisphere's experiences. Since these other experiences are richly unified with experiences based in the nonhemispheric parts, but not with experiences based in the other hemisphere, they will be informatively co-presented by the former but not by the latter. For an idea of what this might mean, consider an example where the patient feels a touch moving across their face (processed subcortically, at least at first) while also seeing the object that touches them as it moves from their left visual field to their right visual field (processed first in the right hemisphere, then in the left). Assuming that there is no integration of contents between the hemispheres here, and assuming that the moving object is in fact seen *as* the source of the touch, one hemisphere subject, Righty, will be conscious at first of being touched by a thing they can see, and then of being touched by the same thing, which they cannot see. This much is not so strange; after all, sometimes we see and feel something, and then feel it continuing to touch us while out of sight. What is strange is that even when Righty has no visual experience of the object, they still feel it *as* something also seen: their tactile experience co-presents a visual experience of that object, and does so quite informatively—the character of Righty's tactile experience reflects that of the visual one just as much when Righty is not undergoing that visual experience as when they are. Yet at the same time the visual experiences they do have (of items in the left visual field) do not co-present any further visual experiences: they carry no information about what is appearing in the right visual field, even though what is appearing there is precisely the object which is "felt as also seen."

Neither the perspective of the whole split-brain subject (with massive indeterminacy between two very complex and definite states) nor that of the hemisphere subjects (with a highly informative co-presentation of something that is not actually experienced) is familiar to us or easy for us to imagine. They both differ from our everyday experience, in which we are neither split internally (unlike the split-brain patient) nor tightly linked to an external subject (unlike the hemisphere subjects). This strangeness, together with the anti-combination intuition, contributes to making the split-brain case so intensely puzzling.

6.3.5. THE TRUTH IN THE SWITCH VIEW

Finally, what about the switch view? This takes its cue from evidence showing that when given certain combinations of left-side and right-side stimulation, split-brain patients seem able to respond only to those on a particular side, with no response to the other stimulus even by the relevant hemisphere's motor organs, even though there would be such a response were the other stimulus presented by itself (Levy 1977, 1990; cf. Teng and Sperry 1973). Following Levy, Bayne (2008, 2010) takes this to support the view that consciousness switches between largely independent streams of processing in the two hemispheres, so that the split-brain patient is first conscious of things on one side, then of things on the other, and so on—but never has any disunified experiences at any single moment. While this view can account for many of the data, it has the implausible implication that much of the content of a single subject's consciousness switches discontinuously several times a second; a version of the view which avoided or softened this implication would be preferable.

Fortunately, functionalist combinationism allows for such a version of the switch view. Since it allows for richer and poorer forms of conscious unity, it can make good sense of the experiences based in one hemisphere becoming, for some period of time, more closely unified with nonhemispheric functions and as a result having better access to various cognitive and behavioral processes, such as memory, report, and motor control. A moment later, that dominance might shift to experiences in the other hemisphere, with the first now being relatively isolated and inert. But we do not need this to be a sharp transition from consciousness to unconsciousness, or from unity to disunity; it can be a diminution along a continuum, in the degree of phenomenal binding between different sets of experiences.

From the perspective of the whole, the switch might be experienced as one set of contents becoming more determinately lined up with the nonhemispheric contents (which are always highly determinate), "coming into sharper focus," so to speak, while the other set fades and blurs a little. In everyday contexts this makes very little difference, because so much of the content in both hemispheres is very similar (with no pesky experimenters trying to segregate inputs). In experimental contexts, there is a significant difference in the experiences before and after a given switch—though even then, there will not be a corresponding experience of difference, since split-brain patients appear entirely oblivious to their own condition until confronted with evidence. This seems odd at first, until we remember that making judgments about change—*noticing* that experiences have changed—is itself one of the cognitive functions which the hemispheres seem to carry out individually, and which in this case neither can carry out by itself.

What makes the split-brain patient perplexing is not simply that it is hard to say whether there are two of something there or just one—this sort of difficulty is common and banal. We might look up at the sky to count the clouds and not be sure whether two partly connected masses of vapor should be called "one cloud" or "two clouds," and then shrug and get on with our day; both descriptions capture something, and we are under no pressure to choose one and reject the other once and for all. What is deeply perplexing about the split-brain patient is that the things we do not know how to count are conscious subjects, and the only way to get the same equanimity about different counts of subjects as we do about different counts of clouds is to adopt combinationism.

6.4. Composite Subjectivity in the Typical Human Brain

What about those of us whose brains have not been split or otherwise tampered with? If "being conscious" is an intrinsic property, and if hemisphere subjects are conscious when they operate in isolation (as the survival of hemispherectomy patients, who lose one hemisphere, suggests), then it seems to follow that we are each three overlapping subjects: two hemisphere subjects and a whole brain. Indeed, if constitutive panpsychism is true, then we are many more subjects than that. But let us start with the relationship between the hemisphere subjects: exploring that will cast light on how we might be even more radically composite.

Moreover, in exploring these possibilities we will discover a novel response to certain arguments advanced by Daniel Dennett (1991), which aim to show that there is no objective fact about what someone is conscious of, because there is no single perfectly integrated stream of processing in the brain: functionalist combinationism allows us to accept much of the substance of Dennett's proposal (what he calls the "multiple drafts" theory) while remaining realists about consciousness.

6.4.1. PHENOMENAL BINDING BETWEEN HEMISPHERE SUBJECTS

To understand the relation between hemisphere subjects, consider again the case where the words "key" and "ring" are flashed to the left and right visual fields. A split-brain patient has a visual experience of "key," which they understand as being about keys, and a visual experience of "ring," which they understand as being about rings; what the corpus callosum accomplishes for a normal subject is that these two visual experiences form a single experience of "key ring," which they understand as being about keyrings. To see what this means for the hemisphere subjects, we must crack open this complex experience and analyze how its parts are related.

According to functionalist combinationism, the normal brain's representational unity among the experiences of "key" and "ring" is a matter of informative co-presentation: each experience referring to the other's content as something continuous with its own, but not given directly through it. So the visual experience of the word "key" presents that word as the left-hand part of something. Rather than presenting the other, right-hand part of that thing, this experience points outside itself to (co-presents) the experience of "ring," which correlatively presents that word as the right-hand side of something, and points back to the first experience as what presents the other, left-hand part of it. And the associated awareness of the words' meanings shows the same structure, though here the relationship between the two contents is harder to label than mere spatial proximity: roughly it is that the rings are rings *for* keys, or rings whose function is somehow key-related.[13] Thus the experience of seeing "key" as being about keys is also an experience of seeing it as being about the key-relatedness of some other object, though it does not itself present that object; it merely refers outward to the experience of seeing "ring" as being about rings, which in turn is an experience of seeing "ring" as being about rings-for-some-particular-purpose, and refers back to the first experience to specify which purpose.

---

[13] What I have said here treats "keyring" as a compositional term synonymous with "ring for keys"; in practice our experience of seeing keyrings and hearing them called "keyrings" gives us to some extent a noncompositional grasp on what "keyring" means. To avoid unnecessarily complicating my analysis I have ignored this fact: we may suppose our subject has not previously encountered keyrings.

All this is experienced by the whole person. What about the hemisphere subjects? Supposing that the detection and interpretation of each word occurs in only one hemisphere, we might conjecture that they each experience only one half of the above set of experiences.[14] So Lefty, for instance, seeing only the right visual field, will have an experience of the word "ring," presented as the right-hand side of a phrase involving another word, and will experience it as being not just about rings, but about rings that are meant for some purpose specified by the other word in the phrase. This is not so hard to imagine: we often see part of a phrase while knowing or assuming that there is more of it unseen, perhaps hidden behind a barrier, and we might in some cases even have a fairly definite idea of how the unknown meaning of the unseen word connects with the meaning of what we do see. What is perhaps a little stranger is that neither hemisphere subject does what we might do in such a situation: wonder what the other word is, and try to find out. Neither seems aware that the further experiences their own experience co-presents belong to another subject. Presumably the reason for this is that the signals they get from the other hemisphere not only give their experience the character of indicating something outside itself, but somehow satisfy, or preempt, any impulse to seek out that something else; because of the way each interacts with the other, both are oblivious to the fact that they are only half of the whole cognitive system. Although there are multiple subjects, their self-consciousness is of only one subject (cf. Uddin et al. 2005; Schechter 2018, 156–180). The explanation of this mutual obliviousness will have to wait for chapter 7's discussion of self-consciousness.

Comparing the relation between hemisphere subjects with and without an intact corpus callosum shows us a particularly clear case of phenomenal binding. Of all the things that Lefty is conscious of, it is the experience of "ring" in particular that is phenomenally bound together with a particular experience of Righty's, namely that of "key." What allows for this specificity of binding is (to label it roughly) the integration of information which is accomplished by the corpus callosum: discovering the details of how this is accomplished requires detailed neuroscientific study. Without this integration of information, the elements of Lefty's experience would have no specific tie to any specific elements of Righty's, so that Righty would have no determinate awareness of what Lefty is experiencing, and vice versa.

---

[14] In most people, the left hemisphere takes over most language-processing, though the right seems to be capable of a degree of comprehension even without production. Thus the left-hemisphere subject probably does experience the whole meaning "keyring," perhaps without seeing the whole image of the word. For simplicity of presentation I have neglected this asymmetry.

6.4.2. THE REPRESENTATIONAL STRUCTURE OF HUMAN EXPERIENCE

Phenomenal binding allows for the construction of complex content from simpler content, and so in principle could construct all the complex contents of human consciousness out of very simple components. The particular example considered here, of course, involves binding fairly complex individual contents (like the concept of a key, which depends on the idea of a lock, etc.) experienced by extremely complex subjects (large sections of the human brain) and so is not such a direct insight into the original construction of complex contents out of simpler ones. What it illustrates, however, is that contents can be combined in such a way that the result is more complex than either component. Other examples make the point more clearly: two component subjects, undergoing mutually referring experiences, one of a circle-as-left-hand-part-of-a-shape and one of a circle-as-right-hand-part-of-a-shape, would form a composite subject with an experience of an "infinity sign" type of shape. This might be true even if neither component subject by itself had the capacity to experience a shape like that but was limited to just circles.

Woodward (2015, 249–250) worries that there are still too many primitive types of content involved in human representation: since they are primitive they cannot be built up by phenomenal binding, and there are too many of them to be plausibly taken as metaphysically fundamental. One response for the functionalist combinationist would be to dispute the claim that this or that particular content-type was primitive, but in fact it is not necessary to engage in this kind of semantic trench warfare. The combinationist need not regard all those contents which are primitive for human development and reflection as primitive in a metaphysical sense: the fact that we cannot analyze a concept into further components does not by itself guarantee that it is not built up out of further components, for those components may be "hardwired" together within the human brain, so that they are robustly confused: only ever represented by us in combination, and never alone.[15]

Thinking about this sort of hardwiring is also relevant to a form of conscious structure mentioned earlier: the division of human experience into five sensory modalities.[16] What explains this division? Chapter 5's account of blending serves as a first step, since it explains how many different sorts of qualities can be experienced. But it is not a full answer, because some modalities feature more than one type of quality (e.g., vision presents both shapes and colors) and because some types of quality can appear in more than one modality (e.g., shape is detected by

---

[15] Strictly speaking, the relation in question would be something more than confusion: confusion means that two elements can be thought of only together, not apart; what I am suggesting is that elements can be thought of only together *in a particular relation*, not apart or in some other relation.

[16] Whether there are really five modalities, or some larger number, is disputed; for discussion see Grice 1962; MacPherson 2011a and b; Matthen 2015. Nothing I say here depends on the answer to this question.

both vision and touch). We see the contours of a fuller answer when we observe that the boundaries between modalities correspond to constraints on what can and cannot be phenomenally bound. For example, we always experience colors as colors of some shape, and never as colors of some sound.[17] We always experience loudness as the loudness of an event with a pitch, and always experience pitch as the pitch of an event with some degree of loudness. In short, there are constraints on the ways that particular experiential contents can be, or must be, phenomenally bound to particular others. These constraints constitute a division among modalities; for each modality there is a set of types of content that, whenever they occur, can or must be bound to each other but not to contents of different modalities.[18]

The distinctively combinationist spin on the above claims is simply that as well as the whole subject experiencing colored shapes there may also be component subjects whose experience is best characterized as something like "redness-as-the-color-of-something-shape-like."[19] Their relationship to other such subjects is thus somewhat like the relationship of one hemisphere subject to the other, but more fixed, since their experiences always co-present particular other subjects' experiences. This relationship is also somewhat like that between two people in a rigidly organized social group, each working on a particular part of a task while maintaining a sketchy background awareness of the larger task, including the portions the other is working on.

Why are our experiences bound in particular ways? Providing a detailed answer to that question is an ongoing area of research in psychology, on the toes of which I have no wish to step. But the basic type of explanation is clear and unmysterious: the causal architecture of the brain puts some neural structures in communication with others, so that information is integrated in certain ways rather than others.

---

[17] Creatures which did not work like this are possible, and perhaps synesthetes are an actual example (or perhaps they are not, and simply [for instance] *see* a color whenever they *hear* a sound). That would simply show that the configuration of modalities in those other subjects was different to the human norm.

[18] Perhaps we can account for the difference between visual shape and tactile shape by observing that some experiences of shape come to us bound with experiences of pressure, texture, etc., but not with experiences of color, while others come to us bound in the opposite way.

[19] This has much in common with Zeki's (2007) suggestion that multiple brain areas independently generate "microconsciousnesses" for different perceived qualities, which are only secondarily unified into "macroconsciousness." Note, however, that Zeki's view is that upon being unified together, the microconsciousnesses cease to exist in their own right (584), while functionalist combinationism says that they continue to exist as components of the macroconsciousness.

6.4.3. FUNCTIONALIST COMBINATIONISM AND THE MULTIPLE DRAFTS MODEL

The constitution of composite experience by many somewhat independent component subjects gives rise to a certain puzzling possibility: that the experiences of the brain's many parts might occur "out of sync" with the other experiences they co-present. For example, a particular object's color might be experienced by one part before the part which detects and experiences its shape has finished its information processing. Not only is this a possibility, but it seems likely to be an actuality. After all, from an evolutionary perspective, a brain which does not force all subsystems to wait for the slowest one will react faster, which might make the difference between life and death. Yet this makes it puzzling that the composite subject seems to experience a single consistent timeline, in which all the features of the object come together at once.

The "smearing-out" of content determinations across various subsystems comes out very clearly in certain perceptual illusions, like the "cutaneous rabbit" (Geldard and Sherrick 1972; Geldard 1982) and "color phi" (Wertheimer 1912; Kolers and von Grünau 1976), where two stimuli appearing at different locations in rapid succession give rise to an experience of a single object moving from one location to another. In the "cutaneous rabbit," for example, a tap at the wrist followed by a tap at the elbow gives rise to an experience as of multiple taps "hopping" along the forearm, even though the forearm was not touched.

What is puzzling about these cases is not simply that there is an illusion of a stimulus which was never present: that can be explained simply as brain systems making rapid, fallible "guesses" about the likely causes of inputs. What is puzzling is that the illusory experience seems to take place *before* the experience of the second actual stimulus, even though the latter is necessary for the illusion to take place at all. Thus it seems that the brain must be detecting the second stimulus, forming a "best guess" model of the cause, and generating an experience of the intermediate, illusory taps—and doing all of this *before* there is any conscious experience of the second tap. While it is not inherently implausible that there is some temporal gap between receiving a stimulus and undergoing an experience, the length of the gap in this particular case seems implausibly large—in particular, it would exceed the time that seems to be required for the construction of experience in other, simpler cases (see, e.g., Efron 1967; Pockett 2002, 2003). This might push us toward an alternative picture: the experience of the second stimulus occurs quickly, but as soon as some brain mechanism computes that the most likely cause of two such rapid stimuli is a single moving object, there is a swift revision of memory, so that the subject falsely remembers having experienced the intermediate stages of the movement.

Dennett (1991, 115–117) labels these two models the "Stalinesque" and "Orwellian," since the first carefully constructs a "show trial" (a false perception) and the second revises "historical records" (a false memory). Rather than supporting one over the other, however, he holds them up as a dilemma that a good theory should save us from. If the brain is a system designed by evolution to do things as quickly and efficiently as possible, why would it "wait" to experience the second stimulus, as the Stalinesque model posits? And equally, why would it bother making rapid, undetected, revisions to its memory records, as the Orwellian model posits? In fact, he thinks, once we reject the misleading image of a central location in the brain where conscious experience is "played" for an observer (the conscious subject), we see that neither the Stalinesque nor the Orwellian model is right. What happens, instead, is that multiple subsystems of the brain are processing different aspects of the stimulus in parallel, not waiting for one another but updating each other with their results as soon as those results are produced, and revising their results when those of other subsystems turn out to conflict. In this ongoing stream of multiple, changing, partial-content determinations, there is a rapid determination of certain features of the second stimulus, and then soon after a determination that the most likely cause was a single moving object, leading to a representation of intermediate stimuli that arises after the representation of the second actual stimulus, but is represented as occurring before it. There exist simultaneously two "drafts" of history: one featuring two stimuli, the other featuring three.

Most radically, Dennett proposes that there is no objective fact as to what the subject is conscious of at any particular moment: all of these multiple, sometimes conflicting content determinations carried out by different subsystems are equally good candidates for being called "what is experienced." Their interactions—checking for consistency and revising what is found inconsistent—are not "pre-publication" checks to ensure that a consistent total content is "presented to consciousness," because there is no further, distinct stage where conscious experience is "played": these messy changing parallel content determinations, these "multiple drafts," are all there is. Our impression of a single consistent timeline of consciousness arises because if someone else *asks* us "What did you experience?," or if we ourselves ask that question for some purpose, our various subsystems will settle on mutually consistent contents *to present as an answer*, i.e., to guide the behavior that answers the question, to be reported, remembered, or otherwise made use of. As Dennett (1991, 138) puts it, any "probe" we give the subject will elicit a single consistent timeline of experienced events, but "there are no fixed facts about the stream of consciousness independent of particular probes." Thus his theory has been viewed, I think rightly, as in effect a sort of "eliminative materialism," a denial of the reality of conscious experience as something existing independently of any particular probe.

Panpsychist combinationism is in some ways radically at odds with the multiple drafts theory: one denies any objective fact about consciousness, the other treats consciousness as a fundamental feature of reality. And functionalist combinationism, though not committed to the fundamentality of consciousness, does presuppose that there are objective facts about it. But in another way the theories are very similar: both identify the seemingly indivisible unity of the mind as masking an underlying multiplicity of somewhat independent parallel processes. In particular, they can all avoid the awkward choice between Stalinesque and Orwellian models of illusions like the cutaneous rabbit. The multiple drafts theory says that there is no objective fact about whether the illusory intermediate touches are inserted into the story "before consciousness" (Stalinesque) or "after consciousness" (Orwellian), because there is no objective fact about what is and isn't conscious. Functionalist combinationism says that it is all conscious, equally, but forms a composite stream of consciousness whose content is at certain points significantly indeterminate. Let me explain a little more fully what this means.

As sensory input is processed by different subsystems, each one is conscious and their experiences reflect the information they are processing. As soon as one subsystem, for instance, determines the result "red" for the color seen at a certain point, its experience of visual red is part of the composite subject's conscious stream. But it is always going to be easier for each subsystem to reach a conclusion than for them all to establish a consistent, integrated timeline of what has been perceived; integration lags behind local content determination, if only because integration will be delayed if some of the subsystems work much faster than others. This delay of integration means a delay between the redness experience being part of the composite's stream of consciousness, and its being fixed to a particular point in that stream—characterizing a particular object, with particular other features, that looked a certain way a moment before, in a particular modality, in sensation as opposed to emotion, etc. The process of its acquiring such a particular phenomenal location is in effect the process of its becoming conscious, because when it is entirely unlocalized it cannot be attended, noticed, or reflected upon: at most it blends with the inarticulate background of consciousness.

The process of making particular experiences properly, usefully conscious is a process of aligning them with other experiences so as to coalesce from the blur, and this process will happen by degrees over a period of hundreds of milliseconds. At certain points there will be no objective fact about whether a given "draft" is integrated enough to be called "an experience of the whole" in the ordinary, everyday sense. And if two subsystems have conflicting contents (e.g., "taps all along the forearm" and "taps only at the wrist and elbow") then, until one or the other is revised, the total stream will include both, representing that it is indeterminate whether there are or are not taps along the forearm.

This proposal does make a phenomenological prediction: it predicts that over short periods of time, the best description of what we are seeing (or hearing, or feeling, etc.) may simply be "something." When surprising things happen quickly, the best way to characterize how things seem to us is first as "something is happening," and swiftly thereafter some more determinate kind of content. This seems to me a correct phenomenological prediction (with all the caveats about the unreliability of such declarations); when I am startled, for instance, it often feels as though I am not aware of what, exactly, I felt, until a half-second or so after I am aware that I am feeling something (cf. Gross and Flombaum 2017). To put it another way, the arising of new experiences often feels more like a coalescing, a rapid progression from blurriness to determinacy, than like the appearance of fully formed images out of nothing.

Of course, it is hard to be confident about any of this, for a reason that both the multiple drafts theory and functionalist combinationism predict: the more we pay attention to a particular perception, the more swiftly and fixedly it becomes integrated and consistent. The period of indeterminacy is hard to detect because it vanishes as soon as we attend to it. My aim is not to commit combinationists to anything resembling the multiple drafts theory, but merely to show functionalist combinationism's flexibility, and its surprising affinity for accounts which are usually regarded as antirealist about consciousness, and to that extent sharply opposed to some of the views, like CRP, which would motivate combinationism.

6.5. Conclusions

My four case studies are only a small selection from the range of cases that I believe would benefit from, or call out for, a combinationist treatment. I cannot here attempt a full analysis of, for example, the possible consciousness of ant colonies (though I suspect they have something in common with the Nation-Brain), or the relationship between consciousness in an octopus's central brain and consciousness in its arms (though I suspect that case is analogous to the split-brain phenomenon in many respects). But I hope that my discussion of these four examples has illustrated how functionalist combinationism can cover and illuminate a wide variety of compositional relationships between intelligent subjects.

4   Combinationism for Persons

7 Composite Subjectivity and Psychological Subjects

INNER CONFLICT IS the first thing that comes to mind for many people when they hear the phrase "parts of the mind": experiences where it feels as though one part of you is struggling against another, as though each is seeking to fulfill its own goals by any means possible, as though each was an agent in its own right. In extreme dissociative cases, they even seem to speak for themselves as separate agents. What are these "parts"? They are probably not the kind of thing covered in divisions 2 and 3—not microsubjects or particular brain regions. So what are they?

In chapter 2 I distinguished a metaphysical and a psychological conception of subjects, and the past four chapters have worked with the former. In this chapter I switch to the psychological conception, outlining "psychological combinationism," a theory of how human psychological subjects (or "personas") can be divided and combined. The two conceptions might be seen as rival theories of what subjects are or as complementary perspectives that bring to prominence different aspects of reality. If they are rivals, then psychological combinationism is an alternative to panpsychist combinationism and functionalist combinationism, a conflicting view of what subjects are and how they combine. If the metaphysical and psychological conceptions are complementary, then psychological combinationists can also be functionalist combinationists or panpsychist combinationists, regarding psychological combinationism as illuminating the world of composite subjectivity from a different angle. They can think that the world contains streams of experiences connected in certain ways and that both the underlying systems which generate these experiences and the structured patterns that coalesce out of these experiences have some claim to being "us."

Section 7.1 outlines psychological combinationism and explores the complexities of the relationship between component personas and component substrates, using as examples variations on the fictional case of Jekyll and Hyde. This involves considering what psychological combinationism can say about the five internal problems for combinationism considered in chapter 2. In the next two sections I then consider two bridging problems that arise specifically for combining *persons*, subjects with self-consciousness and agency. Section 7.2's problem concerns self-consciousness: Are parts of a self-conscious composite subject self-conscious in their own right, each knowing itself distinct from the other parts? Section 7.3's problem concerns agency: generally, what someone else does is not my own action, even if they use my body to do it, so if my parts are themselves agents, I seem to be in competition with them for agency.

My solution to both problems turns on the idea that when the wills of two subjects are related in the right way, they will each experience the other not as distinct but as an extension of themselves, and the actions of both will be attributable to each. When the component subjects within a composite subject are related in these ways, the whole will be conscious of itself as a single entity and will be responsible for certain of the actions taken by its parts. In my final section I consider how the preceding accounts of component personas, and of properly related wills, can cast light on the human experience of inner conflict and dissociation.

7.1. Psychological Combinationism and the Psychological Conception of Subjects

According to what chapter 2 called the "psychological conception of subjects," we conscious beings are not strictly identical with brain, bodies, organisms, or any other object within which consciousness arises. Rather, we are "personas," beings constituted by the interplay between different experiences and psychological states. Can such beings be combined with each other into composite personas?

7.1.1. THE NEO-LOCKEAN ACCOUNT OF PERSONAL IDENTITY

To answer this question we first need to get clearer on what personas are. My starting point is the popular Neo-Lockean analysis of personal identity, which many philosophers have defended in very similar terms, a sample of which I quote:

> Two soul-phases belong to the same soul . . . if they are connected by a continuous character and memory path. . . . Two soul-phases are directly continuous . . . if the character revealed by the constituents of each is closely similar, and if the later contains recollections of some elements of the earlier. Two soul-phases are . . . connected by a continuous character and memory path if there is a series of soul-phases [between them] all of whose members are directly continuous with their immediate predecessors and successors. (Quinton 1962, 398)

> What I mostly want in wanting survival is that . . . my present experiences, thoughts, beliefs, desires, and traits of character should have appropriate future successors. . . . Change should be gradual rather than sudden, and (at least in some respects) there should not be too much change overall . . . [and] such change as there is should conform, for the most part, to lawful regularities concerning the succession of mental states . . . [so that] each succeeding mental state causally depends for its character on the states immediately before it. (Lewis 1976, 17–18)

> Let us say that, between P today and P [in the past], there are direct memory connections if P can now remember having some of the experiences that P had [then]. . . . There are several other kinds of direct psychological connection [such as] that which holds between an intention and the later act in which this intention is carried out [or] those which hold when a belief, or a desire, or any other psychological feature, persists. . . . We can now define psychological continuity . . . as the holding of overlapping chains of such direct psychological connections; and then [say] that P2 at t2 is the same person as P1 at t1 if and only if P2 at t2 is psychologically continuous with P1 at t1. (Noonan 2003, 10–11, paraphrasing Parfit 1984, 205–207)

Despite their differences in emphasis, these definitions agree on the following: the identity of a person (persona) depends on psychological continuity, i.e., a continuous chain of "direct psychological connections," which involve some mix of similarity (your psychology is largely the same from moment to moment), causal dependence (your present state depends on your preceding state), and representational match (your present memories match your past experiences, and your present intentions match your future actions).

I will accept the Neo-Lockean account of personal identity as a starting point for thinking about the combination of personas. It poses the following four questions, which will be discussed in the next four subsections:

1. First, these are definitions of identity across time; they tell us whether someone has survived some process, not how many people are present at a particular time. Thus to make sense of part-whole relations among personas at a given time requires extending the spirit of these proposals to cover identity at a time rather than across time.

2. Second, if we can define personas in an at-a-time fashion, how does the idea of combining personas fare against the five internal problems for combinationism outlined in chapter 2?

3. Third, in particular, this approach seems to imply maximality (anything entirely contained within a persona fails to count as a distinct persona, just because it is contained within a persona), since any putative component persona will presumably be psychologically connected to the other parts, and hence will be counted as identical with the whole. So it is not clear how a persona could contain distinct component personas.

4. Fourth, even if we can make sense of component personas, as well as component substrates, it is unclear how the two are connected—whether a given system's being divisible in one way will have anything to do with its being divisible another way.

7.1.2. IDENTITY AT A TIME AND ACROSS TIME

The Neo-Lockean conception of persons is often motivated by presenting thought experiments of two sorts: those in which a continuous stream of psychological processes is carried on in a sequence of different brains, through each successive brain being somehow rewired so that the new psychology can be "downloaded" (see, e.g., Locke 1836, 229–230; Williams 1970), and those in which two disconnected streams of psychological processes take sequential control of the same brain (see, e.g., Locke 1836, 228–229; Olson 2003). Many find it intuitive that in the former cases a single person has "moved" from one body to another, while in the latter cases two distinct people are "sharing" a single body. A prime example of the second sort of case is that of Dr. Jekyll and Mr. Hyde (Stevenson 1886), where two diametrically opposed personalities alternate in the control of a single body, one baffled and horrified to discover evidence of the atrocities committed by the other.

These across-time examples can be repurposed to illuminate the individuation of personas at a single time. Surely we can make sense of Jekyll and Hyde not alternating in control of their body, but rather coexisting (cf. Olson 2003, 341–342). When we ask that body for a name, we sometimes get an answer like "Dr. Jek—no, Hyde!—no, let me speak—it's Hyde, yes, definitely—agh!—oh all right, go on then—Dr. Jekyll, pleased to meet you." When we give it an opportunity for troublemaking, we observe a few moments of spasms and contortions, as though some sort of struggle is going on, followed by either refusal or embrace of the opportunity, perhaps with one arm trying to interfere with what the rest of the body is doing. At other times we might find the body behaving calmly, striking a middle course between respectability and vice and speaking in the following odd way: "Hello. This is Dr. Jekyll and Mr. Hyde, both pleased to meet you and at your disposal." If pressed, the body explains that "they" have come to a cooperative arrangement, though temptations sometimes prompt a return to squabbling and contests over control of limbs.

Here it seems intuitive to say that we are dealing with two different people (at least if we thought so when Jekyll and Hyde appeared sequentially rather than together). But there might be no distinction between Jekyll and Hyde at the level of substrates: the entire brain might be active in generating both streams of thought. It might even be that each personality sleeps periodically, leaving the brain under the control of the other, and in these states our scans reveal widespread brain activation that differs only subtly from what is detected when the other personality is awake. We might reasonably conclude that both personalities arise from different patterns of activity in the same set of neurons. So if Jekyll and Hyde are two people, it must be because they are two personas.

So what makes Jekyll and Hyde distinct, in this case? It makes no sense to appeal to the above-quoted definitions of identity across time, because those presuppose a definite number of people present at each time who can be compared with one another. But the relations that those definitions appeal to are clearly relevant to what makes Jekyll and Hyde seem distinct. For instance, instead of appealing to the kind of representational matching that obtains between a memory and a past experience, we might appeal to matching between simultaneous beliefs, desires, and decisions. All of Hyde's beliefs are consistent, and all of Jekyll's are, but they might disagree sharply on some points; Hyde desires things to which Jekyll is highly averse, and vice versa; the things Jekyll is attempting to do make sense in light of Jekyll's beliefs and desires, but not Hyde's, and vice versa. Rather than reading these as observations, we could treat them as partly definitional: we assign a belief to Jekyll only if it coheres with the other mental states we assign to Jekyll.

Similarly, whereas the quoted definitions appeal to the causal dependence of one stage on another, we can instead appeal to the causal interdependence of different present mental episodes, in the sense of "causal interdependence" defined in section 2.2 of chapter 2. Readers may by this point have noticed that the sorts of relations that individuate Jekyll and Hyde seem to be just those relations that were discussed in chapter 2 as versions of "the unity of consciousness." Indeed, it is often suggested that subjects are individuated by unified consciousness (see, e.g., Bayne and Chalmers 2003, 55–57; Dainton 2008; Bayne 2010, 289ff.), though this claim will be as ambiguous as the term "unified consciousness": it can mean global consistency, causal interdependence, functional unity, representational unity, or phenomenal unity. Let us suppose that Jekyll and Hyde are as disunified as any two ordinary people, with respect to all these different relations: despite arising in the same brain, their experiences and other mental states are no more representationally unified, conjointly accessible, etc. than mine are with yours. This seems a good basis for distinguishing them from one another, and this distinction would be between personas, not substrates.

So we can supplement the above-quoted definitions of identity of subjects over time with the following:

> Two personas p_1 and p_2 existing at one time are identical if and only if the experiences and other mental states of p_1 are sufficiently unified in various ways with those of p_2.

This definition is limited in that it presupposes that we can already identify two personas and their experiences; a more thorough statement of the same idea would be something like this:

> Two experiences e_1 and e_2 existing at one time belong to the same persona if and only if they are sufficiently unified in various ways.

This definition makes clearer that, according to psychological combinationism, we are to start with experiences and their relations, and on that basis "construct" personas.

7.1.3. PSYCHOLOGICAL COMBINATIONISM DEFENDED AGAINST THE FIVE ARGUMENTS

Psychological combinationism says that personas, constituted by sets of sufficiently unified experiences, can be related as part and whole. In chapter 2 we saw
five arguments that aimed to rule out combinationism of any form: arguments
about subject-summing, unity, privacy, boundaries, and incompatible contexts.
How strong are these arguments applied to psychological combinationism?

First, I think that the subject-summing argument has relatively little force.
Personas are by definition an ontologically nonfundamental sort of thing, something constituted by more basic facts. More specifically, facts about the existence,
identity, and properties of personas are meant to follow from facts about the existence, properties, and interrelations of experiences and other mental states. And facts
about experiences and mental states are surely facts about the intrinsic features of
subjects, if anything is, so a full description of one or more subjects would include a
catalogue of its experiences and their interrelations, which are the right kind of facts
to entail the existence of another subject (cf. Mendelovici 2018, 16).

What about the privacy argument? The experiences which constitute a persona are just those which are ascribed to it, and so any persona constituted by the
experiences of another would also be the subject of those experiences, and would
thus share experiences with that other. If strong privacy (no nonidentical subjects
can share experiences) is true, then it immediately follows that the two subjects
are identical, in which case strong independence (which rules out explanatory relations between nonidentical subjects) is vindicated. But there is no good reason
to accept strong privacy, since we can accept weak privacy (no non-overlapping
subjects can share experiences) instead. In fact, if subjects are personas, then weak
privacy is actually true by definition. Personas are constituted by experiences, so
for them to overlap simply means for them to share experiences. Hence of course
they can only share experiences with other personas they overlap with.[1]

What about the unity argument? Here there is in a sense little to say. Psychological
combinationism says nothing distinctive about conscious unity; it simply explains
how, given experiences and the unity relations among them, personas can be defined and can combine. Thus for a full account of how conscious unity is explained
and grounded, it will need to be supplemented with some other theory.

---

[1] Note that, if subjects are substrates, it is fine for distinct subjects to be experientially identical, because
they can still be distinguished by their nonexperiential properties—human bodies are, for example,
much heavier than brains. By contrast, psychological combinationism rules out complete sharing of
experiences, on the basis that if two personas have all the same experiences there will be nothing to
distinguish them.

For instance, rather than having a distinctive account of phenomenal unity, it might be supplemented with the primitivist account offered by panpsychist combinationism, or with the reductionist account offered by pure functionalist combinationism. If we took a rivalrous view of the metaphysical and psychological conceptions of subject, then this would involve psychological combinationists taking over some elements of these alternative combinationist theories, while rejecting their accounts of subjecthood; if we took a more conciliatory view of the two conceptions, we might instead see this as psychological combinationism adding an extra layer of depth to those theories, without denying the truth of any of their claims.

Finally, what about the paired boundary argument and incompatible contexts argument? Here is where psychological combinationism faces a distinctive sort of objection: the criterion of identity for personas given in the previous section more or less straightforwardly entails the principle of boundedness (premise **D3** from chapter 2). I mentioned this above as the threat of "maximality" and address it in the next subsection. But first let us walk through how this entailment runs. Above I suggested the following criterion:

> Two experiences e_1 and e_2 existing at one time belong to the same persona if and only if they are sufficiently unified in various ways.

This features the phrase "belong to the same persona," which becomes ambiguous if we allow for experiences to be shared by more than one persona. It could mean "belong to one of the same personas" (i.e., there is at least one persona which has both) or "belong to all the same personas" (i.e., any persona which has one has the other). The second disambiguation would give us:

> Two experiences e_1 and e_2 existing at one time belong to all the same personas if and only if they are sufficiently unified in various ways.

This can be rearranged into:

> If (and only if) two experiences e_1 and e_2 (existing at one time) are sufficiently unified, they belong to all the same personas (i.e., any persona p that undergoes one also undergoes the other).

This entails:

> If two experiences e_1 and e_2 are sufficiently unified, then any persona p that undergoes one also undergoes the other.

Which is pretty much equivalent to the following:

Premise D3 (Boundedness): For any experience e_1 belonging to a subject s, if another experience e_2 is unified with e_1, then e_2 must also be had by s.

Consider an example to bring out how the problem works: suppose we have a composite persona (p_1), undergoing experiences e_1 to e_6, and we try to say that it contains two component personas p_2 and p_3, undergoing e_1 to e_3 and e_4 to e_6, respectively. But from the fact that p_1 has all of e_1 to e_6, and from our definition, it follows that all six must be sufficiently unified (otherwise they would not all belong to a single persona). But now consider the relationship between p_2 and p_3: all of p_2's experiences are sufficiently unified with all of p_3's, and so p_2 and p_3 must be the very same persona. Consider also how p_2 (or p_3) relates to p_1: again, all of p_2's experiences are sufficiently unified with all of p_1's, and so it follows that they are the same persona. In effect, by defining personas according to unity, we have ensured that any component persona will "dissolve" into the whole.

7.1.4. ADDRESSING THE BOUNDARY ARGUMENT

The boundary argument against psychological combinationism can be addressed by showing ways that two experiences can be sufficiently unified (to establish the composite persona) and yet not (to keep the component personas distinct). One way to do this is to appeal to the *division-relativity* of various forms of unity, in particular functional unity, in a way that is illustrated by one of the examples discussed in chapter 6: the Nation-Brain. The radio-related experiences (pressing buttons, seeing lights) of two distant citizens are access-unified at the nation-scale but not at the human-scale: they can be jointly accessed to guide the overall functioning of the nation but not to guide the overall functioning of either citizen. Conversely each citizen's radio-related experiences are access-unified with their other, non-radio-related experiences at the human-scale but not at the nation-scale. This means that the psychological combinationist could give an analysis of the Nation-Brain very similar to the functionalist combinationist's: there is one persona for the whole nation, and within it one persona for each citizen.[2]

---

[2] The two forms of combinationism do, however, have different implications for the identity of the Nation-Brain over time: if the citizens were issued a set of radical revisions to their button-pressing instructions, so as to remain in contact but generate very different behavior and cognition at the nation-scale, psychological functionalism would imply that the original Nation-Brain was now gone, replaced by a new subject grounded in the same substrate (like a new mind in an old brain). Functionalist combinationism,

Systems like the Nation-Brain, however, are not very relevant to the question of inner conflict. They rely on a difference in level so extreme that the details of the conscious goings-on at each level are more or less entirely inaccessible to subjects at the other level: the Nation-Brain has no idea it is implemented by citizens (unless we present evidence of this to its robotic avatar—perhaps by letting it tour the nation, i.e., tour its own "brain"), and the citizens have no idea they are implementing a mind (unless we show them evidence about its overall functioning—perhaps by introducing them to the avatar). Can there be component personas that operate on roughly the same scale as the whole they form? I believe there can.

There is another way to evade the boundary argument, allowing for component and composite personas even at the same scale: to appeal to the multidimensional vagueness of the above definition—the looseness of "in various ways" and "sufficiently unified." This allows for subsets of experiences, within a connected set that constitutes a persona, to be more closely connected with each other and thus constitute a component persona. That is, component personas make sense when they correspond to more integrated "clusters" within the larger conscious field.

The messiness in the constitution of personas by streams of psychologically related experiences is not unusual; it is similar to the messiness in the constitution of institutions by streams of socially related human activities, or the messiness in the constitution of organisms by streams of biologically related chemical events. And in all three cases, this multifariousness of relevant criteria and thresholds allows us to make sense of composition among the entities thus constituted.

For instance, citizens of all provinces in a federal state are socially connected in the ways that are required for them to count as members of a single political community. But citizens of each particular state are connected in those ways to a greater degree, given at least some weightings of various factors, and their connections are sustained by distinctive causal mechanisms (e.g., state bureaucracies), and this allows us to say that they are members of a political community that does not also include members of other states. Thus there is a composite political community (the federal nation) composed of component political communities. We can also have composite organisms composed of component organisms, when the events

---

by contrast, would say that the Nation-Brain persists, though with a very different personality. On the other hand, if the radio transmissions were temporarily stopped so that citizens could be progressively replaced with something else—tiny robots, microchips, or even actual neurons—so that afterward the same organizational structure could be started up in a new (and probably smaller) system, functionalist combinationism would imply that the Nation-Brain was gone, even though its persona was now being run on a new substrate. By contrast, psychological combinationism implies that the Nation-Brain would have survived, leaving behind its component personas as it moved to a new substrate but remaining the same subject because it remains the same persona.

in a single component part are biologically connected to a greater degree (given at least some weightings) than they are to events in other parts. One example of such a setup would be colonial animals like the jellyfish of the order Siphonophora; another, arguably, would be multicellular organisms in general, each of whose cells is in some respects an organism in its own right. Indeed, even some organelles within our cells, like mitochondria, show organism-like features.

This multidimensional vagueness of "sufficiently unified" was already present in the notion of "psychological continuity" employed in the Neo-Lockean theory of individuation across time. Clearly, someone can lose some memories, goals, beliefs, etc. while retaining others. But how many can we lose in a short space of time before becoming a different person? As Parfit (1984, 231–233) argues, there must be borderline cases, in between those who retain the same persona despite abandoning a few plans and losing a few memories, and those who lose their persona despite retaining a few plans and keeping a few memories, where someone changes enough to no longer be clearly the same, but not enough to be clearly different.

Not only is there vagueness in the exact threshold for change of personas, but there is also vagueness about the right weighting. One person might lose all their memories of their life and circumstances while retaining allegiance to the goals, values, and projects that had previously animated them; another might keep their memories but cease to see any value in their previous goals. Which has seen the replacement of one persona with another, and which a mere change in a single persona? (Does it depend on what sort of person they were before?) This does not seem like a factual question, but rather a question of how we choose to use concepts—which sorts of continuity we decide to weight more heavily in organizing our thoughts about "people."

To see how this messiness extends to individuation at a time, consider an adjusted version of our Jekyll and Hyde case, where the two have no secrets from each other, even in their most private thoughts. When Hyde indulges in a fantasy of cruel mayhem, Jekyll must experience every grisly detail, and if Jekyll realizes that a vulnerable person is undefended in the next room, Hyde immediately and gleefully jumps into action on this belief. Judged by the standards of access-unity, their experiences are highly unified; judged by the standards of global consistency, they are highly disunified. Should we, then, count them as one or as two?[3] Or suppose that their phenomenology involves a single field of perceptual and bodily

---

[3] The split-brain patient seems to exhibit the reverse condition: two streams of consciousness which are in large part causally independent but which display the same consistent personality, values, and goals. Cf. Schechter (2009), who argues that Tye (2003) is torn between one-subject and two-subjects accounts of the split brain for this reason.

sensations, with distinct sets of urges, feelings, and plans focused on particular parts of them. When we prick the body's finger, a single experience of localized bodily pain is the focus both of Hyde's outrage and desire for vengeance and of Jekyll's perturbed contemplation of possible reasons we might have pricked him. The two might even be aware of the pain as having this dual character, since it co-presents the other's experiences to both subjects: Jekyll contemplates the causes of a pain that he experiences as prompting outrage and anger (from which he studiously distances himself), while Hyde craves revenge for a pain that he feels as calmly contemplated (while dismissing that contemplation as impotent and spineless). Here we seem to have two overlapping sets of mental states, such that it will be hard to say whether, say, Hyde's total set (including both the pain and the anger) is sufficiently unified with Jekyll's contemplation (some elements are, others are not).

It seems to me that the most perspicuous description of cases like this would be to say that there is a single person by low standards (which require only relatively low degrees of relatively few forms of unity), but two people by higher standards (which require higher degrees of more forms of unity). All the experiences associated with this body form a single loose cluster, within which two (possibly overlapping) subclusters can be distinguished. These subclusters are parts of the looser cluster, and Jekyll and Hyde, the personas they constitute, would then qualify as parts of Jekyll-Hyde, the persona it constitutes, by the standards set out in chapter 1, section 1.3. They are simultaneously existing things, in the same ontological category, such that the two parts are existentially independent (except insofar as they overlap), but the whole is existentially dependent on them together. If the Hyde experiences were not occurring (perhaps due to some sort of selective neural inhibition due to a carefully calibrated device invented by Jekyll's scientist friends), the Jekyll experiences could continue, but if neither the Hyde experiences nor the Jekyll experiences were occurring, there would be no Jekyll-Hyde experiences.

For different purposes it might make sense to focus on a different set of standards: when assigning moral responsibility for Hyde's crimes, the inconsistency of their desires might be more important, but when studying perception we might focus on the integration of their sensory experiences, and when holding a conversation their access-unity might matter most. There are innumerable ways that different relations might hold to different degrees among sets of experiences, and for different setups and different purposes there would be innumerably many different versions of the concept "subject" (or "person") that would be most useful to track. No doubt if some new, unfamiliar setup became common, there would be corresponding evolution in the terms we used to think about each other, just as changes in the structure of society prompt changes in the relationship concepts that we employ.

Perhaps it would be most practically useful in everyday life, dealing with mental systems that are fairly sharply differentiated from each other, with no overlap and all the unity relations running together, to individuate personas in a maximal way, with no allowance for part-whole relations among them. But there is no principled reason not to recognize the coherence of a compositional interpretation of the clustering together of experiences in tighter and looser ways. In particular, there is no principled reason not to use this framework (as I do in section 7.4) to make literal sense of everyday talk of component personas.

7.1.5. HOW FAR DO PERSONA DIVISIONS AND SUBSTRATE DIVISIONS LINE UP?

Consider the third question posed at the beginning of this section: What connection is there, if any, between the compositional structure of personas and that of substrates of experience? It is certainly possible to have one without the other. A Cartesian immaterial soul might be strictly simple, admitting of no division into component substrates, and yet be prey to the same sorts of division and dissociation as we are at the level of personas. On the other hand, a collection of objects might all support consciousness both individually and collectively but be so perfectly synchronized with one another, and underlie such a flawless and untroubled psyche, that no division into component personas could be made.

However, we humans, and other conscious evolved animals, are clearly divisible both with respect to the substrates of our experience (organs, ganglia, cells, molecules, etc.) and with respect to our personas (complex personalities, conflicting desires, identities based on different social roles, etc.). How do these two forms of division relate? We can expect them to correlate somewhat, because substrates are relevant to causal interdependence: if two experiences are grounded in the same substrate (e.g., the same brain area), they can more easily affect each other (and less easily avoid doing so), as well as tending to be affected by the same things (anything that influences that brain area). So on at least some dimensions they are likely to be more unified than they are with experiences based in a different substrate. If we weighted the particular sorts of causal interdependence associated with the sharing of substrates very highly, and made the standards for "sufficient unity" high enough, we would have a sense of "persona" such that all the experiences based on that particular substrate counted as belonging to a single distinct persona. We might then speak of the persona corresponding to, say, my left hemisphere system, constituted by all the experiences which are grounded in my left hemisphere and brainstem, individuated by the particular forms of causal interdependence that hold in virtue of sharing this substrate: this persona would be a component of my total persona.

However, these personas that correspond to component substrates are gerrymandered beings, dependent on specifying the standards for identity of personas in a way that ignores all the other forms of unity that hold among my experiences. Moreover, not all experiences can be tied directly to one part of the substrate: they might arise only from the interactions between many, and so would not belong to any of the personas corresponding to the division of the substrate into substrate parts. A final limitation of any division of personas corresponding to that of substrates is that it is likely to be undetectable to the subject themselves, and to anyone lacking a complete and sophisticated neuroscientific understanding of their individual brain. To take a simple example, it appears that the colors of different objects are processed and identified by a single brain area, while other features of the same objects are processed and identified elsewhere (see Zihl et al. 1983; Heeger et al. 1999; Théoret et al. 2002; Anzai et al. 2007). So a division of personas corresponding to substrates would involve a persona constituted by all my color experiences, unbound to shape and motion experiences, but would not involve a persona constituted by all my visual experiences of a particular object. This surprising fact is clearly not something I could tell just by reflecting on my experiences from the inside.

If we make divisions according to what seems important and introspectively detectable (like the division between my identity as a family member and my identity as a professional, for instance), we can have no idea, prior to neuroscientific investigation, whether these component personas correspond to any component substrates. We could of course attempt to define substrates corresponding to those personas, looking for the set of neurons whose activity is necessary and sufficient for the occurrence of the experiences constituting, say, my sense of identity as a family member. But here again, the result will be unhelpfully gerrymandered from the perspective of brain anatomy—it will be "one neuron here, two over here, another one there, etc." (And two distinct personas may have the very same substrate.) Because of the brain's massively interconnected character, top-down and bottom-up divisions will often diverge widely in unpredictable ways.

All this talk of picking whichever specification we want of "sufficient unity" and "various ways," thereby individuating innumerably many subtly different sets of personas, may seem oddly casual. If the psychological conception of subjects is right, then *I* am a certain persona, and my existence, boundaries, and identity across time seem to be objective facts, independent of anyone's decision about which terms or concepts to use. What I experience right now, surely, is not a matter of convention, something that could be equally well decided in many different ways. I feel the force of this intuition, but it seems to me that it is best satisfied outside the framework of the psychological conception (cf. Williams 1970, 176–177; Parfit 1984, 214, 277–280; Thomson 1997, 225), because it seems akin to the intuition that "I," the thing that has experiences, am not myself some kind of collection or system of experiences. If these intuitions are right, then the metaphysical conception of subjects is likely true, and subjects are not personas but substrates. The previous four chapters showed how substrates can combine; here I have tried to show how personas can as well.

7.1.6. ANALOGIES OF SELF AND SOCIETY

Repeatedly in this chapter I will draw analogies between human beings and social groups (army battalions, bands of assassins, and political coalitions, among others). Such analogies are common and natural when thinking in this area, from Plato to the present, and for this reason they deserve some warning comments.

First, are social groups composite subjects, according to psychological combinationism? That is, are they composite personas, constituted by sets of sufficiently unified experiences, for some specification of "sufficiently"? Well, for any social group there are a set of experiences (those of its members), and those experiences interact in a variety of ways, often in ways that share information, connect representations, and partially re-create the functional roles of states like intentions, beliefs, and desires. These relations are somewhat like, though also somewhat unlike, the unity relations among an individual's experiences; in chapter 6's section 6.2 I discussed in more detail the sorts of unity-like relations found in social groups and the ways in which these relations nevertheless fall well short of what is found within a human individual. If we were willing to stretch our notion of a subject to breaking point, we might focus on the forms of unity that do hold among some or all the experiences of the members of some social group, take those forms of unity as our standard for "sufficiently unified," and thus take those experiences to constitute a composite persona, a group subject. This subject would be distinct from the group itself (the substrate of its experiences) in the same way that a human subject, according to the psychological conception, is distinct from their brain and body.

It is probably only by overextending our normal ways of individuating subjects that we could count actual social groups as composite subjects. It is better, then, simply to say this: according to psychological combinationism, social groups often exhibit a sort of clustering and organization of experiences which is similar in kind to that exhibited by a human mind. Individual human personas and the structured mass of experiences that make up the conscious goings-on in a social group differ only in degree of integration, not in their core nature.

There is, however, a very important difference between social groups and human individuals, namely that social groups are divisible into parts (human beings) who *both* are separate substrates of experience and also have separate, sharply distinguishable personas. This contrasts with the cross-cutting of the divisions of a human brain into substrate parts and persona parts. There is consequently something misleading about any representation of inner conflict which pictures the conflicting parts as little people in the head, arguing or fighting or cooperating. Such representations implicitly present the component personas as having separate bodies, i.e., separate substrates, and thus as being distinct prior to the relationships they enter into with each other. But in fact component personas are constructed by relationships among experiences and other mental states: they arise out of the interactions among brain processes rather than simply entering into those interactions. Of course something a little like this is also true of individual human beings' personas: they are formed through the social interactions that the growing human being enters into rather than preexisting those interactions. In this sense individuals are themselves social constructs. But something does preexist social life, namely the sharp difference in physical information conduits for between-brains and within-brain interactions, which makes it nearly inevitable that the experiences which arise during social life and depend on the same brain will be much more unified with one another than they are with experiences in other brains.

If we are to think of component personas in political terms, it is best not to analogize them to individual members of a society, but to political movements, clubs, or parties—subgroups within society which arise out of the patterns of interaction among human individuals. An individual's reconciliation of competing desires or identities, for instance, is not like a "social contract" we might imagine a group of castaways entering into, recognizing a need for cooperation in order to preserve their preexisting lives, because competing desires or identities are already the products of mental development and pattern formation. It is much more like an agreement between rival political parties or gangs, operating within and grounded in the social life of the same population.

7.2. Composite Subjectivity and Self-Consciousness

How do you tell which person you are? How do you distinguish your actions from events that just happen, your thoughts from other people's thoughts you merely detect, your body from someone else's body? This is a large question, and I will not be able to fully answer it, but one thing that is fairly clear is that we do not, in the first instance, accomplish this discernment by first knowing things about various people, and then reasoning our way to identifying one of them as ourselves. Sometimes we do that; for instance, when watching a blurry video of several people involved in a drunken escapade, we might first identify the physical or behavioral traits each person displays, and then, based on knowing that we ourselves have certain traits, identify which of the drunks must be us. But this contrasts sharply with our everyday experience of ourselves, in which questions about which person is us generally do not even arise; in everyday life we distinguish self and other swiftly, automatically, and without thinking, independently of any prior knowledge about what sort of person we are. Each of my actions *feels mine*, for example, and the actions of others don't.

The automaticity of self-identification is what generates a puzzle for combinationists. What happens when there is a composite subject made of several component subjects, and they all distinguish self and other in roughly the way that we do? Does each part identify itself, and distinguish itself from the other parts—which would leave the whole, which shares its experiences with those parts, with a patchwork sense of self and no experience of itself as a whole subject? Or does the whole identify itself and distinguish itself from things outside it—which would leave the parts, which share their experiences with that whole, misled about their own identity, falsely thinking of themselves as the whole? Or do both try to distinguish self and other simultaneously, leading to a contradictory and unstable sense of self?

This puzzle is particularly pressing if the combinationist wonders whether we ourselves might be composite subjects, made of simpler subjects. We seem to have generally fairly consistent self-consciousness as a whole human being: How is this established? Moreover, we generally do not have a sense of ourselves as a composite thing, a sense of our component subjects as distinct from one another: How do our parts fail to identify themselves as distinct from one another?[4]

7.2.1. AN INAPPLICABLE SOLUTION USED BY SOCIAL GROUPS

We can clarify the problem here by considering a social group organized to act as a collective agent,[5] because such social groups typically form a consistent sense of self in a very *different* way from anything we human individuals could be doing.

---

[4] The problems discussed in this section were first suggested to me in conversation by Benj Hellie.

[5] Even if we hold back from accepting chapter 6's argument that social groups share conscious experiences with their members, we can make perfectly good sense of such groups producing and circulating representations which function like thoughts, beliefs, and perceptions, and these often involve either implicit or explicit self-representation.

The individual parts first identify themselves, and then secondarily "identify with" the group while remaining aware that they are not identical with it. Seeing how this solution works for social groups, and why it cannot be extended to us, will throw into relief the combinationist's challenge in explaining how a human individual might be a composite subject.

Suppose, for instance, that an army battalion is trying to ambush the enemy; most of the group have hidden themselves in positions where they can neither see nor be seen, while a small group scouts out the enemy and relays their position to the rest. The ambush must be sprung only when the enemy "is nearby," but the representation of something as "nearby" is implicitly self-specifying, and so means different things for the scouts and for the ambushers. This poses a risk of miscommunication: if the signal "The enemy is nearby" is sent by the scouts when the enemy is near *to them*, but interpreted by the ambushers as meaning the enemy is near *to them*, the ambush will be sprung too soon and the scouting will have been useless.[6] For the signal to play its proper role, being detected and used to guide behavior ("perceived" and "believed") by the group as a whole, it matters which particular subject is implicitly represented. And if each soldier simply relies on their automatic, spontaneous sense of who they are, the resultant confusion will be disastrous.

Of course it is clear how the army battalion avoids this kind of confusion. The scouts can evaluate the enemy using the position of the ambushers as their point of reference, mentally "putting themselves" in that position, and send the "is nearby" signal only when they perceive that the enemy is near the ambushers, not the scouts themselves. The battalion ensures that representations of "self" are consistent in which "self" they are about, by relying on each member's explicit knowledge that although they are a member of the group, they are also an individual agent, distinct from the other members. But this solution is available only because the battalion recognizes the problem—it recognizes that it is made of members, each of which recognizes they are themselves, distinct from each other and from the battalion as a whole. They can then reflect on the content of their own experiences and how that content needs to be translated to be usable by the group as a whole. Their drive toward consistency is founded on a prior recognition of inconsistency.

But this cannot be a fully general account of how a composite subject can have a consistent sense of self, for two reasons. First, it invites the question:

---

[6] Similar problems arise with other implicit self-representations: the scouts should not report how, e.g., dangerous or vulnerable the enemy is by reference to the scouts' own capabilities, but by reference to the larger group's.

How did the members establish the individual self-consciousness that let them recognize their distinctness from the group? Second, it seems clear that individual humans do not in fact work like this; our parts did not first recognize their distinctness from each other, and the problems it poses for coordination, and devise some policy to ensure consistency. If they did, their awareness of being multiple subjects would be inherited by the whole. The intuitive attractiveness of anti-combination reflects that if there are many communicating subjects who compose me, they have no idea that they are many. And this is something that cries out for explanation: people usually notice when they are in constant close interaction with others, so why do the conscious parts of us remain oblivious to each other?

7.2.2. THE PATTERNING PRINCIPLE AND THE DETECTION OF HARMONY

So combinationists must answer two related questions: How can self-consciousness in a composite subject be made consistent *prior to* any self-consciousness in the parts, and how can our parts be capable of self-consciousness *without* becoming aware of their own individuality? I propose the following answer: a given subject's spontaneously occurring self-consciousness refers, by default, not to that subject itself but to the largest composite it belongs to whose parts are all, in a sense to be defined, "harmoniously connected."

The composite subject which is this whole system will self-represent in the strict sense, but all the component subjects within it will refer to something larger than themselves as "me," even when they seem to be self-representing. It follows that those component subjects, in virtue of being harmoniously connected to each other, will perceive each other as extensions of themselves. All the inputs they receive from each other they interpret as telling them either of their own voluntary actions or of events going on "in them."

In this regard they are in something like the position opposite from a schizophrenic suffering from "thought insertion," who perceives their own internally generated thoughts and experiences as produced by outside forces. Where the schizophrenic perceives what is actually "internal" as being "external," the conscious parts of a normal human perceive events that are actually "external" as being "internal." Each thus feels itself to be alone and responsible for all the mental activity in the whole system, which then inherits this unanimous judgment of solitude. (Schechter [2018, 156–180] defends an account of this sort for the split-brain phenomenon: there are two thinkers ["Lefty" and "Righty"], but they each identify themselves with the whole person, self-attributing the actions produced by the other.)

What is harmonious connection, and why would it determine self-consciousness? Rather than defining "harmonious connection" directly, I will progressively flesh out the idea by considering how we usually form spontaneous ideas of self and other. For our parts can employ only the cognitive mechanisms that we do, and so whatever it is that lets them categorize things as internal and external, as "self" and "other," must also be what lets us do that. If combinationists claim that our parts miscategorize each other as "self," they should also think that we could make a similar miscategorization in the right circumstances:

> **Patterning principle:** Our spontaneous impressions of whether an event is external or internal, and of whether it is our voluntary action or not, are determined by the patterns of correspondence and divergence we detect between it and other things.

Since both internal and external events can stand in the same patterns, the patterning principle implies that we might self-ascribe actions, states, or events which in fact occur externally and independently of us, if we detect the right pattern in them. But how plausible is the patterning principle?

I think most of us are inclined, if we reflect on what determines our impressions of internality, externality, and causal responsibility, to accept some role for patterning, but only a limited one. At some point, we tend to think, we fall back on a direct metaphysical insight into certain events beings ours, either in the sense of being our actions or of being "in" our own minds. Thus I think we are normally inclined, on initial reflection, toward a "hybrid" view, with some role for detecting patterns and some role for direct insight. It is this direct insight that poses problems for combinationists: shouldn't each of our parts know automatically that some of the thought processes that guide this human body are *theirs*, while others are not? So the strategy I will pursue on behalf of combinationism is to argue that patterning considerations can in principle entirely explain the relevant class of judgments, making direct metaphysical insight superfluous.

The most plausible role for patterning considerations is determining our impressions of the causal relations among external events. What makes it seem to us that one event we perceive is caused by another? Surely the answer has to be ultimately in terms of some sort of covariation, things either changing at the same time (or in quick succession) or remaining constant together while other things change. If I see the cup hit the floor and at the same moment I hear a noise, it will seem that the collision caused the noise. If I open the oven door and immediately start to feel heat, which ceases when I close the door, it will seem that the door being open caused the heat. If I see a candle being lit and someone across the room suddenly starts screaming, and stops only when the candle is extinguished, it will seem as though the candle was somehow hurting them. Whether we express this in the language of Bayes's Theorem or in that of Humean laws of association, the basic idea seems clear enough: we respond to regularity among the changes we perceive in the world. We might say that we observe "harmony" between events when they are correlated with each other in the relevant ways, with this term serving as a placeholder for whatever the statistical relations are that we respond to.[7]

But even given some idea of which external events are causing which, how do we identify some of these events as *our own* actions? There has been a lot of empirical work on this question, but for the most part it is accepted that we rely on considerations of patterning; the dispute, for instance, between the "comparator model" (see Helmholtz 1866; Blakemore et al. 2002; Frith 2012; Carruthers 2012) and the "multifactorial model" (see Synofzik et al. 2008; Moore and Haggard 2008; David et al. 2008) is a dispute over the particular weighting and mix of factors used, over whether there is a single privileged comparison or not. What is agreed on is that some brain system has to compute, based on signals from perception and from the internal processes that produce action, which events are "done by me." This idea is borne out by the possibility of "tricking" subjects into self-ascribing responsibility for externally caused events by manipulating their perceptions, e.g., by using mirrors to show what looks like their own hand making movements similar to those they intend (Nielsen 1963; Ramachandran and Rogers-Ramachandran 1996; Lynn et al. 2010; Ebert and Wegner 2010; cf. Wegner 2002), or by direct brain stimulation (Desmurget et al. 2009; cf. Fried et al. 1991). We might put the point by saying that we identify external events as our own voluntary actions when and only when we perceive them as harmonizing with our internal decisions and volitions: if we see our arm move just after we've consciously decided to move our arm, the harmony between these two events is what gives us our strong impression that the arm rose *because* we raised it.

But this just pushes the question back a step, to the question of why we self-ascribe the decision itself; clearly we cannot say that we regard it as our own decision because it harmonizes with a prior decision to make that decision!

---

[7] There may or may not be additional, innate or learned "models" we are particularly prone to recognize and perceive as causal. For instance, we might automatically regard the transmission of rectilinear motion as "how things work," and be more sensitive to such patterns than to, say, S-shaped motion (cf. Cheng 1997). But these models cannot be the whole story, since we can identify and recognize causal relations even among unfamiliar or bizarre items.

7.2.3. THE PATTERNING PRINCIPLE AND INTERNAL EVENTS

How can the patterning principle explain our self-ascription of internal events? Some internal events, like imaginations, may fit neatly into the same model as external events. Some experiments suggest that faint sensory stimuli may be miscategorized as imaginary when they match what subjects were independently attempting to imagine, i.e., when they harmonize with a prior intention (Perky 1910; cf. Segal 1972). But many of the events we experience as being "in our minds" are not preceded by any distinct decision to produce them—our decisions, thoughts, impulses, and so on seem to be "ours" *on their own*, with no need for us to compare them with any other events. How can the notion of harmony even apply here? I think there are actually at least three ways for the patterning principle to cover these internal events: harmony with background psychology, lack of resistance to the will, and dedicated comparator mechanisms.

First, we might self-ascribe events not just when they harmonize with particular other events, but also when they harmonize with our background psychology, reflecting the fact that our mental events are typically "caused by a combination of our background beliefs, desires, and interests" (Campbell 1999, 617). We might focus in particular on the mass of dispositional intentions, desires, and goals that could be called "the background will" (as contrasted with "the occurrent will," our present conscious feelings of desire and intention). The background will is the underlying structure of what we want or intend to do in different situations, given different contingencies, when confronted with different stimuli. It is probably impossible to ever fully articulate this structure—we cannot write out a list of what we would want or do in every possible situation—but there does seem to be a set of persistent, determinate facts about us in virtue of which we are inclined to will some things, and in virtue of which we perceive things as unwanted or desirable, frustrating or welcome. I may have never thought before about whether I would like to receive a free pair of glittery gold sneakers or to have all my fingernails double in length, but immediately upon such things happening I would have quite definite reactions, positive or negative. It seems clear that even before they happen, it is an objective fact about me that I "would like" or "would not like" such things—such facts about me are my "background will."

(Note that we are not considering the obviously regressive idea that a subject judges some thoughts to be theirs because of its fitting well with the background psychology that they have already *judged* to be theirs; the background psychology need not be self-ascribed, indeed need not be the object of any kind of thought or awareness, in order to govern and guide what self-ascriptions are in fact made. This evaluation of harmony could be, and probably is, largely inaccessible to reflection:

sometimes the only way we can find out what it is we really want is to expose ourselves to actual or hypothetical cases and see how we react.)

Nevertheless this proposal can be only part of the story, since we can regard
a thought as "ours" despite its content being wildly out of character, just as
we can think that someone *else* is thinking exactly what we would think in the
circumstances (cf. Gerrans 2001, 233ff.; Schechter 2018, 156–180). Being "in character" for us seems neither necessary nor sufficient for being perceived as "ours."
Thus the defender of the patterning principle should supplement the appeal to
background psychology with other factors.

A second option is to appeal to a sort of *instability*: the thoughts and feelings
which we ascribe to ourselves flow into one another, affecting and being affected
by other things we self-ascribe, and by our own decisions and wishes, while external
things remain fixed as our attention, plans, or ideas flow over them. Contrast a
perception of a red square with a mental image of a red square (even one that
arises in the mind unbidden): the latter will shift, recede, disappear, or transform
according as I attend to it, ignore it, suppress it, connect it with something else,
consider something related or something unrelated, and so on. And those changes
which thus affect it are themselves similarly mutable: while we do not choose each
step, we can intensify or inhibit things voluntarily if we try to. By contrast, the
perceived square either stays constant during all those fluctuations, or else changes
in a manner uncorrelated with them.[8] We might say that while neither is positively
voluntary, the perception *resists* my will, whereas the idea does not. (This idea has
a long history: see Descartes 1985, 2:26–27, 55; Locke 1836, 484; Berkeley 2008, 41.)[9]

A final idea is that the "efferent copy" mechanism employed in the monitoring
of motor actions could also be present with thoughts, feelings, and other mental
events. Feinberg (1978) and Campbell (1999) both suggest this, advocating regarding thought "as a motor process." The idea is that the brain processes that
produce actions or thoughts do not just produce those actions or thoughts, but
also produce "efferent copies," signals reporting that such-and-such an action or

---

[8] Again we might worry: doesn't perceiving things as responsive to "our will" require having already self-
ascribed our will? But as with the first suggestion, this misunderstands the proposal. The patterning
principle says that our spontaneous impressions of some X being "in us" or "outside us" are based on
detecting harmony between it and some Ys, but does not require that the Ys be *themselves* the objects of
any judgment or impression. We might be unconscious of the Ys, yet still have our conscious awareness
of X affected by its harmony with them.

[9] Aren't there inner mental states which are stubbornly resistant to our efforts to ignore or induce them
and which display stability over time? What about obsessive or haunting ideas and feelings, which refuse
to go away whatever we do? But these are not, it seems to me, genuinely indifferent to our will. Rather,
they recur and return constantly, in spite of being partially inhibited, or at least modulated, by our
efforts to dispel them.

thought has been produced. These copies are processed by a "comparator," some brain system that also takes in feedback from the actual execution of these actions and thoughts, and from other internal and external events, and monitors the correspondence or lack of correspondence among them. Since the comparator could operate below the level of conscious awareness (cf. Campbell 1999, 617–618), it would easily account for cases where something seems internal to us despite not cohering with other consciously accessible elements of our minds. But it might seem extravagant for every single conscious event to be part of such a monitoring process, with every whim, twinge, flicker of doubt, or snatch of memory generating a copy to be submitted to a comparator mechanism. If so, we might posit a comparator-type monitoring mechanism for some but not all mental events, relying on the first two proposals to explain our impressions of the others.

7.2.4. HARMONY AND HARMONIOUS CONNECTION

I conclude that the sort of "harmony" which leads us to regard events as occurring "in our own mind" can be something less than conformity to a definite prior decision: it can be any combination of conformity to background psychology (especially the background will), sensitivity to a willful stream, or the verdict of a dedicated comparator mechanism, with the particular balance of factors being a topic for empirical research. I will use the term "volitional harmony" for the specific sort of harmony which our minds look for when categorizing things as internal or external (as opposed to when discerning causal relations among external events). The term is still basically a placeholder; we do not know exactly what balance of factors is involved, nor what mechanisms implement and determine volitional harmony in the actual human brain. But it is a placeholder whose place is circumscribed by our limited but nontrivial scientific understanding of how human beings distinguish self and other.

If the patterning principle is true, and the relevant "patterns" are something like what I have called "volitional harmony," it follows that whether some thought or action seems spontaneously to be "mine" depends not on whether it really is, but on its relationship to my will (both occurrent and dispositional) and to other things which seem to me to be "mine." If two subjects, who discern self and other using the same basic mechanisms we do, are interacting harmoniously, so that what each does harmonizes with the psychology of the other, then they will each self-ascribe everything the other does that they are aware of. Let us say that subjects are "harmoniously connected" if they are set up so as to interact in this way all the time: then two harmoniously connected subjects will go their whole lives without ever realizing they are not alone. The self-representations they both form will be based, not specifically on what is true of them, but on what is true of the system that comprises them together with any other subjects they are harmoniously connected to.

I think it is plausible that the parts of a human being are harmoniously connected. The electrical behavior of a brain part, and the physiological structure that underlies that behavior, is very sensitive to that of surrounding parts and has developed in constant interaction with them for years. Moreover, they are alike in their biological requirements (pH, temperature, salinity, etc.), their ways of coding information, the timescale on which they act, and so on. It is hard to imagine better conditions for harmonious connection.

7.3. Composite Subjectivity and Agency

There is a special challenge to combinationism that challenges whether a composite subject who *acts*, in the sense of being genuinely responsible for the things they do, can be composed of parts which also act. Horgan (2007, 190), for instance, points out that "experiencing one's behavior as produced by oneself [i.e., as one's own action] is fundamentally different from experiencing it as caused by internal states of oneself," and if this is true of one's own mental *states*, it seems even more true of one's own mental *parts*. So the combinationist needs to explain how action by our mental parts can ever be enough to really count as action *by us*. (This objection is posed specifically against constitutive panpsychism by Mørch 2014, 198–201.)

This challenge should be distinguished from a couple of nearby issues that are not specific to combinationism, but which also deal with whether our everyday experience of agency is veridical or some form of illusion. The most famous and long-standing issue is whether we act *freely*, and whether our doing so is compatible with our decisions being the effects of prior causes. In the twentieth century, philosophers have also worried about the "causal exclusion" problem mentioned briefly in chapter 1, of whether in the law-governed world revealed by physics, there is room for our decisions, and other mental states, to be causes of behavior at all, free or otherwise: if our behavior is fully explained by the operation of fundamental physical laws governing the microscopic parts of our brain and body, then what work is left for our mental states to do? I will not try to solve these much-discussed problems here;[10] rather, I will try to defuse the specific worry that parts and wholes are always in competition for agency. To do this I will consider

---

[10] Panpsychist combinationists will presumably think that the causal exclusion problem is solved by the Russellian thesis that physical laws are actually realized by the basic experiential properties; functionalist combinationists may prefer to solve the problem in the opposite way, by saying that all mental properties are functional properties realized by underlying physical brain properties. My concern in this book has not been to defend either option, but to show how a combinationist theory can secure

two sorts of relation which are in some ways analogous to the relation between composite and component subjects: the relation between a subject and their own mental states, and the relation between multiple human beings acting at once. In both cases it seems that agential exclusion is sometimes a problem but sometimes not: by considering what makes the difference in these more familiar cases, we may get an idea of what is needed for conscious parts and wholes not to be in agential competition with one another.

7.3.1. AGENTIAL COMPETITION BETWEEN A PERSON AND THEIR STATES

Consider some ways that a movement of my body might fail to be my own action despite being caused by states of me, inspired by Davidson's (1973, 79–80) famous case. A mountain climber is holding his friend on a rope during a climb, and he releases his hold so that his friend falls to his death. But how exactly did this effect come about? Perhaps a gust of wind buffets him so hard that he cannot keep his grip; then releasing his friend is not an action, but something that happens. Or perhaps he decides that, to lighten his load and improve his chances, he will drop his companion. In both cases there are features of him that are causally relevant (e.g., how strong his finger muscles are), but only in the latter case would we call it an *action*, something caused by him as an agent. Davidson famously makes the point that this difference is not simply about whether the cause was a mental state of his: he might let go inadvertently as a result of being startled or afraid, and this would seem to be causation by his mental state but still not action by him. It is not even enough for the cause to be a mental state that rationalized the action: the thought "I could improve my own chances by dropping my friend" might occur to him, and unnerve him so much that he inadvertently drops his friend—again this seems not to be an action attributable to the climber himself. To qualify as his own action, the climber's mental state must cause the movement of his fingers "in the right way." Spelling out this "right way" precisely is not at all easy, but fortunately the combinationist does not need to do so; they simply need to show that there is at least some plausible way of distinguishing cases where the causal role of a subject's mental state does, and does not, exclude the person as a whole from agency, such that conscious parts could also sometimes exclude the whole from agency, and sometimes not.

A first pass might be that in the agential case the action is a result not just of one stray mental state but of the agent's whole set of mental states, of their "whole mind" and thus of "them as a whole." But of course it's rarely, if ever, true that

---

sufficient ontological intimacy between composite subjects and component subjects for either of these views to work, chiefly by having experiences shared between wholes and parts.

every single mental state someone is in makes a difference to their action (most just won't be relevant), and certainly not every single mental state makes a difference in our selfish mountain climber who deliberately drops his friend.

One key difference between the case where the mountain climber seems to act and the cases where he does not is that in the former he makes a *decision* to drop his friend. By 'decision' I mean that there is a process which is both potentially open to many considerations (e.g., motivations to drop or not drop the friend, ideas about alternative options available) and also "unified" in the sense that it generally issues in a consistent plan of action (even if the climber has many conflicting desires to do different, incompatible things, he cannot decide to do them all—he must pick). When actions arise from a mechanism like this, which allows many different motivations to "have their say" but enforces singleness of action, it seems intuitively right to say that the action reflects not just the one mental state that directly motivated it but also all those which "had their say." Of each of the climber's mental states we can at least say that *if* it had been relevant to whether or not to drop the friend, it was in a position to make a difference to the action (which we cannot say about the mental states of other people). In this sense it seems that we can say, roughly, that the deliberate action reflected *all* the climbers' mental states, but when they are startled by an unnerving thought, their behavior reflects only one "stray" mental state.

Could we say then that something counts as someone's action only when it results from a decision they make? No, because so many of our actions are not preceded by a conscious decision, and indeed happen too swiftly and fluidly to be deliberated about. But the "openness" characteristic of decision-making, the sense that any other mental state which was relevant could make a difference to whether the action was performed, *is* still present in such cases. If we found that our fluid everyday actions (our walking, sitting, picking things up, glancing around, and so on) kept happening even when we formed new beliefs or desires which directly spoke against performing them, we would feel vividly as though we were suddenly no longer in control of them, were not acting but just seeing our bodies move. So it might not be too far off the mark to say that something is our action if it is produced by a process that, like conscious decision-making, allows for all of our mental states to have input insofar as they are relevant to it.

One attractive feature of this suggestion is that it ties agency to the defining structure of a persona. According to psychological combinationism, what defines a persona is some set of unity relations among mental states—coherence, interdependence, mutual access, and so on. The details of this structure are variable and complex, but it is clearly bound up with what allows many different mental states to feed into a decision-making process that issues in a single united action. By their mutual submission to this decision-making process, different motivations are made interdependent and coherent with one another, and this mutual submission plausibly requires that they already be mutually accessible. If this is so, then the structure that defines a persona (sufficient unity of various sorts) plays a crucial causal role, and it seems to be just in cases like this that we would intuitively count the agent themselves as having acted.

This is not a full solution to the challenge of defining agency. For one thing, I have not defined "relevance"; for another, what distinguishes the interdependence involved in a decision from that involved in, say, someone's mood? (Perhaps the climber would not have been startled enough to drop his friend if he had been more cheerful and relaxed, and many different mental states could have made a difference to how relaxed he was feeling.) My aim is just to show that something's being caused by a state of me is sometimes compatible with its being my action, and sometimes not, and to gesture in the direction of the sort of factors that make the difference. This will help to illuminate how something's being caused by a *part* of me can also sometimes be compatible with its being my action, and sometimes not, and what makes the difference.

7.3.2. AGENTIAL COMPETITION BETWEEN DISCRETE AGENTS

There is obviously much more to say about the role of psychological structure in agency, but this is not the place to say it. What I have said above is not very surprising and is not specific to combinationism. What is specific to combinationism is that the question changes from "Is there any real agency?" to "Is it *my* agency or *my parts'* agency?" Surely something cannot be my action if it is *someone else's* action?

However, reflection on various forms of social cooperation shows that distinct agents are not always in competition for agency. For example, suppose A hires B to murder C, knowing that B is a very reliable assassin. A is culpable for C's resulting murder, even though their effecting this murder went through B: B is a conduit of A's agency just as a gun or knife would be. But B is also culpable: making themselves a conduit of A's agency does not erase their own. Of course there are circumstances in which the eventual act of murder might seem less fully attributable to one or the other of them, such as if B was coerced into carrying out A's orders, or if A did not really expect B to follow those orders. But at least in some cases it makes sense to regard them both as having agentially caused that outcome, and to that extent as not being in causal or agential competition.

The above example involves something like what in chapter 6 I called "authority relations": one person (B) takes on the expressed intention of another (A) and conforms their own intention to it. But a similar kind of agential noncompetition is plausibly present also in joint action and in actions based on joint commitment. When a team of assassins work together to kill a target, operating based either on their shared intention "that we kill this target" (a joint intention) or on having each committed publicly to the goal of their doing so (a joint commitment), it may be basically random which of them ends up striking the killing blow—and whichever of them does so may well have depended, both for their intention and for their success, on the others. In a case like this it seems artificial to insist on calling one the agent and the others mere accomplices (even if making such a distinction may sometimes be of social use).[11]

In each of these cases, where distinct agents appear not to be in agential competition, there seems to be a kind of "alignment" among the wills of the distinct agents. In authority relations this is asymmetrically established: the obeyer aligns their will to that of the commander. In joint action, the process is multilateral: each member of the group aligns their will to that of the others, until they all share a certain intention. In joint commitment, the alignment is indirect: rather than participants aligning their will to what the other participants intend, they each align theirs to the same public idea, like a constitution, a law, or just a verbal statement. Although there are significant differences in how people's wills come to be aligned in different cases, this common thread is crucial: different agents come to share agential responsibility for particular actions by aligning their wills with each other's.

This answer dovetails with the above suggestion that someone is responsible for the effect their states bring about, if they bring it about through a mechanism that is open to influence from all their other states—if they bring it about, we might say, in a unified way. We can now suggest that mechanisms which display this openness also serve to align the wills of different subjects whose states enter into them. If part of me wants money and part of me wants to relax, the process by which I reach a decision about how to balance these goals is also a process which brings the wills of these two parts of me into alignment. The actions produced by that mechanism are then both attributable to me as a whole (and not just to states of me), and also attributable to both those parts of me.[12]

---

[11] Singling out a single agent might be useful to ensure that each member has an incentive to refrain from executing the murder, even when they have already contributed considerably to the group's pursuit; this is similar to the obvious social interest in distinguishing murder from attempted murder (namely, to give people an incentive not to kill someone, even when they have already tried many times).

[12] I think this model is very intuitive when applied to social decision-making. A decision is usually said to have been made by some group of people, and the resultant actions attributed to them, only if they all "had their say" in its being made, if they all did or *could have* had some appropriate sort of input into the process. But it is also usually attributed to them only if the eventual outcome of that process is carried

7.3.3. ALIGNMENT OF WILLS BETWEEN WHOLE AND PART

In the previous section I defined volitional *harmony* as whatever structural relation of congruence among the wills of distinct subjects served to determine whether they would perceive each other's actions as "mine" or as "someone else's." Two subjects which consistently interact in volitionally harmonious ways are "harmoniously connected," and it is the harmonious connection between the parts of each human brain that stops them from recognizing each other as distinct. What is the relationship between volitional harmony and alignment of wills?

The alignment of wills in various forms of agential cooperation is clearly not harmonious connection, since the participants are fully aware of their distinctness from each other. In part this is because they have had so many other occasions, acting individually, to learn their own identities; in part this is because even when two people share an intention, and communicate regularly on how to implement it, much of the detail of each one's action will still be independent of the other's intentions. (I may tell you to "go over there quickly," but I can hardly specify the particular strides you should take.) Perhaps if these two deficiencies were made up—if some people acted together always, and determined every relevant detail of their actions jointly—the result would qualify as harmonious connection, and they would never need to form individual self-concepts.[13] Alternatively, perhaps harmonious connection requires something more than the alignment of wills involved in things like joint action; I cannot say for sure because both notions are still placeholders, awaiting further empirical and conceptual investigation. But harmonious connection certainly seems *sufficient* for alignment of wills: alignment of wills involves creating, briefly and perhaps in an attenuated sense, something like the volitional harmony that constantly pervades a normal human brain.[14] If this kind of alignment of wills is the key thing that lets distinct agents share responsibility for the same effect, then the harmoniously connected parts of a human brain should eminently qualify for such shared responsibility. They are "working

---

forward, or at least tolerated, by them all, as opposed to being fought by some, enforced by others, and ignored entirely by yet others.

[13] I discuss the possibility of this kind of enormously prolonged and intensified joint action in Roelofs (2017a), rejecting five different arguments that it would either no longer contain multiple agents, or that they would necessarily be impaired or defective when considered as rational agents.

[14] Schechter (2012a) offers an account of the split-brain phenomenon that fits this model: normally our two hemisphere subjects would have their will aligned (or, as she puts it, their agency unified) by direct transfers of information across the corpus callosum, but in the split-brain patient this alignment is achieved only by the pressures imposed by sharing a body: this co-embodiment secures unified agency for the whole patient, but on a different basis than the unified agency of a normal human whole.

together" in such a way that they can share responsibility for the actions they jointly produce.[15]

This is not yet an answer to our question: Even if the parts can share responsibility *with each other* for some or all of their joint effects, what about the whole they form? Though it may sound strange, I think the same basic answer applies: a whole is not in agential competition with its parts as long as its will and their wills are aligned. When one part's will diverges from that of the whole, there is a meaningful question of whether something is the action of one or of the other. When they do not diverge, the question can be answered only "both."

This alignment of wills between whole and part is not quite a matter of authoritative command, or joint action, or any other relation that obtains between discrete agents, because the two wills are constitutively related: the whole's will is grounded in the existence of, and relations among, its parts, and by extension in their wills insofar as those wills are relevant to how they relate. But this does not make alignment of wills automatic: one part's will might diverge considerably from that of all the others, and thus at least partly diverge from the whole's will. In such cases, the whole would experience a strange impression of acting and yet not acting; this is the experience of inner conflict, which I discuss in the next section.

7.4. Composite Subjectivity and Inner Conflict

What should we make of the experience of "inner conflict"? I mean here the broad class of cases in which we would find it natural to say things like "I wasn't myself," "I couldn't control myself," or "I'm at war with myself," or in which we would describe someone as struggling against some mental state of theirs, like addiction, temptation, compulsion, instinct, or conditioning. Cases like this, of varying degrees of severity, have prompted metaphors and theories involving a mind with parts which can oppose one another and struggle for control either against each other or against the person themselves. Such talk is often not interpreted literally, and surely is often not intended literally, in part because it is very hard to make sense of it literally—what are these things that must be fought, and who is it who must fight them?

This is where combinationism can help. I will not try to argue that any particular instance of "inner conflict" talk should be taken literally; rather I will simply ask: What *could* it mean, if it were?

---

[15] This does not mean they necessarily are all the agents of every single action produced by any of them; after all, some might have no causal role to play, or even receive any information about, certain actions produced by the others. How exactly to assign actions to interacting agents is a complex question: my goal is simply to show that there need not be a general principle of competition or exclusion among them.

7.4.1. WHAT ARE THE PARTIES TO AN INNER CONFLICT?

Let us first ask: What, in the most general terms, do people find themselves in inner conflict with—what aspects of their mental life tend to generate this kind of experience? I think the two key factors are (i) incompatible desires and (ii) a "failure of reconciliation" among those desires.

By "incompatible desires" I mean simply desires which, given the agent's perceived situation, cannot both be satisfied in any foreseeable way, but can each be satisfied by some course of action that frustrates the other. They "pull in different directions," motivating incompatible courses of action. But incompatible desires by themselves are not enough for inner conflict; our desires are routinely incompatible in various ways, and while we often regret not being able to satisfy them all, we usually find it easy enough to prioritize, pick a preferred course of action whose benefits outweigh its costs, and carry it out. Inner conflict involves what I call a failure of reconciliation. But what does this mean?

Successful "reconciliation" need not involve the losing desire disappearing, or being revised so as to no longer be incompatible with the winning one (though sometimes it does). Often we continue to feel both desires even while forming and unproblematically executing a plan of action that satisfies only one. What is important is severing any direct link between desire and action: the losing desire is reconciled to the decision when it is denied any power to produce actions in the direction of its satisfaction. When reconciliation fails, the losing desire controls or constrains action in defiance of the decision that frustrates it, either by causing actions which satisfy that desire, or by preventing actions which decisively frustrate it. For example, a heroin addict who has decided to quit cold turkey may find both that their desire for heroin can make them actively consume heroin "in spite of themselves," and also that this desire can prevent them from throwing their heroin away.

Failure of reconciliation seems to be made more likely both by the strength of the desires that must be frustrated and by the relative causal independence of the conflicting desires. Desires which arise from the same sets of mental mechanisms, which "stand and fall together," seem easier to reconcile with one another and less often give rise to inner conflict. By contrast, inner conflict more often arises when two conflicting desires have very different causal bases; for example, classic cases of being overcome by temptation usually involve one of the following three things: a desire based on something bringing pleasure (e.g., desire for food or rest) conflicting with a desire not associated with pleasure (e.g., desire to conform to a training regimen); a desire which is strengthened by stimuli in the immediate environment (e.g., desire for some money right in front of one) conflicting with a desire which requires actively "remembering" something distant or abstract (e.g., desire to avoid pain the next day); or a desire based in simple, developmentally and/or evolutionarily old systems (e.g., danger detection) conflicting with a desire based in later-developing, more distinctively human systems (e.g., adherence to social rules). And plausibly, addiction is so prone to generate inner conflict precisely because it involves a chemical mechanism for forming and maintaining desires independently of the rest of the subject's psychology.

So let us say that inner conflict involves two or more mental things of some sort, distinguished by being associated with incompatible desires which are sufficiently strong or causally independent for reconciliation to fail.

7.4.2. INNER CONFLICT AS INVOLVING COMPONENT SUBJECTS

Let us now suppose, as a combinationist might, that these two opposing mental things are conscious subjects, each a part of the whole person, and the sense in which they are associated with these desires is by "having" them in the same sense that the whole person does. What would follow from such a supposition, given the claims of sections 7.2 and 7.3, that our impressions of self and other track volitional harmony, and that agential competition is avoided by alignment of wills?

It seems clear that a failure of reconciliation involves a failure to align wills, and thus a failure of volitional harmony. The two putative parts have different desires, and neither accepts restriction by the other in their capacity to produce action. They are like two people who not only want incompatible things but insist on pursuing those different things even when it means subverting or opposing the other's efforts. This failure may be only partial, mitigated by alignment of wills on many other matters—rather like squabbling members of a political coalition who nevertheless remain able to act jointly on some issues. Subjects whose wills are not aligned clearly cannot share responsibility for the actions they produce. If my addictive desire for heroin drives me to consume it in spite of the strenuous efforts of "that part of me which wants to quit," the latter entity by supposition is not the agent of the consuming. (Conversely, the addictive part is not the agent of my throwing away my heroin.)

The more significant question is whether the whole subject shares responsibility for such actions, which turns on whether the whole subject's will coheres with that of the particular part responsible, which in turn depends on what counts as the whole subject's "will." And in a case like this, where the whole harbors conflicting desires and cannot reconcile them under any single decision-making mechanism, it is not clear that there will be a single determinate thing answering the description "the whole subject's will." Given this, it will likely be somewhat indeterminate whether the wills of the whole and of a given part are aligned enough to share responsibility, and thus somewhat indeterminate whether the person themselves has acted when that part of them produces an action.

Consider another version of Davidson's mountain climber, who has weighed up their various motives for and against dropping their friend, and found the reasons against far more compelling. Suppose they form a settled intention not to drop their friend, but nevertheless at the last moment find the temptation to save themselves by lightening their load too strong to resist, and drop their friend in a "moment of weakness." The sharp divergence between one element of their psyche and the decision reached by the person as a whole prevents us from seeing this act as equally fully theirs and their parts': it is partly theirs (unlike the case where the same thought or desire simply unnerves them enough to loosen their grip) because it operated through their psychological mechanisms for decision-making and rational action, but not fully theirs because it disrupts and usurps those mechanisms without submitting to the proper protocols.

Of course this result is a matter of degree. If the two conflicting parts are roughly equal in various ways (neither has more control of the decision-making mechanisms, and neither shares more of the whole's desires), it will be harder to say nonarbitrarily that the whole's will either fits or conflicts with either part's will. If one of the parts is considerably "larger" in the sense of comprising far more of the subject's desires—in particular, if all their desires except one can be reconciled to the verdicts of a single decision-making mechanism—then we should think of the whole subject's will as approximating the will of that part, so that whatever that part does is done by the whole subject. The smaller, more "isolated" part, by contrast, is in conflict with the will of the whole (because it is in conflict with the will of the other, larger, part) and so the whole can more reasonably disavow the actions it produces.[16]

Another implication of supposing the mental parts involved in inner conflict to be subjects is that they will recognize each other as distinct, because their conflict

---

[16] The claim that someone is not (determinately) the agent of actions produced by a desire of theirs which is in conflict with their broader psyche may seem to let too many people too easily "off the hook." But it is advanced based on the presumption that the two parts really are resolutely and determinedly opposing each other, i.e., that the person has tried with every ounce of effort to restrain their wayward desire. In many cases people put up a "token effort," or willingly allow an apparently wayward desire to control them because they prefer to act inconsistently, and be in denial about it, than to really give up the prospect of satisfaction. Here there is not really a conflict, fundamentally: the two parts of their mind have the same will, namely to allow there to be the appearance of inner conflict. I will not attempt to fully describe or analyze the subtleties of self-deception in such cases, beyond pointing out that they do not threaten the validity of the preceding analysis of cases where the conflict is entirely genuine; rather, they presuppose it, since if there could never be genuine conflict there would be no sense in "staging" it.

involves a lack of volitional harmony. By the arguments of section 7.2, the effects these component subjects have on one another will appear to each as alien, not as their own actions. (Of course this loss may be only partial, and in a healthy person's life it occurs against the background of a long history of unified self-perception, in which all the person's parts have seen each other as extensions of themselves.) Then the whole, inheriting the judgments and perceptions of each part, will get the following impression (where parts 1 and 2 act on desires A and B):

- I am the one who acts on desire A (inherited from part 1).
- I am not the one who frustrates desire A by acting on desire B (inherited from part 1).
- I am the one who acts on desire B (inherited from part 2).
- I am not the one who frustrates desire B by acting on desire A (inherited from part 2).

For example, suppose A and B are the desire to indulge an addiction and the desire to break an addiction, respectively; the composite subject would then simultaneously feel themselves to be the one trying to indulge the addiction, the one frustrating that effort, the one trying to break the addiction, and the one frustrating that effort.

This inconsistent impression of one's own identity seems to me to accurately capture the phenomenology of inner conflict: there seem to be two distinct things, and yet I seem to be both of them. Of course this contradictory impression may be more or less sharp; as well as fully resolute inner conflict, with both sides giving their all, there are many varieties of half-hearted allowing-oneself-to-succumb, and in the latter case there will be intermediate degrees of volitional harmony, yielding odd impressions as of something's being somewhere between self and other, in ways whose details deserve more empirical and phenomenological study than can be given here.

7.4.3. INNER CONFLICT AMONG SUBSTRATES AND AMONG PERSONAS

But if the mental parts involved in inner conflict are subjects, what sort of subjects are they—brain lobes, neural networks, subpersonalities, or what? In light of the reasonable disagreement over the essence of subjecthood, we should try construing them both as substrates and as personas. It is certainly possible for two substrates of experience to be related in such a way that they form a single subject which experiences inner conflict in the way that we do. Plato (1997, 246a–254e) famously imagines the soul of an internally conflicted person as a team composed of two horses and a man, trying to work together but only sometimes succeeding; if such a team did exist, and its members stood in such intimate relations that they generally perceived each other as extensions of themselves, then we would have a case where the structure of human inner conflict is realized by a collection of discrete substrates (namely, three organisms). But in fact it seems unlikely that the actual brain is organized like this, with separate lobes responsible for different goals and desires. The brain's division seems much more to be functional, with different areas dedicated to different sorts of information processing that can subserve many different desires (e.g., both the desire for money and the desire for self-respect can influence and make use of visual perception, auditory perception, imagination, strategic thought, etc.). Given this, it seems that if we identify the substrate for the desires associated with one side of an inner conflict, it may well turn out to also be the substrate for the desires associated with the other, or at least to overlap significantly with it. If our aim is to illuminate the conflict between these two subjects, these considerations count against construing them as substrates.

Can we, instead, make sense of the subjects involved in inner conflict as personas? Yes, and the very features that characterize inner conflict (incompatible desires and failure of reconciliation) provide a guide on how to do so. Their incompatible desires, and consequent incompatible drives to action, constitute an important failure of global consistency between the contents of their mental states; the failure of reconciliation indicates a lack of causal interdependence. If we weight these forms of unity highly, we will find two sharply distinguished clusters of experiences within the overall consciousness of the conflicted person. By a high-threshold definition of personas, these clusters will constitute two distinct personas, contained within the whole persona constituted by the whole cluster which meets a lower-threshold definition of personas. And this will be true whatever the division of the underlying substrates—even if these different personas arise out of activity of the same brain areas.

So it does make sense to interpret inner conflict as involving a literal conflict between distinct subjects. Of course there are some major caveats to this literal construal: the distinct parts are subjects only according to the psychological, not the metaphysical, conception; they are psychological subjects only given particular ways of weighting forms of unity, and particular thresholds for these forms; and, most interestingly, they may be sharply distinguished only "on one border," so to speak. This is because the forms and degrees of unity that define them may not be transitive: experience A might be largely consistent with, and interdependent with, experience B, which is likewise consistent and interdependent with experience C, even though A and C are too contradictory or independent to meet the same standards. The two incompatible desires involved in inner conflict might therefore both qualify as sufficiently unified with many of the same other desires and experiences, despite not being sufficiently unified with one another. We would then have difficulty individuating the personas involved; there could be thought to be one, or to be two, with the choice between those descriptions being to some extent arbitrary (cf. the problem posed by "ring species" for the biological definition of a species, e.g., Moritz et al. 1992).

7.4.4. INNER CONFLICT AND IDENTITY OVER TIME

Further complexities arise when we consider identity across time: How long do the component personas involved in inner conflict survive? If the same pattern of conflict recurs frequently (e.g., someone is driven to self-destructive acts by uncontrollable anger every time they feel insulted), the Neo-Lockean account of personal identity suggests that the rival parts on each occasion are identical to those on the other occasions. The defiant part on one occasion is both very similar to and causally dependent on the defiant part on the previous occasion; that is, the two are psychologically continuous in the same way that the whole persona is psychologically continuous across time. This is why it can make sense to think of someone as engaged in an ongoing, recurrent struggle with a persisting part of themselves (e.g., "their anger").

But what about times when there is no inner conflict, either because the stimulus is absent or because the person has been able to achieve reconciliation among all their desires? Does the defiant persona (e.g., the person's "anger") still exist—that is, is it identical to (by being psychologically continuous with) any persona which exists at this time? On the one hand, it may seem not, because on those more peaceful occasions there is no subcluster of experiences that stands out from the rest on account of being more tightly unified—not because there has been any loosening of the unity that had previously tended to obtain between the experiences associated with the defiant part (e.g., the person's perceptions of offense, impulses to become angry, feelings of simmering grudgeful resentment against particular people), but because of a strengthening of the unity between them and other experiences. That is, the component persona seems to have disappeared by "dissolving into" the whole, rather like a black-and-white drawing which is "erased" by filling in the white spaces with black ink.

On the other hand, we seem to miss something if we just say that the angry subpersona has ceased to exist. That would imply that if the person ever achieves full integration, so as to no longer be troubled by inner conflict, their component personas have been permanently destroyed—turning what seems like a happy reconciliation into a sort of intrapsychic fratricide. We want to say that integrating all aspects of one's personality is, at least sometimes, a laudable and rational aim, not that it is rational for conflicting component personas to obstruct integration as a means of self-preservation. One thing we could try saying is that whenever inner conflict is not occurring, the component persona is identical to the whole person. After all, there is no shortage of psychological continuity between the two, even if the inner conflict involves a limited form of discontinuity. But this turns the process of overcoming inner conflict (or just temporarily ameliorating it) into a "fusion case" of the sort which has proven endlessly paradoxical for theories of personal identity. The basic problem is that if the part has become the whole, then they are the same thing. But the whole was the whole all along, and if it's the same thing as the part, then the part was the whole all along. Yet we started by saying that it was not. This sort of logical problem arises whenever two things go from being distinct to being identical; I will not here attempt to solve it (though in chapter 8 I suggest some ways that combinationism may affect the plausibility of different solutions), only to note the present case as one instance of this general form.

A final possibility is to keep the component personas in existence, but also keep them distinct from the whole, by saying that even when no inner conflict is occurring—even when all unity relations hold just as strongly between the experiences constituting that component persona and those not—the component persona still exists just *because* it existed earlier and was distinguishable from its surroundings then. That is, we might permit ourselves to individuate entities by first looking for patterns that stand out at a particular time, and then tracing the development of that pattern over time, continuing to see it as existing even when it is better connected with its surroundings and thus no longer stands out. After all, personas are not metaphysical bedrock; they are high-level patterns, and it is perfectly appropriate for us to construct our criteria and definitions for their individuation in a flexible way, to enable us to capture whichever high-level patterns we have reason to care about.

7.4.5. INNER CONFLICT AND DISSOCIATION

Finally, what about dissociative identity disorder (DID), in which a single body manifests multiple "alters," rather like Jekyll and Hyde in our earlier thought experiment? DID is usually treated as a disorder afflicting a single individual, whose therapeutic goal should be integration of all their alters so as to no longer have DID. Yet on the face of it, psychological accounts of personal identity, like the Neo-Lockean accounts discussed earlier, imply that the alters are distinct people, and thus entitled to be recognized and respected as such. This tension between popular philosophical accounts of personal identity and the practical approach generally taken to DID has been recognized (e.g., Bayne 2002), and I believe that one of the merits of combinationism is that it can simultaneously do justice to both sides. DID is indeed a condition affecting a single individual,[17] while at the same time involving a literal plurality of component individuals. In fact, combinationism can make sense of DID as just a radical extension of ordinary inner conflict: two or more sets of brain processes consistently give rise to clusters of experiences that are well-unified internally, but strikingly disunified with those arising from the other processes. Because the personas constituted by these clusters at different times are psychologically continuous, they should be recognized as real, distinct, enduring subjects—at least on the psychological conception of what subjects are. If integration is achieved, the same three options as above are available for describing what has happened: that the alters no longer exist, that they are now all identical to the whole subject and thus to each other, and that they still exist but without standing out from the rest of the subject's mental life as distinct entities.

The biggest difficulty in giving this combinationist account of DID is explaining why the disunity involved is not just volitional but also extends to thought, memory, and knowledge. Some hypotheses link DID with traumatic experiences in childhood (see, e.g., Ellason et al. 1996), which would make sense if volitional disunity is the crucial factor. Intensely unpleasant experiences are ones whose subject intensely desires not to be having them, and thus for another subject to volitionally harmonize with them will require the latter to come to also intensely desire that this ongoing state not obtain—which subjects will understandably resist doing, since it amounts to taking on some of the other's intense unhappiness. But how this leads into a situation where the different alters are unaware of each other, and lack memory access to each other's experiences, is much less clear. Indeed the whole topic of how cognition relates to the will is a perplexing one: in general we maintain a clear distinction between what we want to be true and what we think is true, but our occasional failures (manifested by "wishful thinking" on the one hand, and "adaptive preferences" on the other) show that this distinction is not guaranteed. Moreover, DID need not always originate in trauma and may have multiple different sorts of cause. To say anything positive here would be to speculate about a matter best studied empirically.

---

[17] I remain agnostic on whether DID is necessarily a disorder when it does not cause dysfunction or distress; its status as disorder is denied by those who describe themselves as simply "being multiple" (e.g., Amorpha 2010; Astraea 2017).

7.5. Conclusions

A division into component personas works differently from a division of the neural substrates of experience, in that it looks at the pattern of relations among experiences even if they bear little resemblance to the structure of the underlying mechanisms that enable them. Because it is defined by the high-level information processing that enables introspection, agency, and self-consciousness, it is more readily visible to us introspectively, and to the view of others who observe our behavior. The occasions when we spontaneously find it natural and useful to think of people as having person-like parts will tend to be of this sort, involving component personas, not component substrates.

Nevertheless the combining of personas faces the same five internal problems as the combining of substrates, most especially the boundary argument, which I addressed in section 7.1. It also, however, throws into relief some special bridging problems concerning self-consciousness and agency, defining characteristics of the special sort of subjects we call "persons."

The problem around self-consciousness was this: How could any composite whose parts were all self-conscious achieve self-consciousness as a single whole? And would it not automatically thereby be aware of its own compositeness, in a way which we humans seem not to be? Yet if some composite subjects (like us, presumably) do not have individually self-consciousness parts, why don't those parts reflect on and identify themselves as distinct?

The problem around agency was this: When my body moves, is it me or some part of me that performs this action? Intuitively we would like to say that I am the agent, even if parts of me participate as well, but how is this compatibility to be ensured? Doesn't the causation of my actions by some smaller agent within me imply a lack of control on my part?

In trying to solve these problems, I gave a central role to the volitional relations among component subjects, the way that the will of one relates to the will of the other. In so doing I could not help but frame individual reflection and decision-making as something like a social process, a meeting and conversation among many beings. I am thus led toward the idea that "the higher mental functions have their origin in and, therefore, share important features with, interpersonal activity" (Fernyhough 1996, 48; cf. Gregory 2017). The process by which each of us matures and becomes a rational person is, according to psychological combinationism, essentially a social process conducted so successfully as to no longer appear to be social.

However, knowing what lessons to draw from the deep analogy between individuals and groups depends on a topic I have not even touched here: the value of *autonomy*, of making up "your own" mind and living according to "your own" will. It is a truism that to live together in society, people must accept some limitation to their autonomy in this sense. Questions about how far autonomy must or should be restricted, and how such restrictions are justified, are central to political philosophy, and combinationism only makes them deeper by pushing them down into the psyche itself: for many component subjects to live together as a well-integrated composite subject, they must forswear their own individual control over action, and even their own capacity to know their identity. Conversely, if individual parts of the self have *independent* wills, letting them know themselves and act individually, the whole's autonomy is compromised: they are no longer "master of themselves," but act inconsistently based on caprice or circumstance, as one desire or another wins out and directs their actions. Indeed combinationism goes beyond expanding the range of cases where this kind of conflict over autonomy occurs: it unsettles the very idea of "your own mind," since a composite subject's mind is not *just* theirs but also "belongs" to their parts. To evaluate the values involved in these conflicts, and how they should be resolved, is a major undertaking in moral and political philosophy. I have not tried to do any of that ethical work, but merely to lay out the metaphysical and psychological framework within which we can best appreciate what is at stake.

8 What It Is Like for Two to Become One

CHAPTER 7 OUTLINED psychological combinationism, on which subjects are constituted by sets of unified experiences and component subjects are constituted by clusters of experiences which are either *more* unified than the larger mass that contains them or unified relative to a different scale. Because there are so many ways that experiences can be called "unified," there are many valid ways to divide a subject into component subjects—many different patterns within the stream of their consciousness that are worth recognizing. Of particular relevance for humans are unity relations that involve the will: when component subjects' wills are "aligned," as those of cooperating humans are, the behavior that results is a genuine action by all of them, and by the whole they form. And when their wills are also "harmonized," covarying reliably and in detail, they will each experience the other as extensions of themselves. When sharply opposed wills arise within a human mind and cannot be brought into harmony or alignment, the human being's unified sense of self and of agency begins to break down.

In this chapter I seek to illustrate and enrich psychological combinationism, along with the other theories of combination I have been developing, by applying them to an extended thought experiment involving the fusion of two persons into one—or, in combinationist terms, two persons becoming conscious parts of a composite person. Over the course of this thought experiment, subjects like us become subjects like our parts, and it is one of the advantages of combinationism that it can make sense of this as a gradual change of status rather than an abrupt transition.

8.1. Introducing Mind-Fusion

The best way to get a sense of what it is like to be a component subject in a unified mind is to imagine becoming one, and so most of this chapter is devoted to a thought experiment involving the fusion of two minds into one. My primary aim is to make vivid the abstract principles defended in previous chapters; my secondary aim is to argue that combinationism expands our options for understanding survival and identity in cases of fission and fusion.

8.1.1. MARS NEEDS FUSED HUMANS

Suppose that some technologically advanced Martians decide, for reasons best known to themselves, that they would like to be able to combine many humans into a sort of "hive mind" creature, with a single consciousness controlling many bodies and drawing upon the cognitive resources of many brains. Suppose that a team of their best scientists gets funding for a series of experiments aimed at creating such a "multihuman."

They do this by implanting specially designed pairs of electrodes into the brains of two human participants, such that when a certain circuit in one brain fires, it activates an electrode, which sends a radio signal to the other, which immediately generates a surge of current in the other brain. This allows activity in one brain to produce or influence activity in the other brain, and hence allows the thoughts and experiences of one subject to produce or influence thoughts and experiences in the other. If the number and sophistication of these electrodes were increased enough, the causal connections between the two brains could eventually be as fast, as complex, and as reliable as the connections between the two hemispheres of either brain individually. At this point the only thing stopping us from saying there is a single, highly integrated nervous organ, with parts in two different skulls, is that the electrical signals are traveling via radio, not along an axon.[1]

---

[1] Churchland (1981, 87–88) briefly discusses this sort of procedure in a futuristic human society; Rovane (1998, 141) discusses something similar but conceived of as a voluntary undertaking "something like a marriage arrangement" (cf. Parfit 1971, 19; Roelofs 2017a).

Of course this description simplifies what will be an incredibly fraught and complicated process. The Martians are ahead of us technologically by a few hundred years, but not by thousands, so while they can create and implant these electrodes, they have limited foresight about, and control of, what happens next. To prevent messy failures that only deplete their supply of humans, they run the procedure carefully and gradually, over a period of months or years, so that increases in the bandwidth of the implants are interspersed with periods of exploration, assimilation, and adjustment by the human participants, who can spend time working out what signals they can now send and receive and how to respond to these developments.

Moreover, let us suppose that the experimenters design the implants to mimic nerve cells as closely as possible. Obviously there are limits, since nerve cells do not emit or receive radio signals, but they may incorporate things like neurotransmitters, axons, ion channels, and so on. In particular, the manner in which the implants "multiply," spreading to connect more and more circuits across the two brains, could be made responsive to the way in which the participants use it. Just as neuronal connections become stronger or weaker based on the history of their activity, so can the links between implants, and between each implant and its brain. (As Churchland [1981, 88] says, "We simply trick the normal processes of dendritic arborization into growing their own myriad connections with the active microsurface of the transducer.") This way the experimenters need not constantly be performing repeat surgeries: the first operation puts in a biomechanical device which thereafter grows and expands into the brain.

8.1.2. FOUR OBSERVABLE OUTCOMES

So far I have described the various high-tech interventions which our Martian scientists are making into the brains of their human subjects. The goal of these interventions is to create a single being, with a unified mind and coordinated, intelligent behavior across both bodies, which combines the personality, memories, and values of both humans. But their success in this endeavor is not guaranteed. While I will focus on the "good cases" in which they succeed, other results are possible, and the outcome is determined not simply by the setup and techniques used, but also by the way the humans handle the process. They have to undergo a transformative, potentially traumatic experience, and their temperament and attitudes to each other will make the difference at each stage between experiencing it as communion or as invasion.

We may distinguish four "ideal types" of outcome, allowing that actual outcomes may be intermediate between them or entirely unexpected. The intended outcome can be called "merging"; this is when there is a unified mind (i.e., a single maximal persona) that controls both bodies and is recognizably continuous with both original personas. The combinationist can still say that this is actually one of *three* minds, since the originals can survive as parts of it. But they display no more independent thought or sense of individuality than the conscious parts of a human brain.

The second-best outcome for the Martians is to have a single persona controlling both bodies but displaying recognizable continuity with only one of the original two personas. In such a case, we must surmise that the other persona has been suppressed, assimilated, or somehow subsumed into the resultant being without being at all manifest in that being's behavior. Call this outcome "domination." For instance, one of the two participants might be aggressive, defensive, and unwilling to allow another access to its thoughts, while the other is submissive and deferential and values acceptance over autonomy. The development of the experiment might then involve the former constantly seeking to interfere more and more with the latter's mental processes, while resisting any countervailing interference. By the end, one human has in effect "colonized" and "assimilated" the other's brain into itself, and thereby taken control of their body.

Third, we might end up with two recognizably separate personas, controlling different bodies or alternating in control of both bodies, despite the organic connectedness of their brains. This would be somewhat similar to a case of dissociative identity disorder: two psychologically distinct but internally integrated personalities control (simultaneously or sequentially) a single organic structure. These two would probably be recognizable as the original people, who had built up psychological barriers to replace the physiological ones that had previously separated them; a combinationist might still think there are, strictly, three minds here, but the composite mind they formed would at best be like that of a familiar social group like a club rather than an ordinary human mind. Call this outcome "dissociation."

This might arise if both participants were very concerned to maintain the privacy of their own mental processes but had little desire to explore or enter into those of the other. At each stage of the experiment, they might respond to the new way of influencing each other's minds by setting up, independently or cooperatively, policies and habits to minimize its effect.

Finally, the process might be too traumatic and too invasive for either subject to survive. They might both end up so deeply psychotic and fragmented that the resultant being is not recognizable as either, and perhaps not even as a single individual. This might mean that neither body's behavior was coherently interpretable at all, or even that at a certain point both bodies collapse into catatonia or epilepsy, having somehow killed each other from within, and never wake up. One or both might even become traumatized to the point of violent paranoia, seeking out the other's physical body and stabbing or strangling it in order to silence the voices in their head. (If there is a composite mind here, it is most similar to unstructured aggregates like "all the snakes in Ontario.") Call this outcome "dissolution."

So to get the philosophically most interesting "merging" result, we might need to run the experiment several times. But we may suppose that the Martian experimenters have as much concern for human life as human experimenters have for the life of rodents. My reason for sketching these four possible outcomes is that it will be illuminating to refer to them at various points, noting how the way the participants handle a particular aspect of the process might make one or the other outcome more likely. While I will focus on the responses which most conduce to the merging outcome, these will be best appreciated by contrasting them with those which conduce to domination, dissociation, or dissolution.

8.1.3. WHAT HAS HAPPENED TO THE ORIGINAL PARTICIPANTS?

As well as uncertainty about which of these four outcomes will be observed, there is room for uncertainty about what any of those outcomes would mean for the fate of the original participants. In this respect the procedure is a bit like the famous thought experiment discussed in chapter 2, where two people's bodies are given the other's memories, personality, beliefs, and so on; even once we have established every observable fact, and even once we know exactly what has happened in scientific terms, the question can still be asked whether two people have "switched bodies" or instead "switched minds." Similar things apply to *Star Trek*–style teletransportation thought experiments, where a device scans, records, and disassembles the person who enters, then transmits the recorded information to a device elsewhere which constructs an exact replica of their body out of different particles. Even a full scientific understanding of how the device works is not enough by itself to answer the question whether the device is transporting one individual from place to place, or killing them and making a new but exactly similar person elsewhere. Such questions turn not on the scientific question of what would in fact happen, but on the question of what defines a person.

Particular puzzles are raised by the "merging" outcome of our imagined procedure because of the difference in number of people at the beginning and the end. If we start with two people but end with one, which (if either) of the original people has survived as the resultant person? (A similar question could be asked if we ran the reverse version of the procedure, "splitting" a single person into two people: Which of them, if either, does the original person survive as?) This is the puzzle of fusion and fission, which has been discussed extensively but for which no fully sat-isfying solution seems to be available (see, e.g., Wiggins 1967, 50; Parfit 1971; Perry 1972; Lewis 1976; Nozick 2003). Other science-fictional thought experiments pose the exact same puzzle; the two most often discussed are the "teletransporter mal-function," where a teletransporter, instead of just scanning, disassembling, and then re-creating a person, re-creates them twice over, creating two perfect copies of a single person (Parfit 1984, 199ff.; cf. "Second Chances," S6E24 of *Star Trek: The Next Generation*, and "Tuvix," S2E24 of *Star Trek: Voyager*), and the "double-brain transplant," where someone's brain is safely bisected into two halves each sufficient to support consciousness, and each is then implanted into and given control over a different body (Wiggins 1967; Shoemaker 1984; Parfit 1971, 1984). And in chapter 7 I noted, in passing, that if the alters of a DID patient are distinct subjects, then the dissociation that produces them is a form of "fission," and any therapeutic reintegration they may achieve is a form of "fusion." Let us consider some of the options available for thinking about what happens to the original participants of our Martian experiment, to see both why the puzzle is puzzling and what combinationism might contribute.

On the one hand, it seems as though both of the original participants are gone: they no longer exist, having vanished into the new whole. This would clearly be the right thing to say if the observed result of the procedure was "dissolution." But if the observed result is "merging," with both bodies walking and talking and seem-ingly alive, governed by a single personality, it seems wrong to simply regard this as the destruction of both participants, as though they had simply died. They are learning new ways to communicate, to learn from each other, to work together, and this seems like a basically constructive, not destructive, sort of process. While the participants clearly do change, this change is gradual, organic, and often bene-ficial in terms of overall capacities. In particular, the resultant person still has the memories of both participants' lives, and in that sense will seem to itself to have existed prior to the procedure.

But if the original participants survive, where are they? It might seem attrac-tive to identify them each with the single person who controls both bodies at the end, but this rapidly leads to contradiction: if participant 1 is the same person as the resultant person, and so is participant 2, then participant 1 is the same person as participant 2. But clearly they are distinct people—otherwise we would not even have a case of fusion at all. We could avoid this contradiction by saying that participant 1 survives as the resultant person, but participant 2 does not (or vice versa), and this would seem the right thing to say in a "domination" case, where the resultant person shows psychological continuity with only one of the participants. But in a "merging" case, where each is equally continuous with both, there is no nonarbitrary way to say which participant has survived and which has not.

There is a way to say that both participants equally have survived: to say that they are jointly identical with the resultant person rather than individually identical with it. They are not *each* that resultant person; rather they are it, together. In short, each original person has become a part of a person. In a fission case, where a single person splits in two, the corresponding analysis would be that two parts of them have survived, while they have become a pair of persons. Let us call this "the compositional approach."

The compositional approach is not often explicitly defended (though see Moyer 2008). Parfit (1971, 7) rejects it for "greatly distort[ing] the concept of a person. . . . It is hard to think of two people as, together, being a third person." The thesis of this book is that although this is true (it is indeed hard to think of two people as, together, being a third person), it is a feature of our everyday thinking that needs to be changed, not embraced. In short, the compositional approach "distorts" the concept of a person because it violates the anti-combination intuition.

8.1.4. COMBINATIONISM AND THE FUSION OF PERSONS

The fact that the compositional approach to fusion and fission conflicts with anti-combination does not, of course, mean that combinationists need to accept it. Indeed, combinationists need not endorse a single approach for all sorts of fission and fusion. For instance, teletransporter malfunctions, which make two or more identical copies but do not in any literal sense "split" the original person, might need to be treated differently from things like double-brain transplants or amoeba-like physical "splitting." Part of my aim in distinguishing the metaphysical and psychological conceptions of subjects, and remaining neutral between them, was to emphasize that combinationism does not by itself imply anything about what subjects are or what it means for one of them to survive over some period of time.

I do think, however, that it is worthwhile to explore how the compositional approach might be spelled out, to show the sort of options that combinationism makes available. So in the next two sections I will lay out a compositional way of understanding what has happened in my imagined Martian experiment when the observed result is "merging." I will treat the process not strictly as "two becoming one" but as "three becoming three": at the beginning there is a pair of subjects and the two subjects that compose it, and by the end the former has become an intelligent composite subject, and each of the latter has become a component subject within it. It is like the process of welding two pieces of metal together: nothing has really been created or destroyed, but whereas before the two pieces stood out as units, and the whole that they formed did not, afterward their behavior is sufficiently integrated (e.g., any movement of one will mean a corresponding movement of the other) that the whole now stands out more than either part. The transition is thus not a discontinuous jump from two to one, but a gradual shift in which of the levels exhibits greater integration, and thus stands out as more salient.

8.2. Fusion from the Perspective of the Parts

In this section I discuss my thought experiment of fusion with a focus on the two human individuals involved. My aim is to show that what happens to them can be understood as an extreme form of various familiar relational phenomena: they are each interacting with another person, who they at first perceive as "other" but come eventually to perceive as an extension of themselves.

8.2.1. LET'S TALK, BRAIN TO BRAIN

At first, the two participants will be related somewhat like two conversational partners, or two people with pagers. Each can, by thinking a certain way, produce a certain kind of experience in the other. Depending on where the implants are first put, this might be one seeing lights when the other thinks hard about math, or one hearing words whenever the other feels sad, or something else. Each participant may struggle, at first, to distinguish "normally occurring" experiences from those produced by the other. But suppose we give them a supportive environment, where they can talk normally with each other (so as to ask "Do you feel anything when I do *this*?"), and have the time and inclination to practice controlling and interpreting the implants. This will probably let them devise a mutually understood "language" and come to perceive implant-generated experiences as signals betokening another mind, just as we perceive words, hand gestures, or facial expressions.

In learning this language, the participants would be employing the correlation or lack thereof between their own volitions, the reported volitions of the other, the experiences they undergo, and the reported experiences of the other, thereby conforming to the patterning principle from chapter 7. Assuming that each was honest and open, they could distinguish experiences arising spontaneously, experiences voluntarily produced by them, and experiences produced voluntarily or unintentionally by the other. But they could do this only because these various experiences were generated by "unsynchronized" systems, which varied independently rather than being volitionally harmonized at all times.

With time, they will also be able to reliably discern, from incoming signals, what effects they are producing in the other—paralleling the ability to, for instance, read in someone's face how they feel about one's utterances. Even before this they can guess, infer, or wonder about their effects on the other—including how the other is judging them based on "hearing their thoughts." Each may thus become "self-conscious" about whether the other finds the electronic relaying of their thoughts impressive, amusing, disgusting, etc. They may then make efforts to reduce or control the amount of information they send out, either by avoiding the thoughts which send out signals, by using feedback information to find ways of thinking those thoughts without being detected, or by learning which thoughts the other finds hardest to identify. Each might, that is, try to develop a "poker brain" in the same way that we can develop a "poker face."

Participants could also try to control the other's knowledge of their mind by asking the other to deliberately ignore the signals they receive, to direct their attention away from them. If they trust each other, they may simply request this, much as we might request that someone look away while we change clothes or type a password. If these ways of politely ignoring the other, and the ways of establishing a "poker brain," became habitual, they might eventually lead to the "dissociation" outcome, with the individuals surviving as two separate minds supported by one substrate. But if they do not trust each other, then in order to ensure their privacy, each participant must ascertain whether the other is attending to the signals they are receiving via the implant. But then each must, to protect their own privacy, invade the other's privacy. This prepares the way for a conflict which might end in "domination," if one wins conclusively, in "dissociation," if both manage to repel the other, or in "dissolution," if each psychologically cripples the other.

Fortunately, the participants may display emotional responses besides defensiveness. In the right circumstances, humans strongly desire both to know others and to be known by them. So if the right circumstances can be contrived, the participants may relish the connection which their implants give them and spend much of their time engaged in silent but energetic conversation. No doubt they will also want a degree of privacy, so expedients like the "poker brain" will be employed to some extent, but not so as to become automatic and inflexible. What will secure this happy result? Primarily it will be the temperaments of and relationships between the participants selected; perhaps for best results they should be a pair who have already established a strong and stable friendship or romantic partnership, who feel comfortable exposing their own mental lives and are enthusiastic about getting to see the other's. Psychological health and stability will also be important, to handle productively the tensions and arguments which will inevitably arise when two people, even people who love each other, are installed permanently inside each other's skulls.

8.2.2. IS THIS TELEPATHY?

Suppose that the experimenters have, by luck, wise choice, or trial and error, selected two stable and mature human beings who are willing to be merged with each other but refuse to either conquer or be conquered. One interesting question is whether the communication they become capable of counts as "telepathy"—or rather, since that term could mean many things, is it a fundamentally different form of communication from the ways that people communicate normally?

If "telepathy" just meant communication not by any of the specific mechanisms that humans normally use—in particular, those that operate through the sense organs—then of course the participants are engaged in telepathy. But if telepathy means direct, *unmediated* awareness of another's experiences, then they are not; the access is mediated by the electrical connections (radio waves or nerve signals) which link the two subjects. This means that the access is fallible, for something may interfere with the signals traveling along those connections. In this sense, what the two participants have is no more telepathic than is an everyday spoken conversation: one subject's thoughts are encoded in some form of energy signal that is picked up and decoded by the other. When the energy signal is sound waves between mouth and ear, or light waves between face and eye, the communication is comparatively slow, unreliable, and low in information: when it is nerve impulses from one part of the brain to another, it is comparatively fast, reliable, and rich in information. Over the course of the Martian experiment, the radio communication between the participants goes from being more like the former to being more like the latter, but the difference is only one of degree.

Is the electrical communication perhaps somehow "less filtered"? It might be, especially at first. When we talk, we can exert a lot of control over the signal that gets to the other person, letting us craft it to be misleading or uninformative. But when the implants are first put in, there is none of that: each receives a signal that varies based simply on what the other is *actually* thinking or feeling, not on what they wish to claim they are thinking and feeling. But deliberate control, and with it insincerity and deception, can arise simply from each coming to understand how the connection works. Later on, as they become so used to each other that they slowly cease to think of themselves as distinct, this capacity for insincerity and deception might fade away again. So in a sense we might say that the participants have telepathic access at first (when they are probably unable to make sense of it) but then lose it as they become more aware of the implants' workings, and may regain it once they become so attuned that filtering the signals they send to the other comes to seem perverse.

In another sense, telepathy might mean literally sharing experiences. Are there particular mental events which both subjects undergo? Of course there may be experiences that guide the behavior of both participants, but this differs only in degree from the way that my decision might guide the behavior of many other people, via my verbal instructions to them. I maintain that two discrete subjects cannot literally undergo a single experience: whatever is going on in one brain will be an experience of that subject, and not the other. And if an experience is realized in a dispersed manner, spread across both brains, then it belongs to neither individually; rather, that experience belongs to the composite of both, and each has some part of it, some component experience.

So I conclude that "telepathic" communication, in the sense of sharing particular experiences, does not (and probably cannot) occur between discrete subjects. They can communicate in a fast, reliable, and informative way, and they may in some cases do so with little room for insincerity or pretense. Yet they do not know each other's experiences *directly*, the way they know their own experiences, and they do not literally share experiences. This is a consequence of accepting (albeit in weakened form) the privacy of experience. If the two participants are discrete, weak privacy precludes their sharing any single experience.

Because the procedure involves no telepathy, we could not use it for direct between-subjects quality comparisons. Suppose we connect one normally sighted participant and one blind participant. Or suppose we connected two participants who were, unbeknownst to us, spectrum-inverted relative to each other, one seeing green whenever the other would see red, and so on. What would happen?

Maybe one participant would report, with surprise, having a kind of experience whose quality they could not previously have imagined. But this might also happen when two experientially normal subjects are connected, if the signals each received stimulated their brain in previously unknown ways. Or maybe they would simply report experiencing familiar qualities under new circumstances or in new arrangements—because the incoming signal caused the same kind of brain activity as normal sensory stimuli. In either case, the type of quality which the receiving subject experiences is fixed by the signal's effects on their brain, and thus depends on the experiential capacities of that subject and their brain. They may find previously unknown capacities unlocked by the procedure, but this is still not the same as their directly sharing the experiences of the other person. In this respect, the participants are not fundamentally different from any two of us who talk.

8.2.3. UNIFYING THE PARTICIPANTS' EXPERIENCES

What about conscious unity? Here panpsychist combinationism disagrees some-what with other sorts of combinationism, but certain things can be agreed on. In most senses of "unity," the participants' experiences become gradually more and more unified. Before the procedure, the participants' experiences are no more representationally unified, or access-unified, or causally interdependent, or glob-ally consistent, than any other two people's. By the end of the procedure, they are just as unified, in these respects, as the experiences of any ordinary person. This transition is not some sudden magical transformation; there is no crucial moment when unity "switches on" all at once. It is a gradual increase in the amount of in-formation that is shared and integrated between the participants and the way that this establishes feedback that enriches the experiences of each. From each one's perspective, this means that their phenomenology of co-presentation—their awareness of the mental life "behind" the signals they receive from the other— becomes richer and more informative. Each participant comes to be constantly aware, not of the other's experiences as external events, but of how things seem to the other. That is, each participant comes to see the world through the other's eyes and have an awareness of this other perspective constantly in the background of their own perspective.

As the participants learn to tell what kind of experiences in the other mind produce what experiences in their own, they will come to perceive the latter experiences as the revealed aspect of—the expression of—a mental process that is not fully given but whose content they increasingly can discern. By exten-sion, the absence of certain experiences in their own minds, and the particular combinations of experiences they do have, will also come to seem meaningful, like a fragment of a whole other stream of consciousness. Eventually, when each expe-rience of either participant conveys something not just of *their* other experiences, but of the experiences of the other participant, we will be able to call the whole set unified because each experience will be felt as merely one fragment of a conscious whole that includes both minds.

Through this process, we will also find pairs of experiences in the two participants interacting to yield more complex experiences. For instance, when one of the participants perceives something, the signals received by the other may activate a memory of a similar thing perceived in the past, and the signals of this memory received by the first may then contextualize and color their perception of this new thing just as their own memories would. This growing disposition to think together will likely be accompanied by a growing difficulty in thinking separately: when relevant thoughts from the other subject spring to both minds so quickly and readily, it will be hard for either not to be influenced by the other's ongoing thoughts.

The closest we can get to this kind of psychic intimacy is probably "internalization": when someone has exercised a formative influence on us, we can come to involuntarily and unreflectively see the world as they would see it, with this seeing becoming a constant background to our own seeing. What stops that from counting as conscious unity is that it is in virtue of a past interaction, not a present one, which is precisely what the procedure we are imagining changes. Each participant's constant background awareness of the other's perspective is a product of an ongoing interaction—though this need not mean that it snaps into existence simply because the implants are turned on. If the flood of new stimuli is unwelcome, it will prompt defensive measures or cause a traumatic breakdown in one or both psyches. But even if it is welcomed, there will still have to be a process of attunement and mutual learning, to help the two minds communicate more effectively rather than to help one re-create the other in their absence.

But what about phenomenal unity? Intuitively, causal interactions, joint access, and so on, are a very different kind of thing when accompanied by phenomenal unity and when not. When two representationally connected experiences are phenomenally unified, there is a composite experience with the richer representational content; when they are not, the complex content may be represented but not consciously. When two jointly accessible experiences are phenomenally unified, there is a composite experience which is access-conscious; when they are not, information is accessible but not in virtue of any single experience being access-conscious. When do the participants' experiences go from phenomenally disunified to phenomenally unified?

By hypothesis, there is no discontinuous break in the gradual enriching of the participants' interactions, which makes it very awkward to insist that at some precise point the phenomenal transition must suddenly occur; indeed, I do not think there is any such precise point. But different forms of combinationism have different ways to avoid insisting on a precise point of transition. Combinationists who think that consciousness is a nonfundamental property, explained by some underlying physical or functional structure, can say the same about phenomenal unity: it is not a fundamental property, but rather explained by some underlying pattern of causal, functional, or informational relations. This allows them to say that phenomenal unity is vague: there is a midpoint at which it is neither determinately true nor determinately false that the participants' experiences are phenomenally unified, because their relations are neither definitely rich enough nor definitely not.

Panpsychist combinationism cannot take this line: consciousness is a fundamental property, and so cannot be analyzed as meeting some ill-specified threshold on some underlying scale. A state is either conscious or not, and so a pair of experiences is either conscious jointly or not; thus phenomenal unity is not vague. Panpsychist combinationism instead says that there is no precise transition point, because there is not really any transition. Phenomenal unity is pervasive in the universe, and so the participants' experiences will be phenomenally unified even before the procedure begins. They were simply unable to introspectively register this unity because no set of introspective mechanisms could register the experiences in both heads. Eventually this changes, in ways that will be discussed more fully in the next section, and the whole becomes able to register the phenomenal unity among all its experiences. But this is a matter of its discovering something that was there all along.

8.2.4. THE GROWTH OF SHARED RESPONSIBILITY

As the procedure progresses, the two participants are likely to spend less time attending specifically to one another and more time attending jointly to external things. In the early "conversations," each focuses on how to convey things to the other and on how to interpret the other's own expressions. Their goals are to learn about the other, or to cause the other to believe certain things (true or false) about them. This contrasts with shared attention, where they are not attending to each other, but are rather aware of each other in the background of something they are both attending to, and which they are attending to partly because they know the other is attending to it.

To illuminate this shift, we might compare two people first meeting, engaged in "getting to know" one another, with two old friends jointly considering a shared problem. In the latter case, each may ask the other for their view on a particular part of the question, and will maintain a constant awareness of what the other knows, may not know, can do, refuses to do, and so on, but only in the same way that they maintain a constant awareness of their own capabilities and knowledge, without having to focus attention on them.

The growth of shared attention corresponds to one aspect of their growing conscious unity: their experiences tend more and more to transfer attention, so that if one focuses on something, the other's attention will also be drawn to that thing (even if that thing is known to them only via signals from the other). This will contribute to a growing difficulty in assigning responsibility to one participant or the other. Each time one begins to focus on an action, the other becomes aware of this, and has a few related ideas, which the first immediately becomes aware of, and so on. Eventually every action performed by either body will be the product of multiple rounds of feedback between both minds, making it all but impossible to isolate the exact contribution of each. In the terms of chapter 7, they are now consistently "aligning their wills," acting on joint rather than just individual intentions, so that neither can escape responsibility for the actions of either.[2]

A similar difficulty in assigning responsibility may occur with rapid and habitual actions, because at some point it will likely be possible for one participant to initiate actions in the other's body, perhaps acting via a momentary urge it can prompt in the other's consciousness or perhaps bypassing the latter. Even if the second participant is able to inhibit the action just as they can inhibit their own, at this stage they will likely have become fairly comfortable with each other and not prone to automatically inhibiting every impulse they receive from the other. For instance, if one participant is graceful and perceptive and the other clumsy and oblivious, the first may start adjusting the second's posture to avoid the trips and spills they were previously prone to. The second, seeing no reason to block out this helpful intervention, allows it to become habitual, so that every action performed with the second body is a blend of contributions from both minds.

But even while it becomes harder to assign responsibility to just one participant, it also becomes less practically important to do so. One reason we normally care which of two people did something is because we need to know what to expect from those people in the future. But if neither participant will act separately in the future, this prospective need becomes less urgent. It is also normally important to assign responsibility so as to allocate rewards and punishments, but with the two participants so closely linked in body and mind, and likely strongly caring about and empathizing with each other, we cannot cause any pain, joy, or inconvenience to one without affecting both.

There will also be long-term effects on each participant's personality. Just as people often change to reflect and accommodate their families, the participants will be prone to absorb values, beliefs, and habits from each other—while any sharply opposing or incompatible traits are likely to be removed, either violently (in a case tending toward domination) or by persuasion and negotiation (in a case tending toward merging). Any persistence of sharp conflict increases the odds of dissociation or dissolution.

Drawing on my defense of the patterning principle in chapter 7, we might say that their background psychologies and background wills are more aligned with each other. If I am right that human beings perceive events as their own voluntary actions to the extent that those events harmonize with their will, then they may

---

[2] In Rovane's (1998, 141) terms, this is part of their establishing "overall rational unity."

start experiencing each other's actions as their own. For instance, when I decide to picture a yellow flamingo, and the image of a yellow flamingo arises, the close correspondence between what I intended and what happens makes me feel that I imagined the flamingo voluntarily. Now if one participant decides to picture a yellow flamingo, which is noticed by the other, who is generally better at visual imagination, their habitual response might be to form an image of a yellow flamingo and transmit it to the first participant. The first participant, experiencing an intention followed by a matching image, will likely feel as though they have voluntarily imagined that flamingo. The distinction between doing something oneself and doing it with the other's help becomes increasingly irrelevant as these options become indistinguishable in speed and reliability. Arguments over responsibility may still arise, when something goes wrong and each tries to blame the other. But these are unlikely to end with any clear answer; rather, the participants need to be willing to let go of the question. Only if they can think of their actions as "ours," rather than trying to carve out "mine" and "yours" in each case, will the procedure lead to successful merging.

8.2.5. CAN THE PARTICIPANTS STILL KNOW THEIR OWN MINDS?

But couldn't each participant still consciously decide to "take charge" of their own mind and make a decision that is their own, not shared? Supposing the other is supportive and does not deliberately interfere, isn't individual responsibility still possible, by carefully "screening out" incoming signals?

There are three difficulties facing such efforts at individual responsibility. First, as noted above, it will grow harder and harder to discern which thoughts come from outside and which from inside. Second, many internally generated thoughts will now reflect the past influence of the other, and may even require consultation with the other in order to properly understand them (e.g., one participant may have been persuaded of a certain belief by the other, but remember the conclusion better than they remember the arguments). As a result, evaluating the reasonableness or virtue of one participant's thoughts or actions will require evaluating those of the other that fed into it.

The third and most interesting difficulty is that to decide something "by oneself" requires distinguishing not only between what is one's own and what is another's, but also between what is one's own and what is a random passing whim or chance thought. Occasionally I might get the urge to slap an annoying person, but it does not follow that if I gave into that urge every time it arose I would be acting more autonomously, for it may be that a concern for civility and mutual respect is a far more important part of "who I really am" than this occasional urge.

This is essentially the same point discussed in chapter 7's section 7.3.1, that behavior caused by my mental states are not actions of mine, unless they go through some process which, like deliberate decision-making, is open to all my mental states and so can reach outcomes that reflect the balance of all of them.

This means that in order to find out what we really want, among a certain amount of random statistical "noise," we need to engage in "soul-searching." By this I mean a kind of calm taking stock of one's thoughts and feelings, a conscious effort to be open to all our desires and to discern which are stable and which are fleeting. This effort at "self-consultation" contrasts with the sort of blinkered focusing where we just pursue to completion what we have already embarked upon, pushing aside all new thoughts and feelings that arise, attending only to the implications of a particular line of thought or the means to a particular end. While this makes us more likely to successfully complete our task, it impedes efforts to establish our true wishes, and increases the risk of devoting ourselves to something we do not really want.

So to decide "for oneself" properly requires "soul-searching," which requires openness to one's "whole mind," a lowering of thresholds for admission to attention. But in our thought experiment, this kind of openness will actually invite thoughts stimulated (even if unintentionally) by the other. The attempt to block out or ignore thoughts coming from the other requires the opposite of soul-searching: vigilantly keeping watch over one's thoughts and driving away any that do not fit certain criteria. Thus the distinction "talking to the other person versus doing it myself" comes increasingly to line up with the distinction "soul-searching versus blinkered focusing." We can find parallels to this in real life: talking with someone else is often the best way for us to work out what we really want, as long as they are supportive and open-minded. In a sense "making up my own mind" is an illusion: our autonomy is the product of our relatedness. The participants in the thought experiment just take this to an extreme.

8.2.6. SURVIVING AS PART OF A PERSON

Many people would describe the merging outcome by saying that the two participants are no more; they no longer exist, having been "absorbed" or "dissolved" into the whole. Yet I would like to say that they survive as parts of a person, and combinationism is interesting in part for allowing us to say this sensibly. This does not mean entirely rejecting the idea that the participants are in some sense "gone"; indeed, this idea is correct in at least two superficial senses.

The first superficial sense is that the two participants have ceased to be salient things, or things which it is useful to think in terms of. It is no longer sensible for someone trying to understand the situation to organize their thoughts around "participant 1" and "participant 2." The second superficial sense explains this fact; each participant has lost a significant degree of "independence," in that their body's actions are no longer primarily controlled *only* by their own mental processes, and their mental processes are no longer primarily controlled *only* by their own mental processes a moment before. But despite these facts about the two participants, a defender of the compositional approach will maintain that they still, strictly speaking, exist. The success of fusion is not marked by a change in which things exist, but by a shift in the salient divisions, whereby the distinction between the two individuals becomes increasingly irrelevant. Each one's story is not a story of something being destroyed, but of something growing and forming new connections to an external thing—indeed, an external thing which, if the experiment succeeded, probably managed to elicit intense feelings of friendship, love, and acceptance. It would be perverse to think of this as a form of self-destruction.

Of course, what the participants' survival consists in will depend on what subjects are, and I have tried to make combinationism compatible with both the metaphysical and the psychological conceptions, as well as with mixed views which recognize both conceptions as identifying important senses of "subject." On the metaphysical conception, the original people are the two substrates—crucially, the two brains. Since these two brains clearly still exist, the contentious claim is that they are still subjects. On the psychological conception, the original people are two personas, and the contentious claim is that they persist as two component personas in the overarching persona of the two-bodied being that results. If we had observed the outcome I earlier labeled "dissociation," it will be very clear that this is the case: the two component personas will verbally assure us of their own distinctness and existence. But in the "merging" outcome, things are less obvious; as noted above, the behavior and thought of the two-bodied being shows no salient or obvious division into two personalities but is seamlessly integrated.

But section 7.1 of chapter 7 argued that personas can exist even when they do not stand out sharply from their background, and the mental life of the pair is still likely to show two subclusters, slightly more unified internally than they are with each other.[3] Moreover, experiences arising within one particular brain are likely to show greater causal interdependence with one another than they do with experiences arising in the other brain, because of the simple effect of physical proximity, shared dependence on particular mechanisms, and being the "first port-of-call" for the same streams of incoming sensory information. So even if

---

[3] For an example of an integrated persona which has recognizable component personas from earlier individuals who fused, see "Tuvix" in S2E24 of *Star Trek: Voyager*.

there is no preservation of any discernible boundary between personality quirks, memories, habits of speech, or dispositions inherited from the one participant and those inherited from the other, there is still a sense in which the original personas can be delimited from each other as parts within the whole.

The basic reason to accept the continued existence of the original participants as component subjects is that the type of thing happening in each brain at the end is basically the same as what was happening at the beginning. Neurons fire, stimuli produce responses, information is processed and filtered and integrated to enable a coherent and meaningful worldview. These activities have not been disrupted or stopped, just connected with other such activities so that they work together. Why think that these activities no longer support a conscious perspective of their own?

One might say that they no longer support a perspective of their own because they contribute to supporting a larger conscious perspective. But this follows only given the rejection of combinationism, which claims precisely that supporting a perspective of their own can be a way of contributing to a larger perspective. Or one might say that their psychological integrity has been destroyed, and they no longer display the same psychology as before. But any theory of personal identity must account for the way that our psychologies change over time, and one of my major aims in this section has been to show that what happens to these participants is just an extreme version of things that happen to all of us when we become intensely related to someone: shared attention, long-term shifts in personality, or finding that we best understand our own desires by discussing them with another.

8.3. Fusion from the Perspective of the Whole

In this section I shift to consider the whole composed of the two human participants. Its perspective is, at first, much less familiar to us and harder to make sense of. Nevertheless, I argue, we have conceptual tools available that can give us some idea of what it is like to be a pair of people midway through this process, and perhaps even what it is like, if anything, to be a pair of people prior to this process—i.e., what it is like to be any of the many pairs of people which actually exist.

8.3.1. BEING A PAIR OF PEOPLE

Different combinationists will take different views on whether pairs of people are composite subjects, but all should agree that they are not *intelligent* subjects. The many experiences going on in a pair do not integrate enough information overall to generate structured consciousness; they do not work together to produce intelligent functioning at the pair-level. This is why it seems bizarre to attribute mental states to a pair, once we are clear that this ascription is not to be merely distributive; obviously we can say "There's a happy pair," meaning that each member individually is happy, but the pair cannot really be happy itself. Because intelligent functioning is division-relative, intelligent functioning in each of a thing's parts does not guarantee intelligent functioning in the whole. But it is also not incompatible with it, and human sociality shows a way to connect the two. As discussed in chapter 6, joint intentionality in its various forms effectively allows the many mental states of some group of people to jointly play a certain functional role for the group as a whole. And our two participants are ideally placed to intend, think, and act jointly: they have unfettered access to the other's mental states, time to build up cooperative habits, and (hopefully) a deep bond of trust. Given this, we can expect them, more and more frequently, to each think and behave in ways that are conditional upon the other's "doing their part." When they work together like this, it begins to make more sense to describe the pair in properly psychological ways—as "wanting X," for example, when both participants want X, know the other wants X, and are prepared to work together to get X.

As joint intentionality becomes easier and more automatic, it will approach the ease and automaticity of individual action. At a certain point, the pair will start to qualify as functioning intelligently, and its intelligent functioning will be a natural outgrowth of the intelligent functioning in its parts.[4] In tandem, the increasing integration of information that enables this intelligent functioning will be connecting the participants' experiences in more and more specific ways, until the whole starts to qualify as having structured consciousness. At this point, it will be an intelligent subject—or rather, since "intelligent functioning" and "structured consciousness" are vague, it will first reach a point where it is indeterminate whether it qualifies as an intelligent subject (rather like, perhaps, an insect or a snail, though differing considerably in containing two definitely intelligent subjects as parts), and then later reach a point where it is determinately an intelligent subject.

On pure functionalist versions of combinationism, being an intelligent subject is the only way to be a subject, so the pair becoming an intelligent subject is also its becoming conscious. But this becoming conscious does not involve the appearance

---

[4] Arguably, full-strength ascription of psychological properties to the pair requires it to be a "group agent" in the robust sense described by List and Pettit (2011), which requires not just a succession of temporary joint actions but also a stable and consistent set of collective attitudes. This seems likely to be what happens in our imagined procedure, as each participant becomes more and more able to persuade and be persuaded by the other, and more and more willing to adhere to past joint decisions.

of any new experiences: the experiences themselves were going on in the pair all along, but only when the whole functioned as a subject did it qualify as "having" them. By contrast, panpsychist combinationism allows for subjects which are not intelligent—subjects like fundamental particles, which have experiences but without any cognitive capacity to access, think about, or act on those experiences. And panpsychist combinationism says that in this "stripped-down" sense of subjecthood, all wholes inherit experiences from their parts. On such a view, the pair of people was conscious all along, but without any of the functional and behavioral complexity we normally associate with consciousness. The pair had the same experiences as its parts, but they, and not it, also have their overall behavior intelligently guided by those experiences. It was conscious only in the minimal sense that elementary particles, according to panpsychism, are conscious. Moreover, according to panpsychist combinationism, its experiences were phenomenally unified all along, but prior to the Martian experiment the two clusters associated with the two brains integrated so little information between them that the composite experience they formed was a mere blur, a blend of all their different experiences in which none could be distinguished from the others. As the two brains integrate more and more information, elements of their two conscious fields become phenomenally bound, and structured consciousness slowly coalesces from what was previously a homogeneous blend.

8.3.2. HOW THE PAIR KNOWS ITSELF

Even if the pair is conscious from the beginning, it cannot at first introspect on its consciousness as a whole. In the early stages of the procedure each person has good access to their own experiences, but very limited access to the other's. Each will thus form introspective impressions of only part of the composite's phenomenal field, or at least, introspective impressions in which the rest of the field features hazily and peripherally. This could still be called a sort of "introspection by the composite": the composite is introspecting on half its experiences at a time, using a different brain each time. But this falls short of what we might think of as "proper" introspection and attention, which involve the whole phenomenal field. These, I will argue, become possible for the composite only when it can act simultaneously with both brains and connect its two acts properly.

For proper introspection, the composite needs to not only have each brain introspect but have each inquire with the other about the other's part of the field, and incorporate what they are told into their own view. It may never get a complete survey of the phenomenal field in a single brain, but this does not mean it never gets a complete survey: the complete survey is distributed across the two brains. This allows the composite to think about its own thoughts, but it does so by means of each participant separately identifying and then putting together "what *I* am experiencing" and "what *they* are experiencing." These two impressions will be distinguished as introspective and testimonial, respectively, and so the composite can think of itself as such only on the basis of first thinking of each part as a distinct part.

But as the procedure progresses, the consequent "we-thoughts" will follow the antecedent "I-thoughts" more and more automatically, as any attempt at introspective stocktaking by one participant automatically prompts the other not only to also take stock, but to listen to its partner and share its own results. With increasing automaticity, it will become less salient to each that it is hearing things from someone else. By contrast, the impressions in each brain of what "we" are experiencing will grow more salient, not to mention easier to focus on, for segregating out only the experiences from one's own brain will come to take more and more effort. Eventually, for a participant to introspectively review all and only what they individually are experiencing, without attending also to what the other is experiencing, will come to seem both pointless and nearly impossible, compared to reviewing everything in both minds. The participants come to be conscious of themselves only as a whole, not as parts. And thereby the whole becomes conscious of itself as such.

8.3.3. NEW FORMS OF PHENOMENAL BLENDING

While in one sense the composite has gained new capacities throughout the procedure, there is also a respect in which it has steadily lost capacities. In particular, it has lost various capacities to do one thing *without* a certain other thing happening. The implants ensure that certain mental or bodily actions taken with one body will have automatic consequences in the other body—such as the other participant knowing what was done, or feeling some emotion, or supplying some useful or disruptive feedback. It is often worthwhile and overwhelmingly tempting to prioritize speed and efficiency over carefully scrutinizing every step in a mental process, and so when there is no strong reason to keep things separate, a useful pattern of action may become so habitual that its components cannot occur separately.

This loss of capacities is a form of *confusion*, as defined in chapter 4. The composite mind becomes unable to perform one mental act without simultaneously performing another, just as each participant's mind may be unable to attend to the microexperiences of its microscopic parts without simultaneously attending to many others. At first this confusion will be weak and shallow: shallow because the effect in the second mind might still potentially be inhibited or avoided, and weak because even once both mental actions have occurred, the separateness of the two brains' attentional systems will allow for distinct attention. But over time, as the links become stronger and faster, and as the two brains' capacities for attention become more and more coupled together, there may be instances where it becomes in practice impossible even to attend separately. Obviously this will not happen for all mental events; there are benefits to preserving some separation of function, if only so as to know at each moment which body's eyes are generating which visual experiences. But pairs of events which there is no reason to keep distinguishing may become strongly, robustly, and symmetrically—i.e., radically—confused.

Since confusion is subject-relative, this does not guarantee that the parts suffer the same confusion. They may suffer confusion between a given thought or experience of theirs and the *feedback* that it automatically prompts from the other brain, but this is still confusion among events in their own brain, contrasting with confusion among events in the two brains.

This raises the interesting possibility of the whole experiencing phenomenal qualities which its parts cannot, which are blended out of, and thus nothing over and above, the qualities experienced by its parts. To see this, imagine that one subject has very different color experiences than the other, outwardly responding the same to stimuli but experiencing different qualities—seeing gred, grue, and grurple where the other sees red, blue, and purple. For these to blend they must be both phenomenally unified and radically confused; this is unlikely to happen with perception (due to the separateness of eyes), so we should focus on imagination. Consider the whole visually imagining the color blurple, a blend of gred and blue, by imagining gred in one brain, and blue in the other, without any ability to separate the two. What is this like for the parts, e.g., the subject who can see and imagine blue but not gred? Since their blue-experience is representationally unified with the other's gred-experience, it co-presents that other experience in some fairly informative way. Yet since the link is not telepathic, they do not experience and cannot even imagine gred, and by extension do not experience and cannot imagine blurple. Yet at the same time, this joint imagination is entirely satisfactory within the psychological economy of the merged minds, generating no sense of dissatisfaction or frustration in either part.

Thus the subject imagining blue has an experience which co-presents gred informatively, without actually instantiating the character of gred, and yet generates no further curiosity or sense of lacking access to the quality gred. This is a hard description to make sense of, but not impossible. I think the best way to make sense of how the co-presentation can be highly informative without actually conveying the character of gred is to think of it as a sort of acquaintance that enables recognition but not recall; the subject will recognize next time the other subject is imagining gred, but cannot themselves visualize or otherwise capture the quality—a little bit like when we say "I don't know how to describe it, but I would recognize it if I saw it again." And the best way to make sense of its producing no sense of frustration or curiosity is to appeal to the patterning principle: the subject imagining blue thinks they can imagine gred, and indeed blurple, because whenever they try to (by resolving to imagine "that quality"), this prompts the other to imagine gred, thereby composing blurple, and all the feedback that any subject (composite or component) gets is "Success: quality visualized." In fact much of that feedback is coming to each component subject from the other, but the degree of volitional harmony they have built up makes this fact impossible to detect from the inside.

8.4. Conclusions

When I think about the procedure our two imaginary humans have undergone, I find combinationism more attractive. If minds cannot be parts of minds, then there must be some moment when two become one, and I find it hard to accept any such abrupt transition in a gradual process. If minds can be parts of minds, but component minds do not explain the mentality of their composite, then when we have explained the behavior of the composite in terms of the two original minds closely and automatically cooperating (as I think we can), it would be superfluous to posit a further distinct mind belonging to the whole. Yet if the whole gives as much indication of being an intelligent conscious subject as any of us do, then it seems arbitrary to deny it that status. I find myself forced to look for some account on which the genuine consciousness of the parts and the genuine consciousness of the whole are not only compatible but are two sides of the same coin. Over the course of this work I have attempted to formulate three versions of such an account and to articulate both why they are attractive and why they might be rejected.

9 Concluding Remarks

CAN SUBJECTIVITY BE composite? Can the consciousness of a whole be a mere combination of the consciousness of its parts? My guiding thought in this book has been that there is something difficult to understand in this idea, that makes it tempting to reject it out of hand. This rejection—the thesis I have called "anti-combination"—constrains the way we think about minds, ruling out otherwise promising theories of consciousness (like constitutive Russellian panpsychism) and making consciousness seems like an alien irruption into nature. My aim has been to understand and analyze both what arguments can be made against composite subjectivity and how a positive theory of composite subjectivity—a "combinationist" theory—might be built to resist these arguments. In this final chapter I recap the ideas of the preceding eight chapters and consider where the anti-combination intuition comes from and what gives it its force.

9.1. Many Problems and Many Theories

In the previous eight chapters I have considered, and sought to refute, several arguments for anti-combination, which in chapter 1 I divided into internal problems, bridging problems, and lack-of-theory problems. Chapter 2 surveyed five "internal problems" for combinationism, which seemed to show the in-principle impossibility of any kind of composite subjectivity: the subject-summing argument, the unity argument, the privacy argument, the boundary argument, and the incompatible contexts argument.

I sketched the outlines of responses to these arguments in chapter 2. In particular, I argued for rejecting strong privacy and strong independence (which rule out experience-sharing and grounding between any nonidentical subjects) as overstatements of the more reasonable principles of weak privacy and weak independence (which rule out experience-sharing and grounding between any nonoverlapping subjects). And I argued for distinguishing several sorts of conscious unity, so as to find for each one an appropriate way to thread between the unity, boundary, and incompatible contexts arguments. Chapters 3, 5, and 7 then filled in these outlines in different ways, reflecting different assumptions about conscious subjects and conscious unity.

Subsequent chapters added several "bridging problems," concerned with whether the specific sorts of minds we encounter in the world could combine or arise through combination. More specifically, in chapter 4 I considered the palette argument and the revelation argument, both aiming to rule out the kind of mental combination posited by panpsychism, where human consciousness is constituted by that of the fundamental physical entities; in chapters 4 and 5 I considered the mismatch argument, that combinationism cannot explain the structure and content of human consciousness; and in chapter 7 I considered the arguments that subjects in compositional relations could not have the kind of self-consciousness, or the kind of agency, that we take ourselves to have.

None of these arguments is sound. The palette and revelation arguments fail because diverse elements can be manifest in consciousness in a distinctively qualitative way, as ingredients in a blended quality whose subject cannot intro-spectively isolate them from each other. The mismatch argument fails because complex structured content can arise intelligibly out of the structured superimpo-sition of simple conscious fields, corresponding to the integration of information between the subjects of those simpler fields. And the arguments from self-consciousness and agency fail because distinct subjects who interact in volition-ally harmonious ways, aligning their wills with each other's will, can be expected to perceive each other as extensions of themselves and can be properly regarded as jointly the agents of actions taken by each.

Lying behind these specific objections is the more basic lack-of-theory problem. Nagel (1986, 50), for example, writes, "We cannot at present understand how a mental event could be composed of myriad proto-mental events on the model of our understanding of how a muscle movement is composed of myriad physicochemical events. . . . We lack the concept of a mental part-whole relation." Over the course of the past six chapters I have developed and defended not one but three combinationist theories:

- In Division 1, I presented panpsychist combinationism, on which the material universe is suffused with elemental consciousness, phenomenal unity is the inner nature of (one or all) the fundamental physical relations, and aggregates inherit the elementary experiences of their parts.
- In Division 2, I presented functionalist combinationism, on which when conscious parts of some system interact in such a way that their experiences have control over, sensitivity to, and coordination with other events in the system, the system inherits those experiences.
- In Division 3, I presented psychological combinationism, on which sets of unified experiences constitute subjects, and subsets of *more* unified experiences within them constitute component subjects.

These three theories could be viewed as rivals, with conflicting accounts of consciousness and its combination, or they could be viewed as allies, illuminating different and complementary aspects of reality. (I prefer the latter.) Even if they are seen as rivals, they can "share resources"; for instance, the account of self-consciousness given in chapter 7, the account of representational unity given in chapter 5, and the account of phenomenal blending given in chapter 4, each might be employed in defending any of the three theories.

Fundamentally, my aim has not been to persuade the reader that these theories are true (though I think they are); it has been to use these theories to undermine anti-combination by showing multiple, consistent, plausible ways that minds might combine. In the remainder of this chapter I consider a lingering question about anti-combination: What explains the intuitive attraction so many people have felt toward it—if it is false, why does it seem so compelling?

9.2. The Oddness of Humans

I think the ultimate explanation of the anti-combination intuition depends partly on contingent facts about humans, and partly on necessary facts about consciousness and composition. The contingent fact about humans is that we never have occasion to think about overlapping subjects: all the complex consciousness we have ever encountered comes in very well-defined and well-protected units—human and animal brains, highly integrated internally and sharply separated externally. It has only ever been useful to us to think about the minds of whole animals, which do not overlap with one another, and so we developed (both in the sense of "evolved" and in the sense of "learned") systems for thinking about minds that assumed that any nonidentical minds would also be nonoverlapping.

Reinforcing this, the volitional harmony that obtains between the parts of an animal brain serves to obscure their distinctness from each other, and from the animal itself. "Harmoniously connected" subjects have little evidence that they are many, because they function as one, with one will. Like human beings in a cooperative group, they feel the boundary between "us" and the rest of the world more keenly than the boundary between "me" and the rest of "us"; unlike human beings in a cooperative group, they have never operated alone and have no secure private domain of thoughts they can conceal from the others. Because the many subjects who I am operate in such consistent harmony, their many-ness is never salient to each other, and insofar as they become self-aware, they are aware only of themselves as one.

It is hard to imagine oneself into the perspective of someone who is very different in their temperament and life experiences; it is even harder to imagine oneself into the perspective of someone who is very different in the basic structure of their consciousness. In this book I have discussed subjects who undergo many experiences that are weakly, if at all, unified with their other experiences; I have discussed subjects all of whose experiences are richly unified with the experiences of other subjects. I have discussed subjects with unity only among some parts of their minds, and subjects living through the process of merging with another subject. If human beings struggle to understand what it is like to be, say, a chimpanzee, or even a human being with a very different outlook, how much more will they struggle to make sense of beings like these?

So for creatures constructed like us, it is both extremely hard to identify or track conscious subjects who are not maximal, and also generally of little use. And as far as we know, we are the only creatures who have developed a sophisticated, abstract, understanding of the mind and consciousness. I think in developing this understanding we have often taken genuine insights (such as weak privacy, weak independence, and the observation that the relations between two humans' experiences are quite different from any that obtain among one human's experiences) and mistakenly formulated them into stronger, false principles (such as strong privacy, strong independence, and the idea that the relations between two humans' experiences are fundamentally discontinuous with those that obtain among one human's experiences). Moreover, because there is generally for each human being *both* a well-defined single substrate of experience and a well-defined single persona, we have little need to distinguish the two, and our everyday idea of a conscious subject mingles the metaphysical and psychological conceptions of subjecthood. This makes it hard for us even to grasp clearly what division and composition of subjects would mean.

In short, the problem is that all the philosophy we know of has been done by humans. But this is simply an observation of what has happened so far on this particular planet. There are creatures whose nervous systems do not match our pattern of separate, stable, well-integrated, and well-insulated units: starfish, cephalopods, even eusocial insect colonies. There are rare human beings who also do not match the standard pattern: craniopagus conjoined twins, split-brain patients, and people with dissociative identity disorder. And if and when our technology allows for the creation of intelligent, conscious beings, they are very likely to also violate the human pattern in various ways—shifting between or sharing bodies, saving their minds into one another's like some sort of psychological virus, or even living permanently on the internet, indifferent to their physical realization in any particular server or device.

If creatures like this—whose mental lives are not entirely and permanently carried on in sharply separated, internally well-integrated, easily countable units—became intelligent enough to think about minds as such, to develop an everyday "theory of mind" and a scientific psychology, I think they would not share our inclination to endorse anti-combination. Their form of life would force them to confront some of the complex ways that conscious beings can compose and contain one another, and they would likely develop words, customs, and even emotions specifically designed to manage those complexities.

9.3. Why Is This All So Confusing?

I do not think, however, that less sharply individuated beings would find *no* philosophical difficulties in thinking about mental combination; after all, familiarity with things like linguistic communication, political association, and free choice has not saved humans from deep philosophical perplexity over these topics. And on the topic of composite subjectivity, I think there are some genuine conceptual issues that would impede clear thinking on this topic by any creature, human or not.

At root, the problem is that most of the concepts involved in mental combination (consciousness, composition, subjecthood, unity) are subject to conflicting intuitions, generating opposing conceptions which are both very hard to keep separate and also very different in their implications. In chapter 3, section 3.5, I argued that two particular forms of this kind of conceptual ambivalence contributed to making the subject-summing argument seem stronger than it is. First, the ease of confusing wholes as aggregates and wholes as true units makes it seem conceivable that parts and wholes exist with independent, noncorresponding properties (leading ultimately to the absurd result that tables might not exist, even though particles arranged tablewise do). And second, the ease of confusing access-consciousness with phenomenal consciousness can make the division-relativity of access-consciousness seem like clear evidence of the division-relativity of phenomenal consciousness (even though, according to panpsychist combinationism, phenomenal consciousness is division-invariant).

More generally, the diversity of conceptions available for what conscious subjects are and what conscious unity is has the result that almost none of the five arguments introduced in chapter 2 can be given a single straightforward response. This is why I had to develop multiple combinationist theories, to offer multiple responses to these arguments. The subject-summing argument is a prime example: psychological combinationism and functionalist combinationism both respond to it by analyzing what it takes for a subject to exist, but employ quite different analyses (a functionalist one and a Neo-Lockean one), while panpsychist combinationism treats subjecthood as primitive, and so needs a very different response, based on the substantive indiscernibility of parts and aggregates. Given the starting point of any one of these responses, the other responses will seem completely inappropriate. But all three starting points have some intuitive pull; as a result no response by itself is liable to feel satisfactory.

The same goes for the unity argument: one starting point is the intuition that two beings might interact, converse, and cooperate as much as we like, without that ever being enough to guarantee phenomenal unity between their experiences. Panpsychist combinationism accepts this, and responds that phenomenal unity need not be guaranteed by any pattern of interaction, because it was there all along, a fundamental relation that pervades our universe. But the implication of this, that my experiences are already unified with everyone else's, will seem clearly absurd from the opposite starting point, which sees phenomenal unity as indissociable from various kinds of functional unity. Functionalist combinationism offers an account of unity based on this starting point, but that account will seem to miss the point relative to the first starting point. Again, no response by itself can accommodate all the relevant intuitions.

I think there is an interaction between the previous section's point, that we are familiar only with a particularly neatly packaged sort of consciousness, and that all the concepts involved are hazardously easy to become confused by. When we venture to think about minds less neatly packaged than human ones, we will inevitably encounter perplexities and seeming contradictions, because it is so hard to keep a clear grasp on how to think about composition, consciousness, or any of the other concepts involved. But because our topic is so unfamiliar and speculative, it will seem as though those perplexities and contradictions come from the very idea of mental combination. In this book I have tried to show that mental combination is not the problem; when we settle on consistent ideas about other topics, the objections to it can all be answered.

Bibliography

Aaronson, S. (2014). "Why I Am Not an Integrated Information Theorist (or, The Unconscious Expander)." *Shtetl-Optimized* (blog). http://www.scottaaronson.com/blog/?p=1799.

Akins, K. (1996). "Lost the Plot? Reconstructing Dennett's Multiple Drafts Theory of Consciousness." *Mind & Language* 71 (1): 1–43.

Albahari, M. (2018). "Grounding the World in NonDual Awareness: A Metaphysical Model for Advaita Vedanta." In W. Seager (ed.), *The Routledge Handbook of Panpsychism*. New York: Routledge.

Allen, K. (2011). "Revelation and the Nature of Colour." *Dialectica* 65 (2): 153–176.

Alston, W. (1971). "Varieties of Privileged Access." *American Philosophical Quarterly* 8: 223–241.

Alter, T., and Nagasawa, Y. (2012). "What Is Russellian Monism?" *Journal of Consciousness Studies* 19: 67–95.

Amorpha. (2010). "Collective Phenomenon." *Dreamshore*. http://www.dreamshore.net/amorpha/index.html.

Amsterdam, B. (1972). "Mirror Self-Image Reactions before Age Two." *Developmental Psychobiology* 5 (4): 297–305.

Anderson, M. L. (2015). "Beyond Componential Constitution in the Brain—Starburst Amacrine Cells and Enabling Constraints." In T. Metzinger and J. M. Windt (eds.), *Open MIND: 1(T)*. Frankfurt am Main: MIND Group.

Anzai, A., Peng, X., and Van Essen, D. (2007). "Neurons in Monkey Visual Area V2 Encode Combinations of Orientations." *Nature Neuroscience* 10 (10): 1313–1321.

Aristotle. (2007). *Nicomachean Ethics*. Trans. D. P. Chase (1911). New York: Cosimo.

Armstrong, D. M. (1963). "Is Introspective Knowledge Incorrigible?" *Philosophical Review* 72 (4): 417–432.

Armstrong, D. M. (1978). *Universals and Scientific Realism*. 2 vols. Cambridge, UK: Cambridge University Press.

Asanga. (1992). *The Summary of the Great Vehicle*. Trans. from the Chinese of Paramārtha (*Taishō* vol. 31, no. 1593) by J. Keenan. Berkeley, CA: Numata Center for Buddhist Translation and Research.

Astraea. (2017). "Astraea Multiple Personality FAQ" http://astraeasweb.net/plural/faq.html

Auvray, M., and Spence, C. (2008). "The Multisensory Perception of Flavour." *Consciousness and Cognition* 17: 1016–1031.

Avicenna. (1952). "The Book of Healing" (1027). In *Avicenna's Psychology*. Trans. F. Rahman. Oxford: Oxford University Press.

Ayer, A. J. (1940). *The Foundations of Empirical Knowledge*. New York: Macmillan.

Baars, B. (1988). *A Cognitive Theory of Consciousness*. Cambridge, UK: Cambridge University Press.

Bailey, A. (2015). "The Priority Principle." *Journal of the American Philosophical Association* 1 (1): 163–174.

Baillargeon, R., and De Vos, J. (1991). "Object Permanence in Young Infants: Further Evidence." *Child Development* 62 (6): 1227–1246.

Barnes, E., and Williams, J. R. G. (2011). "A Theory of Metaphysical Indeterminacy." In K. Bennett and D. Zimmerman (eds.), *Oxford Studies in Metaphysics*, vol. 6. Oxford: Oxford University Press.

Barnett, D. (2008). "The Simplicity Intuition and Its Hidden Influence on Philosophy of Mind." *Nous* 42 (2): 308–335.

Basile, P. (2010). "It Must Be True—But How Can It Be? Some Remarks on Panpsychism and Mental Composition." *Royal Institute of Philosophy Supplement* 67: 93–112.

Baxter, D. (1988). "Many-One Identity." *Philosophical Papers* 17 (3): 193–216.

Baxter, D., and Cotnoir, A. (eds.) (2014). *Composition as Identity*. Oxford: Oxford University Press.

Bayle, P. (1991). *The Historical and Critical Dictionary* (1697). Selections trans. and introduced by Richard Popkin. Indianapolis, IN: Hackett.

Bayne, T. (2002). "Moral Status and the Treatment of Dissociative Identity Disorder." *Journal of Medical Philosophy* 27 (1): 87–105.

Bayne, T. (2008). "The Unity of Consciousness and the Split-Brain Syndrome." *Journal of Philosophy* 105 (6): 277–300.

Bayne, T. (2010). *The Unity of Consciousness*. Oxford: Oxford University Press.

Bayne, T., and Chalmers, D. (2003). "What Is the Unity of Consciousness?" in A. Cleeremans (ed.), *The Unity of Consciousness: Binding, Integration, Dissociation*. Oxford: Oxford University Press.

Bayne, T., and Hohwy, J. (2016). "Modes of Consciousness." In W. Sinnott-Armstrong (ed.), *Finding Consciousness: The Neuroscience, Ethics and Law of Severe Brain Damage*. New York: Oxford University Press.

Bayne, T., and Montague, M. (eds.) (2011). *Cognitive Phenomenology*. Oxford: Oxford University Press.

Bechtel, W. (1994). "Levels of Description and Explanation in Cognitive Science." *Minds and Machines* 4: 1–25.

Bedau, M. (1997). "Weak Emergence." *Philosophical Perspectives* 11 (11): 375–399.

Bennett, K. (2004). "Material Coincidence and the Grounding Problem." *Philosophical Studies* 118 (3): 339–371.

Bennett, K. (2011). "Koslicki on Formal Proper Parts." *Analysis* 71 (2): 286–290.

Bennett, K. (2013). "Having a Part Twice Over." *Australasian Journal of Philosophy* 91 (1): 83–103.

Bennett, K. (2015). "'Perfectly Understood, Unproblematic, and Certain': Lewis on Mereology." In B. Lowerer and J. Schaffer (eds.), *Blackwell Companion to David Lewis*. Oxford: Blackwell.

Bennett, M., and Hacker, P. (2003). *Philosophical Foundations of Neuroscience*. Hoboken, NJ: Wiley-Blackwell.

Berkeley, G. (2008). *A Treatise Concerning the Principles of Human Knowledge* (1710). Rockville, MD: Arc Manor.

Bhaskar, R. (1978). *A Realist Theory of Science*. 2nd ed. Brighton, UK: Harvester Press.

Bhat, R., and Rockwood, K. (2007). "Delirium as a Disorder of Consciousness." *Journal of Neurology, Neurosurgery, and Psychiatry* 78 (11): 1167–1170.

Bhattacharya, J., and Petsche, H. (2005). "Phase Synchrony Analysis of EEG during Music Perception Reveals Changes in Functional Connectivity Due to Musical Expertise." *Signal Processing* 85 (11): 2161–2177.

Bingham, A., Birch, G., De Graaf, C., Behan, J., and Perring, K. (1990). "Sensory Studies with Sucrose-Maltol Mixtures." *Chemical Senses* 15 (4): 447–456.

Blackmon, J. (2016). "Hemispherectomies and Independently Conscious Brain Regions." *Journal of Cognition and Neuroethics* 3 (4): 1–26.

Blackmore, S. (2002). "There Is No Stream of Consciousness." *Journal of Consciousness Studies* 9 (5): 17–28.

Blakemore, S., Wolpert M., and Frith, D. (2002). "Abnormalities in the Awareness of Action." *Trends in Cognitive Sciences* 6 (6): 237–242.

Blamauer, M. (2011). "Taking the Hard Problem of Consciousness Seriously: Dualism, Panpsychism and the Origin of the Combination Problem." In M. Blamauer (ed.), *The Mental as Fundamental: New Perspectives on Panpsychism*. Heusenstamm Nr Frankfurt: Ontos.

Block, N. (1981). "Psychologism and Behaviourism." *Philosophical Review* 90 (1): 5–43.

Block, N. (1992). "Troubles with Functionalism." Reprinted with revisions in B. Beakley and P. Ludlow (eds.), *The Philosophy of Mind: Classical Problems/Contemporary Issues*. Cambridge, MA: MIT Press. Originally published 1978 in C. W. Savage (ed.), *Perception and Cognition: Issues in the Foundations of Psychology*. Minneapolis: University of Minneapolis Press.

Block, N. (1995). "On a Confusion about a Function of Consciousness." *Behavioral and Brain Sciences* 18 (2): 227–287.

Block, N. (2003). "Mental Paint." In M. Hahn and B. Ramberg (eds.), *Reflections and Replies: Essays on the Philosophy of Tyler Burge*. Cambridge, MA: MIT Press.

Block, N. (2005). "Two Neural Correlates of Consciousness." *Trends in Cognitive Sciences* 9 (2): 46–52.

Block, N. (2007). "Overflow, Access, and Attention." *Behavioral and Brain Sciences* 30 (5–6): 530–548.

Block, N. (2011). "Perceptual Consciousness Overflows Cognitive Access." *Trends in Cognitive Sciences* 15 (12): 567–575.

Block, N., and Stalnaker, R. (1999). "Conceptual Analysis, Dualism and the Explanatory Gap." *Philosophical Review* 108: 1–46.

Bower, T. G. R. (1974). *Development in Infancy*. San Francisco: Freeman.

Bratman, M. (1997). "I Intend that We J." In R. Tuomela and G. Holmstrom-Hintikka (eds.), *Contemporary Action Theory* vol. II. Dordrecht: Kluwer.

Bratman, M. (2009). "Modest Sociality and the Distinctiveness of Intention." *Philosophical Studies* 144: 149–165.

Bratman, M. (2014). *Shared Agency: A Planning Theory of Acting Together*. Oxford University Press.

Brentano, F. (1987). *The Existence of God: Lectures Given at the Universities of Worzburg and Vienna, 1868–1891*. Ed. and trans. S. Krantz. Leiden: Nijhoff International Philosophy Series.

Briscoe, R. (2011). "Mental Imagery and the Varieties of Amodal Perception." *Pacific Philosophical Quarterly* 92 (2): 153–173.

Broad, C. D. (1925). *The Mind and Its Place in Nature*. London: Kegan Paul.

Broad, C. D. (1971). "Self and Others" (1953). Herbert Spencer Lecture, Oxford University. In D. R. Cheney (ed.), *Broad's Critical Essays in Moral Philosophy*. New York: Routledge.

Brogaard, B. (2017). "In Search of Mentons: Panpsychism, Physicalism and the Missing Link." In G. Brüntrup and L. Jaskolla (eds.), *Panpsychism: Contemporary Perspectives*. Oxford: Oxford University Press.

Brugger, P., Lenggenhager B., and Giummarra, M. (2013). "Xenomelia: A Social Neuroscience View of Altered Bodily Self-Consciousness." *Frontiers in Psychology* 4 (204): 1–7.

Buchanan, J., and Roelofs, L. (2018). "Panpsychism, Intuitions, and the Great Chain of Being." *Philosophical Studies*. https://doi.org/10.1007/s11098-018-1160-1.

Burge, T. (1979). "Individualism and the Mental." In P. French, T. Uehling, and H. Wettstein (eds.), *Midwest Studies in Philosophy, IV*. Minneapolis: University of Minnesota Press.

Burge, T. (2000). "Reason and the First-Person." In C. Wright, B. C. Smith, and C. Macdonald (eds.), *Knowing Our Own Minds*. Oxford: Oxford University Press.

Burke, M. (1994). "Dion and Theon: An Essentialist Solution to an Ancient Puzzle." *Journal of Philosophy* 91 (3): 129–139.

Burke, M. (2003). "Is My Head a Person?" In K. Petrus (ed.), *On Human Persons*. Heusenstamm Nr Frankfurt: Ontos Verlag.

Butler, J. (1860). *The Analogy of Religion, Natural and Revealed, to the Constitution and Course of Nature* (1736). Ed. with an analysis by J. T. Champlin. Boston: J. P. Jowett.

Byrne, A., and Hilbert, D. (2006). "Color Primitivism." *Erkenntnis* 66: 73–105.

Cameron, R. (2011). "Composition as Identity Doesn't Settle the Special Composition Question." *Philosophy and Phenomenological Research* 84 (3): 531–554.

Campbell, J. (1999). "Schizophrenia, the Space of Reasons, and Thinking as a Motor Process." *The Monist* 82 (4): 609–625.

Carruthers, G. (2012). "The Case for the Comparator Model as an Explanation of the Sense of Agency and Its Breakdowns." *Consciousness and Cognition* 21: 32–47.

Carruthers, P. (2004). "Reductive Explanation and the 'Explanatory Gap.'" *Canadian Journal of Philosophy* 34 (2): 153–174.

Carruthers, P. (2005). "Conscious Experience versus Conscious Thought." In *Consciousness: Essays from a Higher-Order Perspective*. Oxford: Oxford University Press.

Carruthers, P., and Schechter, E. (2006). "Can Panpsychism Bridge the Explanatory Gap?" *Journal of Consciousness Studies* 13 (10–11): 32–39.

Cartwright, N. (1980). "Do the Laws of Physics State the Facts?" *Pacific Philosophical Quarterly* 61: 75–84.

Cartwright, N. (1983). *How the Laws of Physics Lie*. Oxford: Oxford University Press.

Chalmers, A. (1987). "Bhaskar, Cartwright and Realism in Physics." *Methodology and Science* 20: 77–96.

Chalmers, D. (1995). "Facing Up to the Problem of Consciousness." *Journal of Consciousness Studies* 2 (3): 200–219.

Chalmers, D. (1996). *The Conscious Mind: In Search of a Fundamental Theory*. Oxford: Oxford University Press.

Chalmers, D. (2002). "Does Conceivability Entail Possibility?" In T. Gendler and J. Hawthorne (eds.), *Conceivability and Possibility*. Oxford University Press.

Chalmers, D. (2003a). "Consciousness and Its Place in Nature." In S. Stich and F. Warfield (eds.), *Blackwell Guide to the Philosophy of Mind*. Oxford: Blackwell.

Chalmers, D. (2003b). "The Content and Epistemology of Phenomenal Belief." in Q. Smith and A. Jokic (eds.), *Consciousness: New Philosophical Perspectives*. Oxford: Oxford University Press.

Chalmers, D. (2006a). *The Character of Consciousness*. Oxford: Oxford University Press.

Chalmers, D. (2006b). "Strong and Weak Emergence." In P. Clayton and P. Davies (eds.), *The Re-Emergence of Emergence: The Emergentist Hypothesis from Science to Religion*. Oxford: Oxford University Press.

Chalmers, D. (2009). "The Two-Dimensional Argument against Materialism." In B. McLaughlin (ed.), *The Oxford Handbook of the Philosophy of Mind*. Oxford: Oxford University Press.

Chalmers, D. (2012). *Constructing the World*. Oxford: Oxford University Press.

Chalmers, D. (2015). "Panpsychism and Panprotopsychism." In Y. Nagasawa and T. Alter (eds.), *Consciousness in the Physical World: Essays on Russellian Monism*. Oxford: Oxford University Press.

Chalmers, D. (2017). "The Combination Problem for Panpsychism." In G. Brüntrup and L. Jaskolla (eds.), *Panpsychism: Contemporary Perspectives*. Oxford: Oxford University Press.

Chalmers, D., & Jackson, F. (2001). "Conceptual Analysis and Reductive Explanation." *Philosophical Review* 110 (13): 315–361.

Cheng, P. (1997). "From Covariation to Causation: A Causal Power Theory." *Psychological Review* 104 (2): 367–405.

Chisholm, R. (1976). *Person and Object: A Metaphysical Study*. London: G. Allen & Unwin.

Chisholm, R. (1991). "On the Simplicity of the Soul." *Philosophical Perspectives* 5: 157–181.

Christoff, K., Cosmelli, D., Legrand, D., and Thompson, E. (2011). "Specifying the Self for Cognitive Neuroscience." *Trends in Cognitive Sciences* 15: 104–112.

Chuard, P. (2007). "Indiscriminable Shades and Demonstrative Concepts." *Australasian Journal of Philosophy* 85 (2): 277–306.

Chudnoff, E. (2013). "Gurwitsch's Phenomenal Holism." *Phenomenology and the Cognitive Sciences* 12 (3): 559–578.

Chudnoff, E. (2018). "Epistemic Elitism and Other Minds." *Philosophy and Phenomenological Research* 96 (2): 276–298.

Church, J. (2016). "Perceiving People as People: An Overlooked Role for the Imagination." In A. Kind and P. Kung (eds.), *Knowledge through Imagination*. Oxford: Oxford University Press.

Churchland, P. (1981). "Eliminative Materialism and the Propositional Attitudes." *Journal of Philosophy* 78 (2): 67–90.

Clark, A. (1989). "The Particulate Instantiation of Homogeneous Pink." *Synthese* 80: 277–304.

Clarke, S. (1978). *The Works* (1738). New York: Garland.

Clarke, T. (1965). "Seeing Surfaces and Physical Objects." In M. Black (ed.), *Philosophy in America*. Ithaca, NY: Cornell University Press.

Clifford, W. (1874/86). "Body and Mind." *Fortnightly Review* 1874, reprinted in L. Stephen and F. Pollock (eds.) *Lectures and Essays*, 1886. London: MacMillan.

Coleman, S. (2009). "Mind under Matter." In D. Skrbina (ed.), *Mind That Abides*. Amsterdam: Benjamins.

Coleman, S. (2012). "Mental Chemistry: Combination for Panpsychists." *Dialectica* 66 (1): 137–166.

Coleman, S. (2014). "The Real Combination Problem: Panpsychism, Micro-Subjects, and Emergence." *Erkenntnis* 79 (1): 19–44.

Coleman, S. (2015). "Neurocosmology." In P. Coates and S. Coleman (eds.), *Phenomenal Qualities: Sense, Perception, and Consciousness*. Oxford: Oxford University Press.

Coleman, S. (2017). "Panpsychism and Neutral Monism: How to Make Up One's Mind." In G. Brüntrup and L. Jaskolla (eds.), *Panpsychism: Contemporary Perspectives*. Oxford: Oxford University Press.

Copeland, B. (1993). "The Curious Case of the Chinese Gym." *Synthese* 95 (2): 173–186.

Corbetta, M., Miezin, F., Dobmeyer, S., Shulman, G., and Petersen, S. (1990). "Attentional Modulation of Neural Processing of Shape, Color, and Velocity in Humans." *Science* 248: 1556–1559.

Cosmides, L., and Tooby, J. (1992). "Cognitive Adaptations for Social Exchange." In J. Barkow, L. Cosmides, and J. Tooby (eds.), *The Adapted Mind*. Oxford: Oxford University Press.

Cotnoir, A. (2013). "Composition as General Identity." In K. Bennett and D. Zimmerman (eds.), *Oxford Studies in Metaphysics*, vol. 8. Oxford: Oxford University Press.

Craver, C. (2015). "Levels." In T. Metzinger and J. M. Windt (eds.), *Open MIND*. Frankfurt a. M.: MIND Group.

Creary, L. (1981). "Causal Explanation and the Reality of Natural Component Forces." *Pacific Philosophical Quarterly* 62: 148–157.

Crick, F., and Koch, C. (1990). "Towards a Neurobiological Theory of Consciousness." *Seminars in Neuroscience* 12: 263–275.

Dainton, B. (1998). "Review of Eric Olson's *The Human Animal: Personal Identity without Psychology*." *Mind* 107: 679–82.

Dainton, B. (2000). *Stream of Consciousness: Unity and Continuity in Conscious Experience*. London: Routledge.

Dainton, B. (2004). "Précis of 'Stream of Consciousness.'" *Psyche* 9 (12): 1–29.

Dainton, B. (2008). *The Phenomenal Self*. Oxford: Oxford University Press.

Dainton, B. (2010). "Phenomenal Holism." *Royal Institute of Philosophy Supplement* 67: 113–139.

Dainton, B. (2011). "Review of Consciousness and Its Place in Nature." *Philosophy and Phenomenological Research* 83 (1): 238–261.

Dasgupta, S. (2014). "The Possibility of Physicalism." *Journal of Philosophy* 111(9): 557–592.

David, N., et al. (2008) "The 'Sense of Agency' and Its Underlying Cognitive and Neural Mechanisms." *Consciousness and Cognition* 17: 523–534.

Davidson, D. (1973). "Freedom to Act." In T. Honderich (ed.), *Essays on Freedom of Action*. New York: Routledge.

Davidson, D. (1980). "Mental Events." In *Essays on Actions and Events*. Oxford: Clarendon Press. Originally published 1970 in L. Foster and J. W. Swanson (eds.), *Experience and Theory*. Amherst: University of Massachusetts Press.

Dayhoff, J., Hameroff, S., Lahoz-Beltra, R., and Swenberg, C. (1994). "Cytoskeletal Involvement in Neuronal Learning: A Review." *European Biophysics Journal* 23 (2): 79–93.

De Courcillon, L., and Timoleon, F. (1684). *Quatre Dialogues: I. Sur l'Immortalité de l'Ame, II. Sur l'Existence de Dieu, III. Sur La Providence, IV. Sur La Religion*. Paris: Sebastian Mabre-Cramoisy.

Delaney, C. (1972). "Sellars's Grain Argument." *Australasian Journal of Philosophy* 50 (1): 14–16.

Della Rocca, M. (2008). *Spinoza*. New York: Routledge.

Dennett, D. (1978a). "Where Am I?" In *Brainstorms*. Montgomery, VT: Bradford Books: 310–323.

Dennett, D. (1978b). "Why the Law of Effect Will Not Go Away." In *Brainstorms*. Montgomery, VT: Bradford Books: 71–89.

Dennett, D. (1991). *Consciousness Explained*. London: Penguin Press.

Dennett, D. (1992). "The Self as Centre of Narrative Gravity." In F. Kessel, P. Cole, and D. Johnson (eds.), *Self and Consciousness: Multiple Perspectives*. Hillsdale, NJ: Erlbaum.

Dennett, D. (2006). "What RoboMary Knows." In T. Alter and S. Walter (eds.), *Phenomenal Concepts and Phenomenal Knowledge: New Essays on Consciousness and Physicalism*. Oxford: Oxford University Press.

DeRosset, Louis. (2010). "Reference and Response." *Australasian Journal of Philosophy* 89 (1):1–18.

Descartes, R. (1985). *Meditations on First Philosophy* (1641). In J. Cottingham, R. Stoothoff, and D. Murdoch (trans and eds.), *The Philosophical Writings of Descartes*. 2 vols. Cambridge, UK: Cambridge University Press.

Desmurget, M., Reilly, K. T., Richard, N., Szathmari, A., Mottolese, C., and Sirigu, A. (2009). "Movement Intention after Parietal Cortex Stimulation in Humans." *Science* 324: 811–813.

De Sousa, R. (1976). "Rational Homunculi." In A. Rorty (ed.), *The Identities of Persons*. Berkeley: University of California Press.

Diamante, S. (2017). "The Octopus and the Unity of Consciousness." *Philosophy of Biology* 32 (6): 1269–1287.

Diaz-Leon, E. (2011). "Reductive Explanation, Concepts, and A Priori Entailment." *Philosophical Studies* 155: 99–116.

Domenech, G., and Holik, F. (2007). "A Discussion on Particle Number and Quantum Indistinguishability." *Foundations of Physics* 37 (6): 855–878.

Dominus, S. (2011). "Could Conjoined Twins Share a Mind?" *New York Times Magazine*, May 29. http://www.nytimes.com/2011/05/29/magazine/could-conjoined-twins-share-a-mind.html.

Doré F. (1986). "Object Permanence in Adult Cats (*Felis catus*)." *Journal of Comparative Psychology* 100 (4): 340–347.

Dretske, F. (1994). "Introspection." *Proceedings of the Aristotelian Society* 94: 263–278.

Dubner, R., and Zeki, S. (1971). "Response Properties and Receptive Fields of Cells in an Anatomically Defined Region of the Superior Temporal Sulcus in the Monkey." *Brain Research* 35 (2): 528–532.

Duke, H. H. (1847). *A Systematic Analysis of Bishop Butler's Treatise on the Analogy of Religion to the Constitution of Nature, so far as relates to Natural Religion. To which is added, some considerations on certain arguments therein advanced*. London: Joseph Masters.

Duncan, J., and Humphreys, G. W. (1989). "Visual Search and Stimulus Similarity." *Psychological Review* 96: 433–458.

Duncan, J., and Humphreys, G. (1992). "Beyond the Search Surface: Visual Search and Attentional Engagement." *Journal of Experimental Psychology: Human Perception and Performance* 18 (2): 578–588; discussion 589–593.

Duns Scotus, J. (1986). "Questions on Aristotle's Metaphysics IX, Q.15." In A. B. Wolter (trans. and ed.), *Duns Scotus on the Will and Morality*. Washington, DC: Catholic University of America Press.

Ebert, J., and Wegner, D. (2010). "Time Warp: Authorship Shapes the Perceived Timing of Actions and Events." *Consciousness and Cognition* 19: 481–489.

Eddington, A. (1929). *The Nature of the Physical World*. Gifford Lectures. Cambridge, UK: Cambridge University Press.

Efron, R. (1967). "The Duration of the Present." *Annals of the New York Academy of Sciences* 138: 713–729.

Ehring, D. (1996). "Causation, Determinables, and Property Instances." *Nous* 30 (4): 461–480.

Eklund, M. (2008). "Deconstructing Ontological Vagueness." *Canadian Journal of Philosophy* 38 (1): 117–140.

Elder, C. (2008). "Against Universal Mereological Composition." *Dialectica* 62: 433–454.

Ellason, J., Ross, C., and Fuchs, D. (1996). "Lifetime Axis I and II Comorbidity and Childhood Trauma History in Dissociative Identity Disorder." *Psychiatry: Interpersonal and Biological Processes* 59 (3): 255–266.

Engel, S., Glover, G., and Wandell, B. (1997). "Retinotopic Organization in Human Visual Cortex and the Spatial Precision of Functional MRI." *Cerebral Cortex* 7 (2): 181–192.

Eriksen, C., and St. James, J. (1986). "Visual Attention within and around the Field of Focal Attention: A Zoom Lens Model." *Perceptual Psychophysics* 40: 225–240.

Evans, G. (1982). *The Varieties of Reference*. Ed. J. MacDowell. Oxford: Oxford University Press.

Evans, J. St. B. T. (2003). "In Two Minds: Dual Process Accounts of Reasoning." *Trends in Cognitive Sciences* 7: 454–459.

Feinberg, I. (1978). "Efference Copy and Corollary Discharge: Implications for Thinking and Its Disorders." *Schizophrenia Bulletin* 4: 636–640.

Fernyhough, C. (1996). "The Dialogic Mind: A Dialogic Approach to the Higher Mental Functions." *New Ideas in Psychology* 14 (1): 47–62.

Field, H. (1977). "Logic, Meaning and Conceptual Role." *Journal of Philosophy* 69: 379–408.

Fine, K. (1975). "Vagueness, Truth, and Logic." *Synthese* 30 (3–4): 265–300.

Fine, K. (1982). "Acts, Events and Things." In W. Leinfellner, E. Kramer, and J. Schank (eds.), *Language and Ontology: Proceedings of the 6th International Wittgenstein Symposium*. Vienna: Holder-Pichler-Tempsky.

Fine, K. (1999). "Things and Their Parts." *Midwest Studies in Philosophy* 23: 61–74.

Fine, K. (2001). "The Question of Realism." *Philosophers' Imprint* 1 (2): 1–30.

Fishman R. (1997). "Gordon Holmes, the Cortical Retina, and the Wounds of war." Seventh Charles B. Snyder Lecture. *Documenta Ophthalmologica* 93: 9–28.

Fodor, J. A. (1983). *The Modularity of Mind*. Cambridge, MA: MIT Press.

Fodor, J. A. (1987). *Psychosemantics*. Cambridge, MA: MIT/Bradford.

Fodor, J. (2007). "The Revenge of the Given." In B. P. McLaughlin and J. D. Cohen (eds.), *Contemporary Debates in Philosophy of Mind*. Oxford: Blackwell.

Frankfurt, H. (1987). "Identification and Wholeheartedness." In F. Schoeman (ed.), *Responsiblity, Character, and the Emotions: New Essays in Moral Psychology*. Cambridge, UK: Cambridge University Press.

Frankish, K. (2010). "Dual-Process and Dual-System Theories of Reasoning." *Philosophy Compass* 5 (10): 914–926.

French, S., and Rickles, D. P. (2003). "Understanding Permutation Symmetry." In K. Brading and E. Castellani (eds.), *Symmetries in Physics: New Reactions*. Cambridge, UK: Cambridge University Press.

Freud, S. (1961). *Beyond the Pleasure Principle* (1920). Trans. James Strachey. New York: Liveright Publishing Corporation.

Freud, S. (1949). *The Ego and the Id* (1923). Trans. J. Riviere. London: Hogarth Press.

Fried, I., et al. (1991). "Functional Organization of Human Supplementary Motor Cortex Studied by Electrical Stimulation." *Journal of Neuroscience* 11 (11): 3656–3666.

Friedman, M. (1974). "Explanation and Scientific Understanding." *Journal of Philosophy* 71: 5–19.

Frith, C. (2012). "Explaining Delusions of Control: The Comparator Model 20 Years On." *Consciousness and Cognition* 21: 52–54.

Gabora, L. (2002). "Amplifying Phenomenal Information: Toward a Fundamental Theory of Consciousness." *Journal of Consciousness Studies* 9 (8): 3–29.

Gallese, V., Keysers, C., and Rizzolatti, G. (2004). "A Unifying View of the Basis of Social Cognition." *Trends in Cognitive Sciences* 8 (9): 396–403.

Gallup, G. (1970). "Chimpanzees: Self Recognition." *Science* 167 (3914): 86–87.

Gaudry, J. (2008). "Does Physicalism Entail Cosmopsychism?" *Panexperientialism* (blog), May 24. http://panexperientialism.blogspot.ca/2008/05/does-physicalism-entail-cosmopsychism.html.

Gazzaniga, M. S. (2000). "Cerebral Specialization and Interhemispheric Communication. Does the Corpus Callosum Enable the Human Condition?" *Brain* 123 (7): 1293–1336.

Gazzaniga, M., Bogen, J., and Sperry, R. (1962). "Some Functional Effects of Sectioning the Cerebral Commissures in Man." *Proceedings of the National Academy of Sciences* 48 (2): 17–65.

Gazzaniga, M. S., and Freedman, H. (1973). "Observations on Visual Processes after Posterior Callosal Section." *Neurology* 23: 1126–1130.

Geach, P. (1967). "Identity." *Review of Metaphysics* 21 (1): 3–12.

Geldard, F. (1982). "Saltation in Somesthesis." *Psychological Bulletin* 92 (1): 136–175.

Geldard, F., and Sherrick, C. (1972). "The Cutaneous 'Rabbit': A Perceptual Illusion." *Science* 178 (4057): 178–179.

Gerrans, P. (2001). "Authorship and Ownership of Thoughts." *Philosophy, Psychiatry, & Psychology* 8 (2–3): 231–237.

Gertler, B. (2002). "Explanatory Reduction, Conceptual Analysis, and Conceivability Arguments about the Mind." *Nous* 36 (1): 22–49.

Gibbard, A. (1975). "Contingent Identity." *Journal of Philosophical Logic* 4: 187–222.

Gilbert, M. (1990). "Walking together: A paradigmatic social phenomenon." *Midwest Studies in Philosophy* 15: 1–14.

Gilbert, M. (2000). *Sociality and Responsibility: New Essays in Plural Subject Theory*. Lanham: Rowman & Littlefield Publishers.

Gilbert, M. (2002). "Collective Guilt and Collective Guilt Feelings." *Journal of Ethics* 6: 115–143.

Gilbert, M. (2009). "Shared Intention and Personal Intentions." *Philosophical Studies* 144(1): 167–187.

Gillett, C. (2002). "The Dimensions of Realization: A Critique of the Standard View." *Analysis* 62: 316–323.

Gillett, C., and Rives, B. (2005). "The Non-Existence of Determinables: Or, a World of Absolute Determinates as Default Hypothesis." *Nous* 39 (3): 483–504.

Gilmore, C. (2017). "Homunculi Are People Too! Lewis' Definition of Personhood Debugged." *Thought: A Journal of Philosophy* 6 (1): 54–60.

Godfrey-Smith, P. (2012). "Darwinian Individuals." In F. Bouchard and P. Huneman (eds.), *From Groups to Individuals: Perspectives on Biological Associations and Emerging Individuality.* Cambridge, MA: MIT Press.

Godfrey-Smith, P. (2016). *Other Minds: The Octopus, the Sea, and the Deep Origins of Consciousness.* New York: Macmillan.

Goff, P. (2006). "Experiences Don't Sum." *Journal of Consciousness Studies* 13 (10–11): 53–61.

Goff, P. (2009a). "Can the Panpsychist Get Round the Combination Problem? In D. Skrbina (ed.), *Mind That Abides: Panpsychism in the New Millennium.* Amsterdam: John Benjamins.

Goff, P. (2009b). "Why Panpsychism Doesn't Help Us Explain Consciousness." *Dialectica* 63 (3): 289–311.

Goff, P. (2010). "There Is No Combination Problem." In M. Blamauer (ed.), *The Mental as Fundamental: New Perspectives on Panpsychism.* Heusenstamm Nr Frankfurt: Ontos.

Goff, P. (2012). "There Is More than One Thing." In P. Goff (ed), *Spinoza on Monism.* New York: Palgrave Macmillan.

Goff, P. (2013). "Orthodox Property Dualism + Linguistic Theory of Vagueness = Panpsychism." In R. Brown (ed.), *Consciousness Inside and Out: Phenomenology, Neuroscience, and the Nature of Experience.* New York: Springer.

Goff, P. (2015). "Real Acquaintance and Physicalism." In P. Coates and S. Coleman (eds.), *Phenomenal Qualities: Sense, Perception, and Consciousness.* Oxford: Oxford University Press.

Goff, P. (2017a). *Consciousness and Fundamental Reality.* Oxford: Oxford University Press.

Goff, P. (2017b). "Panpsychism." *Stanford Encyclopedia of Philosophy.* Revised July 18. https://plato.stanford.edu/entries/panpsychism/.

Goff, P. (2017c). "The Phenomenal Bonding Solution to the Combination Problem." In G. Bruntrop and L. Jaskolla (eds.), *Panpsychism: Contemporary Perspectives.* Oxford: Oxford University Press.

Goldman, A. (2008). *Simulating Minds.* Oxford: Oxford University Press.

Goodman, N. (1951). *The Structure of Appearance.* Cambridge, MA: Harvard University Press.

Gopnik, A. (2000). "Explanation as Orgasm and the Drive for Causal Understanding: The Evolution, Function and Phenomenology of the Theory-Formation System." In F. Keil and R. Wilson (eds.), *Cognition and Explanation.* Cambridge, MA: MIT Press.

Graff, D. (2000). "Shifting Sands: An Interest Relative Theory of Vagueness." *Philosophical Topics* 28: 45–81.

Graham, G., Horgan, T., and Tienson, J. (2007). "Consciousness and Intentionality." In M. Velmans and S. Schneider (eds.), *The Blackwell Companion to Consciousness.* Oxford: Blackwell.

Grahek, N. (2007). *Feeling Pain and Being in Pain.* 2nd edition. Cambridge, MA: MIT Press.

Gregory, D. (2017). "Is Inner Speech Dialogic?" *Journal of Consciousness Studies* 24 (1–2): 111–137.

Grice, H. P. (1957). "Meaning." *Philosophical Review* 66 (3): 377–388.

Grice, H. P. (1962). "Some Remarks about the Senses." In R. J. Butler (ed.), *Analytic Philosophy.* First series. Oxford: Basil Blackwell.

Grimm, S. (2009). "Reliability and the Sense of Understanding." In H. De Regt, S. Leonelli, and K. Eigner (eds.), *Scientific Understanding: Philosophical Perspectives*. University of Pittsburgh Press.

Gross, S., and Flombaum, J. (2017). "Does Perceptual Consciousness Overflow Cognitive Access? The Challenge from Probabilistic, Hierarchical Processes." *Mind and Language* 32 (3): 257–391.

Grossberg, S., and Mignolla, E. (1985). "Neural Dynamics of Form Perception: Boundary Completion, Illusory Figures, and Neon Color Spreading." *Psychological Review* 92: 173–211.

Gurwitsch, A. (1964). *The Field of Consciousness*. Pittsburgh: Duquesne University Press.

Gutfreund, Y., Matzner, H., Flash, T., and Hochner, B. (2006). "Patterns of Motor Activity in the Isolated Nerve Cord of the Octopus Arm." *Biological Bulletin* 211: 212–222.

Gutnick, T., Byrne, R. A., Hochner. B., Kuba, M. (2011). *"Octopus vulgaris Uses Visual Information to Determine the Location of Its Arm.'* *Current Biology* 21 (6): 460–462.

Hare, C. (2007). "Self-Bias, Time-Bias, and the Metaphysics of Self and Time." *Journal of Philosophy* 104 (7): 350–373.

Harman, G. (1990). "The Intrinsic Quality of Experience." In J. Tomberlin (ed.), *Philosophical Perspectives 4*. Atascadero, CA: Ridgeview.

Hartshorne, C. (1934). *The Philosophy and Psychology of Sensation*. Chicago: University of Chicago Press.

Haugeland, B. (2002). "Authentic Intentionality." In M. Scheutz (ed.), *Computationalism: New Directions*. Cambridge, MA: MIT Press.

Hebb, D. O. (1949). *The Organization of Behavior*. New York: Wiley & Sons.

Heeger, D., Boynton, G., Demb, J, Seideman, E., and Newsome, W. (1999). "Motion Opponency in Visual Cortex." *Journal of Neuroscience* 19: 7162–7174.

Helle, R. (2013). "The Stoic Case for Cosmic Holism and Cosmopsychism in De Natura Deorum II." Master's thesis, University of Oslo.

Heller, M. (2000). "Temporal Overlap Is Not Coincidence." *Monist* 83 (3): 362–380.

Hellie, B. (2005). "Noise and Perceptual Indiscriminability." *Mind* 114: 481–508.

Helmholtz, H. v. (1866). *Handbuch der Physiologischen Optik*. Leipzig: Voss.

Hempel, C. (1965). *Aspects of Scientific Explanation*. New York: Free Press.

Hempel, C., and Oppenheim, P. (1948). "Studies in the Logic of Explanation." *Philosophy of Science* 15 (2): 135–175.

Hirsch, E. (1991). "Divided Minds." *Philosophical Review* 100 (1): 3–30.

Holmes, G. (1944). "The Organization of the Visual Cortex in Man." *Proceedings of the Royal Society*, series B, 132: 348–361.

Horgan, T. (1993). "From Supervenience to Superdupervenience: Meeting the Demands of a Material World." *Mind* 102 (408): 555–586.

Horgan, T. (2007). "Mental Causation and the Agent-Exclusion Problem." *Erkenntnis* 67 (2): 183–200.

Horgan, T., and Potrc, M. (2012). "Existence Monism Trumps Priority Monism." In P. Goff (ed.), *Spinoza on Monism*. New York: Palgrave Macmillan.

Horgan, T., and Tienson, J. (2002). "The Intentionality of Phenomenology and the Phenomenology of Intentionality." In D. Chalmers (ed.), *Philosophy of Mind: Classical and Contemporary Readings*. Oxford: Oxford University Press.

Huebner, B. (2011). "Genuinely Collective Emotions." *European Journal for Philosophy of Science* 1 (1): 89–118.

Huebner, B. (2014). *Macrocognition: A Theory of Distributed Minds and Collective Intentionality*. Oxford University Press.

Huebner, B., Bruno, M., and Sarkissian, H. (2010). "What Does the Nation of China Think about Phenomenal States?" *Review of Philosophy and Psychology* 1: 225–243.

Hume, D. (1888). *Treatise of Human Nature* (1739). Ed. L. A. Selby-Bigge. Oxford: Clarendon Press.

Hurley, S. (1998). *Consciousness in Action*. Cambridge, MA: Harvard University Press.

Husserl, E. (1970). *Logical Investigations*. Trans J. N. Findlay. London: Routledge and Kegan Paul.

Husserl, E. (1982). *Ideas Pertaining to a Pure Phenomenology and to a Phenomenological Philosophy: First Book*. Trans F. Kersten. Dordrecht: Kluwer Academic.

Husserl, E. (1989). *Ideas Pertaining to a Pure Phenomenology and to a Phenomenological Philosophy: Second Book*. Trans R. Rojcewicz and A. Schuwer. Dordrecht: Kluwer Academic.

Husserl, E. (2001). *Analyses concerning Active and Passive Synthesis: Lectures on Transcendental Logic*. Trans. A. Steinbock. New York: Springer.

Hutchins, Edwin. (1995). *Cognition in the Wild*. Cambridge, MA: MIT Press.

Hutto, D., and Myin, E. (2017). *Evolving Enactivism: Basic Minds Meet Content*. Cambridge: The MIT Press.

Jackson, F. (1975). "On the Adverbial Analysis of Visual Experience." *Metaphilosophy* 6 (April): 127–135.

Jackson, F. (1982). "Epiphenomenal Qualia." *Philosophical Quarterly* 32: 127–136.

Jackson, F. (1993). "Block's Challenge." In J. Bacon, K. Campbell, and L. Reinhardt (eds.), *Ontology, Causality and Mind: Essays in Honour of D. M. Armstrong*. New York: Cambridge University Press.

Jackson, F. (1996). "Mental Causation." *Mind* 105: 377–413.

Jackson, F. (1998). *From Metaphysics to Ethics*. Oxford: Oxford University Press.

Jackson, F. (2003). "From H$_2$O to Water: The Relevance to A Priori Passage." In H. Lillehammer and G. Rodriguez-Pereyra (eds.), *Real Metaphysics*. London: Routledge.

Jackson, F., and Pettit, P. (1988). "Functionalism and Broad Content." *Mind* 97: 381–400.

Jackson, F., and Pettit, P. (1990). "Program Explanation: A General Perspective." *Analysis* 50: 107–117.

James, W. (1890). *The Principles of Psychology*. Cambridge, MA: Harvard University Press.

James, W. (1909). *A Pluralistic Universe*. London: Longman, Green.

James, W. (1916). *Talks to Teachers on Psychology; and to Students on Some of Life's Ideals*. New York: Henry Holt.

Jaskolla, L., and Buck, A. (2012). "Does Panexperientialistic Holism Solve the Combination Problem?" *Journal of Consciousness Studies* 19 (9–10): 190–199.

Jaynes, J. (1976). *The Origin of Consciousness in the Breakdown of the Bicameral Mind*. New York: Houghton Mifflin.

Jenkins, C. S. I. (2011). "Is Metaphysical Dependence Irreflexive?" *The Monist* 94: 267–276.

Johansson, I. (2004). "On the Transitivity of the Parthood Relations." In H. Hochberg and K. Mulligan (eds.), *Relations and Predicates*. Frankfurt: Ontos.

Johnston, M. (1992). "How to Speak of the Colours." *Philosophical Studies* 68 (3): 221–263.

Johnston, M. (2007). "Humans Beings Revisited: My Body Is Not an Animal." In D. Zimmerman (ed.), *Oxford Studies in Metaphysics*, vol. 3. Oxford: Oxford University Press.

Johnston, W., and Dark. V. (1986). "Selective Attention." *Annual Review of Psychology* 37: 43–75.

Jorba, M. (2016). "Attitudinal Cognitive Phenomenology and the Horizon of Possibilities." In T. Breyer and C. Gutland (eds.), *The Phenomenology of Thinking: Philosophical Investigations into the Character of Cognitive Experiences*. New York: Routledge.

Kahneman, D. (2011). *Thinking, Fast and Slow*. New York: Farrar, Straus and Giroux.

Kant, I. (1997). *Critique of Pure Reason* (1781). Trans. and ed. P. Guyer and A. W. Wood. In *The Cambridge Edition of the Works of Immanuel Kant*. Cambridge, UK: Cambridge University Press.

Kellman, P., and Shipley, T. (1991). "A Theory of Visual Interpolation in Object Perception." *Cognitive Psychology* 23: 141–221.

Kelly, S. (2003). "Edmund Husserl on Phenomenology." In R. C. Solomon (ed.), *Blackwell Guide to Continental Philosophy*. Oxford: Blackwell.

Kelly, S. (2004). "On Seeing Things in Merleau-Ponty." In T. Carmon (ed.), *The Cambridge Companion to Merleau-Ponty*. Cambridge, UK: Cambridge University Press.

Kibble, T., and Berkshire, F. (2004). *Classical Mechanics*. 5th edition. London: Imperial College Press.

Kim, J. (1984). "Epiphenomenal and Supervenient Causation." *Midwest Studies in Philosophy* 9: 257–270.

Kim, J. (1998). *Mind in a Physical World*. Cambridge, MA: MIT Press.

Kim, J. (1999). "Making Sense of Emergence." Philosophical Studies: An International Journal for Philosophy in the Analytic Tradition 95 (1–2): 3–36.

Kim, S. (2011). "Multiple Realization and Evidence." *Philosophical Psychology* 24 (6): 739–749.

Kind, A. (2001). "Putting the Image Back in Imagination." *Philosophy and Phenomenological Research* 62 (1): 85–109.

Klein, C. (2015). "What Pain Asymbolia Really Shows." *Mind* 124 (494): 493–516.

Knobe, J., and Prinz, J. (2008). "Intuitions about Consciousness: Experimental Studies." *Phenomenology and Cognitive Science* 7: 67–83.

Koksvik, O. (2014). "Three Models of Phenomenal Unity." *Journal of Consciousness Studies* 21: 105–131.

Kolers, P., and von Grünau, M. (1976). "Shape and Color in Apparent Motion." *Vision Research* 16 (4): 329–335.

Korsgaard, C. (1989). "Personal Identity and the Unity of Agency: A Kantian Response to Parfit." *Philosophy and Public Affairs* 18 (2): 109–123.

Korsgaard, C. (2009). *Self-Constitution: Agency, Identity, and Integrity*. Oxford: Oxford University Press.

Koslicki, K. (2008). *The Structure of Objects*. Oxford: Oxford University Press.

Kriegel, U. (2004). "Consciousness and Self-Consciousness." *Monist* 87: 182–205.

Kriegel, U. (2007). "Intentional Inexistence and Phenomenal Intentionality." *Philosophical Perspectives* 21: 307–340.

Kriegel, U. (2009). *Subjective Consciousness: A Self-Representational Theory*. Oxford: Oxford University Press.

Kriegel, U. (ed.). (2013). *Phenomenal Intentionality*. Oxford: Oxford University Press.

Kripke, S. (1980). *Naming and Necessity*. Cambridge, MA: Harvard University Press.

Krueger, J. (2012). "Seeing Mind in Action." *Phenomenology and Cognitive Science* 11: 149–173.

Langland-Hassan, P. (2015). "Introspective Misidentification." *Philosophical Studies* 172 (7): 1737–1758.

Langland-Hassan, P. (N.d.). "Craniopagus Twins and the Possibility of Introspective Misidentification." *Consciousness Online*. http://consciousnessonline.files.wordpress.com/2013/02/langland-hassan-c05.pdf.

Lederman, L. (1993). *The God Particle: If the Universe Is the Answer, What Is the Question?* New York: Houghton Mifflin.

Lee, A. (N.d.). "The Deep Structure of Experience."

Leibniz, G. W. (1967). *The Leibniz-Arnauld Correspondence* (1686–1687). Trans. and ed. by H. T. Mason. Manchester, UK: Manchester University Press.

Leibniz, G. W. (1981). *New Essays on Human Understanding* (1765). Trans. and ed. P. Remnant and J. Bennett. Cambridge, UK: Cambridge University Press.

Leibniz, G. W. (1989). *Philosophical Essays* (Various). Ed. and trans. R. Ariew and D. Garber. Indianapolis, IN: Hackett.

Leibniz, G. W. (2012). "The Discourse on Metaphysics" (1686). In R. Latta and G. Montgomery (trans.), revised by P. Loptson (ed.), *The Discourse on Metaphysics and Other Writings*. Broadview Press.

Lennon, T., and Stainton, J. (eds.). (2008). *The Achilles of Rationalist Psychology*. Vol. 7 of *Studies in the History of Philosophy of Mind*. New York: Springer.

Leonard, H., and Goodman, N. (1940). "The Calculus of Individuals and Its Uses." *The Journal of Symbolic Logic* 5 (2): 45–55.

Leopold, A. (1949). *A Sand County Almanac*. New York: Oxford University Press.

Levine, J. (1983). "Materialism and Qualia: The Explanatory Gap." *Pacific Philosophy Quarterly* 64: 354–361.

Levy, J. (1977). "Manifestations and Implications of Shifting Hemi-Inattention in Commisurotomy Patients." *Advances in Neurology* 18: 83–92.

Levy, J. (1990). "Regulation and Generation of Perception in the Asymmetric Brain." In C. Trevarthen (ed.), *Brain Circuits and Functions of the Mind: Essays in Honour of Roger W. Sperry*. Cambridge, UK: Cambridge University Press.

Levy, J., Trevarthen, C., and Sperry, R. W. (1972). "Perception of Bilateral Chimeric Figures Following Hemispheric Deconnexion." *Brain* 95: 61–78.

Lewis, D. (1971). "Counterparts of Persons and Their Bodies." *Journal of Philosophy* 68: 203–211.

Lewis, D. (1976). "Survival and Identity." In A. Rorty (ed.), *The Identities of Persons*. Berkeley: University of California Press.

Lewis, D. (1979). "Attitudes De Dicto and De Se." *Philosophical Review* 88 (4): 513–543.

Lewis, David. (1980). "Mad Pain and Martian Pain." In N. Block (ed.), *Readings in the Philosophy of Psychology*, vol. 1. Cambridge, MA: Harvard University Press.

Lewis, D. (1986). *On the Plurality of Worlds*. Oxford: Blackwell.

Lewis, D. (1988). "Vague Identity: Evans Misunderstood." *Analysis* 48 (3): 128–130.

Lewis, D. (1990). "What Experience Teaches." In W. G. Lycan (ed.), *Mind and Cognition*. Oxford: Blackwell.

Lewis, D. (1991). *Parts of Classes*. Oxford: Basil Blackwell.

Lewis, D. (1993). "Many, but Almost One." In J. Bacon, K. Campbell, and L. Reinhardt (eds.), *Ontology, Causality, and Mind: Essays in Honour of D. M. Armstrong*. Cambridge, UK: Cambridge University Press.

Lewis, D. (1995). "Should a Materialist Believe in Qualia?" *Australasian Journal of Philosophy* 73 (1): 140–144.

Lewis, D. (2003). "Things qua Truthmakers." In H. Lillehammer and G. Rodriguez-Pereyra (eds.), *Real Metaphysics: Essays in Honor of D. H. Mellor*. New York: Routledge.

Lewis, M., and Brooks-Gunn, J. (1979). *Social Cognition and the Acquisition of Self*. New York: Plenum Press.

Lewtas, P. (2013). "What Is It Like to Be a Quark?" *Journal of Consciousness Studies* 20 (9–10): 39–64.

Lindsay, R. Bruce. (1961). *Physical Mechanics*. 3rd edition. New York: Van Nostrand.

Lipton, P. (2009). "Understanding without Explanation." In H. De Regt, S. Leonelli, and K. Eigner (eds.), *Scientific Understanding: Philosophical Perspectives*. Pittsburgh: University of Pittsburgh Press.

List, C., and Pettit, P. (2011). *Group Agency: The Possibility, Design, and Status of Corporate Agents*. Oxford: Oxford University Press.

List, C. (2018). "What is it Like to be a Group Agent?" *Noûs* 52 (2): 295–319.

Loar, B. (1990). "Phenomenal States." *Philosophical Perspectives* 4: 81–108.

Locke, J. (1836). *An Essay Concerning Human Understanding* (1689). London: T. Tegg and Son.

Lockwood, M. (1989). *Mind, Brain, and the Quantum*. Oxford: Oxford University Press.

Lockwood, M. (1993). "The Grain Problem." In H. Robinson (ed.), *Objections to Physicalism*. Oxford: Oxford University Press.

Lockwood, Michael. (1994). "Issues of Unity and Objectivity." In C. Peacocke (ed.), *Objectivity, Simulation and the Unity of Consciousness: Proceedings of the British Academy 83*. Oxford: Oxford University Press.

Lotze. (1894). *Microcosmus: An Essay Concerning Man and His Relation to the World*. Trans. E. Hamilton and E. E. C. Jones. New York: Charles Scribner's Sons.

Lovelock, J. (2000). *Gaia: A New Look at Life on Earth*. Oxford: Oxford University Press.

Lowe, E. J. (1996). *Subjects of Experience*. Cambridge, UK: Cambridge University Press.

Lycan, G. (1979). "A New Lilliputian Argument against Machine Functionalism." *Philosophical Studies* 35: 279–287.

Lycan, William G. (1995). *Consciousness* (1987). Cambridge, MA: MIT Press.

Lynn, M., Berger, C., Riddle, T, and Morsella, E. (2010). "Mind Control? Creating Illusory Intentions through a Phony Brain-Computer Interface." *Consciousness and Cognition* 19: 1007–1012.

MacArthur, R., and Wilson, E. O. (1967). *The Theory of Island Biogeography*. Princeton, NJ: Princeton University Press.

MacKenzie, Matthew. (2007). "The Illumination of Consciousness: Approaches to Self-Awareness in the Indian and Western Traditions." *Philosophy East and West* 57: 40–62.

Macpherson, F. (2011a). "Introduction: Individuating the Senses." In *The Senses: Classical and Contemporary Philosphical Perspectives*. New York: Oxford University Press.

Macpherson, F. (2011b). *The Senses: Classical and Contemporary Philosphical Perspectives*. New York: Oxford University Press.

Madden, R. (2012). "The Naive Topology of the Conscious Subject." *Nous* 100: 1–15.

Maitra, S., Weatherson, B., and Ichikawa, J. (2012). "In Defense of a Kripkean Dogma." *Philosophy and Phenomenological Research* 85 (1): 56–68.

Mallon, R., Machery, E., Nichols, S., and Stich, S. (2009). "Against Arguments from Reference." *Philosophy and Phenomenological Research* 79 (2): 332–356.

Margulis, L. (1998). *Symbiotic Planet: A New Look at Evolution*. London: Weidenfeld & Nicolson.

Markosian, E. (1998). "Brutal Composition." *Philosophical Studies* 92 (3): 211–249.

Marks, C. (1980). *Commissurotomy, Consciousness, and Unity of Mind*. Cambridge, MA: MIT Press.

Marr, D. (1982). *Vision*. San Francisco: Freeman Press.

Masrour, F. (2014). "Unity of Consciousness: Advertisement for a Leibnizian View." In C. Hill and D. Bennett (eds.), *Sensory Integration and the Unity of Consciousness*. Cambridge, MA: MIT Press.

Matey, J. (2013). "Representing the Impossible." *Philosophical Psychology* 26 (2): 188–206.

Matthen, M. (1988). "Biological Functions and Perceptual Content." *Journal of Philosophy* 85 (1): 5–27.

Matthen, M. (2015). "The Individuation of the Senses." In M. Matthen (ed.), *The Oxford Handbook of Philosophy of Perception*. Oxford: Oxford University Press.

Matthews, F. (2003). *For Love of Matter: A Contemporary Panpsychism*. Albany, NY: SUNY Press.

Maxwell, G. (1979). "Rigid Designators and Mind-Brain Identity." In C. Savage (ed.), *Perception and Cognition: Minnesota Studies in the Philosophy of Science*. Vol. 9. Minneapolis: University of Minnesota Press.

McBurney, D. H. (1986). "Taste, Smell, and Flavor Terminology: Taking the Confusion Out of Fusion." In H. MeisIlman and R. Rivkin (eds.), *Clinical Measurement of Taste and Smell*. New York, NY: Macmillan.

McGinn, C. (1989). "Can We Solve the Mind-Body Problem?" *Mind* 98: 349–366.

McGinn, C. (2006). "Hard Questions." In A. Freeman (ed.), *Consciousness and Its Place in Nature: Does Physicalism Entail Panpsychism?*. Exeter/Charlottesville: Imprint Academic.

McLaughlin, B. (1992). "The Rise and Fall of British Emergentism." In A. Beckermann, H. Flohr, and J. Kim (eds.), *Emergence or Reduction? Prospects for Nonreductive Physicalism*. Berlin: De Gruyter.

McLaughlin, B. (1997). "Emergence and Supervenience." *Intellectica* 25 (2): 25–43.

McQueen, K. (2013) . "A Priori Entailment and the Metaphysics of Science." PhD dissertation, Australian National University. Accessed November 2018. https://pdfs.semanticscholar. org/c24e/146869c9370168f823b041088fbc9dd9fa21.pdf.

McQueen, K. (2015). "Mass Additivity and A Priori Entailment." *Synthese* 192 (5): 1373–1392.

McTaggart, J. (1988). *The Nature of Existence*. Vol. 1. Ed. C. D. Broad. Cambridge, UK: Cambridge University Press.

Melloni, L., Molina, C., Pena, M., Torres, D., Singer, W., and Rodeiguez, E. (2007). "Synchronization of Neural Activity across Cortical Areas Correlates with Conscious Perception." *Journal of Neuroscience* 27 (11): 2858–2865.

Melnyk A. (2003). *A Physicalist Manifesto: Thoroughly Modern Materialism*. Cambridge, UK: Cambridge University Press.

Melnyk, A. (2014). "Pereboom's Robust Non-Reductive Physicalism." *Erkenntnis* 79 (5): 1191–1207.

Mendelovici, Angela. (2018). "Panpsychism's Combination Problem Is a Problem for Everyone." In W. Seager (ed.), *Routledge Handbook of Panpsychism*. New York: Routledge.

Mendelssohn, M. (2002). "Phaedon or, The Death of Socrates" (1767). Trans. C. Cullen, 1789. Schiller Institute. Accessed July 2013. http://www.schillerinstitute.org/transl/mend_phadn_cullen.html.

Merleau-Ponty, M. (1962). *The Phenomenology of Perception* (1945). Trans. Colin Smith. New York: Routledge and Kegan Paul.

Merricks, T. (2001). *Objects and Persons*. Oxford: Oxford University Press.

Merricks, T. (2005). "Composition and Vagueness." *Mind* 114: 615–637.

Michotte, A., Thines, G., and Crabbe, G. (1991). "Amodal Completion of Perceptual Structures" (1964). In G. Thines, A. Costall, and G. Butterworth (eds.), *Michotte's Experimental Phenomenology of Perception*. Hillsdale, NJ: Erlbaum.

Mijuskovic, B. L. (1984). *The Achilles of Rationalist Arguments: The Simplicity, Unity, and Identity of Thought and Soul from the Cambridge Platonists to Kant. A Study in the History of an Argument.* Leiden: Martinus Nijhoff.

Mill, J. S. (1882). *A System of Logic, Ratiocinative and Inductive* (1843). 8th edition. New York: Harper & Brother.

Miller, G. (2017). "Can Subjects Be Proper Parts of Subjects? The De-combination Problem." *Ratio* 30 (2): 1–18.

Miller, G. (2018). "Forming a Positive Concept of the Phenomenal Bonding Relation for Constitutive Panpsychism." *Dialectica* 71 (4): 541–562.

Miller, H., Gipson, C., Vaughan, A., Rayburn-Reeves, R., and Zentall, T. (2009). "Object Permanence in Dogs: Invisible Displacement in a Rotation Task." *Psychonomic Bulletin and Review* 16 (1): 150–155.

Millikan, Ruth G. (1989). "Biosemantics." *Journal of Philosophy* 86 (6): 281–297.

Mizrahi, V. (2009). "Is Colour Composition Phenomenal?" In D. Skusevich and P. Matikas (eds.), *Color Perception: Physiology, Processes and Analysis.* Hauppauge, NY: Nova Science.

Mole, C. (2010). *Attention Is Cognitive Unison: An Essay in Philosophical Psychology.* Oxford: Oxford University Press.

Molnar, G. (2003). *Powers.* Oxford: Oxford University Press.

Montero, B. (2017). "What Combination Problem?" In G. Brüntrup and L. Jaskolla (eds.), *Panpsychism: Contemporary Perspectives.* Oxford: Oxford University Press.

Moore, J., and Haggard, P. (2008). "Awareness of Action: Inference and Prediction." *Consciousness and Cognition* 17: 136–144.

Mørch, H. H. (2013). "Comments On Sebastian: 'What Panpsychists Should Reject: On the Incompatibility of Panpsychism and Organizational Invariantism.'" *Consciousness Online.* http://consciousnessonline.files.wordpress.com/2013/02/hassel-comments-on-sebastian.pdf.

Mørch, H. H. (2014). "Panpsychism and Causation: A New Argument and a Solution to the Combination Problem." PhD dissertation, University of Oslo.

Moritz, C., Schneider, C., and Wake, D. (1992). "Evolutionary Relationships within the *Ensatina eschscholtzii* Complex Confirm the Ring Species Interpretation." *Systematic Biology* 41 (3): 273–291.

Morris, K. (2017). "The Combination Problem: Subjects and Unity." *Erkenntnis* 82 (1): 103–120.

Moyer, M. (2008). "A Survival Guide to Fission." *Philosophical Studies* 141 (3): 299–322.

Nagasawa, Y., and Wager, K. (2017). "Panpsychism and Priority Cosmopsychism." In G. Brüntrup and L. Jaskolla (eds.), *Panpsychism: Contemporary Perspectives.* Oxford: Oxford University Press.

Nagel, E. (1961). *The Structure of Science: Problems in the Logic of Scientific Explanation.* New York: Harcourt, Brace & World.

Nagel, E. (1963). "Wholes, Sums, and Organic Unities." In D. Lerner (ed.), *Parts and Wholes.* New York: Free Press.

Nagel, T. (1971). "Brain Bisection and the Unity of Consciousness." *Synthese* 22: 396–413.

Nagel, T. (1974). "What Is It Like to Be a Bat?" *Philosophical Review* 83: 435–450.

Nagel, T. (1986). *The View from Nowhere.* Oxford: Oxford University Press.

Nagel, T. (2004). "Panpsychism" (1979). In D. S. Clarke (ed.), *Pansychism: Past and Recent Selected Readings.* Albany: State University of New York Press.

Nanay, B. (2010). "Perception and Imagination: Amodal Perception as Mental Imagery." *Philosophical Studies* 50: 239–254.

Nedelsky, J. (2012). *Law's Relations: A Relational Theory of Self, Autonomy, and Law*. Oxford: Oxford University Press.

Nieder, A. (2002). "Seeing More than Meets the Eyes: Processing of Illusory Contours in Animals." *Journal of Comparative Physiology A* 188: 249–260.

Nielsen, T. (1963). "Volition: Towards a New Experimental Approach." *Scandinavian Journal of Psychology* 4: 225–230.

Noë, A. (2005). "Real Presence." *Philosophical Topics* 33: 235–264.

Noonan, H. (2003). *Personal Identity* (1989). 2nd edition. New York: Routledge.

Noonan, H. (2010). "The Thinking Animal Problem and Personal Pronoun Revisionism." *Analysis* 70 (1): 93–98.

Nozick, R. (2003). "Personal Identity through Time" (1981). In R. Martin and J. Barresi (eds.), *Personal Identity* Oxford: Blackwell.

Oizumi, M., Albantakis, L., and Tononi, G. (2014). "From the Phenomenology to the Mechanisms of Consciousness: Integrated Information Theory 3.0." *PLOS Computational Biology* 10 (5). Online.

Olson, E. (1997). *The Human Animal: Personal Identity without Psychology*. Oxford: Oxford University Press.

Olson, E. (2003). "An Argument for Animalism." In R. Martin and J. Barresi (eds.), *Personal Identity*. Oxford: Blackwell.

O'Madagain, C. (2012). "Group Agents: Persons, Mobs, or Zombies?" *International Journal of Philosophical Studies* 20 (2): 271–287.

Parfit, D. (1971). "Personal Identity." *Philosophical Review* 80: 3–27.

Parfit, D. (1984). *Reasons and Persons*. Oxford: Oxford University Press.

Parfit, D. (1995). "The Unimportance of Identity." In H. Harris (ed.), *Identity*. Oxford: Oxford University Press.

Parfit, D. (1999). "Experiences, Subjects, and, Conceptual Schemes." *Philosophical Topics* 26: 217–270.

Paul, L. A. (2002). "Logical Parts." *Nous* 36 (4): 578–596.

Pautz, A. (2015). Comment on John Horgan, "Consciousness and 'Crazyism': Responses to Critique of Integrated Information Theory." *Scientific American*. http://blogs.scientificamerican.com/cross-check/consciousness-and-crazyism-responses-to-critique-of-integrated-information-theory/.

Pautz, A. (N.d.) "A Dilemma for Russellian Monists."

Pereboom, D. (2011). *Consciousness and the Prospects of Physicalism*. New York: Oxford University Press.

Perky, C. (1910) "An Experimental Study of Imagination." *American Journal of Psychology* 21: 422–452.

Perry, J. (1972). "Can the Self Divide?" *Journal of Philosophy* 69: 463–488.

Perry, J. (1979). "The Problem of the Essential Indexical." *Nous* 13: 3–21.

Pettit, P. (2007). "Responsibility Incorporated." *Ethics* 117: 171–201.

Phillips, I. (2014). "The Temporal Structure of Experience." In V. Arstila and D. Lloyd (eds.), *Subjective Time: The Philosophy, Psychology, and Neuroscience of Temporality*. Cambridge, MA: MIT Press.

Pianka, E. R. (1970). "On r and K Selection." *American Naturalist* 104 (940): 592–597.

Pinto, Y., Neville, D., Otten, M., Corballis, P., Lamme, V., de Haan, E., Foschi, N., and Fabri, M. (2017). "Split Brain: Divided Perception but Undivided Consciousness." *Brain: A Journal of Neurology* 140 (5): 1231–1237.

Plato. (1997). *Phaedrus*. Trans. A. Nehamas and P. Woodruff. In J. M. Cooper (ed.), *Plato: Complete Works*. Indianapolis: Hackett.

Plato. (2000). *The Republic*. Trans. T. Griffith. Ed. G. R. F. Ferrari. Cambridge, UK: Cambridge University Press.

Ploner, M., Freund, H. J., and Schnitzler, A. (1999). "Pain Affect without Pain Sensation in a Patient with a Postcentral Lesion." *Pain* 81: 211–214.

Plotinus. (1956). *Enneads*. Trans. and ed. S. Mackenna and B. S. Page. London: Faber and Faber. Internet Archive. Accessed July 2013. http://archive.org/stream/plotinustheennea033190mbp#page/n11/mode/2up.

Plotnik, J., De Waal, F., and Reiss, D. (2006). "Self-Recognition in an Asian Elephant." *Proceedings of the National Academy of Sciences of the United States of America* 103 (45): 17053–17057.

Pockett, S. (2002). "On Subjective Back-Referral and How Long It Takes to Become Conscious of a Stimulus: A Reinterpretation of Libet's Data." *Consciousness and Cognition* 8: 45–61.

Pockett, S. (2003). "How Long Is 'Now'? Phenomenology and the Specious Present." *Phenomenology and the Cognitive Sciences* 2: 55–68.

Polger, T. (2008). "Two Confusions concerning Multiple Realization." *Philosophy of Science* 75: 537–547.

Powell, C. T. (1990). *Kant's Theory of Self-Consciousness*. Oxford: Oxford University Press.

Prescott, J. (2012). "Multimodal Chemosensory Interactions and Perception of Flavour." In M. Murray and M. Wallace (eds.), *The Neural Bases of Multisensory Processes*. Boca Raton, FL: CRC Press.

Prete, F. (ed.). (2004). *Complex Worlds from Simpler Nervous Systems*. Cambridge, MA: MIT Press.

Priel, B., and de Schonen, S. (1986). "Self-Recognition: A Study of a Population without Mirrors." *Journal of Experimental Child Psychology* 41 (2): 237–250.

Prinz, J. J. (2006). "Is the Mind Really Modular?" In R. Stainton (ed.), *Contemporary Debates in Cognitive Science*. Oxford: Blackwell.

Prinz, J. (2011). "Is Attention Necessary and Sufficient for Consciousness?" In C. Mole, D. Smithies, and W. Wu (eds.), *Attention: Philosophical and Psychological Essays*. Oxford: Oxford University Press.

Prinz, J. (2012). *The Conscious Brain: How Attention Engenders Experience*. Oxford: Oxford University Press.

Proclus. (1963). *The Elements of Theology*. Trans. and ed. E. R. Dodds. Oxford: Clarendon Press.

Puccetti, R. (1973). "Brain Bisection and Personal Identity." *British Journal for the Philosophy of Science* 24 (4): 339–355.

Puccetti, R. (1981). "The Case for Mental Duality: Evidence from Split-Brain Data and Other Considerations." *Behavioral and Brain Sciences* 4 (1): 93–123.

Putnam, H. (1975). "The Meaning of Meaning." In *Philosophical Papers*. Vol. 2: *Mind, Language, and Reality*. Cambridge: Cambridge University Press.

Putnam, H. (2003). "The Nature of Mental States" (1965). In T. O'Connor, D. Robb, and J. Heil (eds.), *Philosophy of Mind: Contemporary Readings*. New York: Routledge.

Quinton, A. (1962). "The Soul." *Journal of Philosophy* 59 (15): 393–409.

Raffman, D. (1994). "Vagueness without Paradox." *Philosophical Review* 103 (1): 41–74.

Raffman, D. (2012). "Indiscriminability and Phenomenal Continua." *Philosophical Perspectives* 26 (1): 309–322.

Raffman, D. (2013). *Unruly Words: A Study of Vague Language*. Oxford: Oxford University Press.

Ramachandran, V. S. (1995). "Filling in the Gaps in Logic: Reply to Durgin et al." *Perception* 24: 841–843.

Ramachandran, V. S., and Rogers-Ramachandran, D. (1996). "Synaesthesia in Phantom Limbs Induced with Mirrors." *Proceedings of the Biological Sciences* 263 (1369): 377–386.

Rasmussen, S., Karampurwalab, H., Vaidyanathb, R., Jensenc, K., and Hameroff, S. (1990). "Computational Connectionism within Neurons: A Model of Cytoskeletal Automata Subserving Neural Networks." *Physica D: Nonlinear Phenomena* 42 (1–3): 428–449.

Raymont, P. (2005). "Conscious Unity." *PhilPapers*. http://philpapers.org/archive/RAYCU.1.pdf.

Recanati, F. (2012). "Immunity to Error through Misidentification: What It Is and Where It Comes From." In S. Prosser and F. Recanati (eds.), *Immunity to Error through Misidentification*. Cambridge, UK: Cambridge University Press.

Robinson, H. (2016). *From the Knowledge Argument to Mental Substance: Resurrecting the Mind*. Cambridge, UK: Cambridge University Press.

Roelofs, L. (2014a). "Phenomenal Blending and the Palette Problem." *Thought* 3 (1): 59–70.

Roelofs, L. (2014b). "What Are the Dimensions of the Conscious Field?" *Journal of Consciousness Studies* 21 (7–8): 88–104.

Roelofs, L. (2016). "The Unity of Consciousness, within and between Subjects." *Philosophical Studies* 173 (12): 3199–3221.

Roelofs, L. (2017a). "Rational Agency without Self-Knowledge: Could 'We' Replace 'I'?" *Dialectica* 71 (1): 3–33.

Roelofs, L. (2017b). Review of *Panpsychism: Contemporary Perspectives*. Ed. Godehard Brüntrup and Ludwig Jaskolla. Dialogue.

Roelofs, L. (2018a). "Seeing the Invisible: How to Perceive, Infer, and Imagine Other Minds." *Erkenntnis* 83 (2): 205–229.

Roelofs, L. (2018b). "Can We Sum Subjects? Evaluating Panpsychism's Hard Problem." In W. Seager (ed.), *The Routledge Handbook of Panpsychism*. New York: Routledge.

Roelofs, L. (N.d.). "Consciousness, Revelation, and Confusion: Are Constitutive Panpsychists Hoist by Their Own Petard?" Unpublished manuscript.

Rosen, G. (2010). "Metaphysical Dependence: Grounding and Reduction." In B. Hale and A. Hoffman (eds.), *Modality: Metaphysics, Logic, and Epistemology*. Oxford: Oxford University Press.

Rosenberg, G. (1998). "The Boundary Problem for Phenomenal Individuals." In S. Hameroff, A. Kaszniak, and A. Scott (eds.), *Toward a Science of Consciousness: The First Tucson Discussions and Debates (Complex Adaptive Systems)*. Cambridge, MA: MIT Press.

Rosenberg, G. (2004). *A Place for Consciousness: Probing the Deep Structure of the Natural World*. Oxford: Oxford University Press.

Rosenberg, G. (2017). "Land Ho? We Are Close to a Synoptic Understanding of Consciousness." In G. Brüntrup and L. Jaskolla (eds.), *Panpsychism*. Oxford: Oxford University Press.

Rosenberg, J. (1994). "Comments on Bechtel, 'Levels of Description and Explanation in Cognitive Science.'" *Minds and Machines* 4: 27–37.

Rosenthal, D. (1986). "Two Concepts of Consciousness." *Philosophical Studies* 49: 329–359.

Rosenthal, D. (2005). *Consciousness and Mind*. Oxford: Oxford University Press.

Rosenthal, D. (2007). "Phenomenological Overflow and Cognitive Access." *Behavioral and Brain Sciences* 30 (5–6): 522–523.

Ross, P. (1999). "The Appearance and Nature of Colour." *Southern Journal of Philosophy* 37 (2):227–252.

Rovane, C. (1990). "Branching Self-Consciousness." *Philosophical Review* 99 (3): 355–395.

Rovane, C. (1998). *The Bounds of Agency: An Essay in Revisionary Metaphysics*. Princeton, NJ: Princeton University Press.

Rovane, C. (2005). "Alienation and the Alleged Separateness of Persons." *Monist* 87 (4): 554–572.

Rovane, C. (2012). "Does Rationality Enforce Identity?" In A. Coliva (ed.), *Self and Self-Knowledge*. Oxford: Oxford University Press.

Rozemond, M. (2008). "The Achilles Argument and the Nature of Matter in the Clarke Collins Correspondence." In T. Lennon and J. Stainton (eds.), *The Achilles of Rationalist Psychology*. Vol. 7 of *Studies in the History of Philosophy of Mind*. New York: Springer.

Russell, B. (1903). *The Principles of Mathematics*. Cambridge, UK: Cambridge University Press.

Russell, B. (1919). *Introduction to Mathematical Philosophy*. London: Routledge.

Russell, B. (1927). *The Analysis of Matter*. London: Kegan Paul.

Russell, B. (1985). "The Philosophy of Logical Atomism." In D. Pears (ed.), *The Philosophy of Logical Atomism*. LaSalle, IL: Open Court.

Ryle, G. (1949). *The Concept of Mind*. London: Hutchinson.

Śaṅkara (ācārya). (1994). "The Vedānta Sūtras (Brahma Sūtra Bhāṣya)." In *Sacred Books of the East*. Vol. 38. Delhi: Motilal Banarsidass.

Sartre, J. (1956). *Being and Nothingness: An Essay in Phenomenological Ontology* (1943). Trans. H. E. Barnes. New York: Philosophical Library.

Sato, A., and Yasuda, A. (2005). "Illusion of Sense of Self-Agency: Discrepancy between the Predicted and Actual Sensory Consequences of Actions Modulates the Sense of Self-Agency, but Not the Sense of Self-Ownership." *Cognition* 94 (3): 241–255.

Schachter, J. (2002). "Pierre Bayle, Matter, and the Unity of Consciousness." *Canadian Journal of Philosophy* 32 (2): 241–265.

Schaffer, J. (2010). "Monism: The Priority of the Whole." *Philosophical Review* 119: 31–76.

Schaffer, J. (2012). "Why the World Has Parts." In P. Goff (ed.), *Spinoza on Monism*. New York: Palgrave Macmillan.

Schear, J. (2009). "Experience and Self-Consciousness." *Philosophical Studies* 144 (1): 95–105.

Schechter, E. (2009). "Persons and Psychological Frameworks: A Critique of Tye." *Journal of Consciousness Studies* 16 (2–3): 141–163.

Schechter, E. (2010). "Individuating Mental Tokens: The Split-Brain Case." *Philosophia* 38 (1): 195–216.

Schechter, E. (2012a). "Intentions and Unified Agency: Insights from the Split-Brain Phenomenon." *Mind and Language* 27 (5): 570–594.

Schechter, E. (2012b). "The Switch Model of Split-Brain Consciousness." *Philosophical Psychology* 25 (2): 203–226.

Schechter, E. (2013). "Two Unities of Consciousness." *European Journal of Philosophy* 21 (2): 197–218.

Schechter, E. (2015). "The Subject in Neuropsychology: Individuating Minds in the Split-Brain Case." *Mind and Language* 30 (5): 501–525.

Schechter, E. (2018). *Self-Consciousness and "Split" Brains: The Minds' I*. Oxford: Oxford University Press.

Schechtman, M. (2009). "Getting Our Stories Straight: Personal Identity and Self-Narration." In H. Bok, D. J. H. Mathews, and P. V. Rabins (eds.), *Personal Identity and Fractured Selves: The Self, Personal Identity, and the Brain*. Baltimore: Johns Hopkins University Press.

Schiffer, S. (1987). *Remnants of Meaning*. Cambridge, UK: Cambridge University Press.

Schilder, P., and Stengel, E. (1931). "Asymbolia for Pain." *Archives of Neurology & Psychiatry* 25 (3): 598–600.

Schopenhauer, A. (1969). *The World as Will and Representation*. Vol. 1 (1818). Trans. E. F. J. Payne. New York: Dover.

Schwitzgebel, E. (2015). "If Materialism Is True, the United States Is Probably Conscious." *Philosophical Studies* 172: 1697–1721.

Seager, W. (1990). "The Logic of Lost Lingens." *Journal of Philosophical Logic* 19: 407–428.

Seager, W. (1995). "Consciousness, Information and Panpsychism." *Journal of Consciousness Studies* 2–3: 272–288.

Seager, W. (2001). "The Constructed and the Secret Self." In A. Brook and R. DeVidi (eds.), *Self-Reference and Self-Knowledge*. Amsterdam: John Benjamins.

Seager, W. (2006). "The 'Intrinsic Nature' Argument for Panpsychism." *Journal of Consciousness Studies* 13 (10–11): 129–145.

Seager, W. (2010). "Panpsychism, Aggregation and Combinatorial Infusion." *Mind and Matter* 8 (2): 167–184.

Seager, W. (2017). "Panpsychist Infusion." In G. Brüntrup and L. Jaskolla (eds.), *Panpsychism: Contemporary Perspectives*. Oxford: Oxford University Press.

Searle, J. (1990). "Collective Intentions and Actions." In P. R. Cohen, J. Morgan, and M. E. Pollack (eds.), *Intentions in Communication*. Cambridge, MA: MIT Press.

Searle, J. (2000). "Consciousness." *Annual Review of Neuroscience* 23: 557–578.

Searle, J. (2003). "Minds, Brains, and Programs" (1980). In T. O'Connor, D. Robb, and J. Heil (eds.), *Philosophy of Mind: Contemporary Readings*. New York: Routledge.

Sebastian, M. (2013). "What Panpsychists Should Reject: On the Incompatibility of Panpsychism and the Principle of Organisational Invariance." *Minding the Brain* (blog). http://mindingthebrain.files.wordpress.com/2013/02/ppoi.pdf.

Segal, S. (1972). "Assimilation of a Stimulus in the Construction of an Image: The Perky Effect Revisited." In P. W. Sheehan (ed.), *The Function and Nature of Imagery*. New York: Academic Press.

Selfridge, O. (1959). *Pandemonium: A Paradigm for Learning*. Symposium on the Mechanization of Thought Processes. London: HM Stationery Office.

Sellars, W. (1963). *Science, Perception and Reality*. London: Routledge and Kegan Paul.

Setiya, K. (2008). "Practical Knowledge." *Ethics* 118 (3): 388–409.

Shani, I. (2010). "Mind Stuffed with Red Herrings: Why William James' Critique of the Mind-Stuff Theory Does Not Substantiate a Combination Problem for Panpsychism." *Acta Analytica* 25 (4): 413–434.

Shani, I. (2015). "Cosmopsychism: A Holistic Approach to the Metaphysics of Experience." *Philosophical Papers* 44 (3): 389–437.

Shani, I., and Keppler, J. (Forthcoming). "Beyond Combination: How Cosmic Consciousness Grounds Ordinary Experience." *Journal of the American Philosophical Association*.

Shannon, C. (1948). "The mathematical theory of communication." *Bell System Technical Journal* 27: 379–423.

Shapiro, J. (2014). "Massively Shared Agency." In M. Vargas and G. Yaffe, (eds.), *Rational and Social Agency: The Philosophy of Michael Bratman*, Oxford: Oxford University Press.

Shoemaker, S. (1970). "Persons and Their Pasts." *American Philosophical Quarterly* 7 (4): 269–285.

Shoemaker, S. (1984). *Personal Identity*. Oxford: Basil Blackwell.

Shoemaker, S. (1997). "Parfit on Identity." In J. Dancy (ed.), Reading Parfit. Oxford: Blackwell.

Shoemaker, S. (2000). "Realization and Mental Causation." In B. Elevich (ed.), *Proceedings of the 20th World Congress*. Vol. 9: *Philosophy of Mind*. Bowling Green, OH: Philosophy Documentation Center.

Shoemaker, S. (2002). "Kim on Emergence." *Philosophical Studies* 108 (1): 53–63.

Shoemaker, S. (2003). "Consciousness and Co-Consciousness." In Axel Cleeremans (ed.), *The Unity of Consciousness*. Oxford: Oxford University Press.

Sider, T. (1997). "Four-Dimensionalism." *Philosophical Review* 106 (2): 197–231.

Sider, T. (2001). "Maximality and Intrinsic Properties." *Philosophy and Phenomenological Research* 63 (2): 357–364.

Sider, T. (2007a). "Against Monism." *Analysis* 67 (293): 1–7.

Sider, T. (2007b). "Parthood." *Philosophical Review* 116: 51–91.

Sider, T. (2011). *Writing the Book of the World*. Oxford: Oxford University Press.

Sider, T. (2013). "Against Parthood." In K. Bennett and D. Zimmerman (eds.), *Oxford Studies in Metaphysics*. Vol. 8. Oxford: Oxford University Press.

Siegel, S. (2006). "Which Properties Are Represented in Perception?" In T. Szabo Gendler and J. Hawthorne (eds.), *Perceptual Experience*. Oxford: Clarendon Press.

Siewert, C. (2014). "Speaking up for Consciousness." In U. Kriegel (ed.), *Current Controversies in Philosophy of Mind*. New York: Routledge.

Simons, P. (1987). *Parts: A Study in Ontology*. Oxford: Clarendon Press.

Skrbina, D. (2005). *Panpsychism in the West*. Cambridge, MA: MIT Press.

Smart, J. J. C. (1981). "Physicalism and Emergence." *Neuroscience* 6: 109–113.

Smith, J. (2010). "Seeing Other People." *Philosophy and Phenomenological Research* 81 (3): 731–748.

Smith, J. (2015). "The Phenomenology of Face-to-Face Mindreading." *Philosophy and Phenomenological Research* 90 (2): 274–293.

Smithies, D. (2011). "Attention Is Rational-Access Consciousness." In C. Mole, D. Smithies, and W. Wu (eds.), *Attention: Philosophical and Psychological Essays*. Oxford: Oxford University Press.

Smolensky, P. (1987). "The Constituent Structure of Connectionist Mental States: A Reply to Fodor and Pylyshyn." *Southern Journal of Philosophy* 26 (Supplement): 137–161.

Soames, S. (2010). *Philosophy of Language*. Princeton: Princeton University Press.

Soteriou, M. (2007). "Content and the Stream of Consciousness." *Philosophical Perspectives* 21 (1): 543–568.

Sperry, R. (1964). "Brain Bisection and Mechanisms of Consciousness." In J. Eccles (ed.), *Brain and Conscious Experience*. Berlin: Springer-Verlag.

Sperry, R. (1984). "Consciousness, Personal Identity, and the Divided Brain." *Neuropsychologia* 22 (6): 661–673.

Spinoza, B. (1994). "Ethics Demonstrated in Geometrical Order" (1677). In E. Curley (ed. and trans.), *A Spinoza Reader*. Princeton, NJ: Princeton University Press.

Sprigge, T. (1983). *The Vindication of Absolute Idealism*. Edinburgh: Edinburgh University Press.

Stephens, G. L., and Graham, G. (2000). *When Self-Consciousness Breaks: Alien Voices and Inserted Thoughts*. Cambridge, MA: MIT Press.

Sterne, C. (1891). "Five Souls with but a Single Thought: The Psychological Life of the Star-Fish." *The Monist* 1 (2): 245–262.

Stevenson, R. L. (1886). *Strange Case of Dr. Jekyll and Mr. Hyde*. London: Longmans, Green.

Stoljar, D. (2001). "Two Conceptions of the Physical." *Philosophy and Phenomenological Research* 62 (2): 253–281.

Stoljar, D. (2006a). "Comments on Galen Strawson—Realistic Monism: Why Physicalism Entails Panpsychism." *Journal of Consciousness Studies* 13 (10–11): 170–176.

Stoljar, D. (2006b). *Ignorance and Imagination*. Oxford: Oxford University Press.

Stoljar, D. (2013). "Four Kinds of Russellian Monism." In U. Kriegel (ed.), *Current Controversies in Philosophy of Mind*. New York: Routledge.

Strawson, G. (1989). "'Red' and Red." *Synthese* 78: 193–232.

Strawson, G. (2006). "Realistic Monism—Why Physicalism Entails Panpsychism." *Journal of Consciousness Studies* 13 (10–11): 3–31.

Strawson, G. (2009). *Selves: An Essay in Revisionary Metaphysics*. Oxford: Oxford University Press.

Strawson, G. (2015). "Self-Intimation." *Phenomenology and the Cognitive Sciences* 14 (1): 1–31. http://link.springer.com/article/10.1007%2Fs11097-013-9339-6/fulltext.html.

Strawson, P. F. (1974). "Imagination and Perception." In *Freedom and Resentment and Other Essays*. London: Methuen.

Sumbre, G., Gutfreund, Y., Fiorito, G., Flash, T., and Hochner, B. (2001). "Control of Octopus Arm Extension by a Peripheral Motor Program." *Science* 293: 1845–1848.

Sutton, C. S. (2014). "The Supervenience Solution to the Too-Many-Thinkers Problem." *Philosophical Quarterly* 64 (257): 619–639.

Swinburne, R. (1984). *Personal Identity: The Dualist View*. Oxford: Blackwell.

Swinburne, R. (1986). *The Evolution of the Soul*. Oxford: Oxford University Press.

Synofzik, M., Vosgerau, G., and Newen, A. (2008). "Beyond the Comparator Model: A Multifactorial Two-Step Account of Agency." *Consciousness and Cognition* 17: 219–239.

Szanto, T. (2014). "How to Share a Mind: Reconsidering the Group Mind Thesis." *Phenomenology and the Cognitive Sciences* 13 (1): 99–120.

Teng, E. L., and Sperry, R. W. (1973). "Interhemispheric Interaction during Simultaneous Bilateral Presentation of Letters or Digits in Commissurotomized Patients." *Neuropsychologia* 11: 131–140.

Théoret, H., Kobayashi, M., Ganis, G., Di Capua, P., and Pascual-Leone, A. (2002). "Repetitive Transcranial Magnetic Stimulation of Human Area MT/V5 Disrupts Perception and Storage of the Motion Aftereffect." *Neuropsychologia* 40 (13): 2280–2287.

Thomasson, A. (2009). "Answerable and Unanswerable Questions." In D. Manley, D. Chalmers, and R. Wasserman (eds.), *Metametaphysics*. Oxford: Oxford University Press.

Thomson, J. (1997). "People and their Bodies." In J. Dancy (ed.), *Reading Parfit*, Oxford: Blackwell.

Titchener, E. B. (1909). *A Textbook of Psychology*. New York: Macmillan. Internet Archive. Accessed August 26, 2013. http://archive.org/stream/textbookofpsychoooedwa/textbookofpsychoooedwa_djvu.txt.

Tollefsen, D. (2014). "A Dynamic Theory of Shared Intention." In S. Chant and F. Hindriks (eds.), *From Individual to Collective Intentionality: New Essays*. Oxford: Oxford University Press.

Tononi, G. (2004). "An Information Integration Theory of Consciousness." *BMC Neuroscience* 5 (1): 42–64.

Tononi, G. (2008). "Consciousness as Integrated Information: A Provisional Manifesto." *Biological Bulletin* 215 (3): 216–242.

Tononi, G. (2012). "Integrated Information Theory of Consciousness: An Updated Account." *Archives Italiennes de Biologie* 150 (2–3): 56–90.

Tononi, G. (2014). "Why Scott Should Stare at a Blank Wall and Reconsider (or, The Conscious Grid)." Scott Aaronson website. http://www.scottaaronson.com/tononi.docx.

Tononi, G., and Balduzzi, D. (2009). "Qualia: The Geometry of Integrated Information." *Computational Biology* 5 (8): 1–24.

Tononi, G., and Koch, C. (2014). "Consciousness: Here, There, but Not Everywhere." Cornell University Library. http://arxiv.org/ftp/arxiv/papers/1405/1405.7089.pdf.

Treisman, A., and Gelade, G. (1980). "A Feature-Integration Theory of Attention." *Cognitive Psychology* 12 (1): 97–136.

Treisman, A., and Sato, S. (1990). "Conjunction Search Revisited." *Journal of Experimental Psychology: Human Perception and Performance* 16 (3): 459–478.

Treue, S., and Maunsell, J. (1999). "Effects of Attention on the Processing of Motion in Macaque Middle Temporal and Medial Superior Temporal Visual Cortical Areas." *Journal of Neuroscience* 19 (17): 7591–7602.

Trout, J. (2002). "Scientific Explanation and the Sense of Understanding." *Philosophy of Science* 69 (2): 212–233.

Tuomela, R. (2007). *The Philosophy of Sociality: The Shared Point of View.* New York: Oxford University Press.

Turing, A. (1950). "Computing Machinery and Intelligence." *Mind* 49: 433–460.

Tye, M. 1992. "Visual Qualia and Visual Content." In T. Crane (ed.), *The Contents of Experience.* Cambridge, UK: Cambridge University Press.

Tye, M. (2003). *Consciousness and Persons: Unity and Identity.* Cambridge, MA: MIT Press.

Tye, M. (2009). "A New Look at the Speckled Hen." *Analysis* 69 (2): 258–263.

Uddin, L., Rayman, J., and Zaidel, E. (2005). "Split-Brain Reveals Separate but Equal Self-Recognition in the Two Cerebral Hemispheres." *Consciousness and Cognition* 14 (3): 633–640.

Unger, P. (1979). "There Are No Ordinary Things." *Synthese* 41 (2): 117–154.

Unger, P. (1980). "The Problem of the Many." *Midwest Studies in Philosophy* 5 (1): 411–468.

Unger, P. (1990). *Identity, Consciousness, and Value.* Oxford: Oxford University Press.

Unger, P. (2004). "Mental Problems of the Many." In D. Zimmerman (ed.), *Oxford Studies in Metaphysics.* Vol. 1. Oxford: Clarendon Press.

Unger, P. (2006). *All the Power in the World.* Oxford: Oxford University Press.

Van Cleve, J. (1990). "Mind-Dust or Magic? Panpsychism versus Emergence." *Philosophical Perspectives* 4: 215–226.

Van Essen, D. C., and Deyoe, E. A. (1995). "Concurrent Processing in the Primate Visual Cortex." In M. Gazzaniga (ed.), *The Cognitive Neurosciences.* Cambridge, MA: MIT Press.

Van Inwagen, P. (1990). *Material Beings.* Ithaca, NY: Cornell University Press.

Varzi, A. (2006). "A Note on the Transitivity of Parthood." *Applied Ontology* 1 (2): 141–146.

Velleman, D. (1997). "How To Share An Intention." *Philosophy and Phenomenological Research* 57 (1): 29–50.

Viola, M., and Zanin, E. (2017). "The Standard Ontological Framework of Cognitive Neuroscience: Some Lessons from Broca's Area." *Philosophical Psychology* 30 (7): 945–969.

Watzl, S. (2010). "The Significance of Attention." PhD dissertation, Columbia University.

Watzl, S. (2011). "Attention as Structuring of the Stream of Consciousness." In C. Mole, D. Smithies, and W. Wu (eds.), *Attention: Philosophical and Psychological Essays*. Oxford: Oxford University Press.

Wegner, D. (2002). *The Illusion of Conscious Will*. Cambridge, MA: MIT Press.

Wertheimer, M. (1912). "Experimentelle Studien über das Sehen von Bewegung [Experimental Studies on Motion Vision]." *Zeitschrift für Psychologie* 61 (1): 161–265.

Westergaard, G., and Hyatt, C. (1994). "The Responses of Bonobos (*Pan paniscus*) to Their Mirror Images: Evidence of Self-Recognition." *Human Evolution* 9 (4): 273–279.

Wiggins, D. (1967). *Identity and Spatio-Temporal Continuity*. Oxford: Oxford University Press.

Williams, B. (1957). "Personal Identity and Individuation." *Proceedings of the Aristotelian Society, New Series* 57: 229–252.

Williams, B. (1970). "The Self and the Future." *The Philosophical Review* 79 (2): 161–180.

Williamson, T. (1994). *Vagueness*. London: Routledge.

Wilson, A. (2009). "Disposition-Manifestations and Reference-Frames." *Dialectica* 63: 591–601.

Wilson, J. (1999). "How Superduper Does Physicalist Superdupervenience Need to Be?" *Philosophical Quarterly* 49 (194): 33–52.

Wilson, J. (2005). "Supervenience-Based Formulations of Physicalism." *Nous* 39 (3): 426–459.

Wilson, J. (2010). "Non-Reductive Physicalism and Degrees of Freedom." *British Journal for Philosophy of Science* 61: 279–311.

Wilson, J. (2013). "Nonlinearity and Metaphysical Emergence." In S. Mumford and M. Tugby (eds.), *Metaphysics and Science*. Oxford: Oxford University Press.

Wilson, J. (2014). "No Work for a Theory of Grounding." *Inquiry* 57 (5–6): 1–45.

Wilson, J. (2015). "Metaphysical Emergence: Weak and Strong." In T. Bigaj and C. Wuthrich (eds.), *Metaphysics in Contemporary Physics: Poznan Studies in the Philosophy of the Sciences and the Humanities*. Leiden: Koninklijke Brill.

Wilson, M. (1999). "Objects, Ideas, and 'Minds': Comments on Spinoza's Theory of Mind." In *Ideas and Mechanism: Essays on Early Modern Philosophy*. Princeton, NJ: Princeton University Press.

Wimsatt, W. C. (1976). "Reductionism, Levels of Organization, and the Mind-Body Problem." In G. Globus, G. Maxwell, and I. Savodnik (eds.), *Consciousness and the Brain: A Scientific and Philosophical Inquiry*. New York: Plenum.

Wittgenstein, L. (1958). *The Blue and Brown Books*. New York: Oxford University Press.

Woodward, P. (2015). "The Emergence of Mental Content: An Essay in the Metaphysics of Mind." PhD dissertation, University of Oslo.

Wu, W. (2011). "Attention as Selection for Action." In C. Mole, D. Smithies, and W. Wu (eds.), *Attention: Philosophical and Psychological Essays*. Oxford: Oxford University Press.

Yi, B.-U. (1999). "Is Mereology Ontologically Innocent?" *Philosophical Studies* 93 (2): 141–160.

Zahavi, D., and Kriegel, U. (2015). "For-me-ness: What It Is and What It Is Not." In D. Dahlstrom, A. Elpidorou, and W. Hopp (eds.), *Philosophy of Mind and Phenomenology: Conceptual and Empirical Approaches*. London: Routledge.

Zaidel, E., Iacoboni, M., Zaedel, D. W., and Bogen, J. E. (1993). "The Callosal Syndromes." In K. M. Heilman and E. Valenstein (eds.), *Clinical Neuropsychology*. Oxford: Oxford University Press.

Zeki, S. (2007). "A Theory of Micro-Consciousness." In M. Velmans and S. Schneider (eds.), *The Blackwell Companion to Consciousness*. Oxford: Blackwell.

Zihl, J., von Cramon, D., and Mai, N. (1983). "Selective Disturbance of Movement Vision after Bilateral Brain Damage." *Brain* 106: 313–340.

Zuboff, A. (1982). "The Story of a Brain." In D. R. Hofstadter and D. C. Dennett (eds.), *The Mind's I: Fantasies and Reflections on Self and Soul*. New York: Basic Books.

Zuboff, A. (1990). "One Self: The Logic of Experience." *Inquiry* 33 (1): 39–68.

Index